WILLIAM KOENIG

EYE TO EYE

EYE TO EYE

FACING THE CONSEQUENCES OF DIVIDING ISRAEL

Copyright © 2008 by William R. Koenig

16th Printing (revised and updated version)

Published by *About Him Publishing*

McLean, VA 22102

About Him Publishing
P.O. Box 9124
McLean, VA 22102
http://abouthim.org

ISBN 0-9717347-0-4

Logo design: Claudia Koenig, Janelle Robertson

Eye to Eye

How beautiful upon the mountains are the feet of him that bringeth good tidings, that publisheth peace; that bringeth good tidings of good, that publisheth salvation; that saith unto Zion, Thy God reigneth!; Thy watchmen shall lift up the voice; with the voice together shall they sing: for they shall see eye to eye, when the LORD shall bring Zion; Break forth into joy, sing together, ye waste places of Jerusalem: for the LORD hath comforted His people, He hath redeemed Jerusalem (Isaiah 52:7-9, KJV).

They [the watchmen] shall see an exact agreement between **the prophecy and the event,** the promise and the performance; they shall see how they look one upon another **eye to eye,** and be satisfied that the same God spoke the one and did the other (*The Matthew Henry Commentary* on Isaiah 52:8).

Koenig's International News
For biblically relevant news go to:
http://watch.org

For events from 2007-2010, and for future events,
visit http://watch.org/eyetoeye
and see the "Eye to Eye" section.

TABLE OF CONTENTS

Catastrophes & Events: 1991 – 2005

U.S. Administrations of
George H. W. Bush, William J. Clinton, and George W. Bush

MAPS

Introduction

In *"Eye to Eye – Facing the Consequences of Dividing Israel"* you will gain a greater understanding of the biblical significance of what is occurring today in the nation of Israel.

You will read about the consequences that the leaders and their nations have experienced after pressuring Israel to divide her land.

The Jewish people have a 3,900-year history with the land of Israel and a 3,000-year connection with the city of Jerusalem.

Jerusalem is mentioned 812 times in the Old and New Testaments of the Bible.

Every world power that has controlled and occupied the land of Israel has become a former world power, or has lost power, such as Britain.

Since Israel became a nation again on May 14, 1948, her neighbors have instigated wars against her in 1948, 1956, 1967, 1973, and 1982 and during the 2000-2004 Intifada.

In May of 1967, the hostile forces of Jordan, Egypt, Lebanon and Syria surrounded Israel. The political rhetoric had reached a fevered pitch as Egyptian President Gamal Abdel Nasser pledged two years earlier: "We shall not enter Palestine with its soil covered in sand. We shall enter it with its soil saturated in blood."

Syria frequently used the Golan Heights, which towers 3,000 feet above the Galilee, to shell Israeli farms and villages. While Egypt's Nasser continued to make speeches threatening war, Arab terrorists stepped up their attacks against Israel from 35 in 1965 to 41 the following year, and 37 in just the first four months of 1967.

Syria's continued shelling from the Golan Heights provoked a retaliatory strike on April 7, 1967, during which Israeli planes shot down six Syrian MiGs. On May 15, Israel's Independence Day, Egyptian troops began moving into the Sinai and massing near the Israeli border. Nasser ordered the United Nations Emergency Force (UNEF), stationed in the Sinai since 1956, to withdraw on May 16. Without bringing the matter to the attention of the UN General Assembly, as his predecessor had promised, Secretary-General U Thant complied with the demand.

After the withdrawal of the UNEF, the Voice of the Arabs proclaimed (May 18, 1967):

As of today, there no longer exists an international emergency force to protect Israel. We shall exercise patience no more. We shall not complain any more to the UN about Israel. The sole method we shall apply against Israel is total war, which will result in the extermination of Zionist existence.

Two days later, Syrian Defense Minister Hafez Assad said,

Our forces are now entirely ready not only to repulse the aggression, but to initiate the act of liberation itself, and to explode the Zionist presence in the Arab homeland. The Syrian army, with its finger on the trigger, is united. ... I, as a military man, believe that the time has come to enter into a battle of annihilation.

By May 18, Syrian troops were prepared for battle along the Golan Heights.

After telling the world they were about to attack Israel, the Soviet-backed militaries of Egypt, Syria, and Jordan were hit first. After just six days of fighting, Israeli forces broke through the enemy lines and were in a position to march on Cairo, Damascus and Amman. A ceasefire was invoked on June 10. But five months later, on November 22, 1967, the UN Security Council passed UN Resolution 242 calling on Israel to give back the land that they had obtained in the war of self-defense.

Here is an excerpt from UN resolution 242:

Affirms that the fulfillment of Charter principles requires the establishment of a just and lasting peace in the Middle East which should include the application of both the following principles:

- Withdrawal of Israeli armed forces from territories occupied in the recent conflict;
- Termination of all claims or states of belligerency and respect for and acknowledgement of the sovereignty, territorial integrity and political independence of every State in the area and their right to live in peace within secure and recognized boundaries free from threats or acts of force;
- For guaranteeing freedom of navigation through international waterways in the area; for achieving a just settlement of the refugee problem;
- For guaranteeing the territorial inviolability and political independence of every State in the area, through measures including the establishment of demilitarized zones....

The world's leaders continue to call on Israel to divide her land with an adversary committed to the annihilation of Israel. Israel's neighbors speak peace in English and war and destruction of Israel in Arabic.

In January 2006, Hamas gained control of 74 of 132 Palestinian parliamentary seats. Hamas was founded in 1987 for the express purpose of destroying Israel, and since joining politics has publicly clung to that goal. They deny

Israel's right to exist. They consider all previously signed agreements with Israel void. The new Palestinian Authority Prime Minister, Ismail Haniyeh, plans (as a first step) to drive Israel back to the 1967 borders and establish an Arab state with Jerusalem as its capital. His cabinet brims with hard-line terrorists.

Most other Muslim nations in the Middle East do not accept Israel's right to exist and a few nations are outwardly calling for the elimination of the nation of Israel and the Jewish people.

Iran and Syria are attempting to develop weapons of mass destruction and are funding the terrorist organizations that are attacking Israel.

There are other Middle Eastern nations that are covertly funding terrorist organizations. Some of these nations are arming themselves with weapons from Russia, China and North Korea.

Replacement theology churches that teach that the church has completely replaced Israel in God's redemptive plan for the world, and believe that the Jews are no longer God's chosen people, and that God does not have specific future plan for the nation of Israel, are also calling on Israel to leave the occupied land.

A very large majority of President George W. Bush's political problems and the many record-setting catastrophes and political disruptions that he has experienced during his time in office have a direct connection to his involvement with the Israeli-Palestinian peace process.

Despite their good intentions, President Bush and previous American president's, and to a lesser degree the international community, are accountable for:

- Dividing the land God gave to Abraham, Isaac and Jacob and their descendants;
- A peace plan that would position Israel in indefensible borders;
- Interfering with God's plan of having Jews move home to Israel and Judea and Samaria – the biblical heartland of Israel; and
- Participating in the eviction of Jews from their homes within the biblical heartland of Israel.

Furthermore, Israel is a very small nation—the size of New Jersey—and makes up less than one percent of the land of the Middle East. It is 271 miles long and 81 miles wide at its widest point. The land in dispute is much smaller, but vital to Israel's security and survival.

In Genesis 12:2-3, the Bible proclaims that God "will bless them that bless thee, and curse him that curseth thee: and in thee shall all families of the earth be blessed."

Thus, God promised that He would bless those who bless Abraham and his descendants and curse those who cursed them. He also promised that through them all of the families of earth would be blessed.

Many world leaders believe that Israel is the key to peace when in reality the continued pressure upon Israel and the subsequent events will rapidly lead the world into the final battle: the battle of Armageddon – the battle for Jerusalem.

We hope and pray this book helps you become better aware of why the world is rapidly moving into her final days and nearing the return of the Messiah to Jerusalem.

Let's pray for the peace of Jerusalem (Psalm 122:6).

—William Koenig
    May 2006

Statement by
United States Senator James Inhofe

March 4, 2002

In a speech before the U.S. Senate, Senator James Inhofe (R-Oklahoma) stood against world opinion and offered seven reasons why Israel alone is entitled to possess the Holy Land.

The other day ... the de facto ruler, Saudi Arabian Crown Prince Abdullah, made a statement which was received by many in this country as if it were a fact, as if it were something new, a concept for peace in the Middle East that no one had ever heard of before. I was shocked that it was so well received by many people ....

I suggest to you that what Crown Prince Abdullah talked about a few days ago was not new at all. ... Under the Abdullah plan, Arabs would normalize relations with Israel in exchange for the Jewish state surrendering the territory it received after the 1967 Six-Day War ... He went on to talk about other land that had been acquired by Israel.

I remember so well on December 4 [2001] when we covered all of this, and the fact that there isn't anything new about the prospect of giving up land that is rightfully Israel's land in order to have peace.

When it gets right down to it, the land doesn't make that much difference, because Yasser Arafat and others don't recognize Israel's right to any of the land. They do not recognize Israel's right to exist.

I will discuss seven reasons why Israel is entitled to the land they have, and that it should not be a part of the peace process.

If this is something that Israel wants to do, it is their business to do it. But anyone who has tried to put pressure on Israel to do this is wrong.

We are going to be hit by skeptics who are going to say we will be attacked because of our support for Israel, and if we get out of the Middle East—that is us—all the problems will go away. That is just not true. If we withdraw, all of these problems will again come to our door.

I have some observations to make about that. But I would like to reemphasize once again the seven reasons that Israel has the right to their land.

The first reason is that Israel has the right to the land because of all of the archeological evidence. That is reason No. 1. All the archeological evidence supports it.

Every time there is a dig in Israel, it — does nothing but support the fact that Israelis have had a presence there for 3,000 years. The coins, the cities, the pottery, the culture reveal they have been there for a long time. The coins, the cities, the pottery, the culture. There are other people groups that are there, but there is no mistaking the fact that Israelis have been present in that land for 3,000 years.

It predates any claims that other peoples may have in the region. The ancient Philistines are extinct. Many other ancient peoples are extinct. They do not have the unbroken line to this date that the Israelis have.

Even the Egyptians of today are not racial Egyptians of 2,000 or 3,000 years ago. They are primarily an Arab people. The land is called Egypt, but they are not the same racial and ethnic stock as the old Egyptians of the ancient world.

The first Israelis are in fact descended from the original Israelites. The first proof, then, is the archeology.

The second proof of Israel's right to the land is the historic right. History supports it totally and completely. We know there was an Israel up until the time of the Roman Empire. The Romans conquered the land. Israel had no homeland, although Jews were allowed to live there. They were driven from the land in two dispersions: one was in A.D. 70 and the other was in A.D. 135. But there was always a Jewish presence in the land.

The Turks, who took over about 700 years ago, ruled the land up until about World War I. Then the British conquered the land. The Turks entered World War I on the side of Germany. The British knew they had to do something to punish Turkey, and also to break up that empire that was going to be a part of the whole effort of Germany in World War I. So the British sent troops against the Turks in the Holy Land.

One of the generals who was leading the British armies was a man named Allenby. Allenby was a Bible-believing Christian. He carried a Bible with him everywhere he went and he knew the significance of Jerusalem.

The night before the attack against Jerusalem to drive out the Turks, Allenby prayed that God would allow him to capture the city without doing damage to the holy places.

That day, Allenby sent World War I biplanes over the city of Jerusalem to do a reconnaissance mission. You have to understand that the Turks had at that time never seen an airplane. ... They looked in the sky and saw these fascinating inventions and did not know what they were; they were terrified by them. Then they were told they were going to be opposed by a man named Allenby the next day, which means, in their language, "man sent from God" or "prophet from God." They dared not fight against a prophet from God, so the next morning, when Allenby went to take Jerusalem, he went in and captured it without firing a single shot.

The British government was grateful to Jewish people around the world, particularly to one Jewish chemist who helped them manufacture niter. Niter is an ingredient that was used in nitroglycerin, which was sent over from the New World. But they did not have a way of getting it to England.

The German U-boats were shooting on the boats, so most of the niter they were trying to import to make nitroglycerin was at the bottom of the ocean. But a man named Weitzman, a Jewish chemist, discovered a way to make it from materials that existed in England. As a result, they were able to continue that supply.

The British at that time said they were going to give the Jewish people a homeland. That is all a part of history. It is all written down in history. They were gratified that the Jewish people, the bankers, came through and helped finance the war.

The homeland that Britain said it would set aside consisted of all of what is now Israel and all of what was then the nation of Jordan—the whole thing. That was what Britain promised to give the Jews in 1917.

In the beginning, there was some Arab support for this action. There was not a huge Arab population in the land at that time, and there is a reason for that. The land was not able to sustain a large population of people. It just did not have the development it needed ... Nobody really wanted this land. It was considered to be worthless land.

I want the presiding officer to hear what Mark Twain said. And, of course, you may have read *Huckleberry Finn* and *Tom Sawyer*. Mark Twain—Samuel Clemens—took a tour of Palestine in 1867. This is how he described that land. We are talking about Israel now. He said:

> A desolate country whose soil is rich enough but is given over wholly to weeds. A silent, mournful expanse. We never saw a human being on the whole route. There was hardly a tree or a shrub anywhere. Even the olive and the cactus, those fast friends of a worthless soil, had almost deserted the country.

Where was this great Palestinian nation? It did not exist. It was not there. Palestinians were not there. Palestine was a region named by the Romans, but at that time it was under the control of Turkey, and there was no large mass of people there because the land would not support them.

This is the report made by the Palestinian Royal Commission (created by the British). It quotes an account of the conditions on the coastal plain along the Mediterranean Sea in 1913. They said:

> The road leading from Gaza to the north was only a summer track, suitable for transport by camels or carts. No orange groves, orchards or vineyards were to be seen until one reached the Yavnev village. Houses

were mud. Schools did not exist. The western part toward the sea was almost a desert. The villages in this area were few and thinly populated. Many villages were deserted by their inhabitants.

That was 1913. The French author Voltaire described Palestine as "a hopeless, dreary place."

In short, under the Turks the land suffered from neglect and low population. That is an historic fact.

The nation became populated by both Jews and Arabs because the land came to prosper when Jews came back and began to reclaim it. ... If there had never been any archaeological evidence to support the rights of the Israelis to the territory, it is also important to recognize that other nations in the area have no longstanding claim to the country either.

Did you know that Saudi Arabia was not created until 1913, Lebanon until 1920? Iraq did not exist as a nation until 1932, Syria until 1941. The borders of Jordan were established in 1946, and Kuwait in 1961. Any of these nations that would say Israel is only a recent arrival would have to deny their own rights as recent arrivals as well. They did not exist as countries. They were all under the control of the Turks.

Historically, Israel gained its independence in 1948.

The third reason that land belongs to Israel is the practical value of the Israelis being there. Israel today is a modern marvel of agriculture. Israel is able to bring more food out of a desert environment than any other country in the world. The Arab nations ought to make Israel their friend and import technology from Israel that would allow all the Middle East, not just Israel, to become an exporter of food. Israel has unarguable success in its agriculture.

The fourth reason I believe Israel has the right to the land is on the grounds of humanitarian concern. You see, there were 6 million Jews slaughtered in Europe in World War II. The persecution against the Jews had been very strong in Russia since the advent of communism. It was against them even before then under the Czars.

These people have a right to their homeland. If we are not going to allow them a homeland in the Middle East, then where? What other nation on Earth is going to cede territory, is going to give up land?

They are not asking for a great deal. The whole nation of Israel would fit into my home state of Oklahoma seven times. It would fit into the presiding officer's State of Georgia seven times. They are not asking for a great deal. The whole nation of Israel is very small. It is a nation that, up until the time that claims started coming in, was not desired by anybody.

The fifth reason Israel ought to have their land is that she is a strategic ally of the United States. Whether we realize it or not, Israel is a detriment, an impediment, to certain groups hostile to democracies and hostile to what we believe in, hostile to that which makes us the greatest nation in the history of the world. They have kept them from taking complete control of the Middle East. If it were not for Israel, they would overrun the region. They are our strategic ally.

It is good to know we have a friend in the Middle East on whom we can count. They vote with us in the United Nations more than England, more than Canada, more than France, more than Germany—more than any other country in the world.

The sixth reason is that Israel is a roadblock to terrorism. The war we are now facing is not against a sovereign nation; it is against a group of terrorists who are very fluid, moving from one country to another. They are almost invisible. That is whom we are fighting against today.

We need every ally we can get. If we do not stop terrorism in the Middle East, it will be on our shores. We have said this again and again and again, and it is true.

One of the reasons I believe 'the spiritual door was opened for an attack against the United States of America is that the policy of our Government has been to ask the Israelis, and demand it with pressure, not to retaliate in a significant way against the terrorist strikes that have been launched against them.

Since its independence in 1948, Israel has fought four wars: The war in 1948 and 1949—that was the war for independence; the war in 1956, the Sinai campaign; the Six-Day War in 1967; and in 1973, the Yom Kippur War, the holiest day of the year, and that was with Egypt and Syria.

You have to understand that in all four cases, Israel was attacked. They were not the aggressor. Some people may argue that this was not true because they went in first in 1956, but they knew at that time that Egypt was building a huge military to become the aggressor. Israel, in fact, was not the aggressor and has not been the aggressor in any of the four wars.

Also, they won all four wars against impossible odds. They are great warriors. They consider a level playing field being outnumbered 2 to 1.

There were 39 Scud missiles that landed on Israeli soil during the gulf war. Our president asked Israel not to respond. In order to have the Arab nations on board, we asked Israel not to participate in the war. They showed tremendous restraint and did not. Now we have asked them to stand back and not do anything over these last several attacks.

We have criticized them. We have criticized them in our media. Local people in television and radio often criticize Israel, not knowing the true facts. We need to be informed.

I was so thrilled when I heard a reporter pose a question to our secretary of state, Colin Powell. He said:

"Mr. Powell, the United States has advocated a policy of restraint in the Middle East. We have discouraged Israel from retaliation again and again and again because we've said it leads to continued escalation—that it escalates the violence. Are we going to follow that preaching ourselves?"

Mr. Powell indicated we would strike back. In other words, we can tell Israel not to do it, but when it hits us, we are going to do something.

But all that changed in December [2001] when the Israelis went into the Gaza Strip with gunships and into the West Bank with F-16s. With the exception of last May [2001], the Israelis had not used F-16s since the 1967 Six-Day War. And I am so proud of them because we have to stop terrorism. It is not going to go away. If Israel were driven into the sea tomorrow, if every Jew in the Middle East were killed, terrorism would not end. You know that in your heart. Terrorism would continue.

It is not just a matter of Israel in the Middle East. It is the heart of the very people who are perpetrating this stuff. Should they be successful in overrunning Israel—which they won't be—but should they be, it would not be enough. They will never be satisfied.

No. 7, I believe very strongly that we ought to support Israel; that it has a right to the land. This is the most important reason: because God said so. As I said a minute ago, look it up in the book of Genesis. It is right up there on the desk.

In Genesis 13:14-17, the Bible says:

> The Lord said to Abram, "Lift up now your eyes, and look from the place where you are northward, and southward, and eastward and westward: for all the land which you see, to you will I give it, and to your seed forever. . . . Arise, walk through the land in the length of it and in the breadth of it; for I will give it to thee."

That is God talking.

The Bible says that Abram removed his tent and came and dwelt in the plain of Mamre, which is in Hebron, and built there an altar before the Lord. Hebron is in the West Bank. It is at this place where God appeared to Abram and said, "I am giving you this land"—the West Bank.

This is not a political battle at all. It is a contest over whether or not the Word of God is true. The seven reasons, I am convinced, clearly establish that Israel has a right to the land.

Eight years ago on the lawn of the White House, Yitzhak Rabin shook hands with PLO Chairman Yasser Arafat. It was a historic occasion. It was a tragic occasion.

At that time, the official policy of the government of Israel began to be, "Let us appease the terrorists. Let us begin to trade the land for peace." This process continued unabated up until last year. Here in our own nation, at Camp David, in the summer of 2000, then prime minister of Israel Ehud Barak offered the most generous concessions to Yasser Arafat that had ever been laid on the table.

He offered him more than 90 percent of all the West Bank territory, sovereign control of it. There were some parts he did not want to offer, but in exchange for that he said he would give up land in Israel proper that the PLO had not even asked for.

And he also did the unthinkable. He even spoke of dividing Jerusalem and allowing the Palestinians to have their capital there in the East. Yasser Arafat stormed out of the meeting. Why did he storm out of the meeting? Everything he had said he wanted was offered there. It was put into his hands. Why did he storm out of the meeting?

A couple of months later, there began to be riots, terrorism. The riots began when Prime Minister Ariel Sharon went to the Temple Mount. And this was used as the thing that lit the fire and that caused the explosion.

Did you know that Sharon did not go unannounced, and that he contacted the Islamic authorities before he went, and secured their permission to be there? It was no surprise.

The response was very carefully calculated. They knew the world would not pay attention to the details.

They would portray this in the Arab world as an attack upon the holy mosque. They would portray it as an attack upon that mosque and use it as an excuse to riot. Over the last eight years, during this time of the peace process, where the Israeli public has pressured its leaders to give up land for peace because they are tired of fighting, there has been increased terror.

In fact, it has been greater in the last eight years than any other time in Israel's history. Showing restraint and giving in has not produced any kind of peace. It is so much so that today the leftist peace movement in Israel does not exist because the people feel they were deceived.

They did offer a hand of peace, and it was not taken. That is why the politics of Israel have changed drastically over the past 12 months [since March 2001]. The Israelis have come to see that, "No matter what we do, these people do not want to deal with us . . . They want to destroy us." That is why even yet today the stationery of the PLO still has upon it the map of the entire state of Israel, not just the tiny little part they call the West Bank that they want. They want it all.

We have to get out of this mind set that somehow you can buy peace in the Middle East by giving little plots of land. It has not worked before when it has been offered. These seven reason show why Israel is entitled to that land.

PREFACE

In the Bible, God speaks to Abraham, father of the Jews and the nation of Israel, and directs him to the land of Canaan. In the first book of the Bible, God says to Abraham,

> I will make of thee a great nation, and I will bless thee and make thy name great; and thou shalt be a blessing. And I will bless them that bless thee and curse him who curseth thee: and in thee shall all the families of the earth be blessed (Genesis 12:2-3).

Later in the same book, God promises Abraham,

> Unto thy seed have I given this land, from the river of Egypt unto the great river, the river Euphrates (Genesis 15:18).

And two chapters later, God tells Abraham,

> And I will establish My covenant between Me and thee and thy seed after thee in their generations for an everlasting covenant to be God unto thee and to thy seed after thee (Genesis 17:7).

The Bible also says Israel must be mindful of God's covenant with Abraham,

> O ye seed of Israel His servant, ye children of Jacob, His chosen ones. He is the LORD our God; His judgments are in all the earth. Be ye mindful always of His covenant; the word which He commanded to a thousand generations; Even of the covenant which He made with Abraham, and of His oath unto Isaac; And hath confirmed the same to Jacob for a law, and to Israel for an everlasting covenant, Saying, Unto thee will I give the land of Canaan, the lot of your inheritance (I Chronicles 16:13-18).

America is now experiencing the consequences (curses) of Middle East policies, which have been opposed to God's Word and to the preservation of His covenant land. Ever since the Madrid Conference of October 1991, the United States participation in Israel's destiny has been flawed when put in context of Holy Scripture.

The events of September 11, 2001, were a national wake-up call. However, if this nation continues to support the Road Map, affirming a "land for peace" approach, America can expect to experience the further lifting of the Lord's protective hand in an even greater measure.

> I will also gather all nations, and will bring them down into the valley of Jehoshaphat, and will plead with them there for My people and for My heritage Israel, whom they have scattered among the nations, and parted My land (Joel 3:2).

It is a fact that Israel's very existence is in grave danger because of our nation's sponsorship of "land for peace" plans, which have led her to the brink of war.

What is happening in the world, and especially in the Middle East, these days is truly remarkable. But then again, Bible believers shouldn't be surprised, because the Old Testament prophet, Zechariah, pre-warned us about these times over 2,500 years ago:

> And in that day will I make Jerusalem a burdensome stone for all people: all that burden themselves with it shall be cut in pieces, though all the people of the earth be gathered together against it (Zechariah 12:3).

> And it shall come to pass in that day, that I will seek to destroy all the nations that come against Jerusalem (Zechariah 12:9).

The Bible is very clear that our loving and just God will always warn His people before judgment comes.

—William Koenig
  Watch.org

CHAPTER 1

Historical Basis for Israel's Right to Its Land

God Gave The Land To Abram; From Abram Will Come A Great Nation

Genesis 12

[1]Now the LORD had said unto Abram, "Get thee out of thy country, and from thy kindred, and from thy father's house, unto a land that I will she thee: [2]And I will make of thee a great nation, and I will bless thee, and make thy name great; and thou shalt be a blessing...." [3]And the LORD appeared unto Abram, and said, "Unto thy seed will I give this land...."

Genesis 13

[14]And the LORD said unto Abram, after that Lot was separated from him, "Lift up now thine eyes, and look from the place where thou art northward, and southward, and eastward, and westward: [15]For all the land which thou sees, to thee will I give it, and to thy seed for ever. [16]And I will make thy seed as the dust of the earth; so that if a man can number the dust of the earth, then shall thy seed also be numbered. [17]Arise, walk through the land in the length of it and in the breadth of it; for I will give it unto thee."

God Created A Land Covenant With Defined Borders

Genesis 15

[18]In the same day the LORD made a covenant with Abram, saying, "Unto thy seed have I given this land, from the river of Egypt unto the great river, the river Euphrates...."

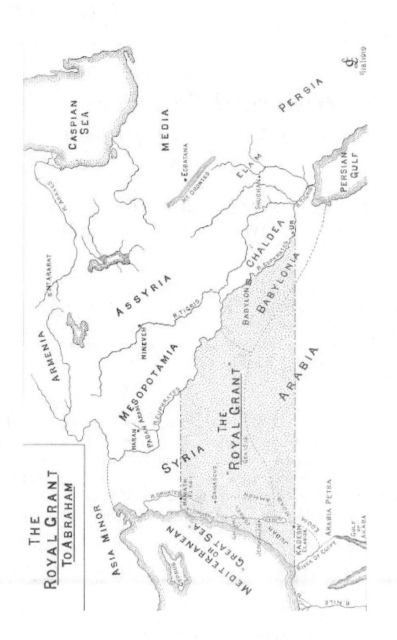

Map: Larkin, Clarence. "The Royal Grant to Abraham," The Book of Revelation. Blue Letter Bible. 1 Apr 2002. 3 Mar 2006. <http://blueletterbible.org/study/larkin/lark03.html>.

God Reinforces That The Covenant Is Forever

Genesis 17

[1]And when Abram was ninety years old and nine, the LORD appeared to Abram, and said unto him, "I am the Almighty God; walk before me, and be thou perfect. [2]And I will make My covenant between Me and thee, and will multiply thee exceedingly." [3]And Abram fell on his face: and God talked with him, saying, [4]"As for Me, behold, My covenant is with thee, and thou shalt be a father of many nations. [5]Neither shall thy name any more be called Abram, but thy name shall be Abraham; for a father of many nations have I made thee. [6]And I will make thee exceeding fruitful, and I will make nations of thee, and kings shall come out of thee. [7]And I will establish My covenant between Me and thee and thy seed after thee in their generations for an everlasting covenant, to be a God unto thee, and to thy seed after thee. [8]And I will give unto thee, and to thy seed after thee, the land wherein thou art a stranger, all the land of Canaan, for an everlasting possession; and I will be their God." ...

[15]And God said unto Abraham, "As for Sara thy wife, thou shalt not call her name Sarai, but Sarah shall her name be. [16]And I will bless her, and give thee a son also of her: yea, I will bless her, and she shall be a mother of nations; kings of people shall be of her." ... [19]And God said, "Sarah thy wife shall bear thee a son indeed; and thou shalt call his name Isaac: and I will establish My covenant with him for an everlasting covenant, and with his seed after him. ... [21]But My covenant will I establish with Isaac."

God Specifically Declared "No Peace Deals"

Exodus 23

[32]"Thou shalt make no covenant with them, nor with their gods. [33]They shall not dwell in thy land, lest they make thee sin against Me: for if thou serve their gods, it will surely be a snare unto thee."

God Commands Israel Not To Give the Land Away

Ezekiel 48

[14]And they shall not sell of it, neither exchange, nor alienate the first fruits of the land: for it is holy unto the LORD.

[29]This is the land which ye shall divide by lot unto the tribes of Israel for inheritance, and these are their portions, saith the Lord GOD.

Jewish Connection to the Land of Israel

Abraham Joshua Heschel, on the Jewish Connection to Israel:

The land was taken from the Jewish people by violence, and we have never abandoned hope of regaining it. Throughout the ages we said No to all the conquerors of Palestine. We said No before God and man emphatically, daily. We objected to their occupations, we rejected their claims; we deepened our attachment, knowing that the occupation by the conquerors was a passing adventure, while our attachment to the land was an eternal link. The Jewish people have never ceased to assert its right, its title, to the land of Israel. This continuous, uninterrupted insistence, an intimate ingredient of Jewish consciousness, is at the core of Jewish history, a vital element of Jewish faith.

MYTH[1]

"The Jews have no claim to the land they call Israel."

FACT:

A common misperception is that all the Jews were forced into the Diaspora by the Romans after the destruction of the Second Temple in Jerusalem in the year 70 AD; and then, 1,900 years later, suddenly returned to Palestine demanding their country back. In reality, the Jewish people have maintained ties to their historic homeland for more than 3,700 years.

The Jewish people base their claim to the Land of Israel on at least four premises:

1. the Jewish people settled and developed the land;
2. the international community granted political sovereignty in Palestine to the Jewish people;
3. the territory was captured in defensive wars; and
4. God promised the land to the patriarch Abraham.

Even after the destruction of the Second Temple in Jerusalem and the beginning of the exile, Jewish life in the Land of Israel continued and often flourished. Large communities were reestablished in Jerusalem and Tiberias by the ninth century. In the 11th century, Jewish communities grew in Rafah, Gaza, Ashkelon, Jaffa, and Caesarea.

The Crusaders massacred many Jews during the 12th century, but the community rebounded in the next two centuries as large numbers of rabbis and Jewish pilgrims immigrated to Jerusalem and the Galilee. Prominent rabbis established communities in Safed, Jerusalem and elsewhere during the next 300 years. By the early 19th century—years before the birth of the modern Zionist movement—more than 10,000 Jews lived throughout what is today Israel. The 78 years of nation-building, beginning in 1870, culminated in the reestablishment of the Jewish State.

Israel's international "birth certificate" was validated by:

- the promise of the Bible;
- uninterrupted Jewish settlement from the time of Joshua onward;
- the Balfour Declaration of 1917;
- the League of Nations Mandate, which incorporated the Balfour Declaration;
- the United Nations partition resolution of 1947;
- Israel's admission to the UN on May 11, 1949;
- the recognition of Israel by most other states; and,
- most of all, the civilization created by Israel's people in decades of thriving, dynamic national existence.

Abba Eban, a member of the Knesset Committee on Foreign Affairs and Security, in a November 11, 1981, *New York Times* article entitled "The Saudi Text," wrote the following:

Nobody does Israel any service by proclaiming its 'right to exist.'

Israel's right to exist, like that of the United States, Saudi Arabia and 152 other states, is axiomatic and unreserved. Israel's legitimacy is not suspended in midair awaiting acknowledgement....

There is certainly no other state, big or small, young or old, that would consider mere recognition of its 'right to exist' a favor, or a negotiable concession.

Jewish Connection to Jerusalem[2]

The connection between the Jewish people and Jerusalem dates back to the period of King David, who lived approximately three thousand years ago, and who established Jerusalem as the capital of Israel.

Jerusalem has represented not only the geographical center of the Jewish people, but also the center of their faith and identity. The relationship between Jerusalem and the Jewish people is entirely unique in the annals of history.

Jerusalem was the site of the two Temples—the first built by King Solomon during the tenth century B.C. and destroyed in 586 B.C. during the Babylonian conquest; and the second built less than a century later, and subsequently refurbished by King Herod, but destroyed in 70 A.D. by Roman forces.

As the psalmist wrote,

If I forget thee, O Jerusalem, let my right hand wither; let my tongue stick to my palate if I cease to think of thee, if I do not keep Jerusalem in memory even at my happiest hour.

Though in forced dispersion for nearly nineteen hundred years, Jews never stopped yearning for Zion and Jerusalem.

In addition to expressing this through prayer, there were always Jews who lived in the land of Israel, and especially Jerusalem. Indeed, since the nineteenth century, Jews have constituted a majority of the city's population. For example, according to the Political Dictionary of the State of Israel, Jews comprised 61.9 percent of Jerusalem's population in 1892.

The historical and religious link to Jerusalem is especially important because some Arabs seek to rewrite history and assert that Jews are "foreign occupiers" or "colonialists" with no actual tie to the land. Such attempts to deny Israel's legitimacy are demonstrably false and need to be exposed for the lies they are. They also entirely ignore the "inconvenient" fact that when Jerusalem was under Muslim (i.e., Ottoman and, later, Jordanian) rule, it was always a backwater.

Hope For Their Own Nation[3]

The Balfour Declaration—a letter from British Foreign Secretary Arthur James Balfour to Lord Rothschild in which the British made public their support of a Jewish homeland in Palestine—was a product of years of careful negotiation. After centuries of living in a Diaspora, the 1894 Dreyfus Affair in France shocked Jews into realizing they would not be safe from arbitrary anti-Semitism unless they had their own country.

In response, Jews created the new concept of political Zionism in which it was believed that through active political maneuvering, a Jewish homeland could be created. Zionism was becoming a popular concept by the time World War I began.

During World War I, Great Britain needed help. Since Germany (Britain's enemy) had cornered the production of acetone—an important ingredient for arms production—Great Britain might have lost the war if Chaim Weizmann had not invented a fermentation process that allowed the British to manufacture their own liquid acetone.

It was this fermentation process that brought Weizmann to the attention of David Lloyd George (minister of ammunitions) and Arthur James Balfour (previously the British prime minister but at this time first lord of the admiralty).

Both Lloyd George and Lord Balfour were devout Christians who attached great religious significance to the proposed reinstatement of the Jews in their ancient homeland

Chaim Weizmann was not just a scientist; he was also the leader of the Zionist movement. Weizmann's contact with Lloyd George and Balfour continued, even after George became prime minister and Balfour was transferred to the Foreign Office in 1916. Additional Zionist leaders such as Nahum Sokolow also pressured Great Britain to support a Jewish homeland in Palestine.

Though Balfour, himself, was in favor of a Jewish state, Great Britain particularly favored the declaration as an act of policy. Britain wanted the United States to join World War I and the British hoped that by supporting a Jewish homeland in Palestine, world Jewry would be able to sway the U.S. to join the war. Though the Balfour Declaration went through several drafts, the final version was issued on November 2, 1917, in a letter from Balfour to Lord Rothschild, president of the British Zionist Federation. The main body of the letter quoted the decision of the October 31, 1917 British Cabinet meeting. This declaration was accepted by the League of Nations on July 24, 1922, and embodied in the mandate that gave Great Britain temporary administrative control of Palestine.

The **Balfour Declaration** was a letter to Lord Rothschild (Walter Rothschild, 2nd Baron Rothschild), a leader of the British Jewish Community, for transmission to the Zionist Federation, a private Zionist organization.

The Balfour Declaration

(its entirety)

Foreign Office
November 2nd, 1917

Dear Lord Rothschild,

I have much pleasure in conveying to you, on behalf of His Majesty's Government, the following declaration of sympathy with Jewish Zionist aspirations which has been submitted to, and approved by, the Cabinet.

His Majesty's Government view with favour the establishment in Palestine of a national home for the Jewish people, and will use their best endeavours to facilitate the achievement of this object, it being clearly understood that nothing shall be done which may prejudice the civil and religious rights of existing non-Jewish communities in Palestine, or the rights and political status enjoyed by Jews in any other country.

I should be grateful if you would bring this declaration to the knowledge of the Zionist Federation.

Yours sincerely,
Arthur James Balfour

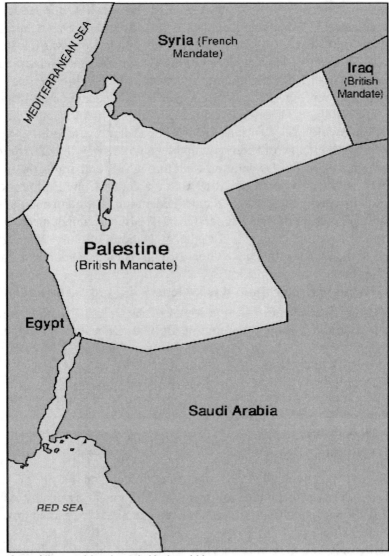

Area Allocated for Jewish National Home
San Remo Conference, 1920

Mandate for Palestine[4]

In July 1922, the League of Nations entrusted Great Britain with the
Mandate for Palestine (the name by which the country was then known).
Recognizing the historical connection of the Jewish people with Palestine, Great
Britain was called upon to facilitate the establishment of a Jewish national home
in Palestine-Eretz Israel (Land of Israel). In September 1922, the British govern-
ment presented a memorandum to the League of Nations stating that

Transjordan would be excluded from all the provisions dealing with Jewish settlement. This memorandum was approved on September 11, 1922.

From that point forward, Britain recognized the land west of the Jordan River as Palestine (which was 23% of the entire territory), and the land east of the Jordan River as Transjordan (constituting 77% of the mandated territories). Technically they remained one mandate but most official documents referred to them as if they were two separate mandates. Transjordan remained under British control until 1946.

In 1923 Britain transferred a part of the Golan Heights to the French Mandate of Syria, in exchange for the Metula region.

Proposed Creation of Jordan, Strong Arab Opposition, and British Restrictions

The Jewish national revival and the community's efforts to rebuild the country were strongly opposed by Arab nationalists. Their resentment erupted in periods of <u>intense violence</u> (1920, 1921, 1929, 1936-39) when Jewish transports were harassed, fields and forests set on fire, and unprovoked attacks were launched against the Jewish population. Attempts to reach a dialogue with the Arabs, undertaken early in the Zionist endeavor, were ultimately unsuccessful, polarizing Zionism and Arab nationalism into a potentially explosive situation. Recognizing the opposing aims of the two national movements, the British recommended (1937) dividing the country into two states, one Jewish and one Arab. The Jewish leadership accepted the idea of partition and empowered the Jewish Agency to negotiate with the British government in an effort to reformulate various aspects of the proposal. The Arabs were uncompromisingly against any partition plan.

Continuing large-scale Arab anti-Jewish riots led Britain (May 1939) to issue a White Paper imposing drastic restrictions on Jewish immigration, despite its consequence of denying European Jewry a place of refuge from Nazi persecution. The start of World War II soon after caused David Ben-Gurion, later Israel's first prime minister, to declare: "We will fight the war as if there were no White Paper, and the White Paper as if there were no war."

After the war, the British intensified their restrictions on the number of Jews permitted to enter and settle in the Land. The Jewish community responded by instituting a wide network of "illegal immigration" activities to rescue Holocaust survivors. Between 1945 and 1948, some 85,000 Jews were brought to the Land by secret, often dangerous routes, in spite of a British naval blockade and border patrols set up to intercept the refugees before they reached the country. Those who were caught were interned in detention camps on the island of Cyprus, or returned to Europe.

Road to Independence Through Creation of Two States, Israel and Jordan

    Britain's inability to reconcile the conflicting demands of the Jewish and Arab communities led the British government to request that the "Question of Palestine" be placed on the agenda of the United Nations General Assembly (April 1947). As a result, a special committee was constituted to draft proposals concerning the country's future. The UN called for the creation of independent Arab and Jewish states in Palestine on November 29, 1947, with Jerusalem to be placed under international administration.

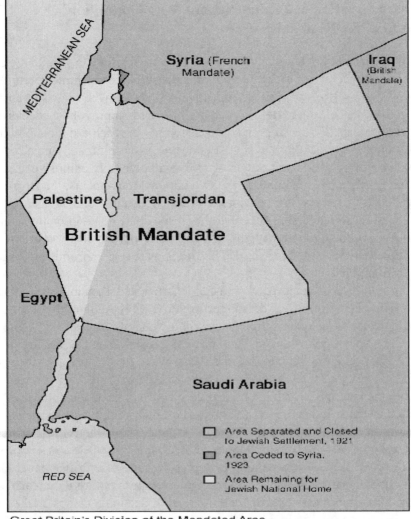

Great Britain's Division of the Mandated Area,
1921-1923

The partition plan was rejected by the leadership of the Palestinian Arabs and by most of the Arab population.

Most of the Jews accepted the proposal, in particular the Jewish Agency, which was the Jewish state-in-formation. Several Jews, however, declined the proposal. Menachem Begin, Irgun's leader (Irgun became the Israeli Defense Force—IDF), announced:

> The partition of the homeland is illegal. It will never be recognized. The signature by institutions and individuals of the partition agreement is invalid. It will not bind the Jewish people. Jerusalem was and will for ever be our capital. The Land of Israel will be restored to the people of Israel.

Following the UN vote, local Arab militants, aided by irregular volunteers from Arab countries, launched violent attacks against the Jewish community in an effort to frustrate the partition resolution and prevent the establishment of a Jewish state. After a number of setbacks, the Jewish defense organizations routed most of the attacking forces, taking hold of the entire area allocated for the Jewish state.

On May 14, 1948, when the British Mandate came to an end, the Jewish provisional government declared the formation of the State of Israel, and the provisional government said that it would grant full civil rights to all within its borders, whether Arab, Jew, Bedouin or Druze. Thus, upon creating the state, any inhabitants inside the newly formed State of Israel, whether Palestinian Jews or Palestinian Arabs, became Israeli. The Jewish population in the Land numbered some 650,000, comprising an organized community with well-developed political, social and economic institutions—in fact, a nation in every sense and a state in everything but name.

The British mandate over Transjordan ended on May 22, 1946; on May 25, the country became the independent Hashemite Kingdom of Transjordan.

Transjordan opposed the creation of Israel in May 1948, and took part in the warfare between the Arab states and the newly founded State of Israel.

In 1950, Transjordan annexed the West Bank, and the country was renamed "the Hashemite Kingdom of Jordan." The annexation was recognized only by the United Kingdom.

Israel Becomes a Nation[5]

In later years, President Harry Truman's daughter Margaret would say it was the most difficult decision her dad ever faced as president. Should he support the creation of a Jewish homeland or shouldn't he?

When Eddie Jacobson—a Jewish American businessman who was a U.S. Army associate, business partner, and friend of President Truman—first heard about what was happening to the Jews in Germany, before and during World War II, he took to discussing it with Truman. After he heard the post-war reports regarding the Nazi Holocaust and its survivors, his talks with Truman about how to help the Jewish people became more intense. Since Jewish leaders in the U.S. knew Jacobson was a friend of the President's, they approached him to lobby Truman with even more fervor. Jacobson went to the White House on March 13, 1948, and at that meeting persuaded Truman to meet with the leader of the Zionist movement, Dr. Chaim Weizmann.[6]

Truman's advisers were split. Clark Clifford—his debonair legal counsel—fervently believed he should meet with Weizmann. Clifford argued the Jews

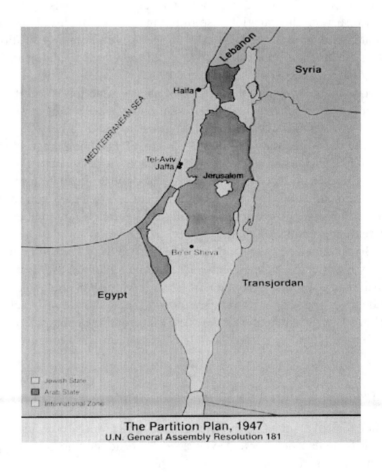

The Partition Plan, 1947
U.N. General Assembly Resolution 181

deserved a sanctuary after the horror of the Holocaust. Besides, the new state would likely come to pass whether or not Truman urged it.

Secretary of State George Marshall felt otherwise. The retired general was a towering figure in the capital: Truman himself said "there wasn't a decoration big enough" to honor Marshall's leadership during World War II. At a White House meeting on May 12, 1948, Marshall objected to quick U.S. recognition of a Jewish homeland. It would look as if Truman was angling for Jewish votes, he said, and might endanger access to Arab oil. He went so far as to say that if Truman went ahead and recognized the new state, then he, personally, would vote against him in the coming election.

It was an extraordinary rebuke to a sitting chief executive—and it didn't work. Two days later, Israel was born at the stroke of midnight, Jerusalem time. The United States announced its recognition of the new nation 11 minutes later.

The United States Holds Back Support[7]

Although the United States vigorously supported the partition resolution, the State Department did not want to provide the Jews with the means to defend themselves. "Otherwise," U.S. Undersecretary of State Robert Lovett argued, "the Arabs might use arms of U.S. origin against Jews, or Jews might use them against Arabs." On December 5, 1947, the U.S. had imposed an arms embargo on the region.

Many in the State Department saw the embargo as yet another means of obstructing partition. President Truman nevertheless went along with it hoping it would be a means of averting bloodshed. This was naive given Britain's rejection of Lovett's request to suspend weapons shipments to the Arabs and subsequent agreements to provide additional arms to Iraq and Transjordan.

The Arabs had no difficulty obtaining all the arms they needed. In fact, Jordan's Arab Legion was armed and trained by the British, and led by a British officer. At the end of 1948 and beginning of 1949, British RAF planes flew with Egyptian squadrons over the Israel-Egypt border.

On January 7, 1949, Israeli planes shot down four of the British aircraft.

Arab Nations Attack, Are Defeated by Scarcely Armed Israel (1948), and Sign Armistice Agreements (1949)

The Jews were forced to smuggle weapons, principally from Czechoslovakia. When Israel declared its independence in May 1948, the army did not have a single cannon or tank. Its air force consisted of nine obsolete planes. Although the Haganah, Israel's watchmen, had 60,000 trained fighters, only 18,900 were fully mobilized, armed and prepared for war.

On May 15, 1948, the day the British Mandate over Palestine ended, the armies of five neighboring Arab states invaded the new State of Israel, which had declared its independence the previous day. From the north, east and south the armies of Lebanon, Syria, Iraq, Egypt, and Transjordan came for battle. On the eve of the war, chief of operations Yigal Yadin told David Ben-Gurion: "The best we can tell you is that we have a 50-50 chance." But the Arab war to destroy Israel failed. Indeed, because of their aggression, the Arabs wound up with less territory than they would have had if they had accepted partition.

The cost to Israel, however, was enormous. "Many of its most productive fields lay gutted and mined. Its citrus groves, for decades the basis of the Yishuv's [Jewish community] economy, were largely destroyed." Military expenditures totaled approximately $500 million. Worse yet, 6,373 Israelis were killed, nearly one percent of the Jewish population of 650,000.

Had the West enforced the partition resolution or given the Jews the capacity to defend themselves, many lives might have been saved.

The Arab countries signed armistice agreements with Israel in 1949, starting with Egypt (Feb. 24), followed by Lebanon (March 23), Jordan (April 3) and Syria (July 20). Iraq was the only country that did not sign an agreement with Israel, choosing instead to withdraw its troops and hand over its sector to Jordan's Arab Legion.

1956 Sinai Campaign[8]

The 1949 armistice agreements failed to pave the way to permanent peace and were constantly violated. In contradiction to the UN Security Council resolution of September 1, 1951, Israeli and Israel-bound shipping was prevented from passing through the Suez Canal; the blockade of the Straits of Tiran was tightened; incursions into Israel of terrorist squads from neighboring Arab countries for murder and sabotage occurred with increasing frequency; and the Sinai Peninsula was gradually converted into a huge Egyptian military base.

Upon the signing of a tripartite military alliance by Egypt, Syria and Jordan (October 1956), the imminent threat to Israel's existence was intensified. In the course of an eight-day campaign, the Israeli Defense Forces (IDF) captured the Gaza Strip and the entire Sinai Peninsula, halting 10 miles (16 km.) east of the Suez Canal.

A UN decision to station an Emergency Force (UNEF) along the Egypt-Israel border, and Egyptian assurances of free navigation in the Gulf of Eilat, led Israel to agree to withdraw in stages (November 1956-March 1957) from the areas taken a few weeks earlier. Consequently, the Straits of Tiran were opened to Israel shipping, enabling the development of trade with Asian and East African countries, as well as oil imports from the Persian Gulf.

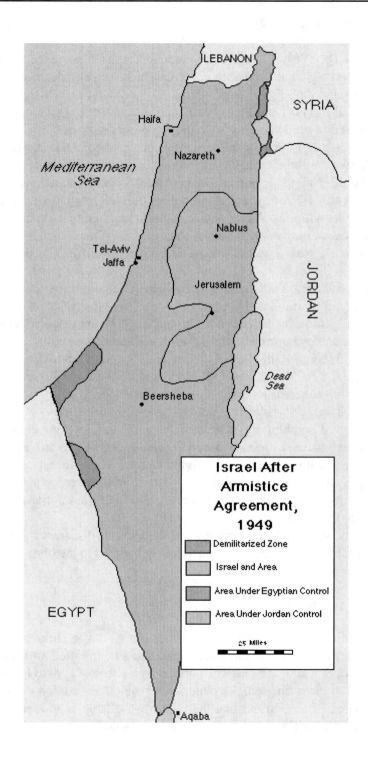

The 1967 Six-Day War[9]

On May 16, 1967, Cairo Radio announced: "The existence of Israel has continued too long. The battle has come in which we shall destroy Israel."

On the same day, Egypt demanded the withdrawal of UN forces that had been stationed in Gaza and Sharm el-Sheikh since 1957. Three days later, the UN announced it would comply with the Egyptian demand.

On May 19, Cairo Radio said: "This is our chance, Arabs, to deal Israel a mortal blow of annihilation...."

On May 23, Egypt's President Gamal Abdel Nasser declared his intention to block the Strait of Tiran to Israeli shipping, thus effectively severing Israel's vital trade links with East Africa and Asia. Israel replied that under international law this was a *casus belli*, an act of war.

On May 27, Nasser said, "our basic objective will be the destruction of Israel."

On May 30, Jordan's King Hussein placed Jordanian forces under Egyptian control. Egyptian, Iraqi, and Saudi troops were sent to Jordan.

On June 1, Iraq's leader added his thoughts: "We are resolved, determined, and united to achieve our clear aim of wiping Israel off the map."

On June 3, Cairo Radio hailed the impending Muslim holy war.

On June 5, 1967, Israel was indeed alone, but its military commanders had conceived a brilliant war strategy. The entire Israeli Air Force, with the exception of just 12 fighters assigned to defend Israeli air space, took off at 7:14 a.m., with the intent of bombing Egyptian airfields while the Egyptian pilots were eating breakfast. In less than 2 hours, roughly 300 Egyptian aircraft were destroyed. A few hours later, Israeli fighters attacked the Jordanian and Syrian air forces, as well as one airfield in Iraq. By the end of the first day, nearly the entire Egyptian and Jordanian air forces, and half the Syrians', had been destroyed on the ground.

The battle then moved to the ground, and some of history's greatest tank battles were fought between Egyptian and Israeli armor in the blast-furnace conditions of the Sinai desert.

Jerusalem Is Attacked

Prime Minister Levi Eshkol sent a message to King Hussein on June 5, 1967, saying Israel would not attack Jordan unless he initiated hostilities. When Jordanian radar picked up a cluster of planes flying from Egypt to Israel, and the Egyptians convinced Hussein the planes were theirs, he ordered the shelling of West Jerusalem. It turned out that the planes were Israel's and were returning from destroying the Egyptian air force on the ground.

Israel Captures Jerusalem

It took only three days for Israeli forces to defeat the Jordanian legion. On the morning of June 7, 1967, the order was given to recapture the Old City. Israeli paratroopers stormed the city and secured it. Defense Minister Moshe Dayan arrived with Chief of Staff Yitzhak Rabin to formally mark the Jews' return to their historic capital and their holiest site. At the Western Wall, the IDF's chaplain, Rabbi Shlomo Goren, blew a shofar to celebrate the event.

A Second Exodus

After Jordan launched its attack on June 5, 1967, approximately 325,000 Palestinians living in the West Bank fled to parts of Jordan, primarily to avoid being caught in the crossfire of a war.

A Palestinian refugee who was an administrator in a UNRWA (United Nations Relief and Works Agency) camp in Jericho said Arab politicians had spread rumors in the camp.

> They said all the young people would be killed. People heard on the radio that this is not the end, only the beginning, so they think maybe it will be a long war and they want to be in Jordan.

Some Palestinians who left preferred to live in an Arab state rather than under Israeli military rule. Members of various PLO factions fled to avoid capture by the Israelis. Nils-Göran Gussing, the person appointed by the UN Secretary-General to investigate the situation, found that many Arabs also feared they would no longer be able to receive money from family members working abroad.

Israeli forces ordered a handful of Palestinians to move for "strategic and security reasons." In some cases, they were allowed to return in a few days; in others, Israel offered to help them resettle elsewhere. The net result, however, was that a new refugee population had been created and the old refugee problem was made worse.

The Stunning Victory

While most IDF units were fighting the Egyptians and Jordanians, a small, heroic group of soldiers were left to defend the northern border against the Syrians. It was not until the Jordanians and Egyptians were subdued that reinforcements could be sent to the Golan Heights, where Syrian gunners commanding the strategic high ground made it exceedingly difficult and costly for Israeli forces to penetrate. Finally, on June 9, after two days of heavy air bombardment, Israeli forces succeeded in breaking through the Syrian lines.

After just six days of fighting, Israeli forces were in a position to march on Cairo, Damascus, and Amman. By this time, the principal objectives of capturing the Sinai and the Golan Heights had been accomplished, and Israeli political leaders had no desire to fight in the Arab capitals. Furthermore, the Soviet Union had become increasingly alarmed by the Israeli advances and was threatening to intervene. At this point, U.S. Secretary of State Dean Rusk advised the Israelis "in the strongest possible terms" to accept a cease-fire. On June 10, 1967, Israel did just that.

The victory came at a very high cost. In storming the Golan Heights, Israel suffered 115 dead—roughly the number of Americans killed during Operation Desert Storm. Altogether, Israel lost twice as many men—777 dead and 2,586 wounded—in proportion to her total population as the U.S. lost in eight years of fighting in Vietnam. Also, despite the incredible success of the air campaign, the Israeli Air Force lost 46 of its 200 fighters. The death toll on the Arab side was 15,000 Egyptians, 2,500 Syrians, and 800 Jordanians.

By the end of the war, Israel had conquered enough territory to more than triple the size of the area it controlled, from 8,000 to 26,000 square miles. The victory enabled Israel to unify Jerusalem. Israeli forces had also captured the Sinai, Golan Heights, Gaza and the West Bank.

Israel now ruled more than three-quarters of a million Palestinians—most of whom were hostile to the government. Nevertheless, more than 9,000 Palestinian families were reunited in 1967. Ultimately, more than 60,000 Palestinians were allowed to return.

1967: UN Security Council adopted Resolution 242

Israel's leaders fully expected to negotiate a peace agreement with their neighbors that would involve some territorial compromise. Therefore, instead of annexing the West Bank, a military administration was created.

Israel then offered to negotiate a peace settlement exchanging the captured lands for peace with Arab neighbors. But a negative response came from Khartoum, Sudan, where Arab leaders met to discuss the outcome of the Six Day War. On September 1, 1967, they issued a resolution announcing the three 'No's': "No peace, no recognition, and no negotiation."

On November 22, 1967, the United Nations Security Council adopted Resolution 242, which established a formula for Arab-Israeli peace whereby Israel would withdraw from territories occupied in the war in exchange for peace with its neighbors. This resolution has served as the basis for peace negotiations and is the foundation of today's Quartet Road Map.

This resolution, often cited in discussions about Arab-Israeli relations, stresses "the inadmissibility of the acquisition of territory by war and the need to work for a just and lasting peace in which every state in the area can live in security."

Further, it calls for "withdrawal of Israeli armed forces from territories occupied in the recent conflict," but deliberately omits use of the word "the" before the word "territories." The U.S. ambassador to the UN at the time, Arthur Goldberg, noted that this was intentional, so that any final settlement could allow for unspecified border adjustments that would take into account Israel's security needs.

The resolution also includes a call for:

> ... termination of all claims or states of belligerency and respect for and acknowledgment of the sovereignty, territorial integrity and political

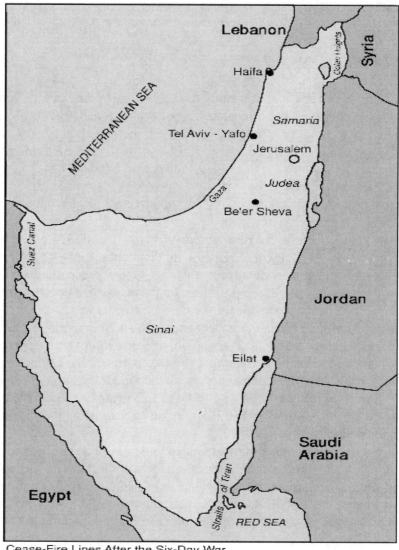

Cease-Fire Lines After the Six-Day War

independence of every State in the area and their right to live in peace within secure and recognized boundaries free from threats or acts of force.

And, not least, it:

... affirms further the necessity (a) For guaranteeing freedom of navigation through international waterways in the area; (b) For achieving a just settlement of the refugee problem*; and (c) For guaranteeing the territorial inviolability and political independence of every State in the area, through measures including the establishment of demilitarized zones.

[*Author's comment: Note the absence of reference to which refugee problem, allowing for more than one interpretation of the refugee populations covered.]

1973 Yom Kippur War[10]

On October 6, 1973—Yom Kippur, the holiest day in the Jewish calendar—Egypt and Syria opened a coordinated surprise attack against Israel. The equivalent of the total forces of NATO in Europe were mobilized on Israel's borders. On the Golan Heights, approximately 180 Israeli tanks faced an onslaught of 1,400 Syrian tanks. Along the Suez Canal, fewer than 500 Israeli defenders were attacked by 80,000 Egyptians.

At least nine Arab states, including four non-Middle Eastern nations, actively aided the Egyptian-Syrian war effort.

A few months before the Yom Kippur War, Iraq transferred a squadron of Hunter jets to Egypt. During the war, an Iraqi division of some 18,000 men and several hundred tanks was deployed in central Golan and participated in the October 16 attack against Israeli positions. Iraqi MiGs began operating over the Golan Heights as early as October 8, the third day of the war.

Besides serving as financial underwriters, Saudi Arabia and Kuwait committed men to battle. A Saudi brigade of about 3,000 troops was dispatched to Syria, where it participated in fighting along the approaches to Damascus. Also, violating Paris's ban on the transfer of French-made weapons, Libya sent Mirage fighters to Egypt. (From 1971-1973, Libyan President Muammar Qaddafi gave Cairo more than $1 billion in aid to rearm Egypt and to pay the Soviets for weapons delivered.)

Other North African countries responded to Arab and Soviet calls to aid the frontline states. Algeria sent three aircraft squadrons of fighters and bombers, an armored brigade and 150 tanks. Approximately 1,000-2,000 Tunisian soldiers were positioned in the Nile Delta. Sudan stationed 3,500 troops in southern Egypt, and Morocco sent three brigades to the front lines, including 2,500 men to Syria.

Lebanese radar units were used by Syrian air defense forces. Lebanon also allowed Palestinian terrorists to shell Israeli civilian settlements from its territory. Palestinians fought on the Southern Front with the Egyptians and Kuwaitis.

The least enthusiastic participant in the October fighting was probably Jordan's King Hussein, who apparently had been kept uninformed of Egyptian and Syrian war plans. But Hussein did send two of his best units—the 40th and 60th Armored Brigades—to Syria. This force took positions in the southern sector, defending the main Amman-Damascus route and attacking Israeli positions along the Kuneitra-Sassa road on October 16. Three Jordanian artillery batteries also participated in the assault, carried out by nearly 100 tanks.

Israel Recovers

Thrown onto the defensive during the first two days of fighting, Israel mobilized its reserves and eventually repulsed the invaders and carried the war deep into Syria and Egypt.

The Arab states were swiftly re-supplied by sea and air from the Soviet Union, which rejected U.S. efforts to work toward an immediate ceasefire.

President Richard Nixon warned Henry Kissinger not to appear so pro-Israel that the Arab oil states, not part of the battle, would break ranks. The president was confident the Israelis would win, as, "thank God, they should." Then he lamented the logical outcome. The Israelis "will be even more impossible to deal with than before," Nixon moaned.

Thus began the 16 sometimes harrowing days of the Yom Kippur War. Israel did not, in fact, win quickly, and the fight bogged down. The American re-supply effort was slow in coming, but when it did come, it was massive. Thanks to General Alexander Haig, the U.S. sent numerous transport planes filled with military supplies and 20 F-4 Phantom jets.

Two weeks later, Egypt was saved from a disastrous defeat by the UN Security Council, which failed to act while the tide was in the Arabs' favor.

The Soviet Union showed no interest in initiating peacemaking efforts while it looked like the Arabs might win. The same was true for UN Secretary-General Kurt Waldheim. (Waldheim's service with a World War II German army unit guilty of war crimes in the Balkans resulted in his being barred from entering the U.S. after his election as President of Austria.)

On October 22, 1973, the UN Security Council adopted Resolution 338 calling for "all parties to the present fighting to cease all firing and terminate all military activity immediately." The vote came on the day Israeli forces cut off and isolated the Egyptian Third Army and were in a position to destroy it.

The resolution also called for implementation of Resolution 242 in its entirety, and the onset of talks between the parties concerned. Resolutions 242 and 338 are normally cited together in connection with any Arab-Israeli peace talks, and are the foundation of today's Quartet Road Map to peace.

Despite the Israel Defense Forces' ultimate success on the battlefield, the war was considered a diplomatic and military failure. A total of 2,688 soldiers were killed.

When it appeared the Arabs weren't serious about peace, Israel's government encouraged the development of settlements (new communities) in the captured lands.

Camp David Accords - 1978

Israel captured Egypt's Sinai Peninsula in the 1967 Six-Day War. After losing badly to Israel again in the 1973 Yom Kippur War, Egypt saw they could not eliminate Israel by war. Egypt's President Anwar Sadat turned to diplomacy.

From September 5 through September 17, 1978, Anwar Sadat and Israeli Prime Minister Menachem Begin, conducted twelve days of intense negotiations at Camp David mediated by U.S. President Jimmy Carter. The negotiations were concluded by the signing of two agreements at the White House. The agreements were based on UN resolutions 242 and 338, and were meant to constitute a basis for peace between Egypt and Israel, as well as to reach "a just, comprehensive, and durable settlement for all neighbors willing to negotiate with Israel."

The first dealt with the future of the Sinai and peace between Israel and Egypt, to be concluded within three months. Israel agreed to withdraw from all of the Sinai, within three years, and to dismantle its air bases near the Gulf of Aqaba and the town of Yamit. Egypt promised full diplomatic relations with Israel, and to allow Israel passage through the Suez Canal, the Strait of Tiran, and the Gulf of Aqaba. The second agreement was a framework establishing a format for the conduct of negotiations for the establishment of an autonomy regime in the West Bank and Gaza to settle the question of the Palestinians.

Enemies of Israel

The world has been on a collision course with the God of Israel. Unbeknown to them they have chosen the wrong side and will be involved in end-time battles which will lead up to the final battle, the battle of Armageddon, the battle for Jerusalem.

Radical Muslim aren't interested in peace. But they are committed to the elimination of Israel and the Jewish people. The peace process for them has one purpose: accumulate enough land from Israel to put them in indefensible borders and move weapons into place so they can destroy them. Anyone who denies this reality is in denial, totally blind, or committed to another agenda.

The U.S. and the international community have spent many years attempting to forge a peace deal between these historic enemies. Yet despite the fact the Palestinians and Israel's neighbors speak peace in English while calling for the elimination of Israel in Arabic, the international community continues to pressure Israel into making dangerous concessions.

United States Policy

U.S. policy in this volatile part of the world has juggled support of Israel with a desire for access to oil supplies controlled by Israel's often-hostile "neighbors." The truth of the matter is that, from Washington's perspective, "supporting Israel while ensuring security of Gulf oil supplies has been a very hard line to walk," says Ruhi Ramazani, a retired professor at the University of Virginia and renowned expert on the history of the modern Middle East.[11]

Empowered Terrorists

The Middle East peace process has not brought peace to Israel or the world, but it has empowered the terrorists and terrorist organizations that operate within the Muslim nations that border Israel, live within Israel, occupy the Middle East, and live within nations around the world.

Israel's problems are now the world's problems. Israel's security concerns are now the world's security concerns. Israel's border problems are now the world's border problems as radical Islam is striking nations throughout the world. This is a judgment against the nations who have pressured Israel into a flawed peace process and empowered radical Islam.

The nations of the world are living under the curse spoken of in Genesis 12:3 (KJV):

And I will bless them that bless thee, and curse him that curseth thee: and in thee shall all families of the earth be blessed.

The nations will be judged for dividing Israel's land as spoken of in Joel 3:2 (ESV):

I will gather all the nations and bring them down to the Valley of Jehoshaphat. And I will enter into judgment with them there, on behalf of my people and my heritage Israel, because they have scattered them among the nations and have divided up my land.

CHAPTER 2

The Error Of Replacement Theology

During the second and third centuries, Christian theologians who mistakenly believed and taught that Bible prophecy was allegorical and not literal ushered in the beginning of biblical error, which has led to nearly 1900 years of anti-Semitism and Jewish persecution. This error led to Jewish persecution from the third century up to the Crusades of the eleventh and twelfth centuries; caused Jews to be blamed for the Black Plague that devastated Europe in the fourteenth century; led to the Spanish Inquisition of the fifteenth century; led to the persecution of Jews in Europe from the fifteenth to nineteenth centuries; and was used as the foundation for Adolph Hitler's activities which led to the horrific Holocaust in the twentieth century.

The Vatican, The World Council of Churches and the National Council of Churches are once again embracing the same biblical error regarding the Jewish people and today's Israel. These church organizations have mistakenly and grossly misinterpreted the role of the church in the Bible, thinking erroneously that since most Jews rejected Christ that today's church supplants Israel as God's chosen people. Nothing could be further from the truth (see Romans 9, 10 and 11 in the Bible).

These church organizations don't believe in the literal interpretation of Bible prophecy and subsequently don't teach the importance of Israel in God's redemptive plan for the world. Moreover, their members have no understanding of the prophetic significance of the events today in Israel and the Middle East.

Due to this error, replacement theology churches, which make up 63% of the American church attendees, have helped mislead national and international political leaders. As a Christian, President Bush's Middle East peace efforts have been greatly affected by this biblical error (as a member of the Episcopalian and the Methodist churches). Furthermore, in their efforts to influence a peace settlement between Arabs and Israel, these church organizations continue to call on Israel to leave the land God gave to Abraham, Isaac, and

Jacob and their descendants through the Abrahamic covenant, an everlasting covenant. Sadly, their error has kept them from educating the U.S., European Union, United Nations, Russia, and the Arab nations on the biblical significance of Israel's covenant land.

President George W. Bush discussed his Middle East peace efforts three times in meetings with Pope John Paul II. (The Pope signed an agreement with Yasser Arafat in February 2000 that called on Jerusalem to be shared between the Muslims, Jews and Christians.)

The National Council of Churches leadership had written numerous letters to President Bush and Secretary of State Colin Powell condemning Israel for refusing to leave the occupied land (instead of calling it disputed land).

The World Council of Churches, the main global body uniting non-Catholic Christians, encouraged members to sell off investments in companies profiting from Israeli control of the West Bank and Gaza.

The Presbyterian Church (USA) is selectively divesting investments in any companies doing business with Israel, and has written a white-paper condemning Christian Zionists. The Episcopalian Church is also considering similar actions. And the story continues ....

The Error Of Replacement Theology[1]

by Clarence H. Wagner, Jr.

Perhaps you have heard of the term Replacement Theology. However, if you look it up in a dictionary of Church history, you will not find it listed as a systematic study. Rather, it is a doctrinal teaching that originated in the early Church. It became the fertile soil from which Christian anti-Semitism grew and has infected the Church for nearly 1,900 years.

What Is Replacement Theology?

Replacement Theology was introduced to the Church shortly after Gentile leadership took over from Jewish leadership in the second and third centuries.

What are its premises?

1. Israel (the Jewish people and the land) has been replaced by the Christian Church in the purposes of God, or, more precisely, the Church is the historic continuation of Israel to the exclusion of Israel.
2. The Jewish people are now no longer a "chosen people." They are no different from any other group, such as the English, Spanish, or Africans.
3. Apart from repentance, the new birth, and incorporation into the Church, the Jewish people have no future, no hope, and no calling in the plan of

God. The same is true for every other nation and group.

4. Since Pentecost (recorded in Acts 2), the term "Israel," as found in the Bible, now refers to the Church.

5. The promises, covenants and blessings ascribed to Israel in the Bible have been taken away from the Jews and given to the Church, which has super-seded Israel. However, the Jews are subject to the curses found in the Bible, as a result of their rejection of Christ.

What happens when the Church replaces Israel?

1. The Church becomes arrogant and self-centered.
2. It boasts against the Jews and Israel.
3. It devalues the role of Israel or has no role for Israel at all.
4. These attitudes result in anti-Semitism in word and deed.
5. Without a true understanding of God's purpose for Israel and the Jewish people today, you cannot explain the Bible prophecies, especially very specific ones being fulfilled in Israel today.
6. Many New Testament passages do not make sense when the Church is viewed as replacing the Jewish people.
7. You can lose the significance of the Hebrew Scriptures, the Old Testament, for today. Many Christians boast of being a New Testament (NT) Christian or a NT Church as in the Book of Acts. However, the Bible of the early Church was not the New Testament, which was not codified until the 4th century, but rather the Hebrew Scriptures.
8. You can lose the Hebraic/Judaic contextualization of the New Testament, which teaches us more about Yeshua and how to become better disciples.
9. The Church loses out on the opportunity to participate in God's plan and prophecy for the Church, Israel and the world today.

What Happens When the Church Relates to Israel?

1. The Church takes its proper role in God's redemptive plan for the world, appreciating God's ongoing covenant relationship and love for Israel and the Jewish people.
2. We can see the consistency of God's redemptive plan from Genesis to Revelation as an ongoing complementary process, not as disconnected snapshots.
3. We show love and honor for God's covenant people, not contempt.
4. We value the Old and New Testaments as equally inspired and significant for the Church today.
5. Bible prophecy makes sense for today and offers opportunities for involvement in God's plan for Israel.
6. We become better disciples of Yeshua [Jesus] as we are able to appreciate

the Hebraic/Judaic roots that fill in the definitions, concepts, words and events in the New Testament that are otherwise obscured. Why? The Jewish writers of the New Testament did not explain many, because they did not feel the need to fill in all the details that were already explained in the Old Testament.

Had the Church understood this very clear message from the beginning, then the sad legacy of anti-Semitic hatred from the Church may have been avoided. The error of Replacement Theology is like a cancer in the Church that has not only caused it to violate God's Word concerning the Jewish people and Israel, but it made us into instruments of hate, not love in God's Name. Yet, it is not too late to change our ways and rightly relate to the Jewish people and Israel today. Through Bridges for Peace you can read, study and learn more, and also give, obeying God's exhortation to us to bless His Covenant People, whom He still loves. Not only do we need to learn and do for ourselves, but also we need to teach others so as to counteract the historical error that has been fostered in the Church for nearly 1900 years.

Thank God, He is a God of mercy, redemption and second chances.

For full commentary go to:
http://www.therefinersfire.org/replacement_theology.htm

Statements by The Vatican, National Council of Churches, World Council of Churches, and Heads of Denominations

Below are agreements, letters and articles that will reveal how deep and serious replacement theology error has become.

If these leaders and organizations were biblically correct, we wouldn't be in the predicament that we are today, but then the Scriptures spoke of a time such as this.

Vatican Signs Agreement With The Palestinians Over Jerusalem

The Vatican and the Palestinians Liberation Organization signed an agreement on February 15, 2000, stating the following:

An equitable solution for the issue of Jerusalem, based on international resolutions, is fundamental for a just and lasting peace in the Middle East, and that unilateral decisions and actions altering the specific character and status of Jerusalem are morally and legally unacceptable;

Calling, therefore, for a special statute for Jerusalem, internationally guaranteed, which should safeguard the following: (a) Freedom of religion and conscience for all; (b) the equality before the law of the three monotheistic religions and their Institutions and followers in the City; (c) the proper identity and sacred character of the City and its universally significant, religious and cultural heritage; (d) The Holy Places, the freedom of access to them and of worship in them; (e) The Regime of "Status Quo" in those Holy Places where it applies.

The Israelis responded by saying:

Israel expresses its great displeasure with the declaration made today in Rome by the Holy See and the PLO, which includes the issue of Jerusalem, and other issues which are subjects of the Israeli-Palestinian negotiations on permanent status. The agreement signed by these two parties constitutes a regretful intervention in the talks between Israel and the Palestinians.

Furthermore, there is no denying that Israel safeguards freedom of conscience and freedom of worship for all, and provides free access to the holy places of all faiths. Similarly, there is no question that the religious and cultural character of Jerusalem is being preserved, as are the rights of all the religious communities and their institutions in the city.

Consequently, Israel flatly rejects the reference to Jerusalem in the aforementioned document. Jerusalem was, is, and shall remain the capital of the State of Israel, and no agreement or declaration by these or any other parties will change this fact.

Letter from 18 U.S. Church Leaders to Secretary Colin Powell[2]

June 7, 2001

The Honorable Colin Powell
Secretary of State
United States Department of State

Dear Mr. Secretary:

We are grateful that you have given us this opportunity to meet with you and are mindful of the additional heads of U.S. churches that joined us in signing this letter. ... We come with support for your effort to end the Israeli-Palestinian cycle of violence and rebuild the trust and mutual confidence that are critical for a negotiated settlement.

There is no higher priority for peacemaking in the world today than that between Israel and the Palestinians. This long and tragic conflict is a cancer that threatens the health of the whole region, U.S. relations with Arab and Muslim countries, and interfaith relations worldwide. We, particularly those of us who have precious partnerships with our sister churches in the Holy Land, offer our prayers and encouragement to our government in this crucial work.

Along with many others, we are deeply concerned that the peace process has broken down so violently and tragically between the government of Israel and the Palestinian leadership. The sobering current reality compels us to take a higher profile in advocacy of U.S. policies conducive to peace.

Few things have done more to destroy the hope and pursuit of peace through negotiations than Israel's unrelenting settlement activity. Over these recent years, we have heard from our Palestinian Christian partners, and seen for ourselves, the destructive impact of Israel's settlement policy—separating village from village, confiscating more and more Palestinian land, creating friction with its military checkpoints.

For over twenty years our churches have appealed to the U.S. government to require Israel to cease this transfer of its civilian population into occupied territory, a clear violation of international law and United Nations resolutions. Each administration has spoken in opposition to the settlement activity, only to watch the settlements increase and expand as Israel ignores the advice.

It is time for the United States to do what it must to bring Israel's settlement activity to an end. We urge you to make clear to Israel and the Palestinians that the United States is committed to a negotiated end of Israel's military occupation of the Gaza Strip, the West Bank and East Jerusalem as called for in U.N.S.C. Res. 242 and that an immediate freezing by Israel of its settlement activity including "natural growth" is imperative. It will likely require considerable diplomatic pressure and possibly economic pressure as well, to convince the government of Israel to recognize that this is a major policy concern of the United States.

Breaking the cycle of violence is fundamental to restarting the peace process and rebuilding the hope and will for peace. While we condemn the violent words and actions of Palestinians, we understand the rage that comes from decades of occupation, dislocation and the feeling of having been betrayed by the peace process. We appeal to the Palestinians, as have you, to abandon violence as a means to end the occupation.

We understand as well Israel's quest for security for the state and its people, but condemn the disproportionately violent and destructive means it is using. Israel's practice of assassination and the economic strangulation of the fledgling Palestinian state are counterproductive to either security or peace. We hope that Israel is responsive to your appeal that it lifts the siege of Palestinian towns and pay the taxes owed to the Palestinian Authority.

We call upon Israel to abandon military force and return to negotiations as the path to security.

A delegation of church leaders on a December pastoral visit saw the destruction wrought by Israel's military might on the homes and livelihood of the Christian towns of Bethlehem, Beit Jala and Beit Sahour. The delegation urged that the United States suspend the current sales of attack helicopters to Israel pending investigation of their use against civilian targets as well as assurances that they will be used in conformity with United States law covering "end-use" in our weapons sales. We ask you to place a hold on any pending delivery of attack helicopters or fighter jets to Israel and to reconsider the promise made by the Clinton Administration that the United States will increase military aid to Israel for each of the next eight years.

While we recognize that it has been U.S policy to support Israel militarily in order to insure its security and to encourage it to move forward with confidence in negotiations, the use of F-16 fighter jets against civilian populations is unacceptable and must be challenged by the U.S. government. Like the U.S. effort to stop settlement activity, stopping the use of these heavy weapons against civilians will require considerable diplomatic pressure and possibly economic pressure.

Although our concern extends to each person suffering from this conflict, we are extremely worried about our Palestinian Christian brothers and sisters. Facing daily threats from violence and economic deprivation and lacking hope for peace and a viable Palestinian state, many feel the pressure to emigrate.

The demise of the living Christian community from the birthplace of the Christian religion would certainly be an irreparable tragedy for the Middle East and the Christian community internationally. For their sake, and for the sake of all, we seek a restoration of hope for a negotiated sharing of the Holy Land and the city of Jerusalem, holy to Jews, Christians and Muslims. We tremble to consider the destructive consequences that would follow the premature moving, as called for by Congress, of the U.S. embassy from Tel Aviv to Jerusalem.

We have heard the cries of fear and mourning of Palestinian Christians and Muslims and of Israeli Jews and pray for their healing and the reconciliation of the Abrahamic family. Be assured of our prayers for you and the President and all others in the Administration as you seek to forge a fair and just policy for the two peoples and three faiths who share a common religious heritage in the land we hold as holy.

[See Addendum 3 for list of signatories.]

Text of Dr. Edgar's Letter to Bush[3]

August 30, 2001

President George W. Bush
The White House
Washington, DC 20500

Dear President Bush:

We write today to express grave concern about recent events in the Middle East, in particular, the recent occupation of the town of Beit Jala by the Israeli military. We appreciate that your Administration called for the Israeli military to withdraw, and urge you to continue to press the government of Israel to comply.

We would especially like to voice our distress regarding the Israeli military's occupation of the Lutheran church in Beit Jala and other of its properties including an orphanage and school. We view this occupation of a Christian site for military purposes as extremely serious, and urge you to communicate with all parties the concern that the violence not spill over into places of worship of any faith. We believe all places of worship are sacred.

On June 7, a delegation of U.S. religious leaders met with Secretary of State Colin Powell taking a letter signed by an additional eighteen heads of U.S. churches and related organizations, myself included. Our views about the situation in the region remain unchanged. If anything, recent events have only served to emphasize these concerns, and to heighten the need for strong American leadership as an irreplaceable factor in resolving this tragic conflict of interests. We urge your Administration to support the deployment of multinational observers with the aim of promoting peace, justice and security in the Occupied Territories.

Since last December, churches across the United States have participated in daily prayer vigils lifting up peace in the region, and the precarious situation of the churches in Jerusalem. We also continue to offer our prayers and encouragement for you, and for your Administration, in your calls to end the cycles of violence and for the opening of new avenues toward a just peace in the region.

Yours in Christ,
Rev. Bob Edgar, General Secretary
National Council of the Churches of Christ in the U.S.A.

Presbyterians Position on Christian Zionists[4]

March 15, 2004

The 216th General Assembly will be asked to oppose Christian Zionism—a movement that says Biblical prophecy requires Christians to support the continued existence of the state of Israel.

That request is part of Overture 04-34 from the Presbytery of Chicago, which calls on the General Assembly "to actively oppose Christian Zionism and to develop a plan to communicate theological and political ramifications it engenders within our denomination, in the mass media, and among U.S. government officials."

Christian Zionism is anchored in a belief that the establishment of the state of Israel in 1948 was the fulfillment of Biblical prophecy. It views Israel as being the focal point for a number of events leading up to the last days—including the second coming of Christ and a worldwide battle at a site known as Har Megiddo in Hebrew and Armageddon in its transliterated form. Christian Zionism also supports the rebuilding of the temple in Jerusalem on land currently being used by Islam's Dome of the Mosque.

Presbyterian Assembly Endorses Israel Divestment[5]

The 216th General Assembly approved several measures opposing the Israeli occupation of Palestine on Friday, July 2, 2004, including a call for the corporate witness office of the Presbyterian Church (USA) to begin gathering data to support a selective divestment of holdings in multinational corporations doing business in Israel/Palestine.

Divestment is one of the strategies that U.S. churches used in the 1970s and '80s in a successful campaign to end apartheid in South Africa.

The vote was 431 to 62 to have the church's Mission Responsibility Through Investment Committee (MRTI) study the matter and make recommendations to the General Assembly Council (GAC).

When a handful of commissioners expressed reservations about the action, the Rev. Mitri Raheb, a Lutheran pastor from Bethlehem, an ecumenical guest at the Assembly, said divestment is important because it is a way for the churches to take direct action. For too long, he said, the churches have simply issued statements—and that is not enough.

"We have to send strong messages to such companies," Raheb said, referring specifically to Caterpillar Inc., the American builder of the armored tractors and bulldozers the Israeli army uses to demolish Palestinian homes.

"Sisters and brothers, this is a moment of truth," Raheb said.

The Rev. Victor Makari, the Presbyterian Church (USA)'s liaison to the Middle East, supported the divestment strategy, saying,

I think the issue of divestment is a very sensitive one with Israel. … If nothing else seems to have changed the policy of Israel toward Palestinians, we need to send a clear and strong message.

The divestment action also **calls for the United States to be an "honest, even-handed broker for peace" and calls for "more meaningful participation" in peace negotiations by Russia, Germany, France and others.** It also encourages the U.S., Israeli and Palestinian governments to "lay aside arrogant political posturing and get on with forging negotiated compromises that open a path to peace."

In other actions related to Israel, the Assembly voted by large margins **to condemn Israel's construction of a "security wall" across the West Bank; disavow Christian Zionism as a legitimate theological stance, and direct the denomination's Middle East and Interfaith Relations offices to develop resources on differences between fundamental Zionism and Reformed theology;** and study the feasibility of sponsoring economic-development projects in Palestine and putting an action plan in place by 2005.

World Council of Churches Calls For Divestment From Israel[6]

February 22, 2005

The World Council of Churches, the main global body uniting non-Catholic Christians, encouraged members Tuesday to sell off investments in companies profiting from Israeli control of the West Bank and Gaza.

The Council's Central Committee, meeting in Geneva, praised the United States Presbyterian Church for examining the possibility of divestment in Israel similar to the financial boycott it used against the apartheid regime in South Africa two decades ago.

But the Central Committee, in a document approved at a week-long meeting at WCC headquarters that ended on Tuesday, February 22, highlighted the divestment push and encouraged other member churches to consider doing the same.

"This action is commendable in both method and manner, uses criteria rooted in faith and calls members to do the 'things that make for peace'," it declared, quoting St Luke's Gospel.

"Economic pressure, appropriately and openly applied, is one such means of action."

It was not clear how many of the WCC's 342 Protestant and Orthodox member churches would heed the call.

No companies targeted yet.

"Multinational corporations have been involved in the demolition of Palestinian homes," the WCC statement said. They were also involved in:

the construction of settlements and settlement infrastructure on occupied territory, in building a dividing wall which is also largely inside occupied territory, and in other violations of international law.

The Presbyterian Church's General Assembly called last July for a "phased, selective divestment" beginning no earlier than July 2006. A dissident group is asking church leaders to place a moratorium on the project as early as next month.

Israel Troubled by World Council of Churches Divestment Campaign

Julie Stahl, Jerusalem Bureau Chief, CNSNews.com,
February 23, 2005

Although the WCC said its declaration was not "one-sided" or "anti-Semitic," Mark Regev Spokesman of the Israel Ministry of Foreign Affairs said it is "clearly both."

"Surely religious groups who claim to support peace and reconciliation should be doing just that and not adopting one-sided partisan attitudes," he said.

The WCC declaration is the latest in a series of attempts over the past four years to urge churches, universities and cities to divest themselves from Israeli companies or companies that do business with Israel.

Statements by Christian Leaders Who Do Not View Nation of Israel as Biblically & Prophetically Significant

Chuck Colson - Prison Fellowship Ministry

Excerpt from Colson's Breakpoint Commentary, No. 030218:
  "Covenant & Conflict—Israel's Place in the World,"
  February 18, 2003

As a Christian and believer in the Abrahamic covenant, I'm a strong supporter of Israel and the Jewish people. I take Genesis 12:3 literally. I also believe that Jesus will return and rule the earth for one thousand years from Jerusalem—a pre-millennial perspective on the second coming. I believe that God has a special plan for the Jewish people and the land of Israel. But I think it is problematic to relate prophecy to current events unfolding in the nation-state of Israel. There may be some relationship, of course. Only God knows. But the secular state of Israel created in 1948 is not, in my understanding, identical with the Jewish people as God's chosen and called-out covenant people.

God clearly has a distinct plan for the Jewish people that the secular state of Israel helps carry out. I don't rule that out, of course. And I strongly support Israel because it is a haven for persecuted Jews—not because I think it fulfills biblical prophecy.

I also support a Palestinian state both from historical and prudential considerations. Given the state of affairs in the Middle East, a Palestinian state is the only practicable solution for peace.

Dr. Joseph F. (Skip) Ryan, Senior Minister, Park Cities Presbyterian Church, Dallas, Texas

Excerpt from Ryan's sermon, "Certain Promises in Uncertain Times" (Ref.: Joshua 21:43-45); presented on March 23, 2003

And here I must run against the grain of what we have been taught. Geo-political Israel today is not to be understood as God's promise of Abraham and Joshua. IT IS NOT!

If you say that the existence of geo-political Israel today fulfills the promise of God that His people will have a land, it raises a question: "How come God's promises fall short, because they are not occupying the land that God promised?" And, "Who are His people"?

It is fair to say, the world owes them a homeland. But, and this is important, there is no biblical right that geopolitical Israel has today to that particular peace of geography in the Middle East.

The world should give Jews a homeland, and I am half Jewish; I don't mean to speak against the Jews or Israel. Look at how the world has mistreated them.

But do they have a biblical right to that particular peace of geography? It is not in the Bible.

For Israel is not a nation state any more; Israel is the church. Israel is the people of God, Jew and Gentile from every nation and every tribe, and every tongue who confesses faith in the Lord Jesus Christ—the new people of God. Ancient Israel is a preview of what God intends for the new Israel.

Parallel: Should we Christians have any concern that a new temple will be built in Jerusalem? ABSOLUTELY NOT! And in fact if such a building were ever built it would be an abomination.

Do you really think there ought to be a place where animals are sacrificed again? Do you really think there should be a place where the old ceremonial laws of the Old Testament are once again reenacted? That is what some people mean when they say, "Rebuild the Temple in Jerusalem." If they say that, I should not be standing before a pulpit preaching to you the word of God . . . I should be standing before an altar with an animal and a knife, and you should hear the scream of the animal, and you should smell the blood.

Because if you don't understand that Jesus Christ has fulfilled all the promises the Temple meant, all the promises Jesus Christ meant, all the promises that the land meant, all the promises that Israel meant, then we have nothing.

Dr. John Piper, Senior Pastor, Bethlehem Baptist, Minneapolis, Minnesota

Excerpt from Piper's sermon titled, "Israel, Palestine, and the Middle East References: Romans 11:25-32"; March 7, 2004

Today I would like to address the issue of Israel's relation to the "Promised Land" in the Middle East. This is not primarily an expository message from Romans 11, but an effort to draw out implications of Romans 11 and the rest of Scripture for a very vexing problem in the world today. The existence of Israel in the Middle East and the extent of her borders and her sovereignty are perhaps the most explosive factors in world terrorism and the most volatile factors in Arab-Western relations.

The Arab roots and the Jewish roots in this land go back for thousands of years. Both lay claim to the land not merely because of historical presence, but also because of divine right. I won't try to lay out a detailed peace plan. But I will try to lay out some biblical truths that could guide all of us in thinking about peace and justice in that part of the world. What we think about this, and what we say, does matter, since politicians are influenced by their constituents in these religiously super-charged situations. And we need to know how to pray. And we need to know how to talk to others in a way that honors the truth. So for all those reasons, and for the reason that God is very much involved in this situation, we should talk about it in the context of Romans 11.

What we've seen in Romans 11 is that Israel as a whole—that is, as an ethnic, corporate people enduring from generation to generation, has a root in the covenant promises made to Abraham and his descendants. Verse 16b: "If the root is holy so are the branches." We interpreted that picture in the light of verse 28: "As regards the gospel, they [Israel] are enemies of God for your [Gentile] sake. But as regards election, they are beloved for the sake of their forefathers." The "forefathers" here correspond to the root in verse 16. So the promises to the forefathers imply that some day the whole tree, with all its branches, will be saved.

Some day. Because verse 28 says, for now "they are enemies." Verse 28a: "As regards the gospel, they [Israel] are enemies of God for your sake." In other words, they are rejecting their Messiah and thus putting themselves against God. This is what Jesus said to Israel in John 8:42: "If God were your father you would love me. Jesus is the litmus test whether anybody's religion is worship of the true God. **But Israel does not**

love Jesus as God's son and her Messiah. So they are, for now, "enemies of God."

So now we ask is the so-called "Promised Land" part of the inheritance and salvation that "all Israel" (v. 26) will receive? And if so, what does that say about the rights of Israel today to the Land?

The following organizations continue to interfere with God's plan for Israel and the Jewish people:

The Jerusalem Sabeel Document Principles For A Just Peace In Palestine-Israel
      http://www.sabeel.org/old/justice/

World Council of Churches
      http://www.oikoumene.org/en/home.html

National Council of Churches
      http://www.ncccusa.org/

CHAPTER 3

U.S. Catastrophes and Events: 1991-1992

U.S. Administration: President George H. W. Bush

Catastrophe #1
Oakland Firestorm: October 20, 1991
Estimated $2.5 (3.5) Billion Damage/Costs

On Friday, *October 18, 1991*, Secretary of State James A. Baker III, at a news conference in Jerusalem, said President George H. W. Bush and Soviet President Mikhail Gorbachev were inviting Israel, the Arab nations, and the Palestinians to attend a Middle East peace conference to be held beginning October 30 in Madrid. Baker said the conference was to be followed by "direct negotiations to achieve real peace."

Oakland Fire

Sunday, *October 20, 1991*, will be remembered as the date of one of this nation's most costly fires, the worst fire involving loss of life and property since the Great San Francisco Earthquake and Fire of 1906. The Oakland fire began within forty-eight hours of the Bush administration's announcement of their Madrid "land for peace" conference, which was to call on Israel to divide God's covenant land in return for promises of peace and security.

The magnitude and scope of what is simply referred to as the "Tunnel Fire" is far beyond the experience of any living American firefighter. According to one fire official, only those who fought the Chicago Fire last century or battled the Great Fire in San Francisco would be able to identify with this conflagration and firestorm.

The 1991 drought affected the entire western U.S. Reduced rainfall caused the area to become unusually dry. Hardest hit was California, where numerous wildfires broke out across the state. The Oakland fire was most devastating.

The unusual weather conditions were described in FEMA's Hazard Mitigation Report as follows:

> (A)n unusual east wind, at speeds in excess of 65 miles per hour, raced down from the crest of the Oakland-Berkeley Hills. Coupled with record high temperatures well into the nineties, the hot, dry winds gusted and swirled through five years of drought-dry brush and groves of freeze-damaged Monterey pines and eucalyptus trees. All the conditions for a major disaster were present that morning of October 20, 1991.

Catastrophe #2
The Perfect Storm: October 30–November 1, 1991

When the Gulf War ended in 1991, President Bush Sr. began a process to formulate a Middle East peace plan involving Israel, the Palestinians, and the countries surrounding Israel.

The current phase of the Middle East peace process was launched at the Madrid conference convened by the United States and the former Soviet Union on *October 30–November 1, 1991*. Former Secretary of State Baker reached agreement on the conference in a series of trips to the Middle East region between *March* and *October 1991*. (As stated in Catastrophe #1, the decision was finalized on *October 18* in Jerusalem.)

President Bush made it clear to the Israelis, with cancellations of loan guarantees on *September 6, 1991*, that America did not accept the permanent occupation of the West Bank and Gaza. Bush stated,

> Throughout the Middle East, we seek a stable and enduring settlement. We've defined what this means. Indeed, I make these points with no map showing where the final borders are to be drawn. Nevertheless, we believe territorial compromise is essential for peace.

The co-sponsors' letter of invitation to the conference laid out the framework for the negotiations, including:

- A just, lasting, and comprehensive peace settlement based on UN Security Council Resolutions 242 and 338 (see Addendum 2);
- Direct bilateral negotiations along two tracks–between Israel and the Arab nations, and between Israel and the Palestinians; and
- Multilateral negotiations on region-wide issues, such as arms control and regional security, water, refugees, environment, and economic development. These talks would complement bilateral negotiations.

The bilateral negotiations were split into four separate negotiating tracks: Israel-Syria, Israel-Lebanon, Israel-Jordan, and Israel-Palestinian.

Perfect Storm

It was later termed "the perfect storm" and was described by meteorologists as one of the most powerful storms ever. Extremely rare weather patterns, which happen only about once every 100 years, came together to create this weather monster, and record-breaking ocean waves were measured over 100 feet high. This storm ran down the East Coast into the Carolinas, causing millions of dollars in damage. It affected the entire East Coast from Maine to Florida.

The "perfect storm" heavily damaged the Bush family home in Kennebunkport, Maine. Eyewitnesses said waves as high as 30 feet smashed into the president's seafront property. The president had to cancel speaking engagements in order to go and inspect the damage done to his home.

The front-page headlines of *USA Today* on November 1 had the stories of the Madrid conference and the "Perfect Storm" next to each other. One article was titled, "One-on-one peace talks next." The article touching it was titled, "East Coast hit hard by rare storm." The connection between dividing the land of Israel and judgment on the nation causing it was made on the front page of America's largest national newspaper.

Catastrophe #3
Hurricane Andrew: August 23-24, 1992
Estimated $27 (35.6) Billion Damage/Costs

On *August 24, 1992,* round six of the bilateral peace talks resumed in Washington, D.C., until *September 3*. On *August 24*, Prime Minister Rabin canceled eleven deportation orders against PLO activists. Israel presented a detailed autonomy plan, defining the role of the Palestinian Administrative Council controlling civilian matters.

That same day, Hurricane Andrew—a phenomenal Category five storm with top winds recorded at 177 miles per hour—smashed into southern Florida and became the worst natural disaster ever to hit America. It was described by the National Hurricane Center as a 25-to-30-mile-wide tornado, and it left 180,000 people in Florida homeless and another 25,000 in Louisiana. Damage was estimated as high as $30 billion.

On *August 24*, the front pages of the *New York Times* and *USA Today* contained adjacent headlines about Hurricane Andrew and the reconvened Middle East peace talks which reportedly resumed "on a positive note." Newspapers that day also ran stories about President Bush's ratings collapsing in the polls, falling behind Bill Clinton (in the presidential election race) by a substantial margin. Only a year before, after the Gulf War victory, Bush (who initiated the Madrid Conference) had a tremendous approval rating as high as 92 percent.

Three major events converged on the same day. The Madrid Conference convened for the first time on American soil; Hurricane Andrew became the worst natural disaster in American history; and the popularity of President Bush began vanishing in the popularity polls. The timing was breathtaking.

Event #4
Perot Candidacy Helped Cost Bush Reelection
October 1–November 3, 1992

Why H. Ross Perot Disliked George H. W. Bush

Reportedly, Perot came to loath George Bush because he believed Bush did not do enough to search for POWs in Vietnam. Perot's hatred for President Reagan's vice president grew during Bush's run for president in 1988. Perot, a native Texan, learned that Bush, the son of a senator from Connecticut, was a resident of Texas only because he rented a hotel suite in Houston.

Four years later, Bush's popularity was temporarily high after Desert Storm and a second Bush term seemed inevitable.

In early 1992, Bush faced a serious challenge from Pat Buchanan, who received 37 percent of the New Hampshire primary vote. Buchanan's prime time "cultural wars" speech at the Republican convention became a media scandal for Bush. His convention had been poorly run because he insisted that Secretary of State Baker resign and run his campaign. Baker resented returning to politics and refused to manage the convention. Also, Bush had lost his brilliant and ruthless campaign manager—Lee Atwater—to a premature cancerous death, and was left without top-drawer campaign advice and operations.

In *February 1992*, Perot appeared on Larry King's CNN TV talk show and said he would consider running against Bush if volunteers could get his name on all 50 state ballots. Millions of U.S. citizens responded by signing petitions, which put Perot on the ballots of all 50 states by *September 12*.

On *April 28*, a *Washington Post*/ABC News poll found Bush at 36 percent, Clinton at 31 percent and Perot at 30 percent. The poll was deemed especially significant because it was the first one that put Perot, an Independent, within striking distance of the major party candidates.

Perot began appearing on more talk shows and produced his own half-hour TV infomercials to explain his positions on national issues.

By being an Independent and attacking Bush, he, in the words of Democratic political operative Paul Tully, "departisanized the critique of Bush," thus giving credibility to Clinton's campaign attacks.

On *July 16,* Perot quit the presidential race saying he decided to withdraw because the Democratic Party had "revitalized" itself. (Perot's supporters continued their efforts to place his name on all state ballots.)

Ross Perot Reentered Presidential Race;
Bush Lost Election 34 Days Later

On *October 1*, Perot reentered the presidential race as an independent, making the announcement at a Dallas press conference.

On *October 11*, he debated Clinton and Bush in St. Louis, the first of three nationally televised debates. Perot's opening line at the first presidential debate—"Well, they've got a point, I don't have any experience running up a $4 trillion debt"— reminded voters why they had initially supported his maverick candidacy. Prior to the debates, Perot earned only 5 percent of voter support in the polls. His performance at the three debates, along with network broadcasts of his highly rated infomercials, helped him win 19 percent of the popular vote on Election Day. It was the best showing of a third-party candidate for president since Theodore Roosevelt's run in 1912 with the progressive Bull Moose Party.

Bill Clinton, with the help of Ross Perot, defeated President Bush. Republicans criticized Perot, believing that his conservative platform appealed to Republican and swing voters and effectively gave the election to Bill Clinton. Moreover, with the election loss, President Bush would no longer be actively involved in the Middle East peace process that he initiated twelve months earlier in Madrid, Spain.

Federal Election Commission (FEC) documents state Perot spent $65.6 million of his personal fortune on the 1992 campaign.

Summary of Actions and
Coinciding Catastrophes or Events
During Presidency of George H. W. Bush
(1991-1992)

Date	Action	Date	Catastrophe
October 18, 1991	U.S. announces upcoming Madrid peace conference with USSR, Israel, Arab nations, and Palestinians	*October 20, 1991*	**Oakland Firestorm**: greatest fire and loss of life since 1906 in U.S.; $2.5 billion.
October 30 - November 1, 1991	Madrid Middle East peace conference	*October 30 - November 1, 1991*	**Perfect Storm**: worst storm in 100 years covered east coast; Pres. Bush home damaged.
August 24, 1992	Round 6 of peace talks resume in Washington, DC.; Israel came with autonomy plan for Palestinians.	*August 23-24, 1992*	**Hurricane Andrew**: worst natural disaster in U.S. history to date; $27 billion.
February - July 16 & October 1- November 3, 1992	H. Ross Perot enters election race for U.S. presidency, drops out, then reenters race.	*Election Day, November 3, 1992*	Perot candidacy **costs President Bush reelection**.

CHAPTER 4

U.S. Catastrophes
and Events: 1993-1996

U.S. Administration:
President William J. Clinton

Catastrophe #5
World Trade Center Bombing
February 26, 1993
Estimated damages $750 million

In the first trip to Israel by a Clinton administration official, United States Secretary of State Warren M. Christopher visited eight Middle East nations from *February 18-25, 1993*.

Upon his arrival in Israel, Secretary Christopher reconfirmed the special relationship, based on shared democratic values and common interests that exist between Israel and the U.S. Citing President Bill Clinton's determination to make the ties binding our two countries "even stronger and more resilient," the Secretary also reaffirmed the United States' unalterable commitment to Israel's security and its qualitative military edge, a commitment based on our recognition of Israel's continuing security challenges.

The Secretary observed that real security for Israel can only be brought about by real peace—not just the absence of war but peace reflected in lasting treaties, normalized relations, and genuine reconciliation with her neighbors and the Palestinians. To that end, and recognizing that obstacles still existed, he reiterated the U.S. commitment to the role of full partner in a reinvigorated peace process. While Christopher was on his way back to Washington, DC, the U.S. was hit by the largest terror event to date in American history.

On *February 26, 1993*, a car bomb exploded underneath the World Trade Center in New York City. The immense blast occurred at 12:18 p.m. EDT, in the

45

Secret Service's section of the car park underneath and between New York's tallest buildings. It ripped through three floors of concrete, scattering ash and debris and set off a fire that sent choking smoke and flames up through one of the 110-story "Twin Towers." The resulting explosion killed six people and injured more than a thousand. More than 50,000 people were evacuated from the Trade Center complex during the hours immediately following the blast.

The bombing shocked America, which had seemed immune from acts of terrorism that plagued other parts of the world.

An emotional Mario Cuomo, New York's state governor, told journalists: "We all have that feeling of being violated. No foreign people or force has ever done this to us. Until now, we were invulnerable."

Catastrophe #6
Storm of the Century: March 12-15, 1993
Estimated $3-6 (3.8-7.6) billion damages/costs

The following is an excerpt of the opening statement made by Secretary Christopher on *March 10, 1993*, at a news conference in Washington, D.C.:

President Clinton has asked me to make an announcement today on our efforts in the Middle East. Events in the Middle East have historically captured the attention of the world. Unfortunately, too often this has been because of war. This is a region that since 1948 had known five Arab-Israeli wars. And every time there has been a war, the world has held its breath because the risk of a super-Power confrontation was ever present.

I believe we now have an opportunity to promote peace that will serve the interests of Israel, the Arab States, the Palestinians, and the entire community. A passive American role is not enough. What is called for is an active, positive effort that will take advantage of what many believe to be a historic moment in that region.

We must now seize this opportunity to play the role of full partner, just as we did in the achievement of the Israeli-Egyptian peace fourteen years ago. We have been repaid in full over the years by strong friendship and ties with both Israel and Egypt. The visits to Washington by [Israeli] Prime Minister Rabin this week and by [Egyptian] President Mubarak in April are testimony to the enduring nature of the relationships that were forged out of this negotiation.

It is time for the people in this region to set aside violence and work together for reconciliation and peace. The important steps taken at the Madrid conference have opened up a wide vista of possibilities. Over the years, Arabs and Israelis have sat together—that is, over the course of the last year they have sat together—in bilateral negotiations, seeking to achieve a comprehensive settlement based upon UN Security Council resolutions 242 and 338 (see Addendum 2).

The resumption of bilateral and multilateral negotiations, which we are announcing today, is important but not an end in itself.

We must now all roll up our sleeves to make 1993 a year marked by real progress toward peace and reconciliation. The United States is prepared to do its part, and now the other parties must be prepared to do theirs.

Israeli Prime Minister Yitzak Rabin visited the United States from *March 15-17, 1993*. On *March 15*, President Clinton and Rabin spoke on the unique bond between the U.S. and Israel in a news conference following their meeting in the White House. The two leaders discussed issues in U.S.-Israeli relations, including U.S. aid to Israel and peace negotiations in the Middle East. Rabin also visited Secretary of State Christopher and Secretary of Defense Les Aspin, congressional leaders, the media, and Jewish leaders.

Storm of the Century

Two days after Secretary Christopher made the above statement, the storm—called the "Storm of the Century"—began and battered the eastern U.S. for four days, from *March 12-15, 1993,* with tornadoes, high winds, record low pressure and heavy snows. On the Saffir-Simpson hurricane scale it would have been a Category 3. The storm affected 26 states, impacting the lives of nearly 100 million people. At one point, the storm covered one-third of the U.S. Damage was recorded from Texas to the Ohio Valley and Maine

There was $3-6 billion ($3.8-$7.6 billion in 2003 dollars) in damages and 270 deaths attributed to the storm on land, with 48 more missing at sea. Fifteen tornadoes in Florida killed 44, while six inches of snow fell on the Florida Panhandle. Hurricane-force winds were reported from Louisiana all the way to Florida, and up the East Coast to New York and New England. The western coast of Florida received hurricane force winds up to 120 mph, with ten-foot storm surges. Winds over 100 mph were reported on the Dry Tortugas (west of Key West, Florida) and on Flattop Mountain in North Carolina, and peak wind speeds of 99 mph were recorded at a drilling station off the coast of Louisiana.

Mount LeConte in Tennessee received 56 inches of snow; Syracuse, New York, 43 inches; Albany, New York, 20 inches; Chattanooga, Tennessee, 20 inches; and Roanoke, Virginia, 16 inches.

Every airport on the East Coast was closed at one time or another for the first time ever, canceling 25 percent of the United States' flights for two days. Snow fell at two to three inches per hour. On the west coast of Florida, along the outer banks of North Carolina, and on Long Island, homes fell into the sea or received wind or wave damage. Fallen tree limbs and power lines left three million people along the storm's path in the dark.

Catastrophe #7
Midwest Flooding: May–September 1993
Estimated $21 (26.7) billion damages/costs

After intense "behind-the-scenes" contacts and negotiations from *April 27* to *September 13, 1993,* between Israeli and Palestinian negotiators in Oslo, an agreement was achieved between Foreign Minister Shimon Peres and Palestinian Liberation Organization (PLO) Chairman Yasser Arafat. The Declaration of Principles on Interim Self-Government Arrangements, which follows, was signed on the South Lawn of the White House on *September 13, 1993.*

> The aim of the Israeli-Palestinian negotiations within the current Middle East peace process is, among other things, to establish a Palestinian Interim Self-Government Authority, the elected Council (the "Council"), for the Palestinian people in the West Bank and the Gaza Strip, for a transitional period not exceeding five years, leading to a permanent settlement based on Security Council Resolutions 242 and 338.

> It is understood that the interim arrangements are an integral part of the whole peace process and that the negotiations on the permanent status will lead to the implementation of Security Council Resolutions 242 and 338 (see Addendum 2).

September 13, 1993

A new page in the history of the Middle East was turned at the White House, as Israeli Prime Minister Rabin and PLO Chairman Arafat met and watched Israeli Foreign Minister Peres and PLO Executive Council Member Abou Abbas sign the agreement. President Clinton, former presidents George H. W. Bush and Jimmy Carter, and 3,000 dignitaries witnessed the signing—on the same desk used in the signing of the Camp David Accords 15 years earlier.

The Great Midwest Flood of 1993

The Great Midwest Flood of 1993 was the "most devastating flood in modern United States history" with economic damages near $21 billion. More than 50,000 homes were damaged or destroyed. The area extent, intensity, and long duration of the flooding made this event unique in the 20th century (National Oceanic and Atmospheric Administration, 1994). At least 38 people lost their lives as a result of this extreme flood (Interagency Floodplain Management Task Force, 1994).

From *May* through *September* of *1993*, major and/or record flooding occurred across North Dakota, South Dakota, Nebraska, Kansas, Minnesota, Iowa, Missouri, Wisconsin, and Illinois. Hundreds of levees failed along the Mississippi and Missouri Rivers.

The magnitude and severity of this flood was simply over-whelming; it ranks as one of the greatest natural disasters ever to hit the United States. Approximately 600 river forecast points in midwestern U.S. were above flood stage at the same time. Nearly 150 major rivers and tributaries were affected.

Putting this into perspective, the Middle East peace efforts intensified in late April and early May, and throughout the summer, with an eventual agreement signed at the White House on *September 13*. At the signing ceremony, President Clinton pledged continued direct engagement of the United States in the peace process. Moreover, the top news in the American newspapers throughout the summer had been the status of the Oslo Middle East peace talks *and* the history-making midwestern U.S. floods. As the heartland of Israel was being negotiated, the heartland of America was being devastated with record rains and floods costing $21 billion.

Catastrophe #8
Northridge Earthquake: January 17, 1994
Estimated $15.3 (18.9) billion damages/costs

On *January 16, 1994*, at Geneva, President Hafez al-Assad of the Syrian Arab Republic and U.S. President Clinton made the following opening statements at their joint news conference:

President al-Assad:

Syria seeks a just and comprehensive peace with Israel as a strategic choice that secures Arab rights, ends the Israeli occupation, and enables our peoples in the region to live in peace, security and dignity. In honor we fought, in honor we negotiate, and in honor we shall make peace. We want an honorable peace for our people and for the hundreds of thousands who paid their lives in defense of their countries and their rights.

There is hardly a home in Syria in which there is no martyr who fell in defense of his country, nation and of Arab rights. For the sake of all those, for their sons, daughters and families, we want the peace of the brave—a genuine peace which can survive and last—a peace which secures the interests of each side and renders all their rights.

President Clinton:

During our meeting, I told President Assad that I was personally committed to the objective of a comprehensive and secure peace that would produce genuine reconciliation among the peoples of the Middle East. I told him of my view that the agreement between Israel and the PLO constituted an important first step by establishing an agreed basis for resolving the Palestinian problem. I also told him that I believe Syria is the key to the achievement of an enduring and comprehensive peace that finally will put an end to the conflict between Israel and her Arab neighbors.

President Assad, as you have just heard, shares this objective—not just an end to war, but the establishment of real and comprehensive peace with Israel that will ensure normal, peaceful relations among good neighbors. Crucial decisions will have to be made by Syria and Israel if this common objective is to be achieved. That is why President Assad has called for a "peace of the brave." And it is why I join him now in endorsing that appeal.

Accordingly, we pledge today to work together in order to bring the negotiations that started in Madrid over two years ago to a prompt and successful conclusion. Critical issues remain to be resolved, especially the questions relating to withdrawals, to peace and security—excuse me, the question of relating withdrawal to peace and security. But, as a result of our conversation today, I am confident that we laid the foundations for real progress in the negotiations between heads of delegations that will begin again next week in Washington.

President Assad and I also discussed the state of relations between the United States and Syria and agreed on the desirability of improving them.

Northridge Earthquake

Less than 24 hours later, on January 17, 1994, at 4:30:55 am PST, a powerful 6.9 earthquake rocked southern California. This $15 billion earthquake was centered in Northridge, about 25 miles from Los Angeles. This quake was the second most destructive natural disaster ever to hit the United States, second only to Hurricane Andrew, and it also occurred at ground zero of the U.S. pornography industry.

Catastrophe #9
Texas Flooding: October 17-21, 1994
Estimated $1 (1.2) billion damages/costs

On *October 17, 1994*, Israeli Prime Minister Yitzhak Rabin and Jordanian Prime Minister Dr. Abdel Salaam Al-Majali initialed the text of a peace treaty. Jordan and Israel signed the full peace treaty in an October 26 ceremony in the Arava Valley of Israel. President Clinton's participation in the signing ceremony underscored the U.S. commitment to the peace process. Israel and Jordan had continued their work to complete the various agreements called for in their peace treaty.

Southeast Texas Flooding

It was the worst flooding to impact southeast Texas on record. Lake Livingston recorded a record height on the 17th of October and a record flow of 110,000 cubic feet per second (cfs). Liberty recorded 30 inches of rainfall in less than 48 hours, and much of the city went underwater due to a failed levee system. Spring Creek and Lake Houston set new flood crest records. Several major highways into and out of Houston were flooded, including I-45 north of Houston and U.S. 59 northeast of Houston. Four fuel pipelines ruptured on the San Jacinto River, causing a massive fuel spill and widespread fires. An estimated 22,000 homes were flooded across southeast Texas during this event, with $900 million in damages reported. Seventeen fatalities resulted from the floods.

Catastrophe #10
Hurricane Opal: September 27–October 5, 1995
Estimated $3.0 (3.6) billion damages/costs

On *September 28, 1995*, the Israeli-Palestinian Interim Agreement on the West Bank and the Gaza Strip was signed in Washington, D.C. The agreement contained thirty-one articles and seven annexes (redeployment and security, elections, civil affairs, legal matters, economic relations, cooperation programs, and prisoner release). Following the signing, President Clinton hosted a summit attended by King Hussein of Jordan, President Hosny Mubarak of Egypt, Prime Minister Rabin, and Chairman Arafat. The leaders reviewed progress toward a comprehensive peace and ways to reinforce and accelerate that progress.

On *September 29, 1995*, Secretary Christopher, Foreign Minister Peres, and Chairman Arafat convened the first meeting of the U.S.-Israel-Palestinian Trilateral Committee. The parties agreed to promote cooperative efforts to foster economic development in the West Bank and Gaza; to explore the means to increase the availability and more efficient use of water resources; to consult on matters of mutual interest; and to promote cooperation on regional issues.

Under the U.S.-Jordan-Israel Trilateral Economic Commit-tee, Israel and Jordan had completed the first phase of the Jordan Rift Valley (JRV) Joint Master Plan.

The second phase, an eighteen-month Integrated Development Study of the JRV, began in *October 1995*. The parties had outlined a number of projects deal-ing with the environment, water, energy, transportation, and tourism. They agreed to establish a tourism development initiative around the Dead Sea and a Red Sea Marine Peace Park with assistance from the U.S. government. They also agreed to explore the establishment of a free-trade zone in Aqaba-Eilat, with a view to making it an economic hub for the northern peninsula of the Red Sea. Israel and Jordan, together with the United States, also agreed to conduct feasibility studies on expanding the Aqaba airport and developing telecommu-nications.

Hurricane Opal

After drifting over the Yucatan Peninsula and the southwestern Gulf of Mexico from *September 27* to *October 2*, Hurricane Opal turned northeast toward the Florida peninsula. National Hurricane Center advisories and satellite imagery from the Louisiana State University Earth Scan Laboratory indicated that the system significantly intensified as it passed over the central Gulf, attain-ing Category 4 status on the Saffir/Simpson scale by 6 a.m. EST on *October 4*.

On *October 4, 1995*, over a thousand miles of coastline stretching from southwest Florida to Louisiana was struck by storm-generated waves as Hurricane Opal moved northward across the Gulf of Mexico toward landfall east of Pensacola Beach, Florida. Approximately twelve hours before landfall on October 4, Opal neared Category 5 strength with sustained wind speeds of over 65 meters per second. Storm surge levels of about five meters were estimated across the Northwest Florida shelf by the National Hurricane Center (NHC), resulting in the over-wash of most of Santa Rosa Island, the most affected sec-tion of coast in the Gulf.

Opal ranked the strongest of the 18 hurricanes that have struck the Pensacola area since 1900, and it was the most devastating. According to the National Oceanic and Atmospheric Administration (NOAA), Hurricane Opal produced $3 billion in damages/costs and 27 deaths.

Summary of Actions and
Resulting Catastrophes or Events
During Presidency of Bill Clinton
1993-1995

Date	Action	Date	Catastrophe
February 18-25, 1993	U.S. Secretary of State Christopher visited Israel and 7 Arab nations to restart peace process.	*February 26, 1993*	**World Trade Center Bombing**: $750 million.
March 10, 1993 *March 15-17*	Sec. Christopher press conference on Israel. Israel PM Rabin met with Pres. Clinton & others.	*March 12-15, 1993*	**Storm of the Century:** 318 dead; up to 120 mph winds & 56" of snow; all east coast airports closed at times; $3-6 billion.
April 27 – September 1993 *September 13*	• Israeli-Palestinian negotiations in Oslo, Norway. • Israel and PLO sign compromise peace agreement at White House.	*May – September 1993*	**Midwest Flooding**: 38 dead; most devastating and widespread floods in modern U.S. history; $21 billion
January 16, 1994	Pres. Clinton and Syrian Pres. al-Assad made statements supporting Oslo agreement as 1st step to peace.	*January 17, 1994*	**Northridge Earthquake**: 2nd most destructive natural disaster in U.S. history; also ground zero of pornography industry in U.S.; $15.3 billion.
October 17, 1994	Israel PM Rabin & Jordan PM Majali sign peace agreement. Pres. Clinton present.	*October 17-21, 1994*	**Texas Flooding**: 17 dead; worst flooding on record in Texas; $1 billion.
September 28, 1995 *September 29*	• In Washington, DC, Israel & PLO sign Interim Agreement on West Bank & Gaza Strip. • Pres. Clinton hosts summit with King Hussein of Jordan, Egypt Pres. Mubarak, Israel PM Rabin, and Chairman Arafat. • Sec. Christopher, FM Peres & Chairman Arafat convene 1st U.S.-Israel-Palestine Trilateral Comm.	*September 27 – October 5, 1995*	**Hurricane Opal:** 27 dead; strongest hurricane to hit Pensacola, FL since 1900, also hit 1,000 miles of the southern U.S. gulf coast; started Sept. 27, hit U.S. October 4; $3 billion.

CHAPTER 5

U.S. Catastrophes
& Events: 1997-2000

U.S. Administration: President William J. Clinton

In *early 1997*, the Israeli government had begun to build 6,500 Jewish housing units in East Jerusalem, a section of the city that was claimed by the Palestinians. Yasser Arafat, Chairman of the Palestine Liberation Organization (PLO), was upset, and he asked for a meeting with U.S. President Bill Clinton to discuss this issue.

Chairman Arafat arrived in Washington, D.C., on Sunday, *March 2*, for meetings with President Clinton.

Clinton told reporters on March 3 that he would have preferred if Israel had not decided to build the Har Homa housing project in East Jerusalem.

> The important thing [is for Arabs and Israelis] to be building confidence and working together. And so I would have preferred the decision not have been made, because I don't think it builds confidence, I think it builds mistrust, and I wish that it had not been made.

Clinton made the remarks in response to reporters' questions as he began a meeting in the Oval Office with Palestinian leader Yasser Arafat.

Arafat said the new settlements are "to squeeze and to isolate Jerusalem." Asked about U.S. views on Jerusalem, Clinton said:

> I do not believe, now that the parties have reached the agreement that they reached in 1993 and they have made this a final status issue, that the United States can serve any useful purpose by saying or especially by doing anything which seems to prejudge what should be a final status issue between the parties. I think that would be a big mistake.

As Arafat left the White House, the Palestinian leader told reporters that he and Clinton had "fruitful, positive, constructive talks. . . . We discussed everything in detail and the most important thing is the very good Palestinian-American relations, including the joint Palestinian-American committee."

Catastrophe #11
Mississippi and Ohio Valley Flooding and Tornadoes
March 1-2, 1997
Estimated $1 (1.1) billion damages/costs

On *March 1, 1997*, a severe weather situation with tornadoes and very heavy rainfall erupted along a nearly stationary front from Texas to West Virginia. At mid-afternoon on Saturday, an outbreak of strong to violent tornadoes in Arkansas, northern Mississippi, and western Tennessee resulted in 29 deaths, including 26 in Arkansas. Several of the tornadoes were estimated as F-4 intensity, with winds in the 207-260 mph range. This was the deadliest U.S. outbreak of tornadoes since March 27, 1994, when 42 were killed in Alabama, Georgia, and South Carolina. Fortunately in this outbreak, the National Weather Service issued tornado warnings from ten to thirty-two minutes before the tornadoes struck, using NEXRAD radar to provide much more lead time than previously possible.

This event also produced unusually heavy rainfall from northeast Arkansas through western Tennessee and southeast Missouri, and into much of Kentucky, southern Indiana and Ohio, and West Virginia. In many areas, the rains fell on nearly saturated ground left by the snows and rainfall of the past few months. In parts of northern Kentucky, rainfall rates averaged at least one inch per hour for a twelve-hour period on March 1.

A total of 67 deaths were attributed to this event, and damages were $1 billion overall. The last significant flooding along the Ohio River occurred in 1964, resulting in 11 deaths and about $50 million damage. Prior to 1964, the "great flood of 1937" was even more severe, with some towns erecting floodwalls shortly thereafter. These floodwalls (including one protecting Louisville) prevented the flooding from taking an even greater toll.

When Chairman Arafat used America as a platform to promote the dividing of Israel, and President Clinton warmly received him, the president's own home state was devastated by tornadoes, and the nation was ravaged by storms and floods soon thereafter.

The connection was again captured and documented by the *New York Times* on *March 4, 1997*. The front-page headlines reported, "In storm's wake, grief and shock" adjacent to a photo of President Clinton with Arafat with the caption reading, "President Clinton rebukes Israel." The *New York Times*, perhaps inadvertently, linked the U.S. action and judgment.

Catastrophe #12
Northern Plains Flooding: April 1–May 14, 1997
Estimated $3.7 (4.1) billion damages/costs

Clinton Tries to Get Middle East Peace Process on Track

President Clinton said he and Israel's Prime Minister Benjamin Netanyahu had "a very specific, frank, candid and long talk" on *April 7* about the stalled peace process in the Middle East.

The two met for nearly two hours in the Oval Office, the first 90 minutes with a small group of their foreign policy advisers present, followed by 25 minutes of one-on-one conversations.

Rather than say too much about what was said, Clinton expressed his desire to work very hard on moving the peace process forward, saying, "and that's what I'm going to do, I'm going to do my best to get it back on track."

Later in the day, the White House announced that the president had invited Netanyahu back to the White House for coffee at 9 p.m.

White House Press Secretary Mike McCurry characterized the earlier meeting as "profoundly important," coming at "a very important juncture in the peace process itself." He said Clinton presented the Prime Minister with "some serious things to think about," and Netanyahu had some ideas too.

Clinton said he was "heavily involved" in the Middle East peace process from the day he became president, would continue to be heavily involved, and wouldn't rule out any reasonable opportunity to make a positive contribution.

Flooding of the Red River Valley and Tributaries

Substantial flooding occurred in the Northern Plains of the United States and southern Manitoba, Canada during *April–May 1997*, with many rivers reaching record high levels during the month.

Residents of the upper Midwest were digging out April 7 from a spring blizzard that began as rain and changed to heavy snow over the weekend. The *April 5* blizzard added much to the weather woes in the upper Midwest.

For parts of Minnesota, the spring snows brought a double whammy to a region already battling floods caused by runoff from melting winter snow.

"We've been planning for the flood since January, so the planning has frankly paid off," said Minnesota Gov. Arne Carlson. "But the combination of snow and ice along with melting rain has really hurt us. Many people say this is the worst they've ever seen."

The primary cause of this flooding was a highly abnormal thaw during *March* and *April* of substantial winter snow and river ice. Characteristics of the thaw included its timing, duration and extent, as well as the diurnal temperature changes during the periods of substantial snow and ice melt.

In the Red River Valley of eastern North Dakota and west-central Minnesota, flooding persisted from *early April* through *mid-May*. At Fargo, North Dakota the Red River peaked at more than 6.6 meters above flood stage during this period, a level reached only once previously in the past 100 years. Farther north, river levels at East Grand Forks also peaked at more than 6.6 meters above flood stage, slightly exceeding the 500-year statistical recurrence interval at that site. Record flooding also occurred in all major tributaries of the Red River during April, including the Wild Rice and Maple Rivers (a record 1.8 meters above flood stage), the Sheyenne River (a record 2.5 meters above flood stage) and the Buffalo River (a record 1.1 meters above flood stage).

The Red River crested at 39.5 feet, 22.5 feet above flood stage at Fargo, N.D. on Thursday, *April 17*, breaking a one-hundred-year-old record. The crest then surged into Grand Forks, N.D., and East Grand Forks, Minn., pushing water levels to 54.2 feet on *April 21*; flood stage is 28 feet. The Red River in Canada crested in Manitoba's Capitol city of 660,000 early on *May 4*, causing the worst flooding the region has seen since 1852.

The Red River, which borders North Dakota and Minnesota and flows north toward Lake Winnipeg in Manitoba, Canada, finally fell below flood levels in the U.S. in early June of 1997. The James River, which flows southward into the Mississippi River, also saw major flooding in 1997.

1997 Red River Flooding at a Glance

EVACUATIONS: Estimated 80,000 people in North Dakota, Minnesota and
    Manitoba, including 47,500 of the 50,000 residents of Grand Forks.
SCHOOLS: Thousands of displaced children enrolled in schools elsewhere in
    North Dakota and Minnesota.
DEATHS: Five flood-related deaths in the two states and Canada.
CAUSE: Record winter snowfall, more than 100 inches in many areas, fol-
    lowed by a quick thaw and then an April 5 blizzard.
LAND: The area is so flat that locals say any heavy precipitation is like pour-
    ing water on a tabletop. In this case, water spread out, creating a shallow
    lake up to 25 miles wide—even wider where the flood joined existing
    pools of standing water.
WATER: Despite the flatness of the land, water rushed by at ten feet per sec-
    ond as it passed Grand Forks. River crested there at 54.2 feet late Monday,
    26 feet above flood stage.

Event #13
Foreign Financial Contagion —
Loss of Hundreds of Billions Worldwide
July 1997–October 1998

The United Nations General Assembly, meeting in an emergency special session *April 27, 1997*, condemned Israel for the Har Homa building project in East Jerusalem, and demanded an immediate halt to the construction of the "new settlement in Jebl Abu Ghneim."

Israel immediately attacked the resolution and the UN session producing it.

"Israel categorically rejects the one-sided resolution adopted by this session, which stands in contradiction to the peace process and its principles," said David Peleg, the Israeli charge d'affaires.

Although the votes of the General Assembly are not binding, they indicate the depth of international anger and unease with the Har Homa housing project. The tally was 134-to-3, with 11 abstentions. The U.S. and Micronesia joined Israel in opposing the resolution, which also called for the "cessation of all forms of assistance and support for illegal Israeli activities" in the "occupied Palestinian territory."

The *April 27* vote, the second on Har Homa in the assembly since *March 13*, came from an emergency session that was requested by Qatar on *March 31*. It was the first such session since 1982 and only the tenth since the Korean War.

Peleg said it was unwarranted. "There was no procedural or substantive justification for the convening of the 'special emergency session' . . . concerning the construction of a residential neighborhood in Jerusalem."

The U.S. does not support the Har Homa project, but had objected to the session on grounds that Israeli-Palestinian disputes should be resolved through direct negotiations. Further, said U.S. Ambassador Bill Richardson, the debate "can only harden the positions of both sides and make their work even more difficult." Richardson said the resolution set "a dangerous precedent" by infringing on the Security Council's authority.

The UN debates began over the building of 6,500 housing units. Once the debate opened, however, it was not confined to Har Homa.

The resolution recommended that the permanent-status talks on Jerusalem reach an agreement that includes "internationally guaranteed provisions to ensure the freedom of religion and of conscience of its inhabitants" as well as "permanent, free and unhindered access to the Holy Places by the faithful of all religions and nationalities."

The Assembly met again to resume its tenth emergency special session on Israeli activities in East Jerusalem and the rest of the West Bank territory. On *July 15*, it condemned Israel's failure to comply with its demands to immediate-

ly cease building the new settlement at Jebel Abu Ghneim, and demanded that
it immediately cease and reverse all illegal actions taken against Palestinian
Jerusalemites.

By a vote of 131 for to 3 against (Israel, Federated States of Micronesia,
United States), with 14 abstentions, the Assembly also demanded that Israel, the
occupying power, make available information about goods produced or manufactured in the settlements, including Jerusalem.

The Assembly recommended that the high contracting parties to the Geneva
Convention on the protection of civilians in time of war convene a conference
on measures to enforce the Convention in the occupied territories, including
Jerusalem, and to ensure respect for it.

In adopting the resolution, the Assembly also recommended that member
nations actively discourage activities that directly contribute to the construction
of or development of Israeli settlements in the occupied territories.

Speaking for the European Union and associated nations, the representative
of Luxembourg, Mr. Wolzfeld, reiterated that settlements in the occupied territories contravened international law, constituted a major obstacle to peace, and
violated the Fourth Geneva Convention.

What Is Financial Contagion?

Financial contagion is the transmission of economic shocks from one country to others, through trade or other economic connections. Financial interde-
pendence can transmit a crisis from one country to another, for example, if countries borrow from the same creditors. Faced with a crisis in one country, banks
and other lenders may lose their nerve and start recalling loans made to borrow-
ers in the region, creating a domino effect and a costly and debilitating credit crisis.

Foreign Financial Contagion

The Asian economic collapse of *1997* sent shivers through world markets
throughout *1998*, threatening even the vigorous U.S. economy. Financial experts
blamed corrupt governments, unregulated banking systems, fickle investors, and
the International Monetary Fund. The turmoil also led the world's financial elite
to debate the need for capital controls in an age when global capital flows evi-
dently can wreak havoc on national economies.

The Asian financial crisis, which erupted in *July 1997* in Thailand, awoke
the world to "contagion," a new peril inherent to highly interconnected financial
markets. Spreading quickly within and outside the region, the crisis brought the
world's 11th largest economy, South Korea, to the brink of bankruptcy, and led
to the defaults by Russia and Brazil.

Following years of stellar performances, Thailand, Malaysia, Indonesia, the Philippines, and South Korea experienced a plunge in their currency values and a sudden reversal of private capital flows beginning in *June 1997.*

Investors had poured massive amounts of funds into Asian countries until the first half of 1997, and then drastically reversed course as investor money streamed out at a staggering pace. The ensuing $100 billion negative capital flow delivered a huge shock to the region.

Russia's Crisis

Meantime, the "currency based" financial contagion created by the Asian crisis of 1997 and 1998 caused investors to become risk averse, reassessing their investment in the rest of the emerging economies, which put pressure on Russian financial markets. As a result, international capital began to leave Russia and interest rates in all emerging economies rose. Russian asset markets plummeted, sparking speculation on the ruble. In addition, Russia's banking sector suffered due to falling asset prices, triggering capital outflows from Russia. Russia found itself unable to service the debt.

By *July 1998*, the Russian government was unable to roll over treasury bills maturing before the end of 1999. The IMF had approved a financial rescue package of $11 billion to support Russia. Within a month, on *August 17, 1998*, Russia abandoned the exchange rate peg and declared unilateral default on $40 billion in short-term domestic treasury debt, of which about one-third was held by foreign investors. Russia had also defaulted on much of its Soviet-era foreign debt of $40 billion to the Paris Club of government creditors on *April 29, 1996,* and of $20 billion to the London Club of commercial creditors at the *end of 1998.*

Brazil's Crisis

Brazil's fiscal deficit continued to be very large forcing the IMF Plan to rely on tight monetary policy. The Asian crisis of *mid-1997* and the Russian crisis of *August 1998* caused investors to be highly risk averse in the emerging economies, which resulted in high interest rates worldwide. Brazil increased the money market rate from 22 percent in *October 1997* to 43 percent in *November 1997,* and from 19 percent in *August 1998* to 42 percent in *October 1998.* In addition, Brazil spent about $35 billion of foreign reserves from *April 1998* to *October 1998* to defend the crawling peg.

[Note: "crawling peg" refers to foreign exchange rates which allow an automatic change in the par value of a nation's currency by way of minor increments either upward or downward, if in actual daily trading on the foreign exchange markets the price in terms of other monies remain on the floor or ceiling of the established range for a given period].

After the failure of the rescue package to Russia, the IMF, on *November 13, 1998*, approved a three-year financial rescue package of $41.5 billion to Brazil, which was designed to stop global financial turmoil from spreading to Latin America. The package was anchored by the IMF with $18 billion; the Inter-American Development Bank with $4.5 billion; the World Bank with $4.5 billion; the U.S. with $5 billion; and Japan, Germany, Britain, France, Spain, Italy, and other wealthy nations with $9.5 billion. The IMF financial package added to Brazil's existing debt, and the total external debt by the *end of 1998* was estimated to be around $305 billion—about 35 percent of GDP.

As the nations of the world called on Israel to make painful concessions to a terrorist state and instructed them how to conduct their internal business, these nations began experiencing an enormous, worldwide financial crisis, causing them to incur hundreds of billions of dollars in losses (and losses in the value of their own currencies) in an unprecedented financial crisis.

Catastrophe #14
Northeast Ice Storm: January 4-9, 1998
Estimated $1.4 (1.5) billion damages/costs

In Jerusalem on *January 7, 1998*, U.S. Special Middle East Coordinator Dennis Ross told the press that he was in the region now to help "prepare the ground" for the upcoming meetings in Washington, D.C. Ross said he had good meetings with Israel's President Weizman.

Transcript of Ross' Remarks:

I just had a chance to speak with President Weizman, part of the effort that I am engaged in out here right now, as I help to prepare the ground for the upcoming meeting. We had a good discussion. I am going to have more discussions, and we are going to keep working towards what is our objective of trying to find a way to put the process back on track.

President Weizman outlined his views and obviously would be part of our efforts to, as I said, prepare the ground, to see how best to move forward as we look to the meetings in Washington.
[Provided by USIS Tel Aviv]

Northeast Ice Storm

One of the most long-lived and damaging ice storms to hit the northeastern United States during the 20th century struck the week of *January 4-9, 1998*. Weather conditions favored the formation of thick icing unusually far north, into the northern parts of New York and Vermont, across New Hampshire and in most of Maine. Much of southeastern Canada was locked in the freezing rain's icy grip all week; about 4.5 million people lost power as the worst natural disaster in Canada's history unfolded.

Event #15
Lewinsky Scandal: January 20-26, 1998

On *January 20*, President Clinton and Israeli Prime Minister Netanyahu met at the White House in yet another effort to break a one-year impasse in the Middle East peace talks. Netanyahu was expected to propose a relatively modest Israeli pullback on the West Bank that would fall far short of Palestinian demands.

On *January 21*, several news organizations reported the alleged sexual relationship between Monica Lewinsky and Clinton. Clinton denied the allegations as the scandal erupted.

In his continuing effort to revive the stalled Middle East peace process, President Clinton met with PLO Chairman Arafat in the Oval Office on *January 22*, two days after his meetings with Prime Minister Netanyahu. He opened the meeting by saying:

> I am very pleased to welcome Chairman Arafat back to the United States as our partner in the peace process. As I did with Prime Minister Netanyahu, I want to emphasize what a critical time this is in the process and the importance of both parties meeting their obligations.

> I'm going to give Chairman Arafat a little report on my meeting with Mr. Netanyahu, and then we're going to go to work.

Clinton outlined for reporters the principles of the peace process:

> (M)utual obligations and the concept of land-for-peace so that Israelis can live in security recognized by all their neighbors, and the Palestinians can realize their aspirations to live as a free people. . . . If we can focus on these principles, I'm convinced we can make some progress.

Arafat responded:

> I hope that Mr. Netanyahu will understand that peace is not only a Palestinian need. It's an Israeli need, it's a Palestinian need, it's an Arab need, it's an international need. And I hope that Mr. Netanyahu will turn his words to deeds and comply with the agreements.

Chronology from CNN:

January 22: Clinton reiterated his denial of the relationship with Lewinsky, and said he never urged her to lie. Starr issued subpoenas for a number of people, as well as for White House records. Starr also defended the expansion of his initial Whitewater investigation. Attorney Vernon Jordan held a press conference to flatly deny he told Lewinsky to lie. Jordan also said Lewinsky told him she did not have a sexual relationship with the president.

January 23: Clinton assured his Cabinet of his innocence. Judge Susan Webber Wright put off "indefinitely" a deposition Lewinsky was scheduled to give in the Paula Jones lawsuit. Clinton's personal secretary, Betty Currie, and other aides were subpoenaed to appear before a federal grand jury. William Ginsburg said Lewinsky was being "squeezed" by Starr and was now a target of the Whitewater investigation.

January 24: Clinton asked former Deputy White House Chief of Staff Harold Ickes and former Commerce Secretary Mickey Kantor to return to the White House to help deal with the controversy. Talks continued between Starr and attorneys for Lewinsky over a possible immunity agreement.

January 25: Ginsburg said Lewinsky would "tell all" in exchange for immunity. Clinton political adviser James Carville said "a war" would be waged between Clinton supporters and Kenneth Starr over Starr's investigation tactics.

January 26: Clinton forcefully repeated his denial, saying, "I did not have sexual relations with that woman, Miss Lewinsky." Ginsburg offered Starr a summary of what Lewinsky was prepared to say to the grand jury in exchange for a grant of immunity from the prosecution.

Netanyahu came to the Clinton meeting with the possibility that his government might be toppled. How ironic that, literally, right after the meeting, it was President Clinton's own administration that was in trouble. The president was humiliated and faced legal action against him. Netanyahu returned to Israel as a "conquering hero" because he did not give away any land.

From this point on, Bill Clinton was in a fight for political survival.

Catastrophe #16
Southeast Severe Weather: January–February 1998
Estimated $1 (1.1) billion damages/costs

During an Oval Office question and answer session with Israeli Prime Minister Netanyahu just before their *January 20* meeting on the status of the Israeli-Palestinian peace talks, President Clinton gave the following assessment. He stated he believed Israel wanted peace and a resolution of the current Middle East crisis; that "it's very much in the interests of the Palestinians and Mr. Arafat to seek to resolve it"; and that he's found that "more often than not, you ultimately have success if you stay at something and keep working at it in good faith."

Clinton also reaffirmed "the strong support of the United States for Israel and the strong support of the United States for the security of Israel and a peace process that proceeds within that commitment."

Albright Tried Again to Jump-Start Middle East Peace

Secretary of State Madeleine Albright planned to stop in Israel, the West Bank, and Gaza in an effort to get the Middle East peace talks back on track.

During a press conference at the State Department on *January 28*, Albright said that during these visits she would attempt to measure whether and how much each side had "absorbed" the ideas President Clinton presented to Prime Minister Netanyahu and Chairman Arafat when they visited Washington the week of January 19.

> I will carry forward the ideas offered by the president and emphasize the urgent need for progress on the four-part agenda, which includes security, further redeployment, a time-out on unhelpful unilateral steps, and launching permanent status negotiations.

Albright acknowledged that at this point she was "neither optimistic nor pessimistic" about the future of these negotiations.

> I cannot be optimistic because leaders in the region remain reluctant to make the hard decisions and to offer the flexibility required to reach an agreement.

> I cannot be pessimistic, because I'm convinced the majority of all faiths and communities in the region desire peace and that a basis exists for an Israeli-Palestinian agreement and, over time, a comprehensive Israeli-Arab settlement.

> The United States remains committed to seeking progress towards Middle East peace, but it's up to the Palestinians and Israelis to make the decisions that would put the process back on track.

Secretary Albright told the Senate Foreign Relations Committee on *February 10* that the Clinton administration had urged those involved:

> to rise above the zero-sum thinking of the past, and to embrace the reality that cooperation by all will yield for all a future of greater prosperity, dignity, and peace. That is certainly our message in the Middle East, where we continue to seek progress towards a just, lasting, and comprehensive settlement.

The secretary acknowledged that, "1997 was not a good year for the peace process." Mutual trust, respect, and recognition had been "rubbed away," and so "what we have been trying to do is to rebuild those bonds of confidence."

1998 Off to a Very Warm, Wet Start in U.S.

The first two months of 1998 were the warmest and wettest in the 104-year record of temperatures and precipitation measurements for the contiguous 48 states, according to preliminary data compiled by the Commerce Department's National Oceanic and Atmospheric Administration. William Brown of NOAA's National Climatic Data Center said,

> During the period January-February, the national average temperature was 37.5 degrees Fahrenheit compared with a normal of 32.1. The previous record was 37.0 in 1990. For precipitation, 6.01 inches fell, compared with a normal of 4.05. The previous record was 5.7 inches in 1979.

NOAA reported that California and North Dakota had their wettest February on record. Florida, Maryland, Nevada, Rhode Island, and Virginia had their second wettest February since 1895. The warmest February on record took place in much of the upper Midwest and parts of the East—including Minnesota, Wisconsin, Illinois, Michigan, Ohio, Pennsylvania, and Connecticut.

"These are the patterns one would typically expect during a strong El Niño event," said Ants Leetmaa, director of NOAA's Climate Prediction Center in Camp Springs, Maryland.

During the month of February 1998, California was struck by a series of storms—due in part to the effects of El Niño. Estimates indicated over $550 million in damages for the state, and 17 storm-related deaths for the winter. Thirty-five counties were declared federal disaster areas. Clear Lake, in northern California, reached its highest level since 1909, flooding portions of Lakeport, about 90 miles north of San Francisco.

During the late evening of *February 22* and early morning of *February 23, 1998*, a series of tornadoes ripped across central Florida. At least one reached an estimated F-4 intensity. Forty-two fatalities occurred, over 800 residences were destroyed, another 700 were left uninhabitable, over 3,500 were damaged to some extent, and 135,000 utility customers lost power at the height of the storms. Damages from the tornado outbreak exceeded $60 million, and Florida's overall storm damage total was approximately $500 million. Hardest hit locations in the tornado outbreak were Winter Garden, Altamonte Springs, Sanford, and Campbell. Overall, 54 of Florida's 67 counties were declared federal disaster areas due to the storms.

Some areas reported at least 20 inches of rain. About 12 inches fell overnight in Waller County; most roads in the county were flooded at some point.

Some communities reported receiving 20 inches of rain, swelling creeks and rivers in the Texas Hill Country near Austin and southward to San Antonio.

Event #17
U.S.-China Technology Scandal: May 1-June 5, 1998

"I came here not only to celebrate Israel's achievements, but also to restate our iron-clad commitment to Israel's security and well-being in its next half-century and beyond," Vice President Al Gore said on *May 1* in Jerusalem.

"There is no distinction between our continued commitment to Israel's security and well-being on the one hand, and our commitment to helping Israel achieve a comprehensive, just, and lasting peace between Israelis and Arabs on the other," the vice president said at a joint press conference with Israeli Prime Minister Netanyahu. "These two commitments are complementary, and the United States is intent on doing all that is within our power and imagination to help fulfill both."

Gore further said, "a moment exists for moving the process forward," and noted that the U.S. had done its best to facilitate progress in the negotiations among the parties themselves. He expressed "high hopes that the process will yield fruit: peace with security."

Asked if the London Round was "the end of the line," Gore responded that the *May 4* meetings in London between Secretary Albright and the Israeli and Palestinian leaders presented an opportunity for potentially significant progress.

I don't wish to entertain any hypothetical based on the assumption that progress will not be made there. I am hopeful that progress will be made there. The efforts to secure peace with security are never ending and do not have an end.

Jerusalem

On the issue of a united Jerusalem, Gore repeated the U.S. position:

[The U.S.] has always been and is now in favor of a united Jerusalem. There are many questions that could be referred to the final status negotiations. The question of whether or not Jerusalem will be united is a settled question, in our view.

Jeddah, Saudi Arabia

Vice President Gore and Saudi Arabia's Crown Prince Abdullah Bin Abdulaziz met on *May 1-2* to discuss topics of mutual interest and concern.

In a joint statement following their meetings, the two leaders pledged to cooperate fully in the search for just and lasting peace in the Middle East, based on Security Council Resolutions 242 and 338 and the concept of land for peace. Further, they agreed that the best way to achieve peace is by full implementation of each side's obligations made at the Oslo and Washington accords.

Clinton under Fire

As the Clinton administration was increasing its pressure on Prime Minister Netanyahu, Congressional Republicans stated on *May 6* that they planned a series of hearings to investigate whether President Clinton's policy on the export of commercial satellites to China had allowed the Chinese to acquire technology to improve the accuracy of their nuclear missiles.

The hearings were to focus on Clinton's decisions to allow two U.S. aerospace companies, Loral Space and Communications Ltd. and Hughes Electronic Corp., to export satellites to be launched atop Chinese rockets. The Justice Department had been investigating a report that Loral improperly gave China advice to upgrade the guidance systems on its rockets after a failed launch in 1996 destroyed a Loral satellite.

Both U.S. House of Representatives Speaker Newt Gingrich (R-Georgia) and Senate Majority Trent Lott (R-Mississippi) took an active interest in the congressional probes, in part because the aerospace firms had been major contributors to the Democratic Party. Loral's chief executive officer, Bernard L. Schwartz, was the single largest donor to the Democratic Party in 1996.

Republican lawmakers were attempting to find a link between the financial contributions and a decision by Clinton in February 1998 that they said effectively undercut the criminal investigation of Loral. The decision allowed Loral to launch another satellite and provide China with the same type of information that was the subject of the Justice Department inquiry.

The Chronology of Clinton Administration's Pressure on Israel: May 1998

May 1, 1998: Vice President Gore and Prime Minister Netanyahu gave toasts at a lunch in Jerusalem.

May 1-2, 1998: Gore and Saudi Arabia's Crown Prince Bin Abdulaziz met to discuss topics of mutual interest and concern.

May 3, 1998: Gore held talks with Netanyahu in London on the Middle East peace process. He also met with Egyptian President Mubarak.

May 4, 1998: Netanyahu and Arafat met separately with British Prime Minister Blair in London and then with Secretary Albright. Israel informally offered the idea of 3 percent Area C in addition to 10 percent further redeployment (FRD). [Area C is a designated area of the West Bank that is scheduled for future evacuation.]

May 5, 1998: Netanyahu and Arafat continued talks with Albright. She invited them to Washington on May 11 for talks on 13 percent FRD and to start final status talks. Arafat accepted the invitation. Netanyahu said he must consult his Cabinet.

May 6, 1998: First Lady Hillary Clinton stated that an eventual Palestinian state was important for Middle East Peace.

May 6, 1998: Netanyahu briefed his Inner Cabinet on the London talks. Israel asked for a visit by Special Envoy Ross. Twenty-one U.S. House of Representatives members called on Clinton not to pressure Israel on the FRD plan.

May 8, 1998: Netanyahu held talks with Ross, and announced he could not attend the Washington summit due to lack of time to prepare for the talks. The meeting in Washington was cancelled. Foreign ministers of the G-8 nations called on Israel to accept the U.S. 13 percent FRD plan.

May 10, 1998: Netanyahu proposed new ideas for the FRD to Ross. The Palestinian Authority (PA) rejected the ideas.

May 12, 1998: Albright expressed hope that permanent status talks were still possible.

May 13, 1998: Netanyahu met in Washington with Albright. He also met congressional leaders, addressed the American Israel Public Affairs Committee (AIPAC) convention, and briefed the media. No visible progress was achieved.

May 14, 1998: Another Netanyahu-Albright meeting yielded no progress.

May 15, 1998: In a meeting with Ross, Netanyahu proposed a two-stage, 13 percent FRD.

May 18, 1998: Albright briefed Arafat on the latest Israeli ideas. He rejected them.

May 23, 1998: A U.S. congressional delegation in Israel to celebrate Israel's Jubilee and Jerusalem Day, headed by House Speaker Newt Gingrich, canceled plans to lay cornerstone for the proposed U.S. embassy building in Jerusalem.

May 25-29, 1998: Prime Minister Netanyahu visited China.

The Chronology of Clinton's Chinese Scandal: May 6–June 5, 1998

May 6, 1998: Congressional Republicans planned a series of hearings to investigate whether President Clinton's policy on the export of commercial satellites to China allowed the Chinese to acquire technology to improve the accuracy of their nuclear missiles, and whether that policy was influenced by campaign contributions.

May 12, 1998: Congress's two top Republicans demanded that the White House provide documents on whether China's nuclear missile capability was aided by an administration policy on exporting commercial satellites.

May 16, 1998: Democratic fund-raiser Johnny Chung told Justice Department investigators that a Chinese military officer who was an executive with a state-owned aerospace company gave him $300,000 to donate to the Democrats' 1996 campaign.

May 17, 1998: The Justice Department's campaign finance task force began to examine whether a Clinton administration decision to export commercial satellites to China was influenced by contributions to the Democratic Party during the 1996 campaign.

May 18, 1998: President Clinton said no foreign policy decisions by his administration affecting China were influenced by political contributions.

May 19, 1998: The major U.S. aerospace company Loral denied that it requested or received "political favors or benefits of any kind" in exchange for campaign donations.

May 20, 1998: House Speaker Gingrich announced he would create a select committee to probe allegations that China illegally obtained missile technology from a U.S. company that received favorable treatment from the administration.

May 21, 1998: In a series of nearly unanimous votes, the House said President Clinton failed to act in "the national interest" when he gave permission to a U.S. aerospace firm (with close Democratic ties) to launch a Chinese satellite, and moved to block him from approving similar exports.

May 22, 1998: The White House said it intended to send documents to the House that officials said would show there was nothing nefarious about a controversial Chinese satellite launch for a U.S. aerospace firm headed by a top Democratic donor.

May 23, 1998: President Clinton gave the go-ahead in February to a U.S. company's satellite launch in China, despite staff concerns that granting such approval might be seen as letting the company "off the hook" in a Justice Department investigation of whether it previously provided unauthorized assistance to China's ballistic missile program. Hughes Electronics and Loral Space & Communications Ltd. are both under investigation by the Justice Department and two Congressional committees for their role in transferring sensitive U.S. space technology to the Chinese after Hughes and Loral satellites were destroyed in two Chinese rocket explosions.

May 23, 1998: Officials from a Chinese satellite launching company denied that they had received any sensitive technology with military applications from U.S. firms.

May 24, 1998: It was revealed this day that Liu Chaoying, the daughter of China's most powerful military official, brokered deals for missile components one day and Sonoma Valley Cabernet the next. Johnny Chung, a glad-handing entrepreneur who boasted of his White House access, became her California business partner in 1996. Today, their short-lived partnership is over and Chung has told federal investigators that some of the money Liu gave him for their dealings actually came from Chinese military intelligence accounts and was meant to influence U.S. political campaigns. Attorneys familiar with his claims say Chung alleges that at least $35,000 of the $100,000 he donated to Democrats in the summer of 1996 came from the Chinese government through Liu. He has said she gave him a total of about $300,000 as part of their business dealings.

His allegations put the 39-year-old Liu—an aerospace executive with a penchant for Chanel suits and oversized glasses—at the center of a Justice Department investigation into the first charge of a direct money trail from the Chinese government to the Democratic Party.

May 25, 1998: Bernard Schwartz says the "confluence" of his own increased contributions and the Clinton administration's favorable treatment of his company was "just coincidence."

May 31, 1998: According to many independent specialists on Chinese forces, the evidence did not amount to a credible case that China's military rockets were better prepared to strike at American cities as a direct windfall from U.S. participation in its satellite launching business.

May 31, 1998: A reconstruction of the administration's handling of the waiver for a 1998 U.S. satellite launch in China revealed a complicated, and in many ways mundane, picture of a bureaucratic process propelled by a policy forged in the Reagan and Bush administrations.

June 3, 1998: Senate Majority Leader Trent Lott said Congress did not intend to use its China investigations as a political club against the Clinton administration.

June 5, 1998: CIA Director George J. Tenet refused to discuss with the Senate Intelligence Committee a secret report about an unauthorized U.S. transfer of information to Chinese missile officials, citing a last-minute request by Attorney General Janet Reno to reserve comment on the case.

Catastrophe #18
Hurricane Georges: September 24-28, 1998
Estimated $5.9 (6.5) billion damages/costs

On *September 24, 1998*, President Clinton announced he was going to meet with both Yasser Arafat and Benjamin Netanyahu when they came to New York City to address the United Nations. The purpose of the meeting was to discuss the stalled peace plan in which Israel was to give away an additional 13 percent of its land. On the same day, the headlines of the national newspapers said that Hurricane Georges was gaining strength and heading toward the Gulf of Mexico. *USA Today* stated, "Georges gaining strength, killer storm zeros in on Key West."

On *September 27*, Secretary Albright met with Chairman Arafat and Prime Minister Netanyahu on the margins of the UN General Assembly in New York City in preparation for the meeting with President Clinton. The same day, Hurricane Georges slammed into the Gulf Coast with 110-mile-per-hour winds and gusts up to 175 miles per hour. The eye of the storm struck Mississippi and did extensive damage eastward into the Florida panhandle, before stalling and moving slowly inland, dumping excessive rain and causing extensive flooding.

On *September 28*, Netanyahu and Arafat met at the White House with Clinton, who announced that Albright would return to the region for a further push to get direct Israeli-Palestinian negotiations back on track. The three agreed to meet again on October 15 to formally announce the agreement of the land giveaway. That day, the headlines of *USA Today* read, "Georges lingers," and the article adjacent was titled, "Meeting puts Mideast talks back in motion." The *New York Times* had the two stories together on the front page.

Arafat addresses UN; Hurricane George hits Gulf Coast

Later that same day, Arafat addressed the United Nations and made a blatant bid for approval of an independent Palestinian state by *May* of *1999*. He was given a rousing and sustained ovation as he addressed the General Assembly; but as he was speaking, Hurricane Georges was smashing the Gulf Coast, causing $1 billion in damage. When Arafat finished his speech and left America, Hurricane Georges began to dissipate.

Event #19
Massive Floods and Tornadoes in Texas
October 17-22, 1998
Estimated $1 (1.1) billion damages/costs

On *October 15, 1998*, Arafat and Netanyahu gathered at the Wye Plantation in Maryland to continue the talks held on *September 28*. These talks were scheduled to last five days and were centered on Israel giving away 13 percent of the West Bank land. Negotiations stalled, and President Clinton pressured them to continue until a settlement was reached. The time frame was extended and continued until *October 22*, when Israel agreed to give away the land for assurances of peace by Arafat.

Floods and Tornadoes

On *October 17*, awesome rains and tornadoes hit southern Texas. The San Antonio area was deluged by twenty inches of rain in one day, causing flash floods and destroying thousands of homes. Rivers swelled to incredible size. The Guadalupe River, normally 150 feet wide, ranged from three to five miles wide. The floods were so powerful that entire small towns were nearly swallowed. These rains and floods continued until *October 22* (the end of the Middle East talks) and then subsided, after ravaging 25 percent of Texas and causing over $1 billion in damage. On *October 21*, President Clinton declared this section of Texas a major disaster area, and directed the Federal Emergency Management Agency (FEMA) to assist in the relief for the flood-ravaged families. This was a record flood that hit Texas.

For almost the entire time of the Middle East talks, these storms were smashing Texas. The national newspapers once again had the Middle East talks and the weather related disasters together on the front pages for all to see. President Clinton was forced to declare a section of America a disaster area at the exact time he was orchestrating a Middle East "land-for-peace" agreement that would carve up God's covenant land in Israel!

Event #20
Middle East Donors Conference; Stock Market Sell-Off
November 30-December 1, 1998

On *November 30*, President Bill Clinton announced that he would be seeking an additional $400 million in U.S. aid to assist the Palestinian people.

The president made the announcement at the second Conference to Support Middle East Peace and Development held at the State Department. Representatives from some 50 countries and international organizations attended. Clinton said,

> I intend to work closely with our Congress on developing a package to provide an additional $400 million to assist the Palestinian people.

> This amount is in addition to the regular annual contribution provided by the United States, which will reach $100 million next year.

State Department sources told United States Information Agency (USIA) that the administration intended to request from the U.S. Congress $100 million in aid for the Palestinians, plus $400 million in a supplemental request for fiscal year 1999. The administration intended to also request $100 million for each year for the remaining four years of the five-year "cycle" (1999 through 2003) covered by the donors conference.

Initial pledges at the donors conference came to more than $3 billion, Secretary Albright told the press at the conference's conclusion.

As President Clinton was meeting with Arafat that day, the stock market was tumbling, and the Dow Jones average fell 216 points. Media news reports on

November 30 and *December 1* had the Arafat declaration and the stock market sell-off as the featured stories.

Arafat also announced that in *May* of *1999*, he was going to declare a Palestinian state with Jerusalem as the capital.

On *December 1*, the European stock markets experienced the third largest sell-off in history. How ironic that as the nations of the world met to promise $3 billion dollars in aid for a Palestinian state, their own financial markets lost hundreds of billions of dollars of market capitalization.

Event #21
Clinton Impeachment: December 11-19, 1998

On Saturday, *December 11*, the House Judiciary Committee approved impeachment articles I, II, and III, which accused President Clinton of perjury in the Paula Jones deposition, perjury in his grand jury testimony, and obstruction of justice in the Jones case.

The president arrived in Israel the evening of *December 12* on a mission to insure the Wye Agreement was implemented.

On Sunday, *December 12*, the headlines in major newspapers trumpeted both the impeachment process and Clinton's trip on their front pages, while radio and television news broadcast the stories back to back. The Associated Press reported that the president went to Israel "under an impeachment cloud." Ironically, the first president to be impeached in 130 years was in Israel pressuring the Jews to give away God's covenant land!

On *December 13*, Clinton and Netanyahu held bilateral meetings. Netanyahu was pressured to begin implementing the Wye River Accord signed in the U.S. in October.

On *December 14*, Clinton arrived at the Palestinians' newly opened international airport, and got the full red-carpet treatment. Arafat's Force 17—a unit involved for decades in PLO terrorism—provided an honor guard, which played "The Star-Spangled Banner" and a strongly nationalist Palestinian anthem, "Biladi," which means "My Homeland."

Everywhere, thousands of U.S. and Palestinian flags were flying, and posters informed Clinton: "We have a dream—free Palestine."

The airport itself, which Clinton was asked to dedicate, is a symbol of the statehood Arafat repeatedly asserted he would declare in *May 1999*—unilaterally, if necessary.

Later that day, the Palestinian National Council reaffirmed the cancellation of articles in the Palestinian National Charter that refer to the destruction of Israel by a show of hands that took place in Gaza in the presence of Arafat and Clinton.

The issue of the Charter was one of the sticking points in implementing peace agreements, as earlier Palestinian statements had not satisfied Israel that the charter items in question had been made null and void in 1996.

Clinton said that the Palestinian decision "issued a challenge" to the Israeli government to move ahead with the peace process. Netanyahu maintained that the Palestinians had not done enough. Israeli Defense Minister Yitzhak Mordechai's media advisor said that Mordechai welcomed the vote, stating that it represented the implementation of a Palestinian responsibility within the Wye River accord. However, Mordechai called for further Palestinian compliance, especially in the area of security.

Clinton said, on *December 15*, that the Middle East peace process was "back on track" after a meeting with Prime Minister Netanyahu and Chairman Arafat at the Israel-Gaza border. However, the summit failed to win an Israeli commitment to withdraw on schedule from more West Bank land.

Prime Minister Netanyahu told his Cabinet that Israel would not withdraw troops from the territory—a move certain to further damage the peace process.

Israel's position frustrated President Clinton and angered the Palestinians. But Netanyahu was under intense domestic political pressures and was struggling to save his government from collapse.

"The Prime Minister (said) that he cannot at this stage report to the government that the Palestinians have carried out their part and that we will be able to implement the withdrawal on the 18th of December," a Cabinet statement said.

At the same time, both Clinton and Netanyahu faced critical challenges: Clinton faced possible impeachment, and Netanyahu was trying to survive a right-wing, no-confidence vote prompted by the Wye deal.

Following Tuesday's visits in the Middle East, Clinton returned to the United States, where he resumed his struggle against impeachment. He arrived in Washington, D.C., on Wednesday.

On Thursday, *December 17*, the House delayed debate on articles of impeachment while the United States launched military strikes against Iraq.

President Clinton's National Security Advisor, Samuel R. "Sandy" Berger, said Saddam Hussein's claim of victory in the aftermath of the "Desert Fox" aerial offensive against him "was a bit of whistling past the graveyard."

The operation "clearly has been a blow," Berger said during a *December 20* interview on CNN. He said the "substantial strike" involved more cruise missiles than in the Gulf war and more than 300 air sorties against over 100 targets.

On *December 19*, the U.S. House of Representatives voted in favor of Impeachment Articles I and III, covering perjury and obstruction of justice, impeaching Clinton. (The case then went to the Senate for trial.)

On Monday, *December 21*, the Israeli Knesset voted to dissolve and hold early elections after Prime Minister Netanyahu failed to win support for his peacemaking policy with the Palestinians.

Event #22
Kosovo War Begins: March 24–June 10, 1999
War Cost Estimated at $3 billion

On *March 23*, Yasser Arafat met with President Clinton again in Washington, D.C., to discuss carving up Israel to create a Palestinian state with Jerusalem as its capital. That same day, the stock market took its biggest tumble since the previous *November 30*, the last time that Clinton and Arafat met in Washington, falling 219 points. The next day, Arafat went to the United Nations to discuss Palestinian statehood, and Clinton authorized the attack on Serbia, resulting in hostile relations between America and both Russia and China.

The U.S.-led NATO forces bombed the Chinese Embassy in Belgrade, Yugoslavia, on *May 7, 1999*. The Clinton administration blamed the event on outdated maps. China stated it was a deliberate provocation, and refused to accept apologies. Ironically, China used this to turn the intense focus off of them for alleged illegal technology transfers and back on to the U.S.

Catastrophe #23
Oklahoma-Kansas Tornadoes: May 3-4, 1999
Estimated $1.6 (1.7) billion damages/costs
May 3, 1999: Highest Wind Speed in U.S. History

On *May 3, 1999*, the most powerful tornadoes ever to hit the United States raged through Oklahoma and Kansas. The wind of one tornado was officially measured at 316 mph, making it the highest ever recorded. The storms included many F-4 and F-5 tornadoes. (F-5 tornadoes have winds over 260 miles per hour, which are extremely rare.)

The damage from these storms was incredible. In Oklahoma City alone, more than 2,000 homes were destroyed, and the town of Mulhall, Oklahoma, ceased to exist. Thousands of automobiles and vehicles were destroyed, and total damage was in the billions of dollars. The National Oceanic and Atmospheric Administration stated, "This is an outbreak of historic proportions, no doubt about it." Oklahoma Governor Frank Keating said, "This is the most calamitous storm we've ever seen."

The storm warnings were sounded that day at 4:47 p.m. (CST). In Israel, this would have been about 1 a.m. on May 4, the date that Arafat had been scheduled to declare a Palestinian state with Jerusalem as its capital. This declaration was postponed until December 1999 at the request of President Clinton, who also stated that the Palestinians should have their own state, that Jerusalem was negotiable, and that he refused to move the United States embassy to Jerusalem.

On *May 4*, Clinton had to declare parts of Oklahoma and Kansas as federal disaster areas, before sending a letter to Arafat, in which he encouraged Arafat's aspirations for his "own land." Clinton stated that the Palestinians had a right to "determine their own future on their own land," and that the Palestinians deserved "to live free, today, tomorrow, and forever."

On *May 6, 1999*, going beyond U.S. policy, First Lady Hillary Clinton told a youth conference on Middle East peace that she supported the eventual creation of an independent Palestinian state. While the Clinton administration officially distanced itself from her remark, a top aide to Arafat was pleased.

"I hope this becomes official policy," Ahmed Abdel Rahman said in Gaza. "There can be no peace, stability or security in the Middle East without a Palestinian state."

"I think it will be in the long-term interests of the Middle East for Palestine to be a state," said Mrs. Clinton. The first lady also said this would be "very important for the Palestinian people" and for the "broader goal of peace in the Middle East."

White House press secretary Mike McCurry then said, "She was not reflecting any administration policy. She was responding to some very heartfelt concerns raised by the young people who were on the program. She was reflecting a personal view."

The policy of her husband's administration was that a Palestinian state was a matter for Israelis and Palestinians to work out for themselves.

The U.S. consulate in Jerusalem, which acted as Washington's diplomatic channel to Arafat's government, distanced the Clinton administration from the first lady's statement, saying, "These remarks are her own personal view. The administration's position on this matter has not changed."

Arafat originally planned to announce a Palestinian state on *May 4, 1999*. Bill Clinton told him not to, but encouraged him with some very positive comments. Hillary stated she favored a Palestinian state on *May 6*, within 48 hours of *May 4*. Was this Bill and Hillary's way of appeasing Arafat while knowing a current declaration would be politically incorrect? The timing of Hillary's comment certainly makes one believe that was the intent.

Catastrophe #24
Hurricane Dennis: August 24–September 7, 1999
Estimated $1 (1.1) billion damages/costs

On *September 1, 1999*, Secretary of State Albright traveled to Morocco, Egypt, Israel, the West Bank/Gaza, Damascus, and Beirut to consult with regional leaders on developments in the peace process, and attended the signing of the Sharm El-Sheikh Accord on *September 4*. The purpose of her visit was to jump-start the Wye Accord, reached in *October* of *1998*, which had stalled. Albright, Arafat, and Barak agreed to resume the talks on *September 13,* and to conclude them within a year with a final agreement.

In late August, Hurricane Dennis began to affect the American east coast. This Category 2 hurricane contained copious rainfall as it moved very slowly up the seaboard, drenching the states of Florida, Georgia, South Carolina, and North Carolina. Dennis lingered off the coast of North Carolina nearly a week, traveling in a bizarre path. At one point, it actually reversed itself; another time, it was heading away from the coast. This hurricane was literally doing circles in the Atlantic Ocean until the meeting in Israel.

Hurricane Dennis was just below hurricane strength when it finally came ashore on September 4, the same day Albright was in Sharm El-Sheikh Egypt for Barak and Arafat's accord signing. Dennis came ashore over the Cape Lookout National Seashore just east of Harkers Island, NC at 2100 UTC that day. Dennis continued inland and weakened to a depression on the 5th over central North Carolina. Even in dissipation, Dennis continued to move erratically.

Dennis did not do tremendous damage; but the enormous rainfall proved extremely significant less than two weeks later.

Catastrophe #25
Hurricane Floyd: September 7-17, 1999
Estimated $6 (6.5) billion damages/costs

On *September 13*, the Israeli Foreign Minister and one of Arafat's deputies met to work out arrangements for the "final status" of Israel's giving away land in exchange for peace. They agreed to present outlines for the borders of the new Palestinian state, plus the status of Jerusalem and Jewish settlements in the West Bank and Gaza Strip, by *February 15, 2000.*

That same day, Hurricane Floyd strengthened into a very dangerous Category 5 storm with sustained winds of 155 miles per hour. Forecasters at the National Hurricane Center were astonished at how quickly Floyd grew in size and strength in one day. Their actual statement was, "Floyd grew unexpectedly into a monster of a storm on Sunday." On *September 16*, Hurricane Floyd slammed into North Carolina, extending hurricane force winds 150 miles inland and causing the greatest evacuation in United States history. However, the most destructive force of this storm came from rains of twenty inches or more over the entire eastern part of North Carolina, where the rivers were still swollen and the land was soaked from Hurricane Dennis less than two weeks before.

While Israeli officials were meeting with the Palestinians to make plans for giving away God's covenant land, a huge section of America's east coast was being ravaged by a monster hurricane, resulting in some of the greatest property devastation in the nation's history. The timing coincided exactly with the implementation of President Clinton's plan to have Israel give away her covenant land in exchange for peace.

Catastrophes and Event #26
Hurricane Irene, Hector Mine Earthquake, and
Major Stock Market Sell-off
October 14-15, 1999

During the week of October 11, Jewish settlers on 15 West Bank hilltops in Israel were evicted as part of the ongoing "land-for-peace" process, which was actively supported by President Clinton. The settlers resisted the eviction; the confrontation was reported in the national media.

While Israel was forcing the settlers off the covenant land, the stock market was melting down, with the Dow having its worst weekly drop since 1989. On *October 15*, the market lost 266 points (the loss of hundreds of billions of dollars in market capitalization). That same day, Hurricane Irene hit North Carolina; and the next morning, the powerful Hector Mine 7.1 earthquake rocked the Southwest, the fifth largest earthquake to hit America in the twentieth century. Neither the hurricane nor the earthquake caused major damage or casualties; but their stories, along with the stock market melt down, shared the nation's front pages with the reports of Jewish settlers being evicted from God's covenant land in Israel.

Catastrophes and Event #27
Trillion-Dollar NASDAQ Loss, Record Fire Season,
and Major Drought: January 1–July 1, 2000

January 3-9, 2000: Israel and Syria Held Negotiations with President Clinton's Active Participation

The latest round of Syrian-Israeli negotiations, conducted in Shepherdstown, West Virginia, from *January 3-9*, quickly became mired in procedural disputes. The Syrian delegation led by Foreign Minister Farouk al-Sharaa insisted that the question of borders be addressed first, while the Israeli delegation led by Prime Minister Ehud Barak demanded that the initial negotiations consider security arrangements and the normalization of bilateral relations. The United States eventually finessed the issue by suggesting that informal talks on the border issue precede formal talks on security issues, after which both issues would be addressed simultaneously.

This procedural impasse, which almost derailed the talks on the second day, reflected a fundamental disagreement: Syria rigidly insisted on the unconditional return of all of the Golan Heights, while Israel maintained that it could not commit to a total withdrawal from the region until it ascertained what kind of security arrangements and peace would follow. With prompting from the U.S., working groups were formed to address four sets of crucial issues: the delineation of the border, security arrangements, the normalization of bilateral relations, and water rights.

Clinton Pressured Israel While NASDAQ Collapsed

It was all but a given that the NASDAQ was going to eventually collapse. But the fascinating coincidence was that NASDAQ's four worst trading days and/or periods on record occurred at the very same time Clinton and/or one of his top staff were in meetings about Israel's covenant land.

The first record-setting NASDAQ drop occurred on Monday, *January 4, 2000*, while Israeli Prime Minister Barak was at the Shepherdstown, West Virginia, meeting with Syrian Foreign Minister al-Sharaa over the Golan Heights. That same day, the stock market plummeted, with the Dow dropping 359 points for its fourth worst one-day decline, and the NASDAQ falling 229 points for its worst drop ever (at that point). The combined losses in money for one day amounted to $600 billion.

On *March 26*, Clinton held a summit with Syrian President Haffez Assad in Geneva to discuss the stalled peace talks with Israel over the Golan Heights. In the second major correction from *March 25–April 1, 2000*, the NASDAQ fell six of seven sessions and was off 17 percent from its record high of 5,048.62 set just three weeks earlier. In the last week of the first quarter of 2000, the NASDAQ lost 8 percent of its value.

U.S. Defense Secretary William Cohen held talks in Israel from *April 3-4*. On *April 3, 2000,* the NASDAQ suffered its largest point drop (349.15) in history and its fifth largest percentage (7.6 percent) drop.

The fourth major correction, which ended up being the worst one-week loss in the 29-year history of NASDAQ, occurred the week Clinton met with Barak at the White House. Clinton had summoned Barak for a lengthy *April 11* meeting, at which time he told Barak he was ready to make an even greater personal commitment to the peace process. The NASDAQ loss for the trading week of *April 10-14* was a record-crushing $2.1 trillion dollars.

"Year of the Wildfires"

The unprecedented number of wild land acres that burned throughout large stretches of the West, the Southwest, and Florida caused the *summer of 2000* to be remembered as the "Year of the Wildfires." The fire season started in *January*, two months earlier than usual. By *March*, over 40,000 acres had already burned. By *September 10, 2000*, there had been close to 93,000 fires for the year, burning just less than 7 million acres according to NOAA. The ten-year annual average for this same period was 63,600 fires burning 3 million acres. Two major factors combined to contribute to the severity of the situation: extreme drought conditions due to La Niña, and decades of management policy of fire suppression.

"That's one of the hallmarks of the 2000 season, the geographical breadth of it," said Don Smurthwaite, a spokesman for the National Interagency Fire Center (NIFC) in Boise. "There were times when we had active fires burning from the crest of the Rocky Mountains to the Pacific coast and from our border with Canada to our border with Mexico.

"Another reason the 2000 season will be remembered was the duration of it," Smurthwaite added. "The first wildfire began burning on *January 1, 2000*, and there were still fires burning into December. It was a long, long season."

The 2000 fire season was the most expensive fire year in U.S. history. The federal government spent a record $1.6 billion fighting the worst wild-fires the U.S. had seen in decades, according to a new report by Taxpayers for Common Sense (TCS), a national budget watchdog organization.

The $1.6 billion figure was nearly double the cost of severe fire years in the past. It was also significantly more than the $1 billion estimated in the fall of 2000 by the Forest Service.

Warmest January to May on Record

The *spring season (March-May) of 2000* as well as *January-May of 2001* were the warmest on record for the United States, according to statistics calculated by NOAA scientists working from the world's largest statistical weather database. The electronic database at NOAA's National Climatic Center, in Asheville, N.C., goes back through 106 years of record keeping.

For the three-month period, over 64 percent of the country averaged much warmer than normal temperatures, while less than one percent averaged much cooler than normal.

During this spring season, every state in the continental U.S. was warmer than its long-term average. It was the warmest spring on record for Texas, second warmest spring since 1895 for New Mexico, and the third warmest spring on record for Nevada. Twenty additional states ranked within the top ten warmest spring seasons on record.

The extremely warm temperatures contributed to worsening drought conditions in many areas of the country. Parts of the Southeast, Midwest, and Southwest experienced severe to extreme drought, causing crop damage and creating the need for water rationing in many areas. Twelve states averaged drier than normal for the spring season. Florida reported its fourth driest spring on record, while Missouri had its eighth driest spring since 1895.

The U.S. drought impacted 30 of the 48 contiguous states, registering from moderate to extreme drought.

Chronology of Events: January 3–June 10, 2000

- *January 3-9, 2000*: Israel and Syria held negotiations in Shepherdstown, near Washington, D.C., with President Bill Clinton's active participation.
- *January 4, 2000*: The NASDAQ plummeted 229 points, and the Dow was off 359 points.
- *January 10, 2000*: The Israel-Syria talks ended after the U.S. proposed a draft agreement.
- *January 17, 2000*: The U.S. announced freezing of the Israel-Syria talks due to fundamental differences.
- *January 19, 2000*: Syria said it would not resume talks with Israel unless Israel pledged to withdraw to the June 5, 1967, lines.
- *January 25, 2000*: Israel canceled plans to send experts to Washington, DC, to discuss a working paper on Syria.
- *March 8, 2000*: Barak and Arafat met with U.S. Special Envoy Dennis Ross in Ramallah.
- *March 8, 2000*: State Department Spokesman Jamie Rubin said Ross report ed to Secretary Albright that the U.S. had agreed to host negotiations between the Israelis and Palestinians in Washington after the Eid al-Adha, which began March 16. Rubin called this "an important development"; and said, "Secretary Albright welcomed this development because it is an indication of a willingness to sit down together with us to try to move us closer to the kind of blueprint that a framework agreement would provide for the permanent peace." Rubin added, "We want to accelerate the process. This is a way to hopefully do that. At the same time, we recognize that the issues are extraordinarily difficult."
- *March 10, 2000*: The NASDAQ reached its all-time high of 5,048.62. Soon after that, it began tumbling and eventually lost 3,500 points. Israel, as a nation, had the third most publicly traded companies on NASDAQ. The major drop cost Israel billions of dollars and has become their greatest economic setback in history (to date).
- *March 21-26, 2000*: Palestinian-Israeli talks commenced at Bolling Air Force Base near Washington, D.C., and lasted one week. The U.S. facilitated discussion of permanent status issues in an effort to help the parties reach a comprehensive agreement by September 13, 2000.

- *March 26, 2000*: President Clinton met Syrian President Hafez Assad in Geneva, Switzerland.
- *March 25–April 1, 2000*: The NASDAQ fell six of the last seven sessions and was off 17 percent from its record high of 5,048.62 set just three weeks earlier. The last week of the first quarter resulted in NASDAQ's losing 8 percent of its value.
- *April 3, 2000*: The NASDAQ suffered its largest point drop ever (349.15) and its fifth largest percentage drop (7.6 percent).
- *April 4, 2000*: U.S. Defense Secretary Cohen held talks in Israel. The U.S. demanded that Israel cancel the Phalcon deal with China.
- *April 4, 2000*: In a wild trading day, and Wall Street's busiest on record, the NASDAQ recovered nearly all of a 574-point, 13.5-percent tumble that would have been the index's biggest percentage drop in history—ahead of the 11.3 percent plunge on Oct. 19, 1987 (Black Monday). The NASDAQ ended down 74.79, or 1.8 percent, to 4,148.89.

  The Dow Jones industrial average nearly emerged from its own deep hole, a 504-point drop that almost matched the tumble of October 1987. The Dow fell 57.09, or 0.5 percent, to 11,164.84.

- *April 11-12, 2000*: President Clinton summoned Israeli Prime Minister Barak to the White House for a four-hour meeting on April 11. Barak met with other Clinton administration officials on April 12.
- *April 10-14, 2000*: It was the worst one-week decline ever posted by a broad U.S. market index. It was worse than the legendary Black Friday week in 1929, and worse than the week of the 1987 crash that sent the Dow industrials down 22.6 percent in a single day. The week ended with an especially tough note on Friday, with stocks losing an amazing $1 trillion of market value, which Wilshire Associates said was the biggest one-day market loss since money was invented. That raised the week's losses to a record $2.1 trillion. The NASDAQ, for the week ending April 14, had fallen 25.3 percent.
- *April 20, 2000*: President Clinton stated:

  > I am very, very glad to have Chairman Arafat back here at the White House, and I'm looking forward to our talks. We've reached a very serious time in the peace process. He and Prime Minister Barak have set for themselves an ambitious timetable to reach a framework agreement as soon as they can, and then a final agreement by the middle of September. So we're working hard on it and I think we'll get some things done today.

- *May 7, 2000*: Barak and Arafat met in Ramallah. Barak said Israel would shortly cede 3 West Bank villages near Jerusalem to Palestinian control.

- *May 15, 2000*: The Cabinet, and later the Knesset, approved the transfer of Abu Dis, Izariyah, and Sawarah al-Sharquiya to Area A.
- *June 1, 2000*: President Clinton and Barak met in Lisbon, Portugal.
- *June 5, 2000*: Secretary Albright and Special Envoy Ross held talks in Israel & Gaza with Barak & Arafat to prepare for Clinton-Barak-Arafat summit.
- *June 6, 2000*: Secretary Albright announced an Arafat-Clinton meeting on June 14. Israel-PA teams planned to resume talks in Washington, D.C., on June 12 to prepare for a summit at the end of June.
- *June 7, 2000*: The Knesset adopted by 61-to-48, 11 absent, a preliminary motion to dissolve itself.
- *June 10, 2000*: Pres. Assad of Syria died; his son Bashar succeeded him.

Event #28
Drought/Heat Wave: July–August 2000
Estimated $4 (4.2) billion damages/costs

At the urging of Israeli Prime Minister Barak, President Clinton announced on *July 5, 2000*, his invitation to Barak and Arafat to come to Camp David to continue their negotiations on the Middle East peace process.

Camp David Summit Convened: July 11, 2000

Between *July 11 and 24*, President Clinton, Prime Minister Barak, and Chairman Arafat met at Camp David in an effort to reach an agreement on permanent status. While they were not able to bridge the gaps and reach an agreement, their negotiations were unprecedented in both scope and detail. Building on the progress achieved at Camp David, Barak and Arafat agreed on the following principles to guide their negotiations:

1) The aim of their negotiations was to put an end to decades of conflict and achieve a just and lasting peace.
2) They would continue their efforts to conclude an agreement on all permanent status issues as soon as possible.
3) Negotiations based on UN Security Council Resolutions 242 and 338 were the only way to achieve such an agreement; and they would seek to create an environment for negotiations free from pressure, intimidation, and threats of violence.
4) They understood the importance of avoiding unilateral actions that would prejudge the outcome of negotiations—and that their differences would be resolved only by good-faith negotiations.
5) They agreed that the United States should remain a vital partner in the search for peace, and therefore agreed to continue to consult closely with President Clinton and Secretary Albright.

The Year of the Drought and Wildfires
Weather Log: July 11-20, 2000 (NOAA)

It was very hot in parts of south-central U.S. and the western states. Media sources reported that the heat wave blanketing the southern U.S. was responsible for at least 12 deaths in Texas and 10 in Alabama. An additional seven were under investigation as heat-related in Louisiana. Arizona, New Mexico, Oklahoma, Arkansas, Mississippi, and Kansas were also suffering from the 100-plus temperatures that lasted for more than a week. An emergency health alert was announced for the Dallas-Fort Worth area; water restrictions were implemented in 120 cities and towns throughout Texas due to drought conditions.

Weather Log: July 21-31, 2000

Fires Raging in Western U.S.: The worst fire season in years continued to worsen as 50 active fires in western U.S. consumed over 500,000 acres as of July 31, 2000. Two of the fires burned over 60,000 acres each—one in the Sierra Nevada/Sequoia National Forest area of California, and another in Nevada about 60 miles northeast of Elko. An estimated nearly 7 million acres burned in fires in the U.S. that year.

Wild land fires dominated the headlines throughout the summer, as they burned out of control in southeastern, southwestern, and western U.S.

In the meteorological record books, the summer of 2000 will be remembered for devastating wildfires that scorched just under 7 million acres across the nation; searing temperatures and drought that plagued parts of the West and South; a historic string of rain-free days in Texas, which rivaled the Dust Bowl of the 1930s; and cooler-than-usual temperatures in the East. For example, the Washington, D.C., area had its coolest summer since 1972; the San Francisco Bay area, by contrast, had hotter-than-usual temperatures, including a heat wave with record temperatures of up to 110 degrees.

States in the Inter-Mountain West were hit hard, with hot and persistently dry conditions giving rise to the worst wildfire season in the past 50 years.

On a national scale, by the end of August over a third (35 percent) of the contiguous U.S. was experiencing severe to extreme drought as measured by the Palmer Drought Index. Based on a real extent, the summer 2000 drought was as widespread as the 1988 drought, but ranks behind the more extensive droughts of the 1950s and 1930s.

As Bill Clinton applied enormous pressure toward dividing God's covenant land, the land of the United States experienced one of the worst droughts and wildfire seasons in history. As Clinton, Barak, and Arafat were meeting at Camp David, much of the Western U.S. was on fire. As the land of Israel was placed at risk, so was the land of the nation attempting to divide her land.

Event #29
U.S. and Israel Political Crisis, Mitchell Committee Appointed, Clinton Tries to Rush Middle East Deal, and Political Chaos in Israel and the U.S.
October 30–December 13, 2000

Former U.S. Senator George Mitchell, who brokered a peace agreement for troubled Northern Ireland in 1998, was selected to head an international commission investigating six weeks of intense violence between Palestinians and Israeli security forces.

The White House announced Mitchell's appointment—along with that of fellow commission members U.S. Senator Warren Rudman, former Turkish President Suleyman Demirel, European Union Foreign and Security Affairs Chief Javier Solana and Norwegian Foreign Minister Thorbjoern Jagland.

The announcement was made on *November 7*, the same day Americans went to the polls to select the man who was to follow President Clinton in office, and two days ahead of planned meetings between Clinton and Chairman Arafat.

Arafat met with Clinton on *November 9*. Israeli Prime Minister Barak canceled his scheduled meeting for *November 13* due to terror events in Israel.

After Arafat's meeting with President Clinton, he headed to the United Nations to seek support for a proposed UN protection force in Gaza and the West Bank.

Speaking on Thursday night, *November 9*, to the Council on Foreign Relations in Washington, Arafat said the force proposal "was one of the major points I presented to, and requested from, President Clinton" when the two met at the White House.

Seeking to counter Israel's refusal to consider a buffer force, Arafat said:

Between Israel and Egypt, there is an international force. Between Lebanon and Israel, there is an international force. Between Israel and Syria, there is an international force.

Israeli Prime Minister Barak responded by saying that Israel was opposed to the idea because such a force would "reward" Palestinian violence.

The White House said that as long as Israel was opposed to such a force, the two sides should focus on where they agreed.

The Bush-Gore 2000 Election Crisis

It was the concession speech that never came.

Campaign officials for Vice President Al Gore released an official blow-by-blow account on Wednesday, *November 8, 2000*, of the Democratic presidential candidate's contacts with his Republican rival, Texas Governor George W. Bush, and his plans to concede following network news projections of a Bush victory in Florida and nationwide. Here is the Gore camp's account of what happened, and when:

- Between 1:30 a.m. and 1:45 a.m. (CST), Gore called Bush to concede the election. Gore's call came after the media reported that Gore was losing Florida by 50,000 votes, and after TV networks called the state—and the election—for Bush.
- Gore left his hotel in Nashville, Tennessee, and began the short motorcade drive to War Memorial Plaza, where he planned to address supporters gathered there.
- When the motorcade was about two blocks from War Memorial Plaza, traveling chief of staff Michael Feldman was paged by field director Michael Whouley. Whouley told Feldman that only 6,000 votes in Florida separated Gore from Bush at that time, according to the Florida secretary of state, with a significant number of votes outstanding.
- Feldman called Gore campaign chairman William Daley and gave him the latest numbers from Florida. Daley informed Gore.
- By the time Gore's motorcade reached War Memorial Plaza, the difference in Florida was fewer than one thousand votes.
- Gore, Daley and other campaign advisers met in the vice president's holding room at the plaza to discuss the situation.
- About 2:15 a.m.: Daley called Bush campaign chairman Don Evans.
- Between 2:30 a.m. and 2:45 a.m., Gore called Bush again, and the two candidates spoke for a few minutes. The conversation's "contents [were] private," the Gore camp said, but officials told CNN that Gore retracted his earlier concession.
- Gore left War Memorial Plaza to return to his hotel. He did not speak to the crowd.
- Daley addressed the plaza crowd. "Our campaign continues," he said, "until a winner is officially declared in Florida." The few hundred people remaining in the plaza cheered: "Stay and fight!" and "Don't give up!"
- Gore met with staff until 3:45 a.m.; then went to bed.
- Bush and President Clinton scrapped planned public statements.

With Florida's election returns in enough of a state of flux to send both major party presidential campaigns into a frenzy early the next morning, Republicans took some measure of comfort in their ability to retain control of both houses of Congress in that general election year.

Governor Bush, however, saw his victory being stripped away—at least temporarily—when discrepancies in the Sunshine State's return numbers were brought to the fore.

CNN retracted its estimate of a Bush win when Florida state officials announced a statewide vote recount. With more than 5,000,000 votes counted in the state, Gore and Bush appeared to be separated by approximately 220 votes.

Florida holds 25 electoral votes—enough to boost either of the two over the required 270-vote total needed for an unquestionable win in the Electoral College.

Florida held the future of the presidency in the balance.

The campaign of Governor Bush opened a variety of legal offensives in a fevered move to counter the unfavorable effects of a ruling by the Florida Supreme Court—requiring immediate manual recounts of thousands of disputed ballots. Bush attorneys filed an appeal with a federal appeals court in Atlanta, and prepared another for the U.S. Supreme Court.

Supreme Court's Decision

On *December 9*, the U.S. Supreme Court, in a 5-to-4 ruling, halted the manual recounts in Florida and set a hearing on the matter two days later.

On *December 11*, Bush's lawyers argued before the U.S. Supreme Court that the Florida high court again overstepped its bounds by ordering a manual recount of under-votes in Gore's election contest. Gore's lawyers argued that the U.S. Supreme Court had no reason to intervene in the state court contest.

The U.S. Supreme Court had to determine whether the Florida Supreme Court overstepped its bounds in ordering a statewide recount of under-votes. Audiotapes of the historic Supreme Court arguments aired nationally. The long wait for the decisive decision began.

A committee of the Florida House voted 5-to-2 to approve a resolution to name presidential electors for George Bush. A half-hour later, a Florida Senate committee approved a similar resolution by a 4-to-3 vote.

On Tuesday, *December 12*, the Associated Press reported that the Florida House had voted to approve 25 electors for George Bush. Just two Democrats joined the 79-to-41 vote.

The U.S. Supreme Court, in a 5-to-4 ruling, split along ideological lines, stepped in to end the election and Gore's quest for a final recount. It reversed the Florida Supreme Court decision ordering a statewide recount of under-votes—stating, in the per curium section of its opinion, that differing vote-counting standards from county to county and the lack of a single judicial officer to oversee the recount violated the Equal Protection clause of the Constitution.

Al Gore Calls Bush to Concede the Presidential Race

Vice President Al Gore conceded the presidential election on Wednesday night, *December 13, 2000*, effectively concluding an election that was supposed to have ended five weeks earlier.

"Tonight, for the sake of our unity of the people and the strength of our democracy, I offer my concession," Gore said in a televised address from the Old Executive Office Building, adjacent to the White House.

Barak Resigned and Then Was Defeated

A two-hour meeting on Sunday, *October 29, 2000*, between Israeli Prime Minister Barak and Ariel Sharon, the right-wing leader of the opposition Likud party, failed to produce an emergency government designed to strengthen Barak's shaky hold on power.

An alliance between Barak and Sharon was bitterly opposed by Palestinians because of Sharon's hard-line stance on the peace process. Yet including Sharon in the government could avert a call from Barak's political opponents to dissolve parliament and call for new elections for prime minister.

Barak held only 30 seats in the 120-member Knesset and an alliance with Sharon's party would have given him enough added support to maintain power. Barak worked to bring the hawkish opposition Likud party into his coalition, but they refused to give Likud leader Ariel Sharon the control he wanted over peace talks with the Palestinians.

Barak told the legislators on *November 28*—just before they voted overwhelmingly to dissolve parliament and hold elections two years ahead of schedule—he was prepared for such an event.

Barak's announcement came just before an overwhelming majority of MKs [Members of Knesset] were poised to vote for the first reading of opposition legislation calling for dissolving the 15th Knesset and holding early elections. The first of the five bills passed by 75-to-1, with 29 abstentions from One Israel and Meretz MKs. The third passed by 79-to-1.

"I see that the Knesset wants elections, and I am willing for general elections for the prime minister and Knesset to be held," Barak said.

Coalition and opposition leaders began talking about setting an election date. The dissolution bill headed to the Knesset Law Committee, set the exact date for the elections, and sent the final draft back to the plenum for its second and third readings.

Sharon slammed Barak for blaming the Knesset for bringing about early elections. "The person who is responsible for the situation that has been created is you, you, you," Sharon said.

Shinui leader Yosef Lapid made a last-ditch effort to bring Barak and Sharon together through a joint principles document; but Barak (primarily) rejected his overtures, since the plan would have given Sharon a veto on security and other matters.

After hours of consultations, Barak concluded that he did not have the option of postponing the vote through a no-confidence motion or calling an immediate confidence vote, since he was very likely to lose in both scenarios.

In a stunning surprise move, Barak announced his resignation on Saturday, *December 9*, apparently pre-empting the Knesset's push for an early general election and opening the door to a vote only for the premiership.

Barak said he would stand for re-election, effectively asking for a vote of confidence from the Israeli people. At a hastily convened televised news conference on Saturday evening at his Jerusalem office, Barak said:

> Due to the emergency situation the country is in . . . and the need to continue reducing the violence and moving forward the chances of peace negotiations, I have decided to ask again for the trust of the people of Israel.

> Tomorrow morning, I'll tell the president of my official decision to resign and lead the Labor Party to special elections for Israeli prime minister. Afterwards I'll submit my letter of resignation to the government, as required by law.

His government had rejected another Israeli prime minister who had been very active in the Middle East peace talks.

In one of the more remarkable comebacks in Israeli political history, former general Ariel Sharon completed the long road back when the voters overwhelmingly chose him as prime minister of Israel on *February 6, 2001*.

Sharon's landslide victory was as much a product of disillusionment—with the peace process, the ongoing Palestinian violence and the personality of incumbent Prime Minister Barak—as it was an endorsement of Sharon himself.

The public's judgment was resounding: 59.5 percent of the vote went to Likud leader Sharon; 40.5 percent to Barak (per exit polls, Israel Television).

By Israeli standards, the margin was of historic proportions, coming just 21 months after Barak swept into office with a seemingly broad mandate.

Yet many Israelis, it appears, were disillusioned with both candidates. Voter turnout was just 62 percent, the lowest in the nation's history. Israeli turnout generally is about 80 percent, among the highest rates in the democratic world.

Middle East Peace Efforts and a Month of Political Chaos

On *November 7, 2000,* President Clinton appointed the Mitchell Committee to come up with a Middle East plan to help deal with the major violence in Israel and bring peace to the Middle East. That *same day*, the Bush vs. Gore 2000 election turned into a five-week political crisis. During the same period, the Barak government in Israel was in a political crisis and on the verge of collapse. Clinton met with Chairman Arafat at the White House on *November 9* to give his peace efforts one more try. That same day, Barak resigned as Israel's prime minister on; and on *December 13*, the U.S. presidential crisis was over, and the new president, George W. Bush, gave his acceptance speech.

Summary of Actions and Coinciding Catastrophes or Events During Presidency of Bill Clinton (1997-2000)

Date	Action	Date	Catastrophe
March 2, 1997 March 3	• In response to Israel building housing units in East Jerusalem, PLO Chairman Yasser Arafat arrived in DC for a meeting he requested with Pres. Bill Clinton. • Clinton and Arafat met, issued public statements critical of Israel.	March 1-2, 1997	Mississippi & Ohio Valley Flooding and Tornadoes: 67 dead (26 in Arkansas); winds up to 207-260 mph & tornadoes brought heavy rains, flooding; $1 billion. • Pres. Clinton's home state of Arkansas was devastated by tornadoes.
April 7, 1997	Pres. Clinton & Israel PM Benjamin Netanyahu met at White House; Clinton said he would work to get peace process back on track.	April 1 – May 14, 1997	Northern Plains Flooding: 5 dead; flooding in North Dakota, up to 26' above flood stage, breaks 100-year record; worst flooding since 1852 in Manitoba, Canada; $3.7 billion.
April 27, 1997 July 15	• UN General Assembly (UNGA) held emergency special session, condemned Israel for building project. • UNGA passed 2nd resolution demanding Israel stop building homes in East Jerusalem.	July 1997 – October 1998	Foreign Financial Contagion: unprecedented worldwide financial crisis; economic collapse in Asia during 1997 extended through most of 1998; loss of hundreds of billions worldwide.

Date	Action	Date	Catastrophe
January 7, 1998	While in Jerusalem to get peace process back on track, after meeting with Israeli Pres. Weizman, U.S. Middle East Coordinator Ross issued statement.	*January 4-9, 1998*	**Northeast Ice Storm**: One of longest & most damaging ice storms to hit northeast U.S.; worst natural disaster in Canadian history; $1.4 billion.
January 20, 1998 *January 22*	• Pres. Clinton met with PM Netanyahu at White House. • Pres. Clinton met with PLO Chairman Arafat at White House, and told reporters plan is "land-for-peace".	*January 21, 1998*	**Lewinsky Scandal** erupted as news organizations reported on alleged sexual relations with Pres. Clinton. For rest of presidency, Clinton fights for survival.
January 28, 1998	Secretary of State Albright made statement in support of Clinton peace plan.	*January – February 1998*	**Southeast Severe Weather**: Warmest & wettest January-February on record; 59 dead; over 5,000 homes damaged or destroyed; $1 billion.
May 1, 1998 *May 1-2* *May 6*	• VP Al Gore met with PM Netanyahu in Jerusalem, reaffirmed commitment to Olso & Washington accords, and land-for-peace plan. • VP Gore met with Saudi Arabia Crown Prince Abdulaziz, agreed to importance of accords & plan. • First Lady Hillary Clinton said Palestinian state essential to peace.	*May 1 – June 5, 1998*	**U.S.-China Technology Scandal**: U.S. Congress investigated whether Clinton Administration export policy allowed China to acquire technology to improve accuracy of nuclear missiles.
Sept. 24, 1998 *Sept. 27* *Sept. 28*	• Clinton said he would meet with PM Netanyahu and Arafat to pressure Israel to accept plan to give up 13% of land. • Secretary Albright met with Netanyahu and Arafat at UN. • Clinton, Netanyahu & Arafat met at the White House. • Arafat addressed UN, called for Palestinian state by 1999.	*Sept. 24-28, 1998*	**Hurricane Georges**: Began in Gulf of Mexico on 24th; hit Gulf Coast on 27th & 28th with 110-mile-per-hour winds, heavy rains, & flooding; dissipated when Arafat left U.S.; $5.9 billion.

Date	Action	Date	Catastrophe
October 15, 1998 October 22	• PM Netanyahu & Chmn. Arafat met at Wye Plantation for 5 days of talks regarding Israel giving up 13% of land; no agreement. Pres. Clinton pressed for continued talks. • Netanyahu agreed to give land for Arafat peace promise.	October 17-22, 1998	**Texas Flooding**: Tornadoes & rains caused record flooding in southern Texas; 25% of big state affeced; many small towns nearly swept away; $1 billion.
Nov. 30, 1998	2nd Middle East Donors Conference at U.S. Dept. of State with 50 countries; $3 billion pledged, including Pres. Clinton pledge of extra $400 million to Palestinians.	Nov. 30 – Dec. 1, 1998	**Stock Market Sell-Off**: Dow falls 216 points; European stock markets experience 3rd largest sell-off in history.
Dec. 12, 1998	Pres. Clinton arrived in Israel to insure Wye Agreement would be implemented; met with PM Netanyahu & Chairman Arafat; received red carpet treatment at new Palestinian airport.	Dec. 11-19, 1998	**Clinton Impeachment**: Dec. 11: President Clinton charged with perjury and obstruction of justice. • Dec. 19: U.S. House of Representatives voted to impeach Clinton (to Senate for trial). **Israel: PM Netanyahu lost support** of Israeli Knesset, which calls for elections.
March 23, 1999 March 24	• Chairman Arafat met with Pres. Clinton to discuss Palestinian State. • President Clinton authorized attack on Serbia.	March 23, 1999 March 24 – June 10	**Stock Market falls again:** 219 points; biggest fall since Nov. 30 sell-off. **Kosovo War Begins**: $3 billion
May 4, 1999 May 6	• Arafat was to declare Palestinian state & Jerusalem as its capital (postponed until Dec. at Clinton request). • Pres. Clinton wrote Arafat, said he had right to "own land." • Mrs. Clinton repeated support for Palestinian state.	May 3-4, 1999	**Oklahoma-Kansas Tornadoes**: most powerful to ever hit U.S.; 316 mph record wind speed; $1.6 billion.
Sept. 1, 1999 Sept. 4	• Sec. Albright traveled to Egypt, Israel, West Bank, Morocco, Lebanon & Syria to restart Wye Accord compliance. • Albright attended Sharm El-Sheikh Accord.	August 24 – Sept. 7, 1999	**Hurricane Dennis**: came ashore on Sept. 4, the same day Albright was observing Barak and Arafat sign the Sharm El-Sheikh Accord.

Date	Action	Date	Catastrophe
Sept. 13, 1999	1st meeting of Israel Foreign Minister & PLO official to work out borders for Palestinian state.	*Sept. 7-17, 1999*	**Hurricane Floyd**: "grew unexpectedly into monster storm" on Sept. 13; greatest evacuation in U.S. history; $6 billion.
Week of October 11, 1999	Israel: Jewish settlers evicted from 15 West Bank hilltops as part of "land-for-peace" deal.	*October 14-15, 1999*	**Hurricane Irene:** hit North Carolina. **Hector Mine Earthquake**: 7.1, 5th largest to hit U.S. **Major Stock Market Sell-off**: Dow - worst drop since 1989, lost 266 pts.; loss of billions of dollars in market capitalization.
January 3-9, 2000 *March 26* *April 3-4* *April 11*	• Israel PM Barak & Syria FM al-Sharaa held talks near DC; Clinton participated; U.S. convinced Israel to yield to Syria demand to discuss borders first. Talks failed. • Pres. Clinton held summit with Syria Pres. Assad to discuss Golan Heights. • U.S. Defense Sec. Cohen held talks in Israel. • Clinton met with and pressured PM Barak.	*January 1 – July 1, 2000*	**NASDAQ Losses**: 4 greatest drop/loss periods occurred on days U.S. pressured Israel (Jan. 4; Mar. 25-April 1; April 3; April 10-14); losses in trillions of dollars. **Fires & Drought**: "Year of the Wildfires"; unprecedented 93,000 wildfires; most expensive fire year in U.S. history; warmest temperatures on record for period; $1.6 billion.
July 11-24, 2000	Pres. Clinton, PM Barak and Chairman Arafat met at Camp David, agreed to broad negotiating principles.	*July – August, 2000*	**Drought/Heat Wave**: 20 dead; 35% of U.S. faced drought conditions; $4 billion.
Nov. 7, 2000 *Nov. 7*	• Election Day in U.S.; White House announced former Sen. Mitchell would head international commission investigating violence in Israel. • Arafat met with Pres. Clinton, then went to UN, proposing UN protection force in Gaza & West Bank.	*October 30 – Dec. 13, 2000*	**U.S. Political Crisis:** Vice Pres. Al Gore lost presidential election to Gov. George W. Bush. **Israel Political Crisis:** PM Barak failed to get adequate support in Knesset, resigned, and then lost re-election bid to Ariel Sharon.

CHAPTER 6

U.S. Catastrophes
and Events: 2001-2004

U.S. Administration: President George W. Bush

President Bush's Original Plan

President George W. Bush originally wanted to be a facilitator and not an active participant in the ongoing Middle East talks. After violence worsened in

Israel in *early 2001*, and at the urging of Egyptian President Hosni Mubarak and Jordan's King Abdullah II, President Bush agreed to become more involved.

Due to the strained relationship with Crown Prince Abdullah of Saudi Arabia, Secretary of State Colin Powell—along with the United States Ambassador to Israel, Daniel Kurtzer—convinced President Bush to develop a comprehensive Middle East plan. The plan was to be given by Powell to the United Nations General Assembly on *September 24, 2001*. However, the *September 11* terror events postponed the delivery of the speech. Powell eventually gave the message in *November 2001*, which was followed by months of horrific violence in Israel and failed peace efforts by retired U.S. Marine General Anthony Zinni.

President Bush, again frustrated with the terror and violence in Israel, brought Zinni home in late *March 2002*, and stopped actively working on the peace process. On *April 3, 2002*, the European Union (EU) called on the United States to step down and let them take over the Middle East peace talks. President Bush hastily called a Rose Garden press conference the next day, *April 4*. He called on the Israelis and the Palestinians to get back to the peace table, and said he was sending Secretary Powell to the region the following week to discuss ways to jump-start the peace process again.

The violence continued, and President Bush's *June 18 and 19* addresses were postponed due to two major suicide bombings in Jerusalem. He finally presented his long-awaited Middle East plan on *June 24*. Bush's plan became the foundation of the Quartet's new plan.

To build international consensus for the Bush Plan or an alternative plan, "The Quartet" was formed: the EU, UN, Russia and the U.S. They began to prepare their plan in late *September 2002*. After three months of work, the great world powers gathered together at the Oval Office on *December 2*0 to formally affirm their plan on how to divide Israel's covenant land. However, there were still differences between the Quartet Plan and the Bush plan. Primarily, the Bush plan required the Palestinians to stop terror first and then the talks would continue. The world community wanted Israel to stop the settlement construction in conjunction with the cessation of terror. (More on this later.)

Finally, a meeting was held in Jordan on *June 3, 2003*, between President Bush, Israeli Prime Minister Ariel Sharon, and Palestinian Prime Minister Mahmoud Abbas.

The Major "Land for Peace" Efforts and the Corresponding Catastrophes or Events March 31, 2001 to November 10, 2004

Event #30
Bush's First International Crisis: March 31–April 11, 2001

Egyptian President Hosni Mubarak arrived in Washington, DC, on Saturday, *March 31, 2001*, for a meeting with President Bush. His plan was to persuade Bush to become more active in the Middle East talks. On the same day [*April 1st* in China]—a U.S. Navy EP-3E surveillance plane with a 21-man, 3-woman crew collided with a Chinese fighter jet sent to intercept it over the South China Sea, well outside China's 19-kilometer (12-mile) territorial sea and airspace. The U.S. Plane made an emergency landing at a military airfield on China's Hainan Island. Admiral Dennis Blair, commander-in-chief of the U.S. Pacific Command, said the collision was caused by a ``pattern of increasingly unsafe behavior'' by China's military plane.

President Mubarak came to the White House on *April 2* for the meeting with President Bush. The same day U.S. diplomats left for Hainan hoping to meet with American crew members. Bush urged China to release the aircraft and let U.S. diplomats meet with crew members, and said failure to do so would violate "standard diplomatic practice."

The resulting political crisis completely overshadowed the visits of both Mubarak and Jordan's King Abdullah II. After King Abdullah spoke with Christian leaders, members of Congress, and others to solicit support for the "land for peace" initiative, he visited the White House on *April 10*, and then returned home to Jordan. On the very next day, the United States and China reached agreement for the crew's release.

Event #31
President Bush and Secretary Powell Endorse Mitchell Plan; Republicans Lost Majority in the U.S. Senate May 21-24, 2001

The Mitchell report was publicly released *May 21*. An international fact-finding committee, headed by former U.S. Senate Majority Leader George Mitchell, had produced the plan over the previous six months. It recommended an immediate ceasefire, a halt to further settlement activity by the Israelis, and more effort by Palestinian leaders to suppress and denounce terrorism. As Secretary Powell said in Washington on *May 21*:

The United States believes the [Mitchell] committee has provided the parties with ideas that can help to find a solution to the terrible tragedy that has trapped the Israeli and Palestinian peoples in a continuing downward spiral of violence for the past eight months, a spiral that has gotten worse in the last few days.

Powell called on Israelis and Palestinians to address the committee's primary recommendations by reaffirming their commitment to existing agreements and undertakings, immediately and unconditionally ceasing violence, and resuming security cooperation. He also said that both sides:

... must avoid unilateral acts that prejudice the outcome of permanent status negotiations and that could be perceived by the other side as provocative during this very delicate time.

According to White House Press Secretary Ari Fleischer, President Bush placed phone calls early *May 22* to President Mubarak and King Abdullah II to discuss the escalating violence in the Middle East, and the recommendations in the Mitchell committee report on ways to halt it and help return the Israelis and the Palestinians to the peace process.

President Bush is committed to trying to facilitate peace in the region, is very concerned about the level of violence, and [believes that] the best way to seize this moment, now that the Mitchell report is out, is for the parties involved to end the violence, so that the cycle of violence can be broken, and that the parties can indeed begin talking, with the United States playing a facilitative role.

[Both Mubarak and King Abdullah] welcome[d] the United States' endorsement of the Mitchell report, and they both told the President they are ready to work with the United States to encourage the parties to implement the report's recommendations.

Bush called Israeli Prime Minister Ariel Sharon and Palestinian Chairman Yasser Arafat on *May 23* and urged them to accept the Mitchell report as a framework to ending violence and resuming peace efforts. He urged both leaders to seize the opportunity offered by the Mitchell committee report to end the violence in the region, and to work with the plan.

Republicans Lost Majority in the U.S. Senate

As rumored on *May 21-22*, Vermont Senator James Jeffords left the Republican Party on Thursday, *May 24*, to become an Independent, which handed majority control of the Senate over to the Democratic Party for the first time since 1994.

Jeffords' decision created a crisis in the U.S. Senate for the Bush administration and the Republican Party. The Republicans lost their majority and their influential committee chairmanships. Jeffords' defection also had a disruptive impact on Bush's judicial appointments and legislative agenda.

Catastrophe #32
CIA Director Tenet Met with Israelis and Palestinians over Ceasefire Agreement: June 5-13, 2001
Tropical Storm Allison
Estimated $5 (5.1) billion damages/costs

Central Intelligence Agency (CIA) Director George Tenet, who arrived in Israel from Egypt after meeting on *June 6* with President Mubarak, met on *June 7* with Prime Minister Sharon and Israeli security chiefs, and later with Chairman Arafat. His goal was to stem the violence that had claimed more than 600 lives since September.

"The prime minister explained Israel's demand for a halting of the violence, terror and incitement, which have not ceased," a Sharon spokesman said after the meeting with Tenet.

Palestinian security sources said Tenet's meeting with Arafat was held in Ramallah, in the West Bank. Also attending were Palestinian negotiators and security chiefs in Gaza and the West Bank, and U.S. Consul Roland Schliker.

Unrest continued in the West Bank and Gaza Strip on *June 8* despite Arafat's call for a ceasefire over that weekend, and Tenet's meetings with Israeli and Palestinian officials. Tenet, Arafat and Sharon agreed to the Tenet ceasefire agreement, but it was never officially signed.

Bush Hailed Israeli-Palestinian Cease-Fire Agreement

President Bush welcomed an Israeli-Palestinian ceasefire plan that was brokered by the U.S. In a brief statement at the outset of a joint press conference with NATO Secretary-General George Robertson in Brussels on *June 13*, Bush said, "I'm encouraged that both Israel and the Palestinian Authority have agreed to a ceasefire plan, and I'm proud of America's role in helping to achieve it."

Tropical Storm Allison Pummeled Houston

Tropical Storm Allison, the first named storm of the 2001 Atlantic hurricane season, devastated portions of southeast Texas with severe flooding, including the Houston Metro area and surrounding communities. Allison hovered over southeast and east Texas for five days, dumping record amounts of rainfall.

There were three distinct heavy rain events. The first event was associated with Allison's landfall on *June 5* and affected northern Galveston and southern and eastern Harris counties. The second event on *June 7* stretched from southern Liberty County southwest into the Houston area and northern Fort Bend County. The third and most devastating event on *June 8 and 9* stretched from Conroe to the Woodlands to Houston and on into northern Galveston County again. At least 22 fatalities associated with the flooding occurred with this third event. Nearly 37 inches of rain was recorded at the Port of Houston during Allison's five-day rampage.

On *October 31, 2001*, the National Weather Service of the National Oceanic and Atmospheric Administration (NOAA) released its Service Assessment for the Texas/Louisiana flood event associated with Tropical Storm Allison. The costliest tropical storm in the nation's history, Allison left 24 dead and caused more than $5 billion in damage in Texas and Louisiana before moving eastward to wreak havoc along the Gulf and East Coasts of the United States.

In Texas, 45,000 homes and businesses were flooded and 28 counties were declared federal disaster areas. In Louisiana, more than 1,000 homes were flooded and a state of emergency was declared in 25 parishes.

"This devastating event reminds us once again that the current state of the science of forecasting and early warnings can only take us so far," said Larry Mooney, NWS service assessment team leader.

The remnants of Tropical Storm Allison finally moved out to sea on *June 18*, after wreaking havoc from Texas to New England for 12 days.

Joe Allbaugh, FEMA director, said on *June 19* that the massive damage from the storm occurred in large part because people were taken by surprise. "[It was] one of those freak accidents. I don't think we can fault the forecasters. No one can predict 36 inches of rain."

He added that flooding was to blame for many of the casualties. Although floods are one of the least-feared disasters among many Americans, they are a major hazard during almost any storm.

Catastrophe #33
World Trade Center and Pentagon Terrorist Attacks
September 11, 2001
Estimated cost: $40 billion and Higher

Total insurance claims—life insurance, workmen's compensation, property damage and business/rental interruption—was about $40 billion; the U.S. government committed an additional $20 billion for infrastructure repair in New York City and in Washington, DC. The U.S. government also committed hundreds of billions of dollars to the war on terror.

On *September 11*, the greatest attack ever on American soil occurred. The hijacking of four airplanes and the attacks on the World Trade Center (WTC) in New York City and the Pentagon left nearly 3,000 people dead. The suicide attacks by Muslim terrorists stunned the country. On this day, America came under the attack of terrorism on a scale not imagined. More Americans died on September 11 than in the attack on Pearl Harbor or the D-Day invasion. The attack was a complete surprise and came with no warning. The 9-11 events have cost the U.S. economy and nation hundreds of billions of dollars. There have been enormous costs associated with developing the office of Homeland Security; the war in Afghanistan; and the war in Iraq ($154 billion). All of these costs had a huge impact on the U.S. government's budget deficit, which was projected to be $450 billion for 2003 and even higher in 2004. [update cost of two wars; give actual deficits for 2003, 2004, and 2005.]

The attack on the WTC was at the very heart of the U.S. financial center. The largest stock brokerage firms in the world were in the WTC, along with many of the international banks. The effect of this attack on the stock market was devastating.

The attack on the Pentagon was at the heart of the U.S. military. The plane intended for the White House or the Capitol Building (depending on news accounts), crashed west of Pittsburgh when Todd Beamer and other passengers attempted to wrestle control from the hijackers.

According to *The Washington Post*, for 17 days prior to the 9-11 terror events, President Bush—with the encouragement and involvement of Secretary Powell and U.S. Ambassador to Israel Daniel Kurtzer, and in cooperation with the Saudis—was working on the most comprehensive plan and message ever to be offered about Israel's covenant land by an American president. Bush and his top officials had completed a majority of their work on *September 10*. Secretary Powell was to present the plan to the United Nations General Assembly on *September 24, 2001*.

Saudi Arabia's Prince Bandar bin Sultan, who had been active in the negotiations, stated he went from being "the happiest man in the world" on Monday night, *September 10*, to experiencing the worst crisis of his career on *September 11*. Dreams of a new Middle East peace initiative evaporated. The realization that most of the hijackers were Saudis "fell on me . . . like the whole house collapsed over my head," Bandar said later. He couldn't imagine a way to "do more damage or worse damage to Islam or to Saudi Arabia." The U.S. war on terror was birthed on *September 11, 2001*, at the very same time President Bush and his administration were completing a comprehensive plan for Israel. What has happened since then speaks volumes. The education president has now become the war president.

Catastrophe #34
Anthrax: October 2-31, 2001
Estimated cost to the U.S. Government: $3 billion range

The estimated cost to the U.S. government from the anthrax attacks was billions of dollars. By October 31, 2001, the U.S. Postal Service had purchased $2.5 billion in inspection and sanitizing equipment, experienced an estimated $300 million in lost income, and had $60 million in damages from the attacks.

President Bush said on *October 2* that a Palestinian state was always "part of a vision" if Israel's right to exist was to be respected. He said the two parties needed to get to work "on the Mitchell process," which he said provided a clear path to solving the crisis in the Middle East.

When asked, he refused to say whether he had been prepared to announce his support for a Palestinian state prior to the *September 11* terrorist attacks on Washington and New York.

State Department and other senior administration officials told CNN on Monday, *October 1, 2001*, that drafts of a major policy speech on the Middle East, to be delivered by Secretary Powell, were circulating in the State Department for review.

Officials said the speech would "clarify its [U.S.] views on an end result" of the peace process, leading to the eventual "creation of a Palestinian state."

Capitol Hill Disrupted by Anthrax Attacks

On *October 2, 2001*, the FBI announced it was preparing to sort through piles of congressional mail for possible cross-contamination from an anthrax-laced letter sent over two weeks earlier to Senate Majority leader Tom Daschle. Traces of anthrax were discovered in several federal buildings interrupting the work of America's executive, legislative and judicial powers:

- White House mail was in quarantine;
- Congressional offices were sealed, with staff having to work from temporary offices around the city;
- Supreme Court judges convened elsewhere for the first time in 66 years since the current Supreme Court building was built during the FDR administration; and
- The State Department cut off mail to 240 embassies and consulates worldwide.

Officials said the government had not been stopped from functioning; but James Thurber, a professor of government at American University, said the terrorists seemed to have succeeded "much beyond their own expectations."

"I can't think of anything that has disrupted government as much since the Civil War," said Mr. Thurber.

Catastrophe #35
American Airlines Flight #587 Exploded over New York City
November 12, 2001

President Bush told the General Assembly of the United Nations in New York City on *November 10, 2001*:

> The American government also stands by its commitment to a just peace in the Middle East. We are working toward the day when two states—Israel and Palestine—live peacefully together within secure and recognized borders as called for by the Security Council resolutions.

On the same day that Bush and Powell were speaking about their positions on Israel's land, the U.S. received clear and ominous nuclear, chemical, and biological retribution warnings from both acknowledged terrorist leader Osama bin Laden and Iraqi dictator Saddam Hussein.

Osama bin Laden may have already shipped weapons of mass destruction to the U.S. Pakistan's *Frontier Post* said the Al-Qaeda network transported nuclear, biological, and chemical weapons there. It claimed at least two briefcases containing nuclear weapons might have reached U.S. shores.

Iraq's Saddam Hussein and Osama bin Laden worked together on the operational coordination of a potential terrorist nuclear attack on the West, according to Debka News of Israel.

Putting this information into perspective, these statements and warnings were not days, weeks, or months apart. They happened almost simultaneously, and within a 48-hour period. As Bush and Powell were speaking to the world of sacrificing God's covenant land for a Palestinian state, archenemies bin Laden and Hussein were threatening the U.S.

Events: Sunday, November 11

- On Sunday, Powell said that Bush's use of "Palestine" in his speech on Saturday was "deliberate and reflected administration policy." Speaking on NBC's "Meet the Press," Powell said, "If one is moving forward with a vision of two states side by side, it's appropriate . . . to call those two states what they will be, Israel and Palestine." No United States president—Republican or Democrat—had ever made such a statement, according to Powell.

- On Sunday, Middle East Newsline reported that United States intelligence agencies and the Pentagon agreed that Saddam Hussein had made the most explicit threats since the 1991 Gulf War, and that he was ready to use nuclear weapons. The assessment was that Iraq was threatening nuclear retaliation for any attack on Saddam's regime.
- On Sunday, in his address before the General Assembly, Chairman Arafat asked the UN to send international peacekeepers to Israel to protect his people from the "aggressors." Also, he called for Israel to fulfill UN Resolutions 242 and 338, calling for "the evacuation of all settlers from the settlements on occupied land." Other Arafat demands included the establishment of a Palestinian state with "Holy Jerusalem" as its capital.

American Airlines Flight #587 Exploded over NYC

The following day, *November 12*, an American Airlines jetliner, leaving New York City en route to the Dominican Republic with 255 people aboard, crashed moments after takeoff from Kennedy Airport, setting homes ablaze. The people that witnessed the plane's crash stated they saw an explosion in the plane's tail section. *USA Today* stated on the day of the accident that if the flight's crash was due to a terrorist incident, it would have been the "last nail" in the coffin of the airline industry. Federal law enforcement and transportation officials stated a short time later that there was no evidence of terrorist involvement, and that it was believed to be a mechanical failure in the tail of the plane.

Catastrophe #36
Maryland's F-5 Tornado: April 28, 2002

President Bush and the State Department Negotiated Arafat's Release from Ramallah Compound

On *April 28, 2002*, President Bush stated from his ranch:

Good afternoon. I am pleased by today's developments in the Middle East and believe they'll prove to be important steps along the path to peace in the Middle East.

I commend the Israeli Cabinet for its decision this morning to allow Chairman Arafat to move freely, to accept international monitoring of six prisoners who are at Chairman Arafat's compound, and to withdraw its forces from Ramallah. The Palestinian Authority has agreed to accept this approach.

This morning I called Crown Prince Abdullah to thank him for his visit to the United States. Our discussions forged a personal bond of friendship and strengthened the 60-year relationship between the United States and Saudi Arabia. The Crown Prince has offered a number of constructive ideas for making political progress between Israel and the Palestinians. We will continue to build on these ideas, as we move forward to fight terror and to promote peace in the Middle East.

Tornadoes Ravage Cities

A tornado left a 24-mile path of destruction in Maryland on *April 28*.

Six people were killed as a huge swarm of thunderstorms rumbled across the Tennessee and Ohio valleys, and all the way to the East Coast. In Maryland, three people died and at least 100 were injured when a tornado plowed through La Plata, a small town in Charles County (20 miles southeast of Washington).

A preliminary assessment by the National Weather Service rated the twister at F5 on the Fujita tornado intensity scale, the most powerful level—a level at which incredible damage occurs, including the disintegration of homes and generation of car-size debris that turns into deadly missiles.

Barbara Watson, a warning coordination meteorologist for the weather service in Sterling, Va., said the Maryland tornado registered in the low end of the F5 category with winds probably around 260 mph (F5 tornado winds begin at 261 mph).

On *May 1*, White House Press Secretary Fleischer released the following statement:

> The President today declared a major disaster exists in the state of Maryland, and ordered federal aid to supplement state and local recovery efforts in the area struck by a tornado on *April 28, 2002*.

Catastrophe #37
Colorado's Hayman Fire: June 8, 2002
Nearly 138,000 Acres Burned

President Bush and President Mubarak Called for a Palestinian State and for Israel to Leave Their Land
—The Hayman Fire Began in Colorado

President Bush, Camp David Address:

> First, I want to thank the president of Egypt [Mubarak] for his country's strong support in our war against terror. I know there's been a lot of focus on obviously the Middle East, and I'll mention that in a second, but we're still in a war against people who want to harm America and people who want to harm Egypt. And we've had—we've got a good

friend, Americans have a good friend, when it comes to this war on terror, in Egypt.

The president understands that we've got a long way to go in order to be successful. He's now been told again by me that my most important job is to secure our homeland, and this country is plenty tough and plenty patient and plenty determined to achieve that objective.

Obviously, we spent time talking about the Middle East, and we share a common vision of two states living side by side in peace. And I appreciated so very much his—listening to his ideas as to how to achieve that objective, that grand goal. The world—the Palestinians hurt, and I know that. And my concern is for the Palestinian people. And my view is, that if the Palestinian people have a government that is transparent and open and willing to serve the people, Israel will be better off, Egypt will be better off, America will be better off, and we're more likely to achieve peace. And we discussed how to achieve those objectives.

Hayman Fire

Beginning in a campfire circle on the morning of *June 8, 2002*, the Hayman Fire quickly grew to become the largest recorded wildfire in Colorado's history. Spurred by record drought and extreme weather, the Hayman Fire burned nearly 138,000 acres over the course of three weeks. Two major fire activity periods, *June 8-10* and *June 17-18*, marked by high winds and record-low relative humidity, accounted for the majority of the total acreage burned, as well as 93 percent of the 132 homes lost.

Catastrophe #38
Arizona's Rodeo and Chediski Fires: June 18-26, 2002
550,000 Acres Burned

President Bush planned to present his Middle East vision on *June 18*. However, his speech was postponed twice due to two major suicide bombings in Jerusalem.

On *June 18*, the Rodeo Fire began in northeast Arizona. The next morning, the Chediski Fire began in the same general area, fast-moving and quickly merging. On *June 24*, Bush finally delivered his much-awaited Middle East vision. The next morning, rather than traveling directly to the G8 Summit in Canada as previously scheduled, he left Washington, DC, early in the morning for Arizona to survey the Rodeo-Chediski Fires. On site, he called these combined wildfires one of the worst in western U.S. history.

Later that day, after Wall Street stopped trading, MCI declared that they had made a $3.6 billion accounting error. This news immediately sent shockwaves through U.S. and world financial markets. MCI soon became the largest bankruptcy filing in U.S. corporate history.

June 18: The Rodeo Fire—Arizona's "Perfect Fire"

Mike Campbell, chief meteorologist, National Weather Service, in Flagstaff, Arizona, said the night of *June 18* was made for the devil's ball that erupted.

Humidity was staggeringly low. Temperatures were dangerously high. The air around Cibecue was poised to suck up flames and spew them hundreds of yards into lush undergrowth that experts say was thicker and drier than almost any time in the past century.

But nature wasn't alone in conjuring disaster that night. The crews called in to fight the fire made a major miscalculation.

Kent Butler, BIA fire management officer for the Fort Apache Reservation, and his crews decided to let the Rodeo fire burn Tuesday night, convinced it would run to waste when it reached a ridge that burned two years ago. If the fire somehow leaped the ridge, Butler felt confident the flames would die at Carrizo Creek, a 20-foot wide swath of shallow, slow-moving waters. Neither happened.

June 19: Chediski Fire Began

Mitch Jacob, news director of KPHO, said the Chediski Fire—Chediski is the Apache word for White Rock—started some time shortly after 7 a.m. on Thursday, *June 19*.

The once-tiny signal fire was the fifth ingredient—converging with geography, weather, public policy, and sheer chance to create a fire like no other. "It's like drawing a royal flush," said Stephen J. Pyne, an environmental historian at Arizona State University. "Everything was in the cards, but it just doesn't happen. It all came together at maximum extenuating circumstances."

Pyne said the worst time for fires in Arizona, historically, is around the summer solstice. Thursday was the day before the solstice.

The steep canyons of the Apache-Sitgreaves National Forests created what amounted to a chain of plumes and chimneys for fires that fed, in some cases, on a century's worth of untended, tinder-dry undergrowth.

Finally, prevailing winds that day were from the southwest, pushing the fires northeast, into south-facing terrain that naturally attracts the highest temperatures and lowest humidity.

"You [had] everything that could possibly go wrong in the extreme," Pyne said. "Then you [had] the second fire set in a place where you [couldn't] control the perimeter of the first one. You can't put crews between them."

June 24: President Bush's Middle East Plan

After two previous delays, at 3:57 p.m. EDT on *June 24*, President Bush began delivering his Middle East vision for peace in the White House Rose Garden. Here is an excerpt:

> In the situation, the Palestinian people will grow more and more miserable. My vision is two states, living side by side in peace and security. There is simply no way to achieve that peace until all parties fight terror. Yet, at this critical moment, if all parties will break with the past and set out on a new path, we can overcome the darkness with the light of hope. Peace requires a new and different Palestinian leadership, so that a Palestinian state can be born.

> I call on the Palestinian people to elect new leaders, leaders not compromised by terror. I call upon them to build a practicing democracy, based on tolerance and liberty. If the Palestinian people actively pursue these goals, America and the world will actively support their efforts. If the Palestinian people meet these goals, they will be able to reach agreement with Israel and Egypt and Jordan on security and other arrangements for independence.

> And when the Palestinian people have new leaders, new institutions and new security arrangements with their neighbors, the United States of America will support the creation of a Palestinian state whose borders and certain aspects of its sovereignty will be provisional until resolved as part of a final settlement in the Middle East.

> In the work ahead, we all have responsibilities. The Palestinian people are gifted and capable, and I am confident they can achieve a new birth for their nation. A Palestinian state will never be created by terror—it will be built through reform. And reform must be more than cosmetic change, or veiled attempt to preserve the status quo. True reform will require entirely new political and economic institutions, based on democracy, market economics, and action against terrorism.

June 25: President Bush Traveled to Arizona to Visit Displaced Families and to Review the Fire Damage

Here is an excerpt of Bush's address, given to displaced families at Eagar, Arizona, at 10:48 a.m. on *June 25, 2002*:

> Thank you. It's nice to see you. I'm sorry we're doing so under these circumstances. But I want you to know that a lot of people in our country are pulling for you. They understand the suffering that families are

going through because of worry about your most precious possession, your home. They understand that a lot of you are living in tents when you'd rather be in your own bed. They cry for you, and they hurt for you. And I'm here to say on behalf of the American people, God bless you.

Today, I signed a declaration declaring this an emergency, which then provides for federal help—which means money to fight the fires. It means temporary housing money and long-term housing money. It means help for small business owners; I understand there's a lot of small business owners who are worried about your business [sic], and I don't blame you. I'd be worried, too. So it provides help.

It helps provide counseling services; and a lot of folks here, I hope if you need counseling, you ask for it. A lot of people we want to help. So, this is the federal govern-ment's way of committing the resources allowed under the law, the full extent of the resources under the law.

You know, one of the great things about this country is that there's a lot of loving people here in this country. I always say. And not only is the Red Cross helping, but the Salvation Army is as well.

Here's what I tell them. What the enemy didn't under-stand is when they attacked America, they didn't under-stand how kind and decent this country is. So I'm here to say thanks on behalf of the volunteers, the people who are doing their best to spread compassion to people who need compassion, to spread love to people who need love, to spread guidance to people who seek guidance.

June 25: Bush Headed to Canada

President Bush then flew to Canada to discuss his Middle East peace plan (along with other business) with G-8 leaders.

The U.S. markets were off on *June 25*, with the NASDAQ losing another 2.2 percent of its value. After the closing bell MSNBC broke a story that stated WorldCom (MCI) had engaged in what people close to the company described as a massive fraud that had only recently come to the attention of its board of directors. According to sources close to the company, WorldCom had inflated its EBITDA (Earnings Before Interest, Taxes, Depreciation and Amortization) by some $3.6 billion over its last five quarters, by taking as capital expenditures costs that should have been treated as ordinary.

Putting All This into Perspective

Arizona's Rodeo Fire began the very same day of a major suicide bombing in Jerusalem, which postponed President Bush's much-anticipated Middle East peace address. On *June 19*, the day the Chediski Fire began, his Middle East address was postponed again by another major suicide bombing in Jerusalem.

Finally, on *June 24*, he delivered his Middle East vision. His next official speech was in Arizona at the site of a massive wildfire. Again, as Bush was promoting the division of Israel's land, America's land was being devastated by massive record-setting wildfires.

Catastrophe #39
Hurricane Lili
Estimated costs $750 Million
Washington, DC-Area Snipers
October 2-31, 2002

Congress Called on President Bush to Move the U.S. Embassy to Jerusalem; the President Refused.

As a candidate in 2000, President Bush backed Israel's claim on Jerusalem as its capital. Once in office, he turned aside a congressional demand for steps toward moving the U.S. Embassy from Tel Aviv to Jerusalem.

"U.S. policy regarding Jerusalem has not changed," Bush wrote in a statement on *September 30, 2002,* as he signed an $8.6 billion spending bill for State Department programs around the world.

He criticized the provision that recommended recognizing Jerusalem as Israel's capital, saying it "impermissibly interferes with the president's constitutional authority to conduct the nation's foreign affairs."

Hurricane Lili and DC Sniper

Hurricane Lili was the first hurricane of the 21st century to strike the U.S.

The hurricane went from a Category 2 on *October 1*, to a Category 4 on *October 2*, and then miraculously back to a Category 2 on Thursday just before it hit land on *October 3*.

National Hurricane Center Director Max Mayfield was at a loss to explain the hurricane's fluctuations in the Gulf of Mexico. While colder water in the northern Gulf might explain why the hurricane weakened on *October 3*, it did not account for why it had gained strength so dramatically the night before. "A lot of PhDs will be writing about this," he said.

Two snipers held Washington, DC, hostage for four weeks. The first shooting was *within 24 hours* of Bush's decision not to move the U.S. embassy to Jerusalem despite Congress's non-binding vote. The security checkpoints on the highways in Washington resembled the security checkpoints of Jerusalem; the DC area was paralyzed with fear over the snipers.

Catastrophe #40
Eighty-Eight (88) Tornadoes: November 6-13, 2002
Estimated $200 Million in damages/costs

On Thursday night, *November 7, 2002*, President Bush hosted a dinner for Muslim leaders and gave a speech to honor the beginning of Ramadan:

> Ramadan is a special time of prayer and fasting, contemplation of God's greatness, and service to those in need. According to Muslim teachings, this season commemorates the revelation of God's word in the holy Koran to the prophet Muhammad. Today this word inspires faithful Muslims to lead lives of honesty and integrity and compassion.

> In hosting tonight's Iftaar, I send a message to all the nations represented by their ambassadors here tonight: America treasures your friendship. America honors your faith.

> We see in Islam a religion that traces its origins back to God's call on Abraham. We share your belief in God's justice and your insistence on man's moral responsibility.

Eighty-Eight (88) Tornadoes

An estimated 88 tornadoes slashed through Arkansas, Tennessee, Alabama, Mississippi, Georgia, Ohio, and Pennsylvania from late Saturday night, *November 9*, through early Monday morning, according to the National Weather Service. Entire communities were reported demolished in Alabama, Tennessee, and Ohio.

The storm system that struck Tennessee and Ohio over the Veteran's Day weekend, *November 9-11*, was ranked as a Category F-4 storm, the second most severe on the Fujita scale. Winds, gusting to more than 200 miles per hour cut a 100-mile swath across northwest Ohio. Meanwhile two waves of tornadoes were generated in Tennessee late on *November 9* and early on the *10th*, and southeast of Nashville that same night.

The occurrence of tornadoes in the South at this time of year was unusual, according to the center. Peak tornado activity historically occurs from March through early July. This storm system, one of the worst November tornado outbreaks on record, was generated when a high-altitude cold front stretching from Texas to New York collided with a broad, warm and moist air mass drifting north from the Gulf of Mexico (per the National Weather Service).

U.S. Official in Israel

On Sunday, *November 10*, U.S. Deputy Assistant Secretary of State David Satterfield was on his way to Israel to apply pressure on Israel to complete their work on the Quartet's "road map" to peace. He had many meetings on Monday and Tuesday with Israeli officials, and met with Palestinian officials.

Israel asked for an extension of the *December 20* Quartet (EU, UN, Russia and the U.S.) deadline until after the elections. The *Financial Times* said no extension was approved. Then Ha'aretz, an Israeli news service, declared the White House had agreed to hold off until February or March—after a scheduled meeting between the head of the Prime Minister's Bureau, Dov Weisman, and National Security Advisor Condoleezza Rice at the White House.

Catastrophe #41
North Carolina Ice Storm: December 5, 2002
Estimated $133 Million damages/costs

President Bush commemorated the end of Ramadan at the Islamic Center of Washington, DC, on Thursday, *December 5*:

> Islam traces its origins back to God's call on Abraham. And Ramadan commemorates the revelation of God's word in the Holy Koran to the prophet Mohammad—a word that is read and recited with special attention and reverence by Muslims during this season.

> The spirit behind this holiday is a reminder that Islam brings hope and comfort to more than a billion people worldwide. Islam affirms God's justice and insists on man's moral responsibility. This holiday is also an occasion to remember that Islam gave birth to a rich civilization of learning that has benefited mankind.

The day before, Prime Minister Sharon had accepted in principle the U.S. Road Map for Israeli-Palestinian peace that envisaged the creation of an independent Palestinian state within a few years.

An ice storm that officials declared the worst in the history of North Carolina and South Carolina cut power to nearly two million homes and businesses Thursday, *December 5*, and threatened to leave many without light and heat. Thousands of people sought warmth in shelters as utilities warned that power could be down for days—or even weeks—to homes in isolated areas.

Cities, counties and governors of both states issued emergency declarations that let officials restrict movement, raid budgets to pay overtime, regulate prices for key commodities and send out the National Guard, if needed. "This storm was obviously devastating," said Bryan Beatty, N.C., secretary of crime control, public safety, and emergency management.

Duke Power declared this storm worse than 1989s Hurricane Hugo, which knocked out power to 696,000 Carolinas customers—some for nearly three weeks, earning a dark spot in the memory of Charlotteans.

Catastrophe #42
Space Shuttle Columbia Disaster: February 1, 2003

President Bush Signaled He Would Become Much More Involved in the Israeli Palestinian Talks
—Space Shuttle Columbia Broke Up over Palestine, Texas

On *February 1, 2003*, the United States shuddered again under the burden of a terrible tragedy, as the news spread about the breakup and loss of the Columbia Space Shuttle 39 miles above Texas, as it was descending from its mission, and just 16 minutes from landing at Cape Canaveral.

The first report from MSNBC declared that the initial search area was around Palestine, Texas. Maps from MSNBC and *USA Today* had the town in the center of the breakup area—and people from around the world saw the same maps centering on Palestine.

The *Houston Chronicle* provided a National Weather radar image of Columbia that showed the majority of the debris falling just east of Palestine between Nacogdoches and Lufkin.

The "pride of America" (our nation's space program) and the "pride of Israel" (Colonel Ilan Ramon, Israeli crew member of Columbia) tragically broke up over Palestine, Texas. Was it symbolic that the "pride of America and of Israel" broke up over Palestine [Texas]? Was this a warning sign to Israelis and Americans alike that Palestine could break up our nations, too?

All seven astronauts on board, including the first Israeli ever to be on a space mission and at least three Christian believers, were pronounced dead. In a short speech to the nation several hours later, President Bush said:

> In the skies today, we saw destruction and tragedy. Yet farther than we can see, there is comfort and hope. In the words of the prophet Isaiah, "Lift your eyes and look to the heavens. Who created all these? He who brings out the starry hosts one by one and calls them each by name. Because of His great power and mighty strength, not one of them is missing."

The same Creator who names the stars also knows the names of the seven souls we mourn today. The crew of the shuttle Columbia did not return safely to Earth; yet we can pray that all are safely home.

We can rejoice in having a president who draws upon God's Word for comfort and solace for the families left behind and for all who grieve for the loss of these seven astronauts. But in our role as watchmen, we would be remiss if we did not call attention to the apparent significance of the sequence of events and seeming coincidences that surrounded and infused this tragedy.

On Friday, Secretary Powell said in a speech that President Bush would become much more involved in the Israel-Palestinian conflict and that the administration "would actively resume its pursuit of a settlement," once the situation with Iraq was dealt with.

He went on to declare that the Bush administration would use the Road Map devised in partnership with the European Union, Russia, and the United Nations. This Road Map, he said, aimed "to create a Palestinian state by the year 2005, carved out of land that Israel has held for more than 35 years."

Also, on the same day, President Bush and British Prime Minister Tony Blair met at the White House over the pending Iraq war. They agreed to give Iraq six more weeks to comply. Ironically, this is the same amount of time Bush had just agreed to give Prime Minister Sharon to form his coalition government and give his formal response to the Quartet's Road Map.

Catastrophe #43
412 Midwest Tornadoes: May 1-11, 2003
Estimated $2.2 billion damages/costs

International mediators presented a long-awaited Middle East peace plan on Wednesday, *April 30, 2003*, just hours after Palestinian Prime Minister Abbas was sworn in.

U.S. Ambassador Kurtzer presented the plan to Prime Minister Sharon at the prime minister's Jerusalem home, and representatives of the four parties in the "quartet" of Middle East mediators delivered it to Abbas in Ramallah.

The so-called Road Map to peace was drafted by the Quartet, made up of the United States, European Union, United Nations, and Russia.

On Saturday, *May 3*, Powell headed to the Middle East for talks about implementing the Road Map peace plan.

On Sunday, *May 4*, Powell committed to Syria a Middle East peace that "would include Syria and Lebanon, and . . . the Golan Heights."

That same day, a deadly swarm of 83 tornadoes ripped through eastern Kansas, Missouri, Arkansas, and Tennessee, killing at least 38 people and doing extensive damage to homes and buildings. It was "the most devastating series of tornadoes we've ever had in the state of Missouri," Gov. Bob Holden said after walking the rubble-strewn streets of Pierce City, where eight of the missing were from.

On Monday, *May 5*, less than 24 hours after the 83 tornadoes and the Powell news, U.S. Middle East Envoy William Burns met with Abbas in Ramallah. He stated that the Palestinians must carry out a decisive fight against terrorism and Israelis must halt settlement activity.

On Saturday, *May 10*, and Sunday, *May 11*, Powell had meetings in Israel with Sharon and Abbas.

During the *first eleven days of May*, there were 412 tornadoes—the most observed since NOAA began recordkeeping in 1950. The previous record for the first eleven of May was 177 tornadoes, set in 1999.

The tornadoes, which swept across parts of the U.S., were the costliest in U.S. history, according to the Insurance Information Institute (I.I.I.). Boston-based AIR Worldwide, which uses a computer-modeling program to estimate insured losses from catastrophes, put the damage at $2.2 billion.

Along with the tornadoes, there were 535 windstorms and 1,385 hailstorms in America's heartland. More than 300 counties in 19 states suffered losses—and more than 40 deaths were blamed on the storms.

The final tornado occurred on *May 11* as Powell was leaving Israel for Jordan and a meeting with King Abdullah II.

Catastrophe #44
Quartet Nations Experienced Record-Setting Heat, Drought, Rains, Floods and Blackouts, Causing Thousands of Deaths
May 1–August 17, 2003

Estimated damages: Billions in Dollars and Euros

The European Union declared that the United States was not the sole author or owner of the Road Map for Israeli-Palestinian peace. On *May 1*, EU foreign policy chief Javier Solana said,

> This is not a problem to be solved by only one country; it is a problem to be solved by the cooperation of members of the international community that have been engaged in this peace process for a long time.

"The Road Map is not the property of one country, it is the property of the Quartet," he told reporters. The Quartet partners include the U.S., Russia and many nations of the world through the European Union and the UN.

A spokeswoman for European External Affairs Commissioner Chris Patten also spoke out against the comments that the Road Map was an U.S. proposal. "I would like to remind you all that although I hear and read quite frequently that this is America's Road Map, it is not America's Road Map," Emma Udwin told a news briefing. "It is the Road Map of the Quartet."

The White House said it is "a set document." Udwin stated, "The Road Map remains what the international community sees as the best option for peace in the foreseeable future."

When the Quartet's Road Map was delivered to the Israelis and Palestinians, weather-related havoc and chaos began—and it intensified throughout the summer as meetings continued.

It started with the United States experiencing the most traumatic tornado outbreak in history during the first ten days of May—412 tornadoes in the Midwest. This was also the beginning of horrible weather related events in Europe. Below are highlights of the events.

Heat Records

Experienced climatologists had never seen such unusual, strong and persistent world weather patterns; and said, clearly irregular jet stream bends were involved. But no clear-cut reason for that pattern emerged. In their hunt for answers, some scientists looked as far away as the monsoons of South Asia for clues to Miami's unseasonable rains and Madrid's outdoor oven.

"The inherent instability of the atmosphere by itself can produce a persistent pattern, such as the one that has dominated over North America and Europe this summer," said Angie Seth, an associate research scientist at the International Institute for Climate Prediction at Columbia University's Earth Institute.

Between *June* and *August of 2003*, Europe experienced its hottest summer for at least 500 years, according to Swiss university researchers. This heat wave triggered several thousand more deaths than usual, and average temperatures eclipsed the previous record set in 1757, according to a study by the University of Bern's geography department. The U.S. was no exception. Joan Lowy of the Scripps Howard News Service wrote:

> While the heat wave gripping Europe in the summer of 2003 was making headlines around the world, the United States was setting its own records for scorching heat in the West and torrential rains in the East. Every western state except California suffered temperatures much warmer than normal . . . Numerous daily and monthly records were shattered, according to the National Oceanic and Atmospheric Administration's National Climatic Data Center in Asheville, N.C. Idaho and the cities of Phoenix, Las Vegas, Cheyenne, Wyoming, and Grand Junction, Colorado, all experienced their warmest July on record.

Conditions were similar to the weather that caused the catastrophic 'dust bowl' of the 1930s depression years.

Nobody seemed to know why this was happening or what, if anything, it meant. It may or may not have been related to the record-breaking heat waves that year in Europe and parts of the American west, said Jim Laver, director of the NOAA Climate Prediction Center in Camp Springs, Maryland. Typically, he and his associate Anthony Barnston said, prolonged climatic anomalies of this scale would be associated with unusual ocean warming or cooling in the tropical Pacific and Indian oceans, the sort of atmospheric domino effect associated with the ocean current known as El Niño.

"But this year, nothing appear[ed] to be going on in the Pacific that would trigger anything," said Laver.

Record-Setting European and World Weather Began the First Week of May 2003

Earthweek reported that one of the causes of the great European heat epidemic was a shift northward of the "meteorological equator" over Africa. This directly caused the killer heat wave, as the hot air mass that usually sits over the Sahara Desert, to shift to Europe. This represented a major new climatic shift in world weather patterns.

One thing was nevertheless certain: Global weather patterns were changing. The increasing heat, which most radically affects the equatorial regions over the planet's oceans, was spawning storms of ever-increasing magnitude.

The Geneva-based World Meteorological Organization (WMO), to which the weather services of 185 countries contribute, took the view that events in Europe, America, and Asia were so remarkable that the world needed to be made aware of it immediately. They pointed to global warming; however, we point to the repercussions of dividing God's covenant land.

To this point, most of the chaotic events in the U.S. occurred because the U.S. was the sole sponsor of record. But this changed when the Quartet came forward with their "land for peace" plan and the EU, the UN, and Russia began experiencing the repercussions of attempting to divide God's covenant land.

The WMO normally confines itself to issuing scientific reports and statistics compiled from climate data. However, the weather events of 2003 proved so remarkable, officials say, that the organization felt compelled to issue a generalized warning of the emerging pattern.

World and European Heat Records: 2003

- Average temperatures over world land areas climbed to the highest levels ever recorded in May, according to the WMO.
- The combined global land and sea average for May was the second highest on record since observations began in 1880, said the WMO.

- A WMO study explained that the world was experiencing record numbers of extreme weather events such as droughts and tornadoes. They blamed global warming; ironically, they also stated this period of extreme weather occurred quickly and caught many experts by surprise.
- Beginning in *May 2003*, there was an all-time record heat wave across parts of Western Europe and the Indian subcontinent, which caused outbreaks of heat stroke and widespread power disruptions.
- On *August 10, 2003*, Britain experienced the highest temperatures in 350 years of recordkeeping—surpassing 100 degrees for the first time ever, which was coupled with high humidity. The previous national record in Britain was 98.8 degrees, set August 3, 1990.
- France was the worst hit. In some French areas, the thermometers reached an incredible 105 degrees; while in the south of France, average temperatures were between five and seven degrees Celsius (nine to 13 degrees Fahrenheit) warmer than the long-term average.
- Germans, too, had record heat. In the Bavarian city of Roth, the temperature hit 105 degrees Fahrenheit, setting a new German record. The previous record of 104 was also in Bavaria, set in 1983.
- Spain and Portugal suffered worst. In some areas of the Iberian Peninsula, temperatures surpassed 43 degrees Celsius, or 110 degrees Fahrenheit.
- Several visitors to the Vatican fainted in St. Peter's Square as the temperature soared to 98 degrees Fahrenheit—the hottest June reading in Rome since recordkeeping began in 1782.
- The heat and drought-driven fires across the continent prompted Pope John Paul II to urge people to pray for rain.
- Switzerland experienced its hottest June in at least 250 years. Some of the lower glaciers melted, sending mudslides down on villages below.
- Records continued to be broken across Europe as temperatures hit 98 in Prague, 100 in Vienna and 105 in parts of northern Italy.
- In Afghanistan, major sandstorms affected more than 12,000 people, and were described as the "worst sandstorms in living memory." Sandstorms began in the region during early June and continued during July. Up to 20 villages had to be evacuated because they were completely covered in sand, and many irrigation canals and waterways were filled.
- A pre-monsoon heat wave that hit India caused peak temperatures of 45 to 49 degrees Celsius (113-120 degrees Fahrenheit); more than 1,400 people died.
- Cold and snowy weather characterized conditions across much of New Zealand during the first week of *July*, where locally 30 cm (twelve inches) of snow fell in parts of the country. The snowstorm was described by local media as the worst in 50 years, causing thousands of power outages to homes and businesses and stranding hundreds of motorists (*New Zealand Herald*).

Crop Loss

The effect of the heat wave on European agriculture was also catastrophic. This was expected to have a domino effect on other factors of European health and economy:

- European Union agricultural experts said that adverse weather conditions since the winter of 2002 were likely to cause crop losses totaling several billion euros.
- The summer's European drought and record heat wave crippled agriculture and triggered a public health crisis.
- Unusually high temperatures and a summer-long dearth of rain wrought serious damage to crops and weather-related deaths throughout Europe, a continent of increasingly scorched earth.
- France's oyster supplies were submerged under the flood of toxic black sludge that poured from the hull of the Prestige oil tanker. Then the Bollinger harvest was ravaged by a freak storm of golf ball-sized hailstones. After further gloomy news about the premature heat-related deaths of millions of prize chickens, the death by suffocation of much of the country's trout stocks, the shriveling of the honey crop, and the withering of thousands of hectares of fruit trees, the latest cause of the French gourmet's *annus horribilis* (terrible year) looks certain to be the truffle. Exceptionally dry weather in May and June meant that few truffle spores germinated; the unprecedented temperatures in July and August meant that those few truffles which had begun to develop were unable to mature, further diminishing France's tiny supply.
- In Italy, the harvests of grapes, olives, peaches and apricots turned out to be 50 percent below normal. Agricultural groups estimated the financial toll on Italian farmers was about $6 billion.
- The German Association of Farmers reported that more than one-half of the year's grain crop in the east of the country was threatened by drought. The halt of fresh water into Germany's river Spree even caused the waterway to begin flowing upstream in some of its lower reaches.
- The worst drought in Croatia's history devastated the country's spring crops and brought about an acute water shortage. Croatia's farmers' union reported that the drought had affected the livelihoods of a million people.

Drought

- In *July 2003*, rivers reached their lowest levels in 100 years across parts of Italy, where officials imposed a 100-euro fine for watering plants.
- Ships plying the Danube River in Eastern Europe carried restricted loads so as not to scrape bottom. Water levels in the river declined so much that in Romania, dredgers deepened some channels so that ships could pass.

- Croatia's major rivers, including the Sava, Drava, Kupa, and Danube, were reported at their lowest levels ever. In neighboring Serbia, the ecology minister reported that the country's rivers were at their lowest levels in 100 years.
- A swarm of locusts forced residents of an Inner Mongolian town to take drastic measures to stop the insects from settling on surrounding pastures and grasslands. Residents of Erenhot, a Chinese border town, maintained a blackout at night, as electric lighting tended to attract the insects.
- The *Yangcheng Evening News* reported that the locusts—which arrived in the region in *June*—were "like snow falling from the sky." Crushed insects blanketed the roads of the remote town, and the swarm engulfed more than 11 million hectares of Inner Mongolia's grasslands. "The affected area was almost all grassland."

Fires

The early summertime warmth caused a devastating wildfire season across Europe and Russia:

- *July's* fires in France, thought to have been started deliberately, were the worst in the region for decades. Fires ravaged the French Riviera, killing four. There were scenes of panic as the flames engulfed caravans, cars and electricity poles, forcing people to ditch their vehicles by the side of the road. Some tourists were stranded wearing nothing but their swimming suits. "There has rarely been such a powerful blaze in the region," said a spokesman for the regional emergency center. French Interior Minister Nicolas Sarkozy flew to the scene of what he described as an "ecological disaster."
- The fires in Portugal, the worst in a generation, came amidst a heat wave stretching from Russia to the Iberian Peninsula.
- Some 431 fires burned across Russia in July 2003.
- The summer drought contributed to 300 forest fires in Germany.

Power Grid

- Britain canceled some trains on busy routes and imposed reduced, temporary speed limits on others to make sure that rails did not buckle in atypically intense temperatures.
- Power grids in many countries were under significant strain, as people in countries normally suspicious of air conditioning suddenly jettisoned their reservations and embraced—or longed for—even a manufactured breeze.
- France called emergency talks on *August 11* due to overheating at nuclear power plants.

- On *August 10, 2003*, Paris sweltered through its hottest night since records began. Temperatures hit around 104 degrees Fahrenheit, spelling trouble for France's nuclear reactors, many of which are cooled by river water. With river levels falling and the mercury rising, authorities faced the choice of spewing out hotter water, risking ecological damage, or cutting output, potentially leading to electricity blackouts.
- Record heat across France and Italy caused widespread power failures as residents strained power grids by firing up air conditioners to escape the scorching conditions.
- Some areas along the Mediterranean saw the highest use of air conditioning on record due to the heat, threatening power blackouts.

Heat-Related Deaths

The heat wave, which saw temperatures consistently above 100 degrees in some parts of Europe, brought a sharp increase in death rates in several countries:

- While the death toll from weeks of unrelenting heat may never be determined, wire services estimated that well over 22,000 had died in 14 countries.
- More than 4,200 elderly Italians died in the summer heat wave.
- France's Health Minister Jean-Francois Mattei said 11,435 more deaths than normal were registered *August 1-15*, when daily temperatures of 40 degrees Celsius and above roasted the country. The French government eventually estimated that more than 15,000 people died as a result of the unusual weather and inability of the health system to cope.
- The Netherlands estimated 1,400 died of heat-related issues; Portugal announced 1,300 deaths; British officials estimated 900 weather-related deaths.

Record-Setting Violent Weather in U.S. Began: May 1, 2003

Violent Weather

- There were 562 tornadoes that hit the U.S. in *May 2003*—a record far higher than the previous record monthly peak of 399 set in June 1992.
- In *June*, twisters tore up fields in South Dakota and Iowa.
- Residents of Aurora, a town in Nebraska, reported hail on *June 24* that looked "like someone dropping volleyballs down." One resident said hail punched a hole in his roof that was large enough for him to crawl through. Dale Obermeier, a weather service spotter in Aurora, said the hail also dug holes in his yard.

Heat

With an average temperature, day and night, of nearly 98 degrees, *July 2003* branded the record books as the hottest month in Phoenix since the National Weather Service started keeping track in 1896. In Phoenix, where 100 degrees in summer is almost balmy, the highs were breathtaking: 15 days over 110 degrees; on *July 15*, the warmest overnight low ever—96 degrees. The days were so hot, windshields were shattering or falling out, dogs were burning their paws on the pavement, and candles were melting indoors.

- July's punishing heat: Almost everywhere in the region, it cooked the record books. Six western cities registered their hottest month ever; six others their warmest July ever.
- Others tallied record strings of 100-degree days, historic highs for numerous July dates, even record-high marks for overnight low temperatures. "There were records on so many levels," said Mark Ressler, a meteorologist for the Weather Channel.
- Places unaccustomed to triple digits suffered multi-day runs at 100 degrees or higher. Salt Lake City had ten in a row, and Boise nine straight and 12 for the month. Others accumulated 100s like never before. Pueblo, Colorado, which had its hottest day ever (109 on *July 13*), reached 100 or more on 23 days in July. Grand Junction reached 100 or more 17 times. Greeley, which set or tied all-time highs on ten dates, hit 100 on 18 days. Redding, California, north of Sacramento, hit 100 on 20 days.
- Temperatures soared to 109 degrees on *August 7*, at Dallas-Fort Worth International Airport, surpassing the old record of 108 set in 1952.
- In west Texas, Lubbock tied its record high for the date of 102; and in south Texas, Rio Grande City was near 104.
- Texans cranked up their air conditioners to cope. The Electric Reliability Council of Texas, which manages the power grid for 85 percent of the state, broke its usage record, said spokeswoman Dottie Roark. Most residents appeared to be handling the heat in stride.

Heavy Rains

- Between *May 1* and *August 17*, Washington's weather station at Reagan National Airport recorded 69 overcast days (63 percent, about double the usual) and nearly twice the usual amount of rain.
- Far colder and wetter conditions than normal also prevailed in the eastern and southeastern part of the U.S. for much of May and June.
- Wilmington, Delaware, and New York City recorded their wettest Junes in more than a century.
- Between *May 1* and *July 31*, nearly forty inches fell on Mobile, Alabama, the most in 123 years.

- During the *May 1–July 31* period, Birmingham, Alabama's largest city, recorded a total of 29.59 inches of rain, making it the wettest since record-keeping began there in 1890. With 39.65 inches, Mobile also set a new record for the period. Again, the total was more than twice the average (17.65 inches) since recordkeeping began there 123 years ago.
- Atlanta experienced its third wettest *May–July* since record keeping started in 1878, with a total of 22.62 inches of rain.
- During that three-month period, NOAA National Weather Service forecast offices in Mississippi, Alabama, and Georgia issued nearly 350 flash flood warnings.
- At the same time, the NOAA forecast 421 flood events in Southeast River Forecast Center, which serves portions of Mississippi, Alabama, Georgia, Florida, North and South Carolina, Virginia, and Tennessee.

Drought

- The combination of generally warmer and drier-than-average conditions during the *June–September* led to an increase in the drought coverage area to about 41 percent of the United States by *October*.
- Spring was very dry in the southern plains, with Texas experiencing the driest *March–May* during 2003 of 109 years of recordkeeping.
- Much of the West was in the sixth consecutive year of drought. Snow pack and stream runoff in the red areas were 30 to 70 percent below normal. The drought contributed to devastating forest fires, increased ground water consumption, and agricultural failure. Water levels in storage reservoirs along the Colorado River, Lake Powell, and Lake Mead were at record low levels.

Eastern U.S. Blackout: August 14-15, 2003

- The Northeast Blackout left millions stranded. More than 5,000 people had to be evacuated from New York subway trains that were stranded deep inside tunnels—some underneath the Hudson River. Hotels with rooms could not rent them to desperate people, because their computers were down and they didn't know which rooms were occupied or empty. Grand Central station was shut down. All the major Northeast airports had to shut down because of unreliable power supplies to run the computers for traffic control and the navigational systems.
- More than 50 million people in the northeastern United States and the province of Ontario, Canada, lost electricity when the system suddenly broke down—causing the greatest blackout in history.
- What caused the catastrophic electrical breakdown is not completely clear. But the heat wave that had lingered for days over the region certainly played a

part, since air conditioners were running at record levels. This placed a great strain on the entire electrical system. When the electrical system was running at near maximum capacity, the margin for error became extremely small. The problem is that the entire infrastructure of modern cities is built around the assumption of an uninterrupted electrical power supply. Most of the transportation system (subways, trains, automobiles, airports, aircraft, and ships) is dependent upon either electrically powered engines or upon equipment that is necessary for their safe operation. Most multi-story buildings do not even have windows and are totally dependent on air-conditioned systems. Elevators are an absolute necessity for many people who cannot walk up and down enormous numbers of flights of stairs. And buildings with upward of 50 stories are rendered virtually useless.

Catastrophe #45
Riyadh Terror Bombing: May 12, 2003

On *May 11, 2003*, Secretary Powell met with King Abdullah II in Amman, Jordan, about Middle East peace. He then flew to Saudi Arabia to visit with Crown Prince Abdullah to discuss the same. On the evening of *May 12*—within eight hours of Powell's scheduled arrival on *May 13* in Riyadh, American interests were bombed in Riyadh. Al Qaeda claimed responsibility for the largest terror event targeting Americans since 9-11.

At least 29 people, including ten U.S. nationals, were killed and about 200 injured when suicide car bombings devastated three housing compounds for foreigners. Washington blamed al Qaeda for the bombings, and President Bush vowed to be relentless in the "war on terrorism" and to hunt down those responsible for the attacks. The attacks were "suicide bombings using booby-trapped cars filled with explosives," said the Saudi Interior Ministry.

Catastrophe #46
Hurricane Claudette: July 15, 2003
Estimated $100 Million in damages/costs

While Palestinian officials were on Capitol Hill meeting with members of Congress about the Bush administration's Road Map, Hurricane Claudette was clobbering President Bush's home state.

According to the Associated Press, ministers in Prime Minister Abbas' cabinet met with members of Congress to discuss the Bush administration's Road Map to end Israeli-Palestinian violence. The meetings ended *July 15*, just over a week before Abbas' arrival in Washington to meet Bush.

Claudette

Hurricane Claudette, the first Atlantic hurricane of 2003, made landfall on the middle of the Texas coast at midday on *July 15*, according to the National Hurricane Center (NHC). It was a Category 1 storm, classified as the least destructive on a scale of 1 to 5. Claudette's winds reached a maximum of 80 mph, and five to eight inches of rain fell as a direct result.

Catastrophe #47
Two High-Profile Suicides: July 17-24, 2003

The Strange Timing of Two High-Profile Suicides.
Are the Tragedies Symbolic?

On *July 17, 2003,* Prime Minister Blair addressed the U.S. Congress. Blair stated that terrorism would not be defeated without peace in the Middle East between Israel and Palestine.

At a joint press conference with President Bush in Washington that night, Blair noted "the first steps, albeit tentative," had now been taken toward achieving a two-state solution.

On the next day, Blair began to face the biggest political crisis in his six years as Britain's prime minister, when the body of Dr. David Kelly, Britain's chief bio-warfare expert, was found dead. The government's chief expert and former weapons inspector in Iraq took his own life.

On *July 24,* Prime Minister Abbas visited Capitol Hill in Washington to meet with senators and congressmen. Later in the day, he gave a speech to members of the Council on Foreign Relations (CFR).

On *July 25*, Abbas and members of his cabinet were guests of Bush at the White House. Following an Oval Office meeting which included Bush, Vice President Cheney, Secretary Powell, National Security Advisor Rice and other staff, Bush and Abbas held a Rose Garden press briefing.

On *July 24*, Bush's friend, oilman Colin McMillan, who was awaiting Senate confirmation as Navy secretary, was found dead from a single gunshot wound; and on *July 25*, investigators said it was self-inflicted. According to Fox News, he died around lunchtime on the *24th*.

Two employees found his body at his southern New Mexico ranch, said Roswell Mayor Bill Owen, a family spokesman and longtime McMillan employee. The 55,000-acre Three Rivers Ranch is on the edge of the White Sands Missile Range.

McMillan had run Permian Exploration Corp. in Roswell, chaired Bush's New Mexico presidential campaign in 2000, and served as an assistant defense secretary under the first President Bush.

Political Suicide?

Are these tragic events symbolic of the political suicide Bush and Blair are bringing on themselves if they continue to involve themselves with the dividing of God's covenant land?

Catastrophe #48
Hurricane Isabel: September 6-19, 2003
Estimated $4 billion in damages

On *September 16, 2003*, the United States told Israel any money spent on settlements would be subtracted from the $9 billion in loan guarantees; the security fence was under discussion, too. On *September 18*, King Abdullah II of Jordan arrived at Camp David to discuss with President Bush the Road Map, Iraq, and bilateral relations. At the time of their meeting, Hurricane Isabel came ashore and devastated North Carolina, Virginia, and Maryland.

Hurricane Isabel became a tropical storm on Saturday, *September 6*, on the very same day Prime Minister Abbas resigned from office.

From its beginning as a tropical storm, Isabel's path went straight westward towards the U.S. Her intensity increased from a Category 4 to a Category 5 on the afternoon of *September 11*, the same afternoon that the U.S. told Israel not to expel Arafat. Isabel's intensity on Friday and Saturday stayed in the Category 5 range (excluding a few hours as a Category 4). Sunday afternoon it dropped to 155 mph (1 mph below beginning of Category 5), making it a Category 4, and was at 140 mph and fluctuating that evening.

According to early computer models, the storm was expected to come ashore between South Carolina and New Jersey, with most models having it heading directly towards the Washington, DC, area once it came ashore.

On Tuesday, *September 16*, the U.S. vetoed a UN Security Council bill that called on Israel to guarantee Arafat's security. The United States' UN Ambassador John Negroponte stated that the United States did not support the elimination or forced exile of Arafat and believed his diplomatic isolation was the best course. However, he said the United States was forced to use its veto because the resolution failed to name groups such as Hamas and the Al-Aqsa Martyrs Brigade, which claimed credit for numerous suicide bombings and other attacks against Israelis.

Also on that day, the U.S., in addition to telling Israel they would deduct money spent on settlements from their $9 billion loan guarantee, also said they were considering whether to reduce money spent on the security fence from the loan guarantees. U.S. Treasury Secretary Jack Snow reminded Israeli Foreign Minister Netanyahu that Israel was required to reduce its debt as another contingency of their loan guarantees. Due to Bush administration pressure, Prime

Minister Sharon delayed his cabinet meeting on Wednesday to discuss the course of the security fence.

Isabel and Abdullah

On Wednesday, *September 17*, President Bush was briefed at the White House on Hurricane Isabel. The federal government called for all offices to be closed on Thursday and Friday. Bush's next official public meeting was to be at Camp David with King Abdullah, in which they were to discuss how to proceed with the Road Map, Iraq, and bilateral relations. Hurricane Isabel caused Bush to rearrange his schedule. He flew to Camp David on Wednesday night instead of Thursday. His joint press availability with King Abdullah was moved up to the morning of *September 18*, from Friday due to Isabel. Bush welcomed Abdullah at Camp David with these words:

> First, I'm so pleased to welcome my friends, King Abdullah and Queen Rania to Camp David. I want to thank them so much for rearranging their schedules to get up here ahead of Hurricane Isabel. Laura and I look forward to spending some quality time with two really fine people.

> We're going to have some serious discussions today, then we'll have a nice lunch, and then we'll batten down the hatches and spend a good evening with our friends.

Hurricane Isabel

North Carolina, Virginia, and Maryland took the brunt of Hurricane Isabel's intensity.

The storm was still an enormous event, a tragedy for those losing family members, but fortunately it didn't hit Washington, DC; Baltimore; Philadelphia; or New York City straight on, which would have killed many people and caused billions of dollars in property damage. The NOAA initially estimated damage at $4 billion (not including flood-related damage covered by federal flood insurance), which would place Isabel as the third most costly U.S. hurricane according to the Insurance Information Institute.

Federal offices in Washington, DC, were closed, as well as the schools in the DC and Baltimore areas. The Metro trains and buses did not run, airports were closed, millions of people were without power and there were major concerns about flooding due to saturated ground from the last ten months of rain. But the cities were mercifully spared.

Even 72 hours after Isabel hit, over one million people were still without power in the Washington, DC, metro area. More than one million homes were told to boil their water due to contamination. The long and arduous cleanup process began.

On Monday, *September 22*, President Bush's next official day at work, he flew to Richmond, Virginia, to visit the Virginia State Police Academy to participate in a briefing on Hurricane Isabel's damage. He also toured the temporary Virginia Emergency Operations Center.

Surrounded by photographs of Hurricane Isabel slamming into the Atlantic coast, Bush offered federal help to states that took the worst hits from the storm.

"The true character of this country comes out in times of stress and emergency. This country has responded once again," Bush said at the Virginia State Police Academy to a room of 250 emergency relief workers from 12 federal agencies who coordinated recovery efforts in the state. "On behalf of a grateful nation, I want to thank people at all levels of our government for working extra hard to help our country when it needed help," said Bush.

In Washington, Senate Appropriations Committee Chairman Ted Stevens (R-Alaska), said he expected the storm to eventually cost the federal government billions of dollars. Stevens said Isabel was "the most major storm we've seen in recent history in terms of damage."

This powerful and costly storm with its intricate tie-in to Israel was another warning judgment to those involved in dividing God's covenant land.

Catastrophe and Events #49
Record Solar Flares and California Wildfires
October 24–November 5, 2003
Wildfires Left an Estimated $3 billion in damages

Bush Said Israeli Security Fence Would Impede Emergence of a Palestinian State, Hosted White House Ramadan Dinner; the Sun Produced Record-Setting Explosions, and Southern California Had Record Wildfires

"The [Israeli security] fence is an opportunity to make it difficult for a Palestinian state to emerge," President Bush said in a news conference on *October 28, 2003,* after being asked about the security fence Israel was constructing with the stated goal of keeping out terrorists.

"There is a difference between security and land acquisition," Bush said, "and we have made our views clear on that issue."

Bush said his problem with the fence, as with Jewish settlements on the West Bank and in Gaza, was whether it would interfere with conditions for setting up a Palestinian state.

President Bush, for the third year in a row, sponsored a Ramadan dinner at the White House on *October 28*, to celebrate the beginning of the Muslims' 30-day fast. He hosted ambassadors and Muslim leaders, and said, in part:

According to the teachings of Islam, Ramadan commemorates the revelation of God's word in the Holy Koran to the prophet Mohammed. In this
season, Muslims come together to remember their dependence on God, and
to show charity to their neighbors. Fasting during Ramadan helps Muslims
focus on God's greatness, to grow in virtue, and cultivate compassion
toward those who live in poverty and hunger.

The White House developed a Ramadan 2003 section for its Web site:
www.whitehouse.gov/infocus/ramadan/index.html.

Record Solar Flares

On Wednesday, *October 29*, scientists warned that communications on
Earth could be disrupted by another spectacular eruption on the surface of the
Sun and that it might even hamper firefighting efforts in California.

"It's headed straight for us like a freight train," said John Kohl, a solar astro-
physicist at the Harvard-Smithsonian Centre for Astrophysics in Cambridge,
Massachusetts. "This is the real thing." A second huge magnetic solar storm hit
Earth on *October 31*, just a day after an earlier one hurtled into the planet in
what one astronomer called an unprecedented one-two punch.

"It's like the Earth is looking right down the barrel of a giant gun pointed at
us by the sun . . . and it's taken two big shots at us," said John Kohl of the
Harvard-Smithsonian Center for Astrophysics in Massachusetts.

On Tuesday, *November 4*, the Sun cut loose with three severe flares and
unleashed its largest recorded solar flare, capping ten days of unprecedented
activity which began on *October 25*.

Paal Brekke, deputy project manager of the SOHO spacecraft, was digest-
ing the significance of the three additional outbursts on top of two back-to-back
monster flares on *October 28 and 29*.

"I think the last week will go into the history books as one of the most dra-
matic periods of solar activity we have seen in modern time," Brekke told
SPACE.com. "As far as I know, there has been nothing like this before."

None of the latest eruptions were aimed directly at Earth, but glancing
blows did occur.

The "Perfect Non-Storm": October 27–November 5

Everything that could go wrong in Southern California did—everything
except rain to help put out the fires. Greg Forbes, a meteorologist with the
Weather Channel, said:

It's the perfect non-storm. Regardless how the fires start[ed], what
[kept] them growing and devastating such huge areas, instead of being
able to be stopped right away . . . [were] the perfect weather conditions
all brought together at the same time.

Meteorologist Forbes ran down the list: Temperatures in the Los Angeles Basin topped 90 degrees. Humidity was as low as 10 percent. Swirling winds gusted at speeds that frequently topped 40 mph.

So, those three factors—very warm, very low humidity, and windy conditions—[were] perfect for rapid development and spread of fires. And they [came] together in an area filled with dry brush—and houses— almost waiting to burn.

On *November 4*, firefighters got a morale boost from a visit by President Bush, who surveyed some of the damage done by the blazes that had killed at least 22 people, destroyed about 3,600 homes and burned more than 740,000 acres of brush and timber.

"This will be the most expensive fire in California history, both in loss of property and the cost of fighting it," Dallas Jones, director of the state Office of Emergency Services, said.

Catastrophes #50, 51, 52 and 53
Hurricanes Charley, Frances, Ivan, and Jeanne
August 9–September 27, 2004
Insured Loss Estimates: $22 billion-$25 billion
(The U.S. government approved an additional $14.5 billion in hurricane aid, including $3 billion for farmers affected by natural disasters and drought.)

From *August 13* to *September 27, 2004*, an unprecedented four major hurricanes damaged more than one of every five Florida homes. Meteorologists described the 2004 hurricane season as among the most destructive in the past one hundred years. The insurance industry expects claims to surpass two million, easily surpassing the 700,000 claims filed in 1992 after Hurricane Andrew, the nation's most destructive hurricane.

Hurricane Jeanne cost insurers $6-8 billion, storm modeler Eqecat Inc. estimated. "The insured loss estimates for Hurricane Jeanne appears to be averaging about $7 billion," said S&P. And insurers already faced as much as $17 billion in damage from Hurricanes Ivan, Frances, and Charley.

On *October 14*, Bush signed a $14.5 billion hurricane relief bill that cleared the way for $11.5 billion for hurricane victims, including an additional $3 billion for farmers and ranchers hurt by natural disasters and draughts.

The bulk of the money, about $6.5 billion, went to FEMA. Other money for damaged facilities or aid went to the Defense Department, Veterans Administration, Small Business Administration (SBA), NASA, and other agencies.

Catastrophe #50
Hurricane Charley: August 9-17, 2004
Estimated cost to insurers: $6.8 billion
(Charley came ashore in Florida on August 13)

Israel, at the beginning of August, headed for a major showdown with the U.S. Especially on *August 1-2* and *August 7-8*, the Bush administration put pressure on Israel to dismantle unauthorized outpost settlements and stop new settlement construction. Elliott Abrams (from Condoleezza Rice's office) and Ambassador Kurtzer were involved in intense negotiations during the first two weeks of August. Moreover, State Department and White House spokespersons made official statements pertaining to Israel's promises and responsibilities.

Israel was strongly reminded during this time period that the removal of security roadblocks was one of four commitments they had made to the American government.

The other three commitments that were urged by the Bush administration were evacuating illegal (unauthorized) outposts, limiting settlement construction to built-up areas, and unfreezing hundreds of millions of shekels in Palestinian Authority tax money.

On *August 7-8*, Abrams made it clear in talks with officials in Israel that the U.S. stood firm on their demand that the illegal outposts must be removed. The Bush administration put significant pressure on Israel to complete the evacuation of unauthorized outposts by the November 2004 U.S. elections.

During the week of *August 8-13*, Kurtzer was close to reaching an agreement with Baruch Spiegel, the Israeli defense minister's adviser, on how many outposts must be evacuated. (The Israeli defense department lists 23 "unauthorized" outposts established in the West Bank since March 2001.)

On *August 9*, State Department spokesman Adam Ereli called on Israel to fulfill settlement commitments. The same day, a tropical depression began forming in the Caribbean Sea. Within 36 hours, it developed into Hurricane Charley.

On *August 10*, President Bush selected Congressman Porter Goss (R-Florida) as his nominee for director of the CIA. On *August 13*, Hurricane Charley made a surprise course change and smashed ashore in Goss's hometown of Sanibel Island and Punta Gorda, Florida. The hurricane caused an estimated $3 billion in property damage to Goss's congressional district.

According to the Associated Press, Hurricane Charley's 145-mph winds took forecasters by surprise and showed just how shaky a science it still is to predict a storm's intensity—even with all the latest satellite and radar technology. Charley quickly grew from a Category 2 to a Category 4 storm; and its course took a sharp turn to the right, which put it about 70 miles south of the originally projected bull's eye.

"There was a sudden intensification and a veering to the right of track, and we're all trying to work out why," said Mark Saunders, a tropical storm expert from Benfield Hazard Centre at University College London, UK.

Bush and his brother, Governor Jeb Bush, toured Charlotte and Lee Counties (Porter Goss's congressional District) by helicopter on *August 15*.

Putting these events into perspective, while Israel was being forced to evacuate 23 settlement outposts, 25 counties in Florida were declared federal disaster areas. At the time the Bush administration was applying enormous pressure on Prime Minister Sharon to "force" the evacuation of the unauthorized settlement outposts of Judea and Samaria, 1.2 million Floridians were being advised to evacuate their homes.

Ironically, the settlements to be evacuated consisted of many mobile homes; while in Polk County, the county with the most mobile homes in Florida, a total of 3,663, sustained major damage and 6,365 had minor damage. Florida also had 10,000 homes destroyed, and 16,000 homes with major damage.

Hurricane Charley Cost Insurers about $6.8 Billion

U.S. property/casualty insurers were expected to pay homeowners and businesses an estimated $6.8 billion for insured property losses from Hurricane Charley, according to preliminary estimates by the Insurance Services Offices' (ISO) Property Claim Services unit.

On *August 27*, Bush said he would submit a supplemental request to Congress of approximately $2 billion to pay for the response and recovery efforts related to Hurricane Charley.

Catastrophe #51
Hurricane Frances: August 24–September 6, 2004
Estimated cost to insurers: $4.4 billion
(Frances came ashore on September 5)

On Tuesday, *August 24, 2004*, Vice President Cheney stated he did not favor a federal marriage amendment. "Lynne and I have a gay daughter, so it's an issue our family is very familiar with," Cheney told an audience that included his daughter. "With the respect to the question of relationships, my general view is freedom means freedom for everyone. . . . People ought to be free to enter into any kind of relationship they want to."

That evening, a tropical depression began forming in the Atlantic Ocean; in less than 48 hours, it became known as Hurricane Frances and began heading west towards Florida.

On *August 31*, Prime Minister Sharon yielded to White House pressure and publicly stated he would accelerate settlement "evacuations" from Gaza. Within

24 hours, Hurricane Frances moved from a Category 2 to a Category 4 hurricane the size of Texas with 140-mph winds. The next day, 2.8 million people in Florida were advised to "evacuate" their homes, the largest evacuation in Florida's history.

Hurricane Frances and Bush's Republican Convention acceptance speech shared the news headlines on *September 1-2*. In Bush's much-awaited speech, he stated that Israel was a very good friend of the United States, with no mention of the Middle East peace process. Shortly thereafter, Frances dropped from a Category 4 to a Category 2 hurricane before coming ashore 72 hours later.

Hurricane Frances Cost Insurers about $4.4 Billion

Homeowners and businesses were expected to file an estimated $4.4 billion claims for insured property losses from Hurricane Frances, according to an estimate by ISO's Property Claim Services unit on September 23, 2004.

Hurricane Frances made landfall between West Palm Beach and Vero Beach in Florida on *September 5*, but weakened into a tropical storm when it reached the Florida Panhandle. Frances then moved north, triggering numerous tornadoes and heavy rain in Georgia, South Carolina, North Carolina and New York, causing 30 deaths along the way.

Florida accounted for $4.1 billion in insured property losses and more than 500,000 claims. U.S. property/casualty insurers expected to process 552,000 claims for insured losses to personal and commercial property and vehicles.

On *September 14, 2004*, Bush submitted a supplemental budget request totaling $3.1 billion to the Congress to help Florida and other affected areas respond to the damage caused by Hurricanes Charley and Frances.

Catastrophe #52
Hurricane Ivan: September 3-18, 2004
Estimated cost to insurers: $6 billion
*(Ivan came ashore September 16 on Rosh Hashanah
—the Feast of Trumpets, a biblical holy day)*

The Bush administration continued to pressure Israel to leave the unauthorized settlements; New Orleans hosted a major gay, bisexual, and transgender event called "Southern Decadence" for 120,000 from *August 31–September 5*; a federal judge in Nebraska called partial-birth abortion legislation unconstitutional on *September 8*; a federal judge in Pennsylvania ruled against the Internet child porn ban on *September 10*; and Governor Arnold Schwarzenegger of California signed legislation guaranteeing insurance benefits for domestic partners on *September 12*.

These events occurred during Ivan's intense journey towards the United States. In another record-setting evacuation, two million people were advised to evacuate their homes from Louisiana to Florida. Ivan caused enormous damage to the southern United States—including the states of Florida, Alabama, Mississippi, Louisiana, Georgia, and North Carolina—plus seven other northeastern states. Ivan impacted the entire state of Alabama. (The Alabama Supreme Court had removed the Ten Commandments from their office corridor 13 months earlier.)

Hurricane Ivan Cost Insurers about $6 Billion

U.S. property/casualty insurers were expected to pay homeowners and businesses an estimated $6 billion for insured property losses from Hurricane Ivan, according to ISO's Property Claim Services unit.

In all, 15 states were affected, producing nearly 600,000 claims for destroyed or damaged insured homes, cars, boats, and businesses.

The lion's share of the losses was reported in five states:

Florida: $3.8 billion
Alabama: $1.2 billion
Georgia: $350 million
Pennsylvania: $225 million
North Carolina: $135 million

Florida residents and business owners filed 285,000 claims—nearly half the total insurers would pay for Hurricane Ivan. U.S. crude oil production fell to a 50-year low in *September* as Ivan battered operations in the Gulf of Mexico, the private American Petroleum Institute said on *October 13, 2004.*

Data collected by the NOAA indicated that some of the heaviest damage may have been caused by a "rogue wave" that reached 90 feet in height, said Chris Oynes, regional director of the U.S. Minerals Management Service. Underwater mud avalanches spawned other damage, he said.

Disruptions in the Gulf of Mexico, along with temporary dips in Alaskan operations, cut output 15 percent from the previous year to 4.85 million barrels per day, the lowest in half a century. The Gulf of Mexico region usually produced about 1.7 million barrels of oil per day. Government figures showed 471,328 barrels per day were still missing.

Oil prices skyrocketed by more than $10 a barrel in the month, primarily over production delays in the Gulf of Mexico.

ChevronTexaco Corp. said damage from Hurricane Ivan to a single $500 million platform in the Gulf of Mexico was responsible for the substantial portion of its loss of oil and gas production from the region. The platform, which is located in 1,754 feet of water, was not pumping any oil or gas. The company's

Gulf oil output was down by the equivalent of 80,000 barrels per day. Hurricane Ivan, which came ashore in Alabama on *September 16*, damaged at least 13 pipelines and toppled production platforms within its 160-mile span.

Catastrophe #53
Hurricane Jeanne: September 13-27, 2004
Estimated cost to insurers: $6 billion-$9 billion
(Jeanne came ashore September 25 on Yom Kippur
—the Day of Atonement, a biblical holy day)

President Bush gave a major foreign policy speech to the UN General Assembly on *September 21* at 11 a.m. EDT. In his speech, he said, "Israel should impose a settlement freeze, dismantle unauthorized outposts, end the daily humiliation of the Palestinian people, and avoid any actions that prejudice final negotiations."

From that point, Hurricane Jeanne began a course change over the next 48 hours, going from its present east-northeast position in the Atlantic Ocean (moving away from the United States) at the time of Bush's speech, to east-southeast shortly thereafter, to southeast, south, and then west toward Florida, where it came ashore four days later as a Category 3 hurricane.

Tuesday evening, after Bush's UN speech, Prime Minister Sharon reiterated that he was staying with the disengagement timetable, and Israeli Foreign Minister Shalom assured the U.S. that Israel wouldn't enlarge settlements. The next day, there was a major suicide bombing in Jerusalem and two major suicide bombings against American targets in Baghdad.

Hurricane Jeanne's 48-Hour Chronology from the NOAA:

- Tuesday, *September 21*:
  - 5 a.m. EDT: Jeanne strengthened slightly while moving **east-northeast**
  - 11 a.m. EDT: President Bush gave his foreign policy speech to the UN General Assembly; he called on Israel to freeze settlements and dismantle outposts on her land
  - 11 a.m. EDT: Jeanne moved **east-southeast**
  - 5 p.m. EDT: Jeanne was now moving **southeast**
  - 11 p.m. EDT: Jeanne moved **southeast**
- Wednesday, *September 22*:
  - 5 a.m. EDT: Jeanne drifted **south** with little change in strength . . . was expected to turn **west**
  - 11 a.m. EDT: Jeanne strengthened well to the east of the Bahamas . . . was expected to turn **west** by Thursday

- • 5 p.m. EDT: Jeanne moved **southwest** and was expected to turn **west**
- Thursday, *September 23*:
    - • 5 a.m. EDT: Jeanne moved toward the **west**
    - • 11 a.m. EDT: Jeanne strengthened while moving slowly **west**
- Saturday, *September 25*: Hurricane Jeanne hit U.S.

Hurricane Jeanne Cost Insurers about $7 Billion

Hurricane Jeanne made landfall near Stuart, Florida, at midnight on *September 25*, and into the early morning hours of *September 26*, with 120-mph winds. Jeanne peeled off roofs, snapped power lines, and left large swaths of coastline knee-deep in sea and rain water as it plowed through parts of Florida already scarred by Hurricane Frances three weeks earlier.

Tree limbs and debris, including mattresses torn out of mobile homes, flowed through flooded streets along the Atlantic shore; and more than two million people were left without electricity as Jeanne—a record fourth hurricane strike for the state in one storm season—moved inland.

Up to three million of Florida's 17 million people were urged to evacuate trailer parks, islands, and flood-prone areas. According to a statement issued by Standard & Poor's Ratings Services (S&P) at that time:

> The insured loss estimates for Hurricane Jeanne appear to be averaging about $7 billion. These, combined with the estimated insured losses from the three earlier storms (Charley, Frances and Ivan), would give a total insured loss from the hurricanes in the low $20 billions. In real terms, this approaches the loss from Hurricane Andrew in 1992.

On *September 27,* Bush submitted to Congress a supplemental budget request totaling $7.1 billion to help Alabama, Florida, Georgia, Louisiana, Mississippi, North Carolina, Ohio, Pennsylvania, West Virginia, and other affected areas respond to damage caused by Hurricanes Ivan and Jeanne.

Summary

- The Bush administration applied major pressure on Israel to evacuate settlements and freeze settlement construction, while four of the largest evacuations in U.S. history occurred in 45 days.
- Four of the five costliest hurricanes in U.S. history occurred within 42 days of Bush administration pressure on Israel.
- Preliminary insured damage estimates were in the $22-$25 billion range.
- Bush and Congress approved $14.5 billion in hurricane aid: $6.5 billion for FEMA, $11.5 billion for hurricane victims, and an additional $3 billion for farmers and ranchers hurt by natural disasters and droughts.

- Bush traveled to Florida four times to view hurricane damage.
- Bush's campaign team said he performed poorly in the first presidential debate because he was exhausted from touring hurricane damaged areas a few hours before the debate.
- Bush's brother Jeb (Governor of Florida) oversaw the largest statewide rebuilding program in U.S. history.
- Bush's CIA nominee Goss's congressional district received the brunt of Hurricane Charley's devastation 80 hours after his selection.
- Mobile homes in Israel were evacuated while thousands of mobile homes in Florida were evacuated, destroyed and/or heavily damaged.
- Israelis' lives were disrupted in the biblical heartland because of U.S. political pressure, while Floridians' lives were disrupted (not to forget those in other southern states) by four record-setting hurricanes.

*Important Note from the Insurance Institute of America

In the 1990s, insurers paid out $107.3 billion for natural disasters—about $700 million per month, many times more than in previous decades. This included well-known events such as Hurricane Andrew and the Northridge earthquake, but also hundreds of smaller disasters associated with tropical storms, wildfires, hail, and snow. The extraordinary costs associated with these disasters is one of the primary reasons for the cost of homeowners' insurance, rising an estimated 9 percent in 2003, according to research conducted by the Institute.

Hurricane Isabel, together with the major tornadoes that hit the Midwest earlier in the year, made 2003 a relatively bad year for catastrophe-related losses. According to the ISO, insured catastrophe losses through August 2003 totaled $7.6 billion. Through October 1, 2004, insurers expected losses in excess of $25 billion.

Summary of Actions and
Resulting Catastrophes or Events
During Presidency of George W. Bush
(2001-2004)

Date	Action	Date	Catastrophe
March 31 - April 11, 2001	Egypt Pres. Mubarak & Jordan King Abdullah II visited Pres. George W. Bush to persuade him to be more involved in Middle East talks and to support the land-for-peace initiative.	*March 31, 2001 (April 1 in China)* *April 11*	**Chinese fighter jet "bumped" into a U.S. reconnaissance plane,** forcing it and 24-member crew to make emergency landing in China. • China agreed to release detained airmen.
May 21, 2001 *May 22* *May 23*	• Sec. of State Powell spoke in support of Mitchell report released this day. • Pres. Bush called Pres. Mubarak & King Abdullah II, who welcomed U.S. endorsement of Mitchell report. • Bush called Israeli PM Sharon & PLO Chmn Arafat urging them to accept Mitchell report.	*May 21-22, 2001* *May 24*	**Rumor** circulated that Vermont Senator Jeffords may leave Republican Party. **Sen. Jeffords became an Independent, causing Republicans to lose their majority in U.S. Senate,** turning control of Senate over to the Democrats for the first time since 1994.
June 6, 2001 *June 7-8* *June 13*	• CIA Director Tenet met with Pres. Mubarak in Egypt. • In Israel, Tenet met with PM Sharon & security chiefs; + with Arafat, PLO negotiators and security chiefs. • Bush pleased both sides agreed to a cease-fire plan. (But agreement not signed.)	*June 5-18, 2001*	**Tropical Storm Allison** hit southeast U.S.: 24 dead; heavy flooding in Texas and Louisiana; 36" of rain; costliest tropical storm in U.S. history; $5 billion.
August 25 - Sept. 10, 2001	Pres. Bush, Sec. Powell, U.S. Amb. To Israel Kurtzer, with Saudi cooperation, prepared most comprehensive plan & message ever offered by a U.S. president for dividing Israel's land. Plan was nearly complete by Sept. 10.	*Sept. 11, 2001*	**Terrorists used 2 airplanes to attack the World Trade Center towers in New York, one to attack Pentagon in Washington, DC,** and one intended for White House or Congress, but crashed in Pennsylvania because of brave passengers like Todd Beamer; nearly **3,000 dead**; $40 billion plus in damages.

Date	Action	Date	Catastrophe
Oct. 1, 2001 *Oct. 2*	• U.S. officials: draft of major speech on Middle East was under review at State Dept., with plan for eventual "creation of a Palestinian state." • Pres. Bush said Palestinian state was always "part of a vision" to respect Israel's right to exist.	*Oct. 2, 2001*	**Anthrax-laden mail** discovered in Senate mail, and traces in other federal buildings, causing Congressional offices to be closed and sealed, Supreme Court to be temporarily relocated, and the White House to quarantine all mail; $3 billion.
Nov. 10, 2001 *Nov. 11*	• Bush spoke to UN General Assembly (UNGA) supporting "two-states–Israel & Palestine" –as just peace solution. (1st time said by a U.S. president) • Sec. Powell reaffirmed Bush policy of two-state solution. • Chairman Arafat spoke to UNGA asking for peace-keepers, evacuation of all Jewish settlers, and Palestinian state with "Holy Jerusalem as its capital."	*Nov. 11, 2001* *Nov. 12*	**Osama bin Laden & Sadam Hussein warned of nuclear, chemical or biological attacks on U.S.** **American Airlines jet, flight #587, crashed** moments after takeoff from Kennedy Airport in New York City; 255 dead.
April 30, 2002	Pres. Bush & State Dept. persuaded the Israelis to withdraw forces from Ramallah Compound and "allow Chmn Arafat to move freely."	*April 28, 2002*	**Tornadoes ravaged cities from Missouri to Maryland**; Maryland hit with F-5 tornado, with winds in 261-318 mph range, causing 6 deaths.
June 8, 2002	Pres. Bush & Egypt Pres. Mubarak called for a Palestinian state & for Israel to leave some of their land.	*June 8, 2002*	**Hayman fire began in Colorado, the largest in the state's history**, burning nearly 138,000 acres; 132 homes lost.
June 18 & 19, 2002 *June 24* *June 25*	• Pres. Bush planned to present his Middle East vision; cancelled twice due to suicide bombings in Jerusalem. • Bush finally delivered vision. • Instead of flying directly to G-8 Summit, Bush first surveyed damage in Arizona.	*June 18 & 19, 2002* *June 25*	**Rodeo and Chediski Fires began in Arizona**; 550,000 acres burned; one of worst fires in western U.S. history. **MCI declared $3.6 billion accounting error**; soon filed **largest bankruptcy in U.S. history**.
Sept. 30, 2002	Pres. Bush refused to move the U.S. Embassy from Tel Aviv to Jerusalem, ignoring the sense of the U.S. Congress expressed in the State Department spending bill.	*October 1, 2002* *October 2-31*	**Hurricane Lili:** first U.S. hurricane to hit land in 21st century. **Two snipers paralyzed DC:** 1st shooting was within 24 hours of Bush decision not to move embassy.

Date	Action	Date	Catastrophe
Nov. 7, 2002 Nov. 10-12	• Pres. Bush hosted a dinner at beginning of Ramadan for Arab ambassadors, honored Islam and "revelation of God's word in the holy Koran." • U.S. official Satterfield flew to Israel to pressure Israeli and Palestinian officials to complete "road map" designed by Quartet.	Nov. 9-11, 2002	**88 tornadoes** slashed through 7 states; Category F-4 with 200 mph winds; one of worst November tornado outbreaks on record. (Tornado season is March-July, *not* November.)
Dec. 4, 2002 Dec. 5	• PM Sharon accepted in principle Road Map envisioning independent Palestinian state. • Bush commemorated end of Ramadan at Islamic Center in DC, saying it "commemorates the revelation of God's word in the Holy Koran to the prophet Mohammad."	Dec. 5, 2002	**Worst ice storm in history of North Carolina and South Carolina:** 2 million homes and businesses without electric power.
Jan. 31, 2003 Feb. 1	• Sec. Powell said Pres. Bush would become more involved in Israeli-Palestinian talks, with goal of creating a Palestinian state in Israel by 2005. • After Columbia disaster, Bush quoted Isaiah and mentioned Creator in statement to comfort Americans and Israelis.	Feb. 1, 2003	**Space Shuttle Columbia broke up over Palestine, Texas,** upon entry into earth's atmosphere; all 7 astronauts, including first Israeli (on space mission) and 3 Christians, died.
April 30, 2003 May 4 May 5 May 10-11 May 1	• U.S. & other international mediators presented Quartet Road Map to PM Sharon & PM Abbas. • Powell, in Syria, said U.S. is committed to peace plan that "would include Syria and Lebanon & ... Golan Heights." • U.S. Envoy Burns met with Abbas, said Palestinians must fight terrorism and Israelis must halt settlement activity. • Powell met with Sharon & Abbas. • EU declared Road Map was "the property of the Quartet," not one country (U.S.).	May 1-11, 2003 May 4 May	**Record 412 tornadoes in 11 days in U.S.** (previous record of tornadoes for same period in May was 177 in 1999); costliest in U.S. history; $2.2 billion. Also, **535 windstorms & 1,385 hailstorms**. 19 states affected. 40 dead. • As part of 412 above, on this day 83 tornadoes ripped through 4 states; 38 dead. **Record-setting heat-weather patterns began in U.S., Europe, and Indian subcontinent.** • U.S.: **record 562 tornadoes** in May (previous record: 399).
continued on next page			

continued on next page

Date	Action	Date	Catastrophe
May – August 2003	Quartet (U.S., EU, UN, & Russia) continued meeting and negotiating Road Map plan for dividing Israel.	*June – August 2003*	**Hottest summer in Europe in 500 years**; **22,000 dead in 14 countries**; **50% of many crops lost**; hundreds of fires; billions lost in agricultural, other economies. • The **"meteorological equator"** –the hot air mass usually over Africa–**shifted north to Europe**. • U.S. experienced record heat in West (like 1930s dust bowl), but torrential rains in East, with some areas receiving double the normal rainfall. • Russia: 431 fires. • Germany: 300 fires. • Locusts descended on Mongolia/ China border towns damaging 11 million hectares of crops.
May 12-13, 2003	Sec. Powell met with King Abdullah II of Jordan & then Crown Prince Abdullah of Saudi Arabia [Middle East peace].	*May 12, 2003*	**Riyadh, Saudi Arabia terror bombing**; 29 killed (10 Americans); 200 injured.
July 15, 2003	Last day of meetings in DC between Palestinian officials and members of Congress & Bush Admin. officials [Road Map & violence].	*July 15, 2003*	**Hurricane Claudette** hit Texas, Pres. Bush's home state; $100 million.
July 17, 2003 *July 24* *July 25*	• United Kingdom PM Blair spoke to U.S. Congress; at press conf. with Pres. Bush, said "first steps" were taken toward a two-state solution. • PM Abbas met with members of Congress in DC; spoke to Council on Foreign Relations. • PM Abbas & cabinet members met with Pres. Bush, VP Cheney, Sec. Powell, and National Security Advisor Rice.	*July 17, 2003* *July 24*	**PM Blair faced greatest political crisis in 6 years**: **dead body** of Dr. David Kelly (UK's chief expert-inspector on Iraq bio-warfare weapons) found. **Colin McMillan, friend of Pres. Bush** awaiting Senate confirmation for Navy secretary, was **found dead** – apparent suicide.

Date	Action	Date	Catastrophe
Sept. 6, 2003 *Sept. 11* *Sept. 16* *Sept. 16* *Sept. 18*	• PM Abbas resigned. • U.S. told Israel not to expel Arafat. • U.S. told Israel that any money spent on settlements (and possibly money spent on the security fence) would be subtracted from $9 billion in loan guarantees. • U.S. vetoed UN Security Council resolution calling on Israel to ensure Arafat's security, but said did not support his elimination or forced exile. • Jordan King Abdullah II arrived at Camp David for talks with Bush on Road Map.	*Sept. 6-19, 2003* *Sept. 11* *Sept. 17* *Sept. 18*	**Hurricane Isabel**: Third most costliest hurricane; hit North Carolina, Virginia and Maryland; millions without power; $4 billion: • Increased in intensity from Category 4 to 5. • Pres. Bush briefed on Hurricane Isabel, drove to Camp David a day early and closed all federal offices in Washington DC area for *Sept. 18-19.* • Hurricane Isabel came ashore during Jordan's King Abdullah II meetings with Pres. Bush.
October 28, 2003	• Pres. Bush said Israel's security fence, as well as Jewish settlements in the West Bank and Gaza, are obstacles to "Palestinian state." Pres. Bush hosted 3rd annual Ramadan dinner at White House.	*October 24-Nov. 5, 2003* *Oct. 29* *Oct. 30* *Oct. 31* *Nov. 4* *Oct. 27-Nov. 5*	**Unprecedented record solar flares** from the sun, plus **most expensive fire in California history**; $3 billion. • Scientists warned that communications on Earth could be disrupted by solar eruptions "headed straight for us like a freight train." • Magnetic solar storm from sun hit earth. • Second magnetic solar storm hit earth. • Sun sent 3 more flares & largest recorded flare. • Hot temperatures, low humidity, high winds, & lack of rain – "perfect non-storm" – created terrible conditions for California fires; 22 dead; 3,600 homes destroyed; 740,000 acres burned.
August 1 - Sept. 21	(see next two pages)	*Aug. 9 - Sept. 27, 2004*	**Unprecedented 4 major hurricanes** (*names & details next 2 pages*) in one season cause **most destruction in past 100 years**; 20% of Florida homes damaged; $22-25 billion cost to insurers; $11.5 billion cost to U.S. government.

Date	Action	Date	Catastrophe
August 1-2 & 7-8, 2004	• U.S. put pressure on Israel to evacuate and dismantle outpost settlements (many mobile homes), and stop construction on new settlements. U.S. reminded Israel of its promise to remove security roadblocks, and release hundreds of millions of shekels in Palestinian Authority tax money.	*August 9-17, 2004*	**Hurricane Charley**; 1.2 million Floridians advised to evacuate homes; 25 counties declared disaster areas; 10,000 homes destroyed & 16,000 had major damage; in Polk County, 2,663 mobile homes received major damage & 6,365 minor damage; $6.8 billion cost to insurers.
August 9	• U.S. State Dept. spokesman called on Israel to fulfill settlement commitments.	*Aug. 13*	• Hurricane Charley changed course, came ashore in Florida; hit Cong. Goss's hometown and district, with $3 billion in property damage in his district.
August 10	• Pres. Bush nominated Cong. Porter Goss (R-Florida) as new CIA director.		
August 24, 2004	• VP Dick Cheney said he opposes Federal Marriage Amendment because he has a lesbian daughter.	*August 24 - Sept. 6, 2004*	**Hurricane Frances**; 30 deaths; largest evacuation in Florida's history; $4.4 billion cost to insurers; $3.1 billion to U.S. gov't.
August 31	• PM Sharon yielded to White House pressure, and said he would accelerate "evacuations" from Gaza.	*Sept. 1*	• Increased in intensity from a Category 2 to 4, and in size to as big as the state of Texas;
Sept. 2	• Pres. Bush delivered speech at Republican Convention, saying U.S. is a very good friend to Israel, but did not mention the peace process.	*Sept. 2*	• In Florida, 2.8 million people advised to "evacuate";
		Sept. 3-5	• Dropped from a Category 4 back to 2;
		Sept. 5-6	• Came ashore in Florida; moved up east coast.
September 2004	• Bush admin. kept up pressure on Israel to leave "unauthorized" settlements. •	*Sept. 3-18, 2004*	**Hurricane Ivan**; 15 southern & northeastern states affected; 2 million advised to evacuate their homes from Louisiana to Florida; Florida hit worst; Alabama (which removed Ten Commandments 13 months earlier) hit second worst; $6 billion cost to insurers.
August 31 - Sept. 5	• New Orleans hosted 120,000 for gay, bisexual & transgender "Southern Decadence" event.		
Sept. 8	• U.S. federal judge in Nebraska ruled partial-birth abortion bill unconstitutional.	*Sept. 16*	• Came ashore same day as Rosh Hashanah — Feast of Trumpets holy Biblical day.
Sept. 10	• U.S. federal judge in Pennsylvania ruled against Internet child porn ban.		**Oil platforms in the Gulf of Mexico were damaged** by hurricane and 90 foot "rogue wave," causing U.S. crude oil production to fall to 50-year low.
Sept. 12	• California Governor Arnold Schwarzenegger signed bill guaranteeing insurance benefits to domestic partners.		

Date	Action	Date	Catastrophe
Sept. 21, 2004	Pres. Bush gave major foreign policy speech to UN General Assembly, saying, "Israel should impose a settlement freeze, dismantle unauthorized outposts, end daily humiliation of Palestinian people ...."	*Sept. 13-27, 2004*	**Hurricane Jeanne**; 3 million in Florida advised to evacuate; $5-9 billion cost to insurers.
		Sept. 21-23	• Changed course (from moving away to moving toward U.S.)
Sept. 21	• PM Sharon promised to keep disengagement timetable; & Israeli Foreign Minister Shalom promised Israel would not enlarge settlements.	*Sept. 25*	• Came ashore as Category 3 hurricane same day as Yom Kippur—the Day of Atonement.
		Sept. 22	**Two major suicide bombings against U.S. targets in Baghdad.**
		Sept. 22	**Major suicide bombing in Jerusalem.**

CHAPTER 7

U.S. Catastrophes and Events: 2005

U.S. Administration: President George W. Bush

President George W. Bush was very pleased to see Israeli Prime Minister Ariel Sharon's disengagement plan completed. He stated numerous times in meetings in August, September and October 2005 how pleased he was with Sharon's courage and commitment to the evacuation of 21 Gaza settlements and four Northern Samaria settlements.

In late August 2005, President Bush went from great hope to being involved in the greatest disaster in U.S. history.

Hurricane Katrina was a devastating $100 billion hit for the U.S. government and $40 billion plus for insurance companies. It was so enormous that our nation's leaders and people worldwide couldn't believe it happened in America.

Hurricane Rita followed in September and then Hurricane Wilma in October. Rita and Wilma's news headlines and updates were sharing the front pages of most newspapers in the U.S. with President Bush and his Administration's Israeli-Palestinian peace efforts, including meetings with Middle East leaders on the division of the land of Israel.

In eight weeks, from August 29 to October 24, Hurricane's Katrina, Rita and Wilma became the sixth, fourth and most intense hurricanes in Atlantic basin history. These Category 5 hurricanes were unprecedented, but so were the discussions pertaining to the land of Israel.

There was also Hurricane Dennis—another billion-dollar event.

Catastrophe #54
Hurricane Dennis: July 4-10, 2005
Estimated Cost to Insurers: $1-2.5 billion

British Prime Minister Tony Blair, the president of the G-8 nations (United Kingdom, France, Germany, Brazil, Italy, Russia, Canada, U.S., and European Union), sponsored a meeting in Perthshire, Scotland, from July 6-8, 2005.

During the G-8 meeting, President George W. Bush and the other leaders agreed to give $3 billion dollars to the Palestinian Authority. On July 7, the day the declaration was to be announced (it was eventually presented the next day by Tony Blair), London was hit by four suicide bombings.

On July 8, Blair made the G-8 Palestinian aid declaration. President Bush, upon his return to Washington, visited the British Embassy to send condolences to the British people. The next day, Hurricane Dennis re-intensified with hurricane warnings for the Florida Panhandle, Alabama and Mississippi. Dennis came ashore in the Florida Panhandle on the afternoon of July 10, causing an estimated $1-2.5 billion in property damage.

London Bombed, Deadliest Bombing Since WW II

The July 7 London bombings were a series of coordinated suicide attacks that struck public transport system during the morning rush hour. The bombings killed 52 civilians, plus the four suicide bombers, and injured over 700 people.

At 8:50 a.m. BST, three bombs exploded within 50 seconds of each other on three London Underground trains. A fourth bomb exploded on a bus at 9:47 a.m. in Tavistock Square. The bombings caused a severe, day-long disruption of the city's transport and mobile telecommunications infrastructure.

The incident was the deadliest bombing in London since World War II.

These bombings were planned by Islamist paramilitary organizations based in the UK; the terrorist organization al-Qaeda claimed responsibility.

The bombings came while the UK was hosting the first full day of the 31st G-8 Summit, and shortly after Britain had assumed the rotating presidency of the Council of the European Union.

Tony Blair's Statement on London Explosions – July 7, 2005

Speaking from the G-8 Summit at Gleneagles Hotel in Scotland, British Prime Minister Tony Blair said his thoughts were with the victims and families of those involved in the 'barbaric events.'

It is important that those engaged in terrorism realise that our determination to defend our values and our way of life is greater than their determination to cause death and destruction to innocent people in a desire to impose extremism on the world.

Later Blair read a statement on behalf of the G-8 nations. They said they 'utterly condemned the barbaric' incidents which were 'an attack on civilized people everywhere' and sent their condolences to the victims and their families.

The statement said their countries had suffered from terrorism; they were united in their resolve to fight it, pledging that 'terrorism would not succeed.'

Tony Blair's Full Statement on London Bombings – July 7, 2005

I am just going to make a short statement on the terrible events that have happened in London earlier today, and I hope you understand that at the present time we are still trying to establish exactly what has happened.

... It is reasonably clear that there have been a series of terrorist attacks in London. There are obviously casualties, both people that have died and people seriously injured, and our thoughts and prayers of course are with the victims and their families.

It is my intention to leave the G-8 within the next couple of hours and go down to London and get a report, face-to-face, with the police, and the emergency services and the Ministers that have been dealing with this, and then to return later this evening.

President Bush Offers Condolences to People of London, Will Not Yield to Terrorists (*Excerpt*)
Gleneagles Hotel – Perthshire, Scotland – July 7, 2005

PRESIDENT BUSH: I spent some time recently with the Prime Minister, Tony Blair, and had an opportunity to express our heartfelt condolences to the people of London, people who lost lives. I appreciate Prime Minister Blair's steadfast determination and his strength. He's on his way now to London here from the G-8 to speak directly to the people of London. He'll carry a message of solidarity with him.

This morning I have been in contact with our Homeland Security folks. I instructed them to be in touch with local and state officials about the facts of what took place here and in London, and to be extra vigilant, as our folks start heading to work.

The war on terror goes on. I was most impressed by the resolve of all the leaders in the room. Their resolve is as strong as my resolve. And that is we will not yield to these people, will not yield to the terrorists. We will find them, we will bring them to justice and at the same time, we will spread an ideology of hope and compassion that will overwhelm their ideology of hate.

Blair Announces G-8 Will Grant PA $3 Billion Aid

On July 8, British Prime Minister Blair announced that the G-8 countries had agreed on a $3 billion package in aid for the Palestinian Authority.

Blair, speaking at the end of the G-8 summit, said the deal would be implemented "in years to come."

Yesterday evening, the G-8 agreed on a substantial package of help for the Palestinian Authority, amounting to up to $3 billion U.S. dollars for the years to come so that two states, Israel and Palestine, two peoples and two religions can live side by side in peace.

President Signs Book of Condolence at British Embassy – July 8

PRESIDENT BUSH: Yesterday [July 7, 2005] was an incredibly sad day for a lot of families in London. It's my honor, Ambassador, to come and represent our great country in extending our condolences to the people of Great Britain. To those who suffer loss of life, we pray for God's blessings. For those who are injured, we pray for fast healing. The British people are steadfast and strong. Long we've admired the great spirit of the Londoners and the people of Great Britain. Once again that great strength of character is coming through.

Thank you, Ambassador, for letting me come by.

AMBASSADOR MANNING: You're welcome. Mr. President, could I just say thank you very much, sir, for coming straight here from the airplane after the summit at the G-8. It's enormously good of you to come here. The gesture is hugely appreciated. And can I say to you that we have had the most wonderful gestures of support from the Americans over the last 36 hours. We're very grateful for that. It's a huge source of comfort, and thank you so much for coming today.

Hurricane Dennis

On July 7, Hurricane warnings were issued for Cuba at 11 a.m. EDT. Dennis made landfall near Punta del Ingles with 140 mph (220 km/h) winds late that day, and dropped down to a Category 3 storm while crossing the peninsula. As it moved back into the Gulf of Guacanayabo, its wind speed increased to a peak of 150 mph (240 km/h). Dennis then slammed into south-central Cuba just west of Punta Mangles Altos on July 8, again with 140 mph (220 km/h) winds.

Crossing Cuba's mountainous terrain disrupted the storm's circulation, weakening Dennis to Category 1 intensity. However, National Hurricane Center (NHC) forecasts continued to indicate the possibility of a return to Category 4 status after convection was re-established. This prediction was borne out when Dennis rapidly re-intensified on the afternoon of July 9, a re-intensification described by NHC as having occurred "at a rate that bordered on insane." The storm reached Category 4 intensity again on the morning of July 10. At 7 am CDT, the storm reached its peak intensity of 930 mbar, setting a new record for the strongest storm to form prior to August.

Dennis Comes Ashore

By the morning of July 10, hurricane warnings were in effect in the U.S. for the Florida Panhandle, Alabama and Mississippi, and with tropical storm warnings extending further east and west along the coast. The NHC predicted a landing at near full strength in the late afternoon. However, much like Hurricane Ivan which struck in the same area the previous year, the storm weakened just before landfall; its maximum sustained winds dropped from 145 mph (235 km/h, Category 4 strength) to 120 mph (195 km/h, Category 3 strength).

Continental landfall occurred at Santa Rosa Island, between Pensacola, Florida and Navarre Beach, Florida, at 2:25 p.m. CDT on July 10. Dennis was a Category 3 hurricane with winds of 115 to 120 mph. The highest official wind speed reported was a 121 mph wind gust at Navarre Beach. The storm lost strength over the day and was a tropical depression by early on July 11. The depression persisted, however, and gained a little strength while stalled over Illinois the next day. It finally dissipated on July 13, with advisories ceasing a full three days after landfall.

Cost Estimates

AIR Worldwide estimates insured losses in the United States from Hurricane Dennis will be between $1 billion to $2.5 billion. NOAA estimated the insured losses at $2 billion in late 2005. Although Dennis made landfall in the same region as Hurricane Ivan in 2004, insured losses from Dennis are expected to be significantly lower than Ivan's, since Dennis differed from Ivan in four important aspects: intensity, size, speed and location.

Catastrophe #55
Hurricane Katrina: August 23-29, 2005
Estimated Cost to Insurers: $40.4 billion
(The U.S. Government has committed $112.8 billion.
Some estimate that could reach $200 billion.)

From August 26 to October 24, 2005, Texas, Louisiana, Mississippi, Alabama, and Florida experienced the fury of three of the six most intense and costly hurricanes in Atlantic Basin history as Israel's land was being negotiated and divided. Once again, as the land and people of Israel were being pressured, the land of the U.S. was being devastated.

On August 15, thousands of Israeli Defense Force (IDF) soldiers began to deliver eviction notices to Israeli settlers who had lived on the land of Gaza and Northern Samaria for 35 years. They were given 48 hours to leave. The notification process also began in four Northern Samaria settlements. Settlers were given the option to leave voluntarily or be removed by force.

Ariel Sharon committed 55,000 soldiers and 8,000 police to the effort. Soldiers who refused to carry out the orders would face a court-martial.

On August 17, despite some resistance, authorities said Israel's historic withdrawal from Gaza was progressing rapidly, predicting that 10 out of 21 Jewish settlements would be cleared by the end of the day.

Unarmed Israeli troops and police went door to door, appealing to settlers to leave and threatening to move them by force. Some soldiers convinced protesters to leave after embracing them and joining them in song and prayer.

That evening, Israeli police said the evacuations of the Kerem Atzmona, Tel Katifa, Bedolah, Morag, Slav, Rufiah Yam, Gadid and Peat Sadeh settlements were completed. Israel Defense Forces Southern Command said that 60 percent of settlers had left Gaza by that afternoon.

At Gaza's largest settlement – Neveh Dekalim – unarmed Israeli soldiers led or carried away settlers or protesters who had infiltrated the settlements. Many of the estimated 4,000 people were angry and tearful. Buses full of troops and policemen were brought in to transport settlers to temporary housing.

After a painstakingly slow start, Israeli officials said soldiers evacuated 583 homes, synagogues and other buildings in the Gaza settlements. Soldiers loaded the evacuees onto dozens of rented tour buses, sending them out of the territory as part of a withdrawal that the Bush administration hoped would revive the Israeli-Palestinian peace process.

Ariel Sharon is a chief architect of the settlement movement. He said he was evacuating Gaza to give Israel more defensible borders and protect the viability of its Jewish majority from a fast-growing Arab population between the Mediterranean Sea and the Jordan River.

On August 17, 2005, U.S. Secretary of State Condoleezza Rice said that while she feels for evacuated settlers, Israel will be expected to make further concessions that would ultimately lead to an independent Palestinian state.

"Everyone empathizes with what the Israelis are facing," Rice said, but added "It cannot be Gaza only."

On August 18, at Neve Dekalim, troops wrestled for hours against some 1,500 people making their last stand inside Gaza's largest settlement. Protesters lay on the synagogue floor with their arms linked, and kicked the Israeli forces while supporters held their shoulders in a tug-of-war.

After breaking the human chain, troops dragged protesters out of the synagogue, holding them by their arms and legs as they twisted and squirmed. Other protesters chanted "blasphemy, blasphemy."

On Friday, August 19, Neve Dekalim was virtually empty by morning, with security forces, journalists, a few rabbis and a small number of pullout resisters the only remaining inhabitants.

"It is terribly sad to see the empty streets," said Eitan Ben-Mor, who had come from his home in the Golan Heights a week ago to lend support to the pull-out resistance, and planned to leave after the morning prayer.

"The children are missing. The parents are missing," he said. "The most simple things of day-to-day life were taken away cruelly, and by force."

In Nissanit, cranes lifted up prefabricated homes and placed them on flatbed trucks, to be driven to Israel. Piles of rubble lined the settlement's main street. More houses were leveled in the settlement of Dugit. Last week, mobile homes were destroyed at the Kerem Atzmona outpost, but Sunday's demolitions marked the first time stone houses were taken down.

In the outpost of Kerem Atzmona, Israeli bulldozers crushed several empty trailer homes. Israel plans on demolishing all homes in the abandoned settlements, removing hazardous waste and turning over other rubble to the Palestinians for construction.

A military bulldozer cleared debris, and troops quickly fanned throughout the settlement.

The scene in Gadid was a sharp contrast to the fierce standoffs between troops and young protesters in the Neve Dekalim and Kfar Darom settlements (where at least 41 police and soldiers and 17 civilians were injured, and about 50 people were arrested).

In Gadid, most of the protesters holed up in the settlement's synagogue, where they were permitted to hold morning prayers. After negotiations with police, the protesters agreed not to resist with force. Police moved into the building and carried the protesters away into waiting buses.

After three days of forced evacuations, 17 of 21 Gaza settlements were empty. Israel's commander for the region, Maj. Gen. Dan Harel, said the remainder could be emptied by August 23—weeks ahead of schedule.

A senior Defense Ministry official said all 21 Gaza settlements would be razed within two weeks, about half the time previously predicted.

On August 19, U.S. Assistant Secretary of State David Welch said the Gaza pullout will re-energize the U.S.-sponsored "Road Map" peace plan, while giving Israelis and Palestinians more security and prosperity.

> The United States views the Israeli disengagement from Gaza as an important opportunity ... to take further steps forward toward a better future for Israelis and Palestinians.

Welsh was the first senior U.S. official to visit Gaza since October 2003 when Palestinians attacked a U.S. diplomatic convoy and killed three Americans.

On Sunday, August 21, Gush Katif, Atzmona and Slav, the remaining communities in the main settlement bloc, were being emptied, as was the northern Gaza settlement of Elei Sinai.

In Katif, an Israeli army bulldozer broke through the locked community gates to clear a blazing fire of hay, tire and wood so troops could move freely.

Residents held prayers and a farewell ceremony in the synagogue, and then filed in a quiet, tearful procession to the waiting buses, led by the rabbi cradling a Torah scroll. Resigned to the inevitable, they had decided at a community meeting earlier to leave with dignity.

On August 22, the last of the 21 Gaza settlements, Netzarim, was evacuated, with the entire Gaza evacuation compressed into just one week, far shorter than the three weeks security forces foresaw.

On August 23, at 5 p.m. Israel time, Israel's disengagement evacuation and eviction ended. Israel evacuated the last settlers and protesters from the West Bank settlement of Homesh, completing its historic withdrawal of civilians from 25 settlements in Gaza and the West Bank.

"Today, we accomplished the first phase of the disengagement process ... related to evacuation of the civilians," said Israel Defense Forces Chief of Staff, Lt. Gen. Dan Halutz.

Israeli forces planned to remove the settlers' belongings, destroy their houses and then withdraw from Gaza.

Authorities used force at times on August 23, to clear the two remaining West Bank settlements—Homesh and Sanur.

What Bush said about Sharon's Disengagement Plan

Yaron Deckel, of Israeli Television Channel 1, asked President Bush the following question on August 11, 2005, in Crawford, Texas:

Deckel: As a believer, Mr. President, what do you say to Jewish believers who think that God sent them to settle in the biblical Israel and they will not obey any decision of elected government?

President Bush: Well, you know, there are admonitions in the Bible that do talk about the role of government relative to man. And Israel is a democracy and democracies are able to express the will of the people. The Prime Minister is expressing what he thinks is in the best interests of Israel and the people will decide, ultimately, whether or not that decision makes sense.

On August 22, 2005, in a speech to the Veterans of Foreign Wars at a National Convention at the Salt Palace Convention Center, Salt Lake City, Utah, President Bush stated:

In the heart of the Middle East, a hopeful story is unfolding. After decades of shattered promises and stolen lives, peace is within reach in the Holy Land. The Palestinian people have expressed their desire for sovereignty and peace in free and fair elections. President Abbas has rejected violence and taken steps toward democratic reform. This past week, Prime Minister Sharon and the Israeli people took a courageous and painful step by beginning to remove settlements in Gaza and parts of the northern West Bank. The Israeli disengagement is a historic step that reflects the bold leadership of Prime Minister Sharon.

Both Israelis and Palestinians have elected governments committed to peace and progress, and the way forward is clear. We're working for a return to the Road Map.

We'll continue working for the day when the map of the Middle East shows two democratic states, Israel and Palestine, living side-by-side in peace and security.

Source: http://www.whitehouse.gov/news/releases/2005/08/print/20050822-1.html

President Bush spoke with White House Press Pool, Tamarack Resort, Donnelly, Idaho, August 23, 2005

President Bush: First of all, I want to congratulate Prime Minister Sharon for having made a very tough decision. As I said in my remarks yesterday in Salt Lake City, the Prime Minister made a courageous decision to withdraw from the Gaza. We have got Jim Wolfensohn; the former head of the World Bank, on the ground, helping President Abbas develop a government that responds to the will of the folks in Gaza. In other words, this is step one in the development of a democracy.

And so to answer your question, what must take place next is the establishment of a working government in Gaza, a government that responds to the people. President Abbas has made a commitment to fight off the violence, because he understands a democracy can't exist with terrorist groups trying to take the law into their own hands.

Along these lines, we've also got General Ward on the ground, helping the Palestinians consolidate their security forces. It turns out that the post-Arafat regime is one of different factions and different security forces that were really in place to kind of maintain his power, but not necessarily to protect the overall security of the Palestinian people. It's in their interest to consolidate the security forces, so that the government has a vehicle and a group of folks by which to help enforce order.

You asked about the Road Map. Of course you want to get back to the Road Map. But I understand that in order for this process to go forward, there must be confidence—confidence that the Palestinian people will have in their own government to perform, confidence with the Israelis that they'll see a peaceful state emerging. And therefore it's very important for the world to stay focused on Gaza, and helping Gaza—helping the Gaza economy get going, helping rebuild the settlements for Gaza—for the people of Gaza.

This is a very hopeful period. Again, I applaud Prime Minister Sharon for making a decision that has really changed the dynamics on the ground, and has really provided hope for the Palestinian people. My vision, my hope, is that one day we'll see two states—two democratic states—living side-by-side in peace.

(www.whitehouse.gov/news/releases/2005/08/20050823.html)

Katrina

On August 23 the same afternoon the final Jews were driven from their homes in Northern Samaria, a tropical depression began to form near the Bahamas. By 11 a.m. on August 24, the newly formed tropical depression 12* was upgraded to Tropical Storm Katrina; and by 5 p.m. on August 25, Katrina became a hurricane. On Friday, August 26, Hurricane Katrina hit Southeast Florida. By August 29, Katrina had become a fierce and enormous Category 3 hurricane that pummeled Louisiana, Mississippi and Alabama—devastating the city of New Orleans. Katrina became the largest disaster in U.S. history.

The storm forced 1 million people from their homes. Over 225,000 homes in Louisiana, Mississippi and Alabama were completely destroyed. As of December 2005, 473,000 people were without work due to the devastation of Hurricane Katrina.

From August 17-23, 2005 and beyond, Israel experienced one of the most excruciating moments in their nation's history. From August 29 forward, the U.S. experienced the largest most devastating disaster in its history.

[*Note: during each season, each tropical depression is numbered, and if it develops into a tropical storm, it is named.]

World Reacts to Katrina's Devastation

The reaction by world leaders spoke volumes about the shock, awe and surprise over the size and magnitude of the devastation of Hurricane Katrina.

The excerpts below are quoted from the Fox News article, *"World Reacts to Katrina's Devastation."*

From papal prayers to telegrams from China, the world reacted with an outpouring of compassion Wednesday, August 31, for the victims of Hurricane Katrina in messages tinged by shock that a disaster of this scale could occur in the United States.

Islamic extremists rejoiced in America's misfortune, giving the storm a military rank and declaring in Internet chatter that "Private" Katrina had joined the global jihad, or holy war. With "God's help," they declared, oil prices would hit $100 a barrel this year.

Venezuela's government, which has had tense relations with Washington, offered humanitarian aid and fuel if requested.

The storm was seen as an equalizer—proof that any country, weak or strong, can be victimized by a natural disaster. Images of flood-ravaged New Orleans earned particular sympathy in central Europe, where dozens died in raging floodwaters only days ago.

"Nature proved that no matter how rich and economically developed you are, you can't fight it," says Danut Afasei, a local official in Romania's Harghita county, where flooding killed 13 people last week.

Throughout Europe, concerned citizens lamented the loss of life and the damage caused to New Orleans, often described as one of North America's most "European" cities.

Pope Benedict XVI said he was praying for victims of the "tragic" hurricane, while China's President Hu Jintao expressed his "belief that the American people will definitely overcome the natural disaster and rebuild their beautiful homeland."

Britain's Queen Elizabeth II also sent a message to Bush saying she was "deeply shocked and saddened" at the devastation caused by the hurricane and expressed her condolences, "especially to the families of those who have lost their loved ones, to the injured and to all who have been affected by this terrible disaster."

Many Parallels between Gaza, Samaria and Katrina

Israel's Gaza and northern Samaria settlements were under Israeli military occupation during the time of the evacuation. So was New Orleans.

New Orleans needed military help to restore order. As in a war zone, military bases were established in the city divided into sectors, while the U.S. Navy moved warships up the Mississippi for helicopter operations.

On August 17, Israeli Prime Minister Ariel Sharon authorized the mandatory evacuation of residents refusing to evacuate Gaza.

On September 7, an hour after New Orleans Mayor Ray Nagin ordered, by force if necessary, mandatory evacuation of the crippled city, soldiers began coaxing some of Katrina's holdouts from their homes due to fire or disease risks.

"We have thousands of people who want to voluntarily evacuate at this time," Police Chief Eddie Compass said, adding that once they all were out, "we'll concentrate our forces on mandatory evacuation."

Israeli settlers stated that the Gaza and Samaria evictions will go down as the worst abandonment of Jews in history and the largest forced evacuation in Israel's modern history.

Katrina produced the largest mass migration and evacuation in U.S. history as hundreds of thousands of people were forced from their homes. The media and the Democrats say the White House abandoned black residents of New Orleans by not getting them help fast enough.

Aaron Brousard, the president of Louisiana's Jefferson Parish, said on NBC's "Meet the Press" that the response to Katrina will go down as one of the worst abandonment's of Americans on American soil ever in U.S. history.

Nine thousand Israelis were evicted by their government. Shortly thereafter, one million Americans were evicted by Hurricane Katrina.

Israeli security teams went from home to home to evict Israelis. So also teams of soldiers went from home to home in New Orleans evicting people.

Buses took Israelis out of Gaza and northern Samaria to their temporary homes, as did buses take New Orleans residents to their temporary homes in Texas and other southern states.

Israel has an evacuee problem with people spread throughout Israel in hotels, lodged in makeshift homes, and living in tents. Texas and other U.S. states absorbed record numbers of Katrina evacuees who were also lodged in hotels, makeshift homes, apartments, shelters and tents.

President Bush's home state of Texas had more than 250,000 evacuees. Houston's Astrodome was filled with 33,000 people. There were 150,000 refugees in Houston hotels, 20 Red Cross facilities and 20 faith-based shelters.

While 2,700 homes were demolished in Gaza and 300 homes in northern Samaria, 225,000 homes were demolished in the Southern U.S., with many more severely damaged.

Businesses were forcefully abandoned in Gaza. Many businesses were completely destroyed and abandoned in Louisiana and other Gulf Coast cities.

Russell Knocke, the Homeland Security spokesman, said up to 60,000 federal employees were sent to the Gulf Coast to respond to Katrina.

Hurricane Katrina produced 90 million tons of solid waste, and 530 inoperable sewage treatment plants.

Sharon saw the largest eviction of Jews in Israel's history. Bush continues to oversee the largest disaster and displacement of people in U.S. history.

Yet despite the enormous influx of government assistance from across the U.S.—National Guard, reservists, Army, Marines, Coast Guard, airmen, firefighters from Los Angeles, and even Texas game wardens in boats—the logistics of evacuating the remaining residents from the flooded suburbs, and collecting possibly thousands of bodies, presented enormous challenges.

Gush Katif was a very important agricultural area for Israel and its exports. The New Orleans' port exported much of the Midwest's agricultural production.

Meanwhile, Senate Majority Leader Bill Frist told NBC's "Meet the Press" on January 29, 2006, that the federal government will spend "well over $100 billion" to help rebuild the Gulf Coast. The government has so far committed $112.8 billion.

Catastrophe #56
Hurricane Rita: September 17-24, 2005
Estimated Cost Insurers: $6.4 billion

Hurricane Rita developed during a very busy week of focused attention on Israel's land and the peace process.

On September 17, the U.S. State Department told Israeli Prime Minister Ariel Sharon not to interfere with Gaza elections even if Hamas was involved.

On September 20, the Quartet (U.S., EU, UN and Russia) had a Road Map meeting in New York City. They congratulated Sharon for implementing his disengagement plan, and called on Israel and the Palestinians to continue forward.

On September 21, Bush praised Sharon at the Republican Jewish Coalition's 20th Anniversary in Washington, DC.

Within a few hours of his speech, Hurricane Rita became a Category 5 hurricane and the third most intense storm in history. That afternoon Texas Governor Rick Perry called for a mandatory evacuation of Galveston and Houston, which eventually numbered 3 million people.

On September 22, President Bush met with Jordan's King Abdullah at the White House to discuss the peace process.

The Miracle of Rita

Hurricane Rita was a multi-billion-dollar event, but could have been much worse had it hit Galveston and Houston, Texas and not the sparsely populated western Louisiana coast and southeastern Texas coast. Prayers were answered.

Rita made landfall between Sabine Pass and Johnson's Bayou on the Louisiana coast at 2:30 CST, September 24, as a Category 3 hurricane. At landfall, Rita had maximum sustained winds of 120 mph.

Hurricane Rita's track took its strongest winds over the sparsely populated western Louisiana coast, resulting in relatively low insured losses for a storm of its intensity and size. The cities of Beaumont and Port Arthur, Texas, and Lake Charles, Louisiana, were hit the hardest.

Hurricane Rita caused more damage to oilrigs than any other storm in history and forced companies to delay drilling for oil in the U.S. and as far away as the Middle East, initial damage assessments show. Kyle Beatty, meteorologist for Risk Management Solutions (RMS), said,

Hurricane Rita is comparable to last year's Charley in that its damage is spread across a low-population-density region of agricultural and fishing-related industries. There is also notable damage to offshore platforms, refineries and by-products industries of petroleum manufacturing.

Catastrophe #57
Hurricane Wilma: October 17-24, 2005
Estimated Cost Insurers: $10.8 billion

Once again, while the Bush Administration was putting pressure on Israel to comply with the Quartet's Road Map mandates, the United States experienced another record-setting disaster in Hurricane Wilma.

Summary of Political Activity Pertaining to Israel

On Friday, October 14, Middle East Newsline reported that Israeli Prime Minister Sharon was weighing a unilateral pullout from 90 percent of the West Bank and had shared that with President Bush.

On Saturday afternoon, October 15, tropical depression 24 formed in the Western Caribbean Sea.

James Wolfensohn, the Quartet's Special Envoy for Disengagement, sent a letter dated October 16 to United Nations Secretary General Kofi Annan and the foreign ministries of Britain, Russia and the United States, stating:

> The Government of Israel, with its important security concerns, is loath to relinquish control, almost acting as though there has been no withdrawal, delaying making difficult decisions and preferring to take difficult matters back into slow-moving subcommittees.

Accompanying the October 16 letter was a report written on Monday, October 17, regarding Wolfensohn's latest visit to Israel, from October 7-12. The introduction stated:

> The Special Envoy was disappointed that none of the key movement issues has been resolved. Without a dramatic improvement in Palestinian movement and access, within appropriate security arrangements for Israel, the economic revival essential to a resolution of the conflict will not be possible.

On October 18, President Bush met with Wolfensohn at the White House to discuss his report.

On October 19, an Air Force reconnaissance plane reported Wilma at 884 Mb—the lowest minimum pressure ever measured in a hurricane in the Atlantic Basin, making Wilma the most intense hurricane in Atlantic Basin history.

On October 19, Secretary Rice made it clear to Israel that settlement construction between Jerusalem and Maali Adumim settlement contradicts the American policy. In a speech before the Senate Foreign Relations Committee, Rice said that the U.S. is concerned about settlement construction and expansion around Jerusalem, adding that the U.S. administration reduced its financial support for Israel as a result of the continuous settlement activities.

On October 19, Secretary met with Palestinian President Mahmoud Abbas in Washington, DC.

On October 20, when President Bush was meeting President Abbas at the White House to discuss the Israeli-Palestinian peace process, Wilma was a Category 5 hurricane.

Below are excerpts from press reports of statements made by Presidents Bush and Abbas in the Rose Garden following their meeting at the White House.

PRESIDENT BUSH: President Abbas is a man devoted to peace and to his people's aspirations for a state of their own. Today the Palestinian people are closer to realizing those aspirations. It's a really interesting period of history, I think. I was just commenting to the President when we were in the Oval Office how much things have changed in the Holy Land. After all, he got elected in January; there were successful Palestinian municipal elections, and then we witnessed the completion of Israel's disengagement from Gaza and parts of the West Bank.

It's been an eventful year. And I say it's an eventful year because the ultimate objective is there—for there to be two states, living side-by-side in peace; two democracies living side-by-side in peace. And I believe that's where we're headed. Israel's withdrawal from Gaza and parts of West Bank was a bold decision, with historic significance. President Abbas and the Palestinian Authority contributed to the success of the withdrawal in significant ways.

Mr. President, thank you.

As I have stated in the past, achieving peace demands action from all parties. Israel must continue to work with Palestinian leaders to help improve the daily lives of Palestinians. At the same time, Israel should not undertake any activity that contravenes its Road Map obligations, or prejudices the final status negotiations with regard to Gaza, the West Bank, and Jerusalem. This means that Israel must remove unauthorized posts and stop settlement expansion. It also means that the barrier now being built to protect Israelis from terrorist attacks must be a security barrier, rather than a political barrier. Israeli leaders must take into account the impact this security barrier has on Palestinians not engaged in terrorist activities.

This is a time of great possibility in the Middle East. And the people of the region are counting on their leaders to seize the opportunities for peace and progress. This work isn't going to be easy, but the path forward is clear. I want to thank President Abbas for his hard work. I appreciate your service, Mr. President. I assured him that the United States will use our influence to help realize a shared vision of two democratic states, Israel and Palestine, living side-by-side in peace and security.

That afternoon, October 20, Florida Governor Jeb Bush called for a mandatory evacuation of the Florida Keys.

On the night of October 23, Wilma strengthened and made landfall at 6:30 a.m., October 24, at Cape Romano, as a Category 3 hurricane with maximum sustained winds of 125 mph. She pummeled both Southwestern and Southeastern Florida.

Florida Power & Light, the state's biggest utility, said Wilma affected more of its 4.3 million customers than any other disaster in the company's history. By Friday, October 28, the utility said it had returned power to roughly 45 percent of the more than 6 million people who lost it, but said restoration of service for all of the remaining 3.6 million people might take until Thanksgiving week.

Wilma was the third costliest hurricane in U.S. history, after Katrina and Andrew.

Hurricane Insurance Losses $57.6 Billion for Katrina, Rita & Wilma — Largest on Record

On December 27, 2005, Advisen Ltd. estimated worldwide insurance and reinsurance losses related to the three major hurricanes that hit the U.S. would amount to $57.6 billion, making the cumulative catastrophe losses the largest on record.

By predicting unreported losses from State Farm Mutual Automobile Insurance Co., the largest personal lines insurer, as well as unreported and unfilled losses elsewhere, Advisen projects pre-tax insured losses per hurricane to be $40.4 billion for Katrina, $6.4 billion for Rita and $10.8 billion for Wilma.

The losses amount to more than twice the annual total for other U.S. natural disasters and one-and-a-half times the losses from the 2001 terrorist attacks in New York and Washington.

Several variables could prompt Advisen's estimates to increase dramatically, the company warned. Flood losses could elevate Advisen's estimates by billions of dollars if lawsuits to force insurers to cover flood damage related to Hurricane Katrina are successful.

Summary of Actions and Coinciding Catastrophes or Events During Presidency of George W. Bush (2005)

Date	Action	Date	Catastrophe
July 6-8, 2005	G-8 Heads of State – from UK, U.S., EU, France, Germany, Brazil, Italy, Russia & Canada – met in Scotland with PM Tony Blair leading as president; decided to give $3 billion to Palestinian Authority.	July 4-10, 2005	Hurricane Dennis: hit Cuba first, then southern coast of U.S., beginning in Florida and traveling up to Illinois; $1-2.5 billion
		July 7	London Terrorist Bombings (4 on same day G-8 planned to announce $3 billion gift to PA); 52 dead, over 700 injured.
August 15, 2005	• 63,000 Israeli soldiers and police delivered eviction notices to Israeli settlers living in Gaza and Northern Samaria.	August 23-29, 2005	Hurricane Katrina: largest disaster in U.S. history affected Louisiana, Mississippi & Alabama; devastated New Orleans; forced 1 million people from their homes; 225,000 homes destroyed; 473,000 people without work; estimated cost to insurers: $40.4 billion; U.S. Government will spend $112-200 billion.
August 15-23	• With tears and multiple protests, 9,000 Israeli settlers completely evacuated 25 communities; most left voluntarily, but many were forcibly removed by Israeli troops; 3,000 homes were destroyed.		
August 17	• Israeli PM Ariel Sharon authorized mandatory evacuation of residents refusing to leave Gaza.		
August 17	• U.S. Secretary of State Condoleeza Rice said evacuation "cannot be Gaza only."		
August 19	• In Gaza, U.S. Asst. Sec. of State David Welch said Gaza pullout would re-energize "Road Map" peace plan.		
August 22	• Pres. Bush said, "We'll continue working for the day when the map of the Middle East shows two democratic states, Israel and Palestine, living side-by-side in peace and security."		
August 22	• Pres. Bush said, "My vision, my hope, is that one day we'll see two states—two democratic states—living side-by-side in peace."		

Date	Action	Date	Catastrophe
Sept. 17, 2005 *Sept. 20* *Sept. 22*	• U.S. State Department told Israeli PM Sharon not to interfere in Gaza election, even if Hamas was involved. • Quartet (U.S., EU, UN & Russia) met in NYC, congratulated Sharon on implementing his disengagement plan. • Pres. Bush met with Jordan's King Abdullah at White House to discuss peace process.	*Sept. 17-24, 2005*	**Hurricane Rita:** Became Category 5 storm day after Quartet meeting with Sharon, and hours after Bush's speech praising Sharon; 3 million evacuated from Galveston and Houston, Texas area; $6.4 billion.
October 14, 2005 *Oct. 17* *Oct. 18* *Oct. 19* *Oct. 19* *Oct. 20*	• Israeli PM Sharon was considering unilateral pullout from 90% of West Bank; shared idea with Pres. Bush. • Quartet Special Envoy James Wolfensohn sent a letter and report to UN Secretary General Kofi Annan & the U.S., UK and Russian foreign ministries criticized Israel for failing to relinquishing control of evacuated areas. • Pres. Bush met with Wolfensohn at White House to discuss report. • Sec. Rice told Israel that continued settlement construction contradicts U.S. policy; and testified before the U.S. Senate Foreign Relations Committee that the U.S. reduced its financial support to Israel because of settlement construction/activities. • In DC, Sec. Rice met with Palestinian Pres. Mahmoud Abbas. • Pres. Bush met with Abbas at White House, and in Rose Garden press conference after reaffirmed his support for a Palestinian state, and called on Israel to remove "unauthorized posts and stop settlement expansion," and not do anything contrary to Road Map.	*October 15, 2005* *October 17-24* *Oct. 20* *Oct. 24*	The 24th tropical depression formed in the Western Caribbean Sea, which developed into a hurricane within 2 days. **Hurricane Wilma:** Category 5 (developed to worst level day Bush met with Abbas at White House); 3rd costliest in U.S. history; $10.8 billion. • Florida Governor Jeb Bush (Pres. Bush's brother) called for mandatory evacuation of Florida Keys. • Wilma hit Southwestern and Southeastern Florida; 6 million people lose electric power to homes and businesses.

Cumulative insurance losses for Katrina, Rita and Wilma hurricanes
estimated to be $57.6 billion
– The largest catastrophe losses on record.

CHAPTER 8

Major U.S. Catastrophes and Events in Perspective

The following information summarizes the record-setting catastrophes or events that occurred during the 1990s and through 2005 when Presidents George H. W. Bush, Bill Clinton, George W. Bush or one of their top staff were applying pressure on Israel to give up her covenant land.

The major catastrophes or events that began with the Madrid Peace Conference of October 30, 1991, and went to October 24, 2005, include:

- The ten costliest insurance events in U.S. history
- The twelve costliest hurricanes in U.S. History
- Three of the four largest tornado swarms in U.S. history
- Thirty of 53 billion dollar U.S. weather disasters, 1991 to 2005 (NOAA)

The odds of these catastrophes or events occurring at the same time as the United States was pressuring Israel to divide her land are astronomical. These are not mere coincidences. When the land of Israel is at risk, so is the land of the nation promoting the "land for peace" process.

Top Ten Catastrophic Losses Involving Insured Property

1. *Hurricane Katrina – August 2005.* Preliminary estimates of over $150 billion in damages/costs, making this the most expensive natural disaster in U.S. history. (Israel completes Gaza and Northern Samaria settlement evacuations; Bush and Rice congratulate Sharon.)

2. *Terrorist Attack – September 11, 2001*. $29.7 billion. (President George W. Bush and Crown Prince Abdullah of Saudi Arabia were completing work on Bush's Middle East plan on September 10, 2001. The Bush Israeli-Palestinian peace plan was to be presented to the UN General Assembly by Secretary of State Colin Powell on September 24, 2001.)

3. *Hurricane Andrew – August 23-24, 1992.* $26.5 billion damages/costs. (The Madrid "land for peace" meeting convened in Washington, DC, on August 24.)

4. *Northridge, California Earthquake – January 17, 1994.* $19.2 billion. (President Clinton and Syria's Hafez Assad met in Geneva, Switzerland. They called on Israel to leave the Golan Heights and agree to peace talks.)

5. *Hurricane Charley – August 2004.* Estimated $15 billion. (Bush administration applied major pressure on Israel to evacuate unauthorized settlements.)

6. *Hurricane Wilma – October 2005.* Estimate of $14.4 billion in damages/costs; estimated 35 deaths. (The U.S. froze Israel's financial aide over settlement construction. Bush hosted Mahmoud Abbas at White House.)

7. *Hurricane Ivan – September 2004.* Estimate of $14.2 billion in damages/costs. (Bush administration continued pressure on Israel.)

8. *Hurricane Rita – September 2005.* Estimate of $9.4 billion in damages/costs. (Bush honored Israeli Prime Minister Ariel Sharon because of the Gaza and Northern Samaria evacuations. Bush hosted Jordan's King Abdullah II at the White House.)

9. *Hurricane Frances – September 2004.* Estimate of $8.9 billion in damages/costs; at least 48 deaths. (Prime Minister Sharon responded to Bush administration pressure by accelerating Gaza evacuations; Frances shared headlines with Bush's convention speech.)

10. *Hurricane Hugo – September 1989.* Estimate of $7.0 billion in damages/costs; 86 deaths. (Rabin met with Cheney, Baker and Scowcroft.)

Billion-Dollar Hurricanes

Eleven of the twelve costliest hurricanes in U.S. history have a direct tie-in to U.S.-Israeli peace efforts.

1. *Hurricane Katrina – August 2005.* Category 3 hurricane initially impacted the U.S. as a Category 1 near Miami, Florida. Then as a strong Category 3, it hit along the eastern Louisiana and western Mississippi coastlines, resulting in severe storm surge damage (maximum surge probably exceeded 25 feet) along the Louisiana-Mississippi-Alabama coasts. Also there was wind damage and the levee system failed in parts of New Orleans. High winds and some flooding occurred in the states of Alabama, Mississippi, Florida, Tennessee, Kentucky, Indiana, Ohio, and Georgia. Preliminary estimates exceed $80 billion in damages/costs, making this the most expensive natural disaster in U.S. history.

There were over 1300 deaths—the highest U.S. total since the major hurricane that hit southern Florida in 1928. **(Israel completed Gaza and Northern Samaria settlement evacuations. Bush and Rice congratulated Sharon.)**

2. *Hurricane Andrew - August 1992.* Category 5 hurricane hit Florida and Louisiana with high winds that damaged or destroyed over 125,000 homes. Approximately $26.5 billion in damages/costs; 61 deaths. **(Sixth round of Madrid conference talks began in Washington, DC.)**

3. *Hurricane Charley – August 2004.* Category 4 hurricane made landfall in southwest Florida, resulting in major wind and some storm surge damage, along with some damage in South Carolina and North Carolina. Estimate of $15 billion in damages/costs; at least 34 deaths. **(Bush administration applied major pressure on Israel to evacuate unauthorized settlements.)**

4. *Hurricane Wilma - October 2005.* Category 3 hurricane hit southwest Florida bringing strong damaging winds and major flooding across southeastern Florida. Prior to landfall, Wilma, as a Category 5, recorded the lowest pressure (882 mb) ever recorded in the Atlantic basin. Preliminary estimates of over $14.4 billion in damages/costs; estimated 35 deaths. **(U.S. froze Israel's financial aide over settlement construction. Bush hosted Abbas at White House.)**

5. *Hurricane Ivan - September 2004.* Category 3 hurricane made landfall on Gulf coast of Alabama, with significant wind, storm surge, and flooding damage on the coasts of Alabama and the Florida panhandle. May states experienced wind and flood damage: Georgia, South Carolina, North Carolina, Virginia, Louisiana, Mississippi, West Virginia, Maryland, Tennessee, Kentucky, Ohio, Delaware, New Jersey, Pennsylvania, and New York. Estimates of over $14.2 billion in damages/costs; at least 57 deaths. **(Bush administration continued pressure on Israel.)**

6. *Hurricane Rita – September 2005.* Category 3 hurricane hit Texas-Louisiana border coastal region, creating significant storm surge and wind damage along the coast, and some inland flooding in the Florida panhandle, Mississippi, Louisiana, Arkansas, and Texas. Prior to landfall, Rita reached the third lowest pressure (897 mb) ever recorded in the Atlantic basin. Preliminary estimates of damages/costs exceed $9.4 billion; 119 deaths reported – most being indirect (many related to evacuations). **(Bush honored Sharon. Bush hosted Jordan's King Abdullah II at the White House.)**

7. *Hurricane Frances – September 2004.* Category 2 hurricane made landfall in east-central Florida, causing significant wind, storm surge, and flooding damage. Considerable flood damage occurred in Georgia, South Carolina, North Carolina, and New York due to 5-15 inch rains. Estimated damages/costs were $8.9 billion; at least 48 deaths. **(Sharon responded to Bush administration**

pressure by accelerating Gaza evacuations; Frances shared headlines with President Bush's convention speech.)

8. *Hurricane Hugo - September 1989.* Category 4 hurricane devastated South and North Carolina with ~ 20-foot storm surge and severe wind damage after hitting Puerto Rico and the U.S. Virgin Islands. Damage costs were $7.0 billion; 86 people died (57 on U.S. mainland, 29 in U.S. islands). **(Rabin meets with Cheney, Baker and Scowcroft.)**

9. *Hurricane Jeanne - September 2004.* Category 3 hurricane made landfall in east-central Florida causing considerable wind, storm surge, and flooding damage in Florida, with some flood damage also in the states of Georgia, South Carolina, North Carolina, Virginia, Maryland, Delaware, New Jersey, Pennsylvania, and New York. Puerto Rico was affected. Estimated damage/costs exceeded $6.9 billion; at least 28 died. **(President Bush called on Israel to freeze settlements and evacuate the disputed part of her land.)**

10. *Hurricane Floyd - September 1999.* Large category 2 hurricane made landfall in eastern North Carolina, brining 10-20 inch rains in 2 days, with severe flooding. Flooding occurred in South Carolina, Virginia, Maryland, Pennsylvania, New York, New Jersey, Delaware, Rhode Island, Connecticut, Massachusetts, New Hampshire, and Vermont. Estimated damage/costs were $6.0 billion; 77 deaths. **(Israel met with the Palestinians over the borders of a future state, the dividing of Jerusalem, and settlements in the West Bank. The final borders would be submitted by February 15, 2000.)**

11. *Tropical Storm Allison - June 2001.* The persistent remnants of Tropical Storm Allison produced rainfall amounts of 30-40 inches in portions of coastal Texas and Louisiana, causing severe flooding especially in the Houston area; then it moved slowly northeastward. Fatalities and significant damage were reported in Texas, Louisiana, Mississippi, Florida, Virginia, and Pennsylvania. Estimated damages/costs were approximately $5.0 billion; at least 43 people died. **(CIA Director George Tenet met with Israelis and Palestinians over a cease-fire agreement.)**

12. *Hurricane Isabel - September 2003.* Category 2 hurricane made landfall in eastern North Carolina, causing considerable storm surge damage along the coasts of North Carolina, Virginia, and Maryland, with wind damage and some flooding due to 4-12 inch rains in these states and Delaware, West Virginia, New Jersey, New York, and Pennsylvania. Estimated damages/costs were approximately $5 billion; at least 55 died. **(President Bush hosted Jordan's King Abdullah II at Camp David to discuss the peace process.)**

Costliest Hurricanes in the United States (mainland)[1]

Rank	Hurricane	Location	Year	Category[2]	Damage (in billions)
1	Katrina	Louisiana / Mississippi	2005	4	$80.0[3]
2	Andrew	Florida / Louisiana	1992	5	$26.5
3	Charley	Florida	2004	4	$15.0
4	Wilma	Florida	2005	3	$14.4[3]
5	Ivan	Alabama / Florida	2004	3	$14.2
6	Rita	Texas / Louisiana	2005	3	$9.4[3]
7	Frances	Florida	2004	2	$8.9
8	Hugo	South Carolina	1989	4	$7.0
9	Jeanne	Florida	2004	3	$6.9
10*	Floyd	North Carolina ++	1999	2	$6.0
11	Allison	Texas	2001	TS[4]	$5.0

NOTE: Damages are listed in U.S. dollars and are not adjusted for inflation.
1. For the period from 1900 to 2005.
2. Saffir-Simpson Hurricane scale: Category 1 = weak; Category 5 = devastating.
3. Estimated.
4. Tropical storm intensity.
Source: National Oceanic and Atmospheric Administration (NOAA).
    http://www.infoplease.com/ipa/A0778285.html
* added to NOAA table

Largest Tornado Outbreaks in U.S. History

Three out of the four largest tornado outbreaks (swarms) in U.S. history coincided with meetings about Israel's land that involved President Bill Clinton, President George W. Bush, or one of their top officials.

Super storm cells with enormous size and power spawned the following major record-breaking tornadoes.

Tornado Outbreak #1: *Eighty-Five (85) Tornadoes*—May 3, 1999
Major tornado swarm with 316-mph record wind speed.

This powerful super-tornado outbreak occurred on the day that PLO Chairman Arafat was scheduled to declare a Palestinian state with Jerusalem as the capital. It was the most powerful tornado storm system ever to hit the U.S. As it swept across Oklahoma and Kansas, the winds were clocked at 316 mph— the fastest wind speed ever recorded on earth. Until then it was not thought that such a wind speed was possible. Over 70 tornadoes touched down in north Texas, central Oklahoma, and southern Kansas, causing $1.2 billion in damages.

Arafat's declaration was postponed from May 3 until December 1999 at the request of President Clinton. The Clinton letter to Arafat encouraged him in his "aspirations for his own land." Clinton also wrote that the Palestinians have a right to "determine their own future on their own land" and that they deserve to "live free, today, tomorrow, and forever."

Tornado Outbreak #2: *Eighty Eight Tornadoes*—Nov. 10-11, 2002

On the weekend of November 10-11, 2002, we heard about and observed enormous storms and tornadoes that hit 13 U.S. states. MSNBC reported that 35 people in five states were killed and 200 others injured. In Tennessee alone, 100 homes were destroyed and 1,000 damaged. The Associated Press reported there were 88 tornadoes. There were also major thunderstorms reported from the Gulf Coast to the Great Lakes.

On Sunday, November 10, 2002, U.S. Deputy Assistant Secretary of State David Satterfield was on his way to Israel to apply pressure on Israel to complete their work and comments on the Quartet's "Road Map" to peace. He had numerous meetings on Monday and Tuesday with Israeli officials. He also met on Sunday with Palestinian officials.

Tornado Outbreak #3: *Four-Hundred-Twelve (412) Tornadoes*
   —May 1-11, 2003

The 412 tornadoes during the first 11 days of May 2003 were the most since NOAA began recordkeeping in 1950. The previous record for the first ten days of May was 177 tornadoes, set in 1999. More than 300 counties in 19 states suffered losses; and more than 40 deaths were blamed on the storms. Boston-based AIR Worldwide, which uses a computer-modeling program to estimate insured losses from catastrophes, put the damages at $2.2 billion.

The Quartet's Road Map was delivered to Israeli and Palestinian officials on April 30, 2003.

On May 3, Secretary Powell told Syrian President Bashar Assad that the U.S. commitment to Middle East peace "would include Syria and Lebanon and would include the Golan Heights," a particularly sensitive issue for Syria.

On Sunday, May 4, Powell announced he would visit Israel on May 10, for talks about implementing the Road Map peace plan.

On May 5, U.S. Middle East Envoy William Burns met with Palestinian Prime Minister Abbas in Ramallah. He stated that the Palestinians must carry out a decisive fight against terrorism and that the Israelis must halt settlement activity. Burns also bashed fundamental Christians and Orthodox Jews for opposing the Road Map in a meeting with Peace Now activists in Jerusalem.

Powell was in Israel on May 10-11, 2003, to meet with Israeli and Palestinian officials, including Sharon and Abbas, to push the Road Map.

1980-2005 Billion Dollar U.S. Weather Disasters
*(Damage Amounts in Billions of Dollars and
Costs Normalized to 2002 Dollars Using GNP Inflation / Wealth Index)*

Year	Disaster 1	Disaster 2	Disaster 3	Disaster 4
1980	*Drought /* *Heat Wave* $48.4 billion ~ 10,000 Deaths			
1983	*Hurricane Alicia* $5.9 billion 21 Deaths	Florida Freeze ~ $4.0 billion No Deaths	Gulf Storms/Flood ~ $2.2 billion 50 Deaths	W Storms / Flood ~ $2.2 billion 45 Deaths
1985	Florida Freeze ~ $2.2 billion No Deaths	Hurricane Elena $2.4 billion 4 Deaths	Hurricane Juan $2.8 billion 63 Deaths	
1986	Drought-Heat Wave: $2.3 billion ~ 100 Deaths			
1988	*Drought /* *Heat Wave* $61.6 billion ~ 7,500 Deaths			
1989	*Hurricane Hugo* > $13.9 billion 86 Deaths	N Plains Drought > $1.5 billion No Deaths		
1990	S Plains Flooding > $1.4 billion 13 Deaths			
1991	Hurricane Bob $2.1 billion 18 Deaths	Calif. Firestorm ~ $3.5 billion 25 Deaths		
1992	**Hurricane Andrew** $35.6 billion 61 Deaths	Hurricane Iniki ~ $2.4 billion 7 Deaths	Nor'easter $2.0 billion 19 Deaths	
1993	*E Storm / Blizzard* $7.0 billion ~ 270 Deaths	SE Drought / Heat Wave ~ $1.3 billion > 16 Deaths	<u>Midwest Flooding</u> ~ $26.7 billion 48 Deaths	Calif. Wildfires ~ $1.3 billion 4 Deaths
1994	SE Ice Storm ~ $3.7 billion 9 Deaths	Tropical Storm Alberto ~ $1.2 billion 32 Deaths	Texas Flooding ~ $1.2 billion 19 Deaths	W Fire Season ~ $1.2 billion No Deaths
1995	Calif. Flooding > $3.6 billion 27 Deaths	*SE/SW Severe Wx* $6.8 billion 32 Deaths	Hurricane Marilyn e $2.5 billion 13 Deaths	Hurricane Opal > $3.6 billion 27 Deaths
1996	Blizzard / Flooding ~ $3.5 billion 187 Deaths	Pacific NW Flooding ~ $1.2 billion 9 Deaths	*S Plains Drought* ~ $6.0 billion No Deaths	Hurricane Fran > $5.8 billion 37 Deaths

Year	Disaster 1	Disaster 2	Disaster 3	Disaster 4
1997	Midwest Flood / Tornadoes e $1.1 billion 67 Deaths	Plains Flooding ~ $4.1 billion 11 Deaths	W Coast Flooding ~ $3.4 billion 36 Deaths	
1998	New England Ice Storm > $1.5 billion 16 Deaths	SE Severe Wx > $1.1 billion 132 Deaths	Minnesota Severe Storms / Hail > $1.7 billion 1 Death	*S Drought / Heat Wave* $8.3 billion > 200 Deaths
1998 cont.	Hurricane Bonnie ~ $1.1 billion 3 Deaths	*Hurricane Georges* e $6.5 billion 16 Deaths	Texas Flooding ~ $1.1 billion 31 Deaths	New England Ice
1999	Arizona-Tennessee Tornadoes ~ $1.4 billion 17 Deaths	Oklahoma-Kansas Tornadoes > $1.7 billion 55 Deaths	E Drought / Heat Wave > $1.1 billion e 502 Deaths	*Hurricane Floyd* e $6.5 billion 77 Deaths
2000	Drought-Heat Wave e > $4.2 billion ~ 140 Deaths	Western Fires > $2.1 billion No Deaths		
2001	*Tropical Storm Allison* e ~ $5.1 billion > 43 Deaths	Midwest-Ohio Valley Hail / Tornadoes > $1.9 billion > 3 Deaths		
2002	*30-State Drought* e > $10.0 billion No Deaths	Western Fires > $2.0 billion ~ 21 Deaths		
2003	Severe Wx / Hail > $1.6 billion 3 Deaths	Severe Wx / Tornadoes > $3.4 billion 51 Deaths	*Hurricane Isabel* ~ $5.0 billion 55 Deaths	S California Wildfires > $2.5 billion 22 Deaths
2004	*Hurricane Charley* e ~ $15.0 billion 34 Deaths	*Hurricane Frances* e ~ $9.0 billion 48 Deaths	*Hurricane Ivan* e > $14.0 billion 57 Deaths	*Hurricane Jeanne* e > $6.9 billion 28 Deaths
2005	Hurricane Dennis e > $2.0 billion > 12 Deaths	***Hurricane Katrina*** e > $100.0 billion > 1300 Deaths	*Hurricane Rita* e > $8.0 billion 119 Deaths	Midwest Drought e > $1.0 billion No Deaths
2005 cont.	*Hurricane Wilma* e > $10.0 billion 35 Deaths			

Key for levels of disasters by billions of dollars:
    < 5 billion: normal text
    5-20 billion: *italicized* text
    20-30 billion: <u>underlined</u> text
    30-40 billion: **bold** text
    > 40 billion: ***bold italicized*** text

Symbols:
    e = estimated
    < = less than
    ~ = approximately / about
    > = greater than / at least
    cont. = year continued

Source: NOAA's National Climatic Data Center, Asheville, NC 28801-5001.
    www.ncdc.noaa.gov/oa/reports/billionz.html or
    http://www.ncdc.noaa.gov/img/reports/billion/disasterssince1980.pdf

Staggering Catastrophe Losses

Below is the Insurance Service Office's (ISO) annual catastrophic loss estimate for the U.S. since 1996. This is insured losses, and does not count uninsured losses or U.S. FEMA related costs.

The U.S. government approved $12.8 billion in 2004 and $112.8 billion in 2005-2006 for hurricane relief expenditures for Charlie, Frances, Ivan, Jeanne, Dennis, Katrina, Rita and Wilma.

Putting these numbers in perspective, from 1996 to 2000 the total is $33 billion in insured catastrophic losses; from 2001 to 2005 the total is $129.4 billion. The catastrophe totals during President George W. Bush's first five years in office are staggering.

Year	Number of Events	Losses
1996	41	$ 7.4 billion
1997	25	$ 2.6 billion
1998	37	$10.1 billion
1999	27	$ 8.3 billion
2000	24	$ 4.6 billion
2001	20	$26.5 billion
2002	25	$ 5.9 billion
2003	21	$12.9 billion
2004	22	$27.3 billion
2005	24	$56.8 billion

ISO's Property Claim Services (PCS) unit defines a catastrophe as an event within a particular territory that causes $25 million or more in insured property losses and affects a significant number of property and casualty policyholders and insurers.

PCS estimates represent anticipated insured losses on an industry wide basis arising from catastrophes, reflecting the total insurance payment for personal and commercial property items, business interruption and additional living expenses. The estimates exclude loss adjustment expenses.

About ISO: ISO is a leading provider of products and services that help measure, manage and reduce risk. ISO provides data, analytics and decision-support solutions to professionals in many fields, including insurance, finance, real estate, health services, government and human resources. Clients use ISO's databases and services to classify and evaluate a variety of risks and detect potential fraud. In the U.S. and around the world, ISO's services help customers protect people, property and financial assets.

CHAPTER 9

Disruptive Period #1:
September 11, 2001

In August and September of 2001, President George Bush made a conscientious attempt to appease Crown Prince Abdullah of Saudi Arabia, who felt Bush favored Israel. President Bush worked with Prince Bandar–the Saudi ambassador to the U.S., Secretary of State Colin Powell and Daniel Kurtzer, the U.S. ambassador to Israel, to develop a comprehensive peace plan that Abdullah would approve. Powell was to deliver the Bush plan to the UN General Assembly on September 24, 2001. The plan divided Israel and created a Palestinian state, in return for "peace and security" guarantees to Israel. The plan's completion and presentation were disrupted by the September 11, 2001 terror events. For a brief moment, the God of Israel lifted His protection as evil people attacked America. That moment was also the beginning of the costly and complex war on terror.

I do not condemn President Bush for his peace efforts, but there are dire consequences for those who advocate dividing Israel. I have documented 57 major catastrophes and events that occurred when Israel's land was at risk. President Bush and the leaders of the Quartet (the U.S., UN, EU and Russia) are unknowingly on a direct collision course with God over the covenant land of Israel.

In chapters 9 to 11, you will read about the periods of disruption that immediately followed President Bush's call for a Palestinian state, or occurred when he pressured Israel to comply with his peace vision.

Bob Kaiser, Associate Editor of the *Washington Post*, and David Ottoway wrote an extremely insightful article detailing what transpired in the Bush administration seventeen days prior to the September 11 terror events. Excerpts from the three-part article (published on February 10, 11, & 12, 2002) appear on the following pages.

On August 24, 2001, Crown Prince Abdullah ibn Abdulaziz, the leader of Saudi Arabia, was in his palace in Riyadh watching President Bush's televised news conference in Texas when Bush was asked about the Israeli-Palestinian "peace process," which had again been undermined by a new round of violence.

The Israelis will not negotiate under terrorist threats, simple as that," Bush said. "And if the Palestinians are interested in a dialogue, then I strongly urge Mr. Arafat to put 100 percent effort into . . . stopping the terrorist activity. I believe he can do a better job of doing that."

Abdullah interpreted the president's remarks as absolving Israel and blaming Yasser Arafat, the Palestinian leader, for worsening conditions, according to a senior Saudi official. An impulsive, emotional man, Abdullah "just went bananas," the same official said. The crown prince picked up the telephone and called his ambassador to the United States, Prince Bandar bin Sultan, who was watching the same news conference at his palatial residence in Aspen, Colorado.

Abdullah said he wanted Bandar to see Bush at once and deliver a harsh message, the culmination of months of tension between Saudi Arabia and the new Bush administration. The message delivered by Bandar to national security adviser Condoleezza Rice and Secretary of State Colin L. Powell was summarized by a senior Saudi official in these terms:

"We believe there has been a strategic decision by the United States that its national interest in the Middle East is 100-percent based on [Israeli Prime Minister Ariel] Sharon." This was America's right, the message continued, but Saudi Arabia could not accept the decision. "Starting from today, you're from Uruguay, as they say. You [Americans] go your way, I [Saudi Arabia] go my way. From now on, we will protect our national interests, regardless of where America's interests lie in the region."

Bandar was instructed to cut off further discussion between the two countries. The time had come to "get busy rearranging our lives in the Middle East."

Bandar's message was a shock to the Bush administration. As had often happened in the past, these two countries—intimate strangers in many respects—had not really been hearing each other. But over the next two days, the United States went to extraordinary lengths to try to repair the relationship, its closest with any Arab country, finally satisfying the Saudis with a personal letter to Abdullah from the president himself. ...

The Saudi embassy thought there might be a U.S. answer within four or five days, but it came in only 36 hours. "We were told there was an answer ready to go back [to Abdullah] that answers every point," one senior official said. [On August 26, 2001] Bandar picked up the letter and took it personally to the crown prince in Riyadh.

For the Saudis, Bush's letter was "groundbreaking ... Things in it had never been put in writing," one Saudi official said. According to Saudi accounts, Bush outlined an even-handed approach to settling the Arab-Israeli dispute that differed considerably from Sharon's positions on the peace process. One Saudi official said this was a key element: a U.S. vision of a peace settlement that was acceptable to the Saudis, and that differed from any Israeli plan.

Bush's letter, according to Saudi officials, endorsed the idea of a viable Palestinian state on the West Bank and Gaza Strip. He expressed a willingness to begin participating more actively in the peace process. Altogether, said Adel Jubeir, a foreign policy adviser to Abdullah, "where he stood was not that much different from where Clinton stood when he left office."

A particularly important passage in Bush's businesslike, two-page letter, Saudi officials said, was his response to Abdullah's complaints about the ways Israelis were treating Palestinians in the occupied territories. In the message to Bush that was conveyed by Bandar, the crown prince said, according to a Saudi official's account: "I reject this extraordinary, un-American bias whereby the blood of an Israeli child is more expensive and holy than the blood of a Palestinian child. I reject people who say when you kill a Palestinian, it is defense; when a Palestinian kills an Israeli, it's a terrorist act." He also referred to the scene he saw on television of the Israeli soldier putting his boot on the head of a Palestinian woman.

In reply, a Saudi official recounted, Bush said he believes the blood of innocent people is the same — Palestinian, Israeli, Jewish, Christian or Muslim. He rejected the humiliation of individuals, which Abdullah took as a response to his comment about the Israeli soldier's boot. "Suddenly, what came through in that letter was the humane part of George W.," said a senior Saudi official.

It is impossible to say what might have happened if Bush had not so quickly mollified the crown prince at the end of August. According to well-placed sources, the Saudis had conveyed to the U.S. their intention to convene an emergency summit meeting of Arab leaders to offer full support to the Palestinians. They alluded to the possibility of ending all law enforcement and intelligence cooperation with the U.S. — of which there had been a great deal. And they signaled their intention to reconsider the Saudi-U.S. military relationship.

Abdullah made this last threat virtually explicit. On August 24, the Saudi chief of staff, Gen. Salih Ali bin Muhayya, arrived in Washington for a high-level review of Saudi-U.S. military collaboration. On the 25th, when he spoke to Bandar by telephone, Abdullah ordered that Salih return immediately to Riyadh, without meeting any Americans. He also ordered a delegation of about 40 senior Saudi officers who were about to leave for Washington to get off their plane. The annual review of military relations was canceled.

"You don't cancel visits like this on the day before," said a senior adviser to the crown prince. "It was a big, big event, and we downplayed it completely." In fact, the cancellation received no public attention at all. But it shocked the Pentagon, according to a senior Defense Department official who had expected to join the meetings with the Saudis.

Bush's letter transformed his reputation in the small circle of Saudis who run their country. Before the letter, these people had come to the conclusion that Bush was a lightweight—"goofy," as one of them put it. After the letter, "he was strong, judicious, deliberate. ... His reputation went from rock bottom to sky high."

Abdullah decided to share his correspondence with Bush—his message delivered by Bandar, which filled 25 pages, and Bush's two-page reply—with other Arab leaders, including the presidents of Egypt and Syria and the king of Jordan. He summoned Arafat, who was in South Africa, to Riyadh to read it.

According to Saudi officials, they extracted from Arafat a written pledge to satisfy Bush's demands for what Arafat had to do to revive the peace talks, and they sent it back to Washington with their own enthusiastic reply to Bush's letter. The crown prince sent Bandar back to Washington to try to convert the letter into policy and action, first by urging the president to publicly say what he told the Saudis in his letter.

Bandar was convinced that Bush could not have adopted the positions outlined in his letter in just 36 hours. "This must have been something . . . the administration was thinking about, that they just didn't share with everybody [but] were waiting for the right time," he said. Before he could pursue the matter, he needed to patch things up with U.S. officials. A knowledgeable source quoted American officials as telling Bandar when he returned to Washington, "Hey, you guys scared us." Bandar reportedly replied: "The hell with you—we scared ourselves."

On Friday, September 7, Bandar told U.S. officials that Saudi Arabia was "pleased and grateful," as one official put it, to discover that it had misread the Bush administration's attitude toward the Middle East. Saudi Arabia would continue to try to protect U.S. interests, he promised. The Americans indicated a willingness to pursue a new Middle East initiative immediately, Saudi officials said—a sharp departure from the administration's policy for seven months.

Over the weekend of September 8 and 9, officials of the two countries discussed what should happen next: a speech by Bush, or by Powell, or perhaps both? There was also discussion of a Bush-Arafat meeting at the United Nations later in September, an important point for the Saudis, who were pleased that Bush seemed willing to have the meeting. Powell left for a previously scheduled trip to Latin America on Monday, September 10, with these decisions still pending.

Even without the final decisions, Bandar was euphoric. After months in what he called "a yellow mood" over the deteriorating situation in the Middle East, "suddenly I felt the same feeling I had as we were going to Madrid [to the peace conference that followed the Gulf War in 1991], that we really were going to have a major initiative here that could save all of us from ourselves, mostly, and from each other."

So "the happiest man in the world" that night, on Monday night, was Bandar bin Sultan. "I was in the [indoor] swimming pool [of the McLean, Virginia residence], smoking a cigar. I gave myself a day off because I worked the whole weekend. I had been to Saudi Arabia . . . out with the [Bush] response, back with our response. I worked on the weekend up to 3 o'clock, 4 o'clock in the morning. . . . I worked all Monday. And I said to my office, Tuesday I'm taking the day off."

Tuesday was September 11. Instead of a day off, Bandar got the worst crisis of his career. Dreams of a new Middle East peace initiative evaporated. The realization that most of the hijackers were Saudis "fell on me ... like the whole house collapsed over my head," Bandar said later. He couldn't imagine a way to "do more damage or worse damage to Islam or to Saudi Arabia."[1]

A Day That Will Live In Infamy
September 11, 2001

On September 11, 2001, terrorist hijackers sent four airliners to devastating crashes into New York's World Trade Center, the Pentagon and the woods of rural Pennsylvania. It was a day of terror and fear, courage and heroism.

On September 10, 2001, President Bush was completing the most comprehensive Middle East peace plan ever drafted, a plan that called for a Palestinian state. No other American president had ever publicly approved of a Palestinian state. President Bush was responding to Saudi Arabia's assertion that he favored Israel in the Middle East peace process. On September 11, instead of finishing his Middle East plan, Bush was confronted with the largest terror event in American history. Furthermore, he assumed a new role as a comforter to America and our leader in the war on terror. The enemy Israel faced at home had now become an enemy America had to face at home. Moreover, life in America had changed forever.

One of Merriam-Webster's definitions for appease is: to buy off (an aggressor) by concessions usually at the sacrifice of principles.

The God of Israel will not allow His covenant land to be divided with the enemies of Israel. The people who continue to appease the enemies of Israel will continue to pay a very dear price. No one is excluded.

America Under Attack: September 11, 2001 Timeline

8:45 a.m. (all times are EDT): A hijacked passenger jet, American Airlines Flight 11 out of Boston, Massachusetts, crashes into the north tower of the World Trade Center, tearing a gaping hole in the building and setting it afire.

9:03 a.m.: A second hijacked airliner, United Airlines Flight 175 from Boston, crashes into the south tower of the World Trade Center and explodes. Both buildings are burning.

9:17 a.m.: The Federal Aviation Administration shuts down all New York City area airports.

9:21 a.m.: The Port Authority of New York and New Jersey orders all bridges and tunnels in the New York area closed.

9:30 a.m.: President Bush, speaking in Sarasota, Florida, says the country has suffered an "apparent terrorist attack."

9:40 a.m.: The FAA halts all flight operations at U.S. airports, the first time in U.S. history that air traffic nationwide has been halted.

9:43 a.m.: American Airlines Flight 77 crashes into the Pentagon, sending up a huge plume of smoke. Evacuation begins immediately.

9:45 a.m.: The White House evacuates.

9:57 a.m.: Bush departs from Florida.

10:05 a.m.: The south tower of the World Trade Center collapses, plummeting into the streets below. A massive cloud of dust and debris forms and slowly drifts away from the building.

10:08 a.m.: Secret Service agents armed with automatic rifles are deployed into Lafayette Park across from the White House.

10:10 a.m.: A portion of the Pentagon collapses.

10:10 a.m.: United Airlines Flight 93, also hijacked, crashes in Somerset County, Pennsylvania, southeast of Pittsburgh.

10:13 a.m.: The United Nations building evacuates, including 4,700 people from the headquarters building and 7,000 total from UNICEF and UN development programs.

10:22 a.m.: In Washington, the State and Justice departments are evacuated, along with the World Bank.

10:24 a.m.: The FAA reports that all inbound transatlantic aircraft flying into the U.S. are being diverted to Canada.

10:28 a.m.: World Trade Center's north tower collapses from the top down as if being peeled apart, releasing a tremendous cloud of debris and smoke.

10:45 a.m.: All federal office buildings in Washington are evacuated.

Greatest loss of American lives in a single day since the Civil War battle at Gettysburg

Nearly 3,000 people died on September 11th who were either in the commercial airplanes used as terrorist weapons or in the buildings they struck. While recognizing the enormity of this tragedy, it is amazing to realize that tens of thousands more could have died who were in the World Trade Center towers or surrounding buildings in New York City.

How much did the September 11 terrorist attacks cost America?

Counting the value of lives lost, property damage and lost production of goods and services, including the loss in stock market wealth—the market's own estimate arising from expectations of lower corporate profits and higher discount rates for economic volatility—the price tag approaches $2 trillion.

(Source: Institute for the Analysis of Global Security: www.iags.org/costof911.html).

Among the big-ticket items:

- The loss of four civilian aircraft valued at $385 million.
- The destruction of major buildings in the World Trade Center with a replacement cost of from $3 to $4.5 billion.
- Damage to a portion of the Pentagon: up to $1 billion.
- Cleanup costs: $1.3 billion.
- Property and infrastructure damage: $10 to $13 billion.
- Federal emergency funds (heightened airport security, sky marshals, government takeover of airport security, retrofitting aircraft with anti-terrorist devices, cost of operations in Afghanistan): $40 billion.
- The amount of damaged or unrecoverable property hit $21.8 billion.
- Losses to the city of New York (lost jobs, lost taxes, damage to infrastructure, cleaning): $95 billion.
- Losses to the insurance industry: $40 billion.
- Loss of air traffic revenue: $10 billion.

Total of above estimated costs: $222,485,000,000.

Additional Loss Breakdown

The Milken Institute estimated 1,300,000 jobs were lost across the country as a result of September 11 by the end of 2002, and a concomitant decrease of $150 billion in annual income or Gross Domestic Product (GDP).

As a consequence of September 11, the federal government and the states budgeted for nearly $40 billion in 2003 for anti-terror and security related items. U.S. non-governmental agencies and businesses spent about $33 billion in 2002 for added security measures.

In spite of a $15 billion government bailout, a couple of U.S. airlines filed for bankruptcy. All of the carriers combined lost about $11 billion in large part due to a passenger fear of flying following September 11.

Money Appropriated for Homeland Security: October 1, 2003

President Bush signed the Homeland Security Appropriations Act of 2004 at the Department of Homeland Security in Washington, DC on October 1, 2003. In his remarks, Bush said,

The Homeland Security bill I will sign today commits $31 billion to securing our nation, over $14 billion more than pre-September 11 levels. The bill increases funding for the key responsibilities at the Department of Homeland Security and supports important new initiatives across the Department.

CHAPTER 10

The Washington Post

Weather
Today: *Partly sunny, humid.*
High 82, Low 69.
Thursday: *Some sun, late*
showers. High 82, Low 72.
Details, Page 88

WEDNESDAY, JULY 30, 2003

HOME
EDITION

Inside: food, Classified
Today's Contents on Page A2

Bush Urges Israelis to Help Revitalize Peace Process

President Bush and Israeli Prime Minister Ariel Sharon meet at the White House, the eighth visit there by Sharon in the Bush presidency. In Oval Office session, Bush pressed Sharon to support Palestinian counterpart Mahmoud Abbas. **Story, Page A12.**

Bush Won't Release Classified 9/11 Report

Saudi Foreign Minister Calls Accusations an 'Outrage'

By MIKE ALLEN
Washington Post Staff Writer

President Bush rejected a personal appeal from Saudi Arabia's foreign minister yesterday to release a classified section of a congressional report that has led accusations the kingdom aided the attacks of Sept. 11, 2001.

Foreign Minister Prince Saud Faisal called it "an outrage to any sense of fairness" that the 28 blacked-out pages were causing Saudi Arabia to be "wrongfully and unfairly accused of complicity in the tragic terrorist attacks.

"This accusation is based on misguided speculation, and is born of poorly diagnosed malicious intent," he said after a hastily arranged White House meeting.

Saud said his nation is being "indicted by insinuation" and cannot reply to wordless pages: "We have nothing to hide," he said. "We do not seek, nor do we need, to be shielded."

The formal request was contained in a letter from Crown Prince Abdullah, who has developed a bond with Bush.

Saud's stinging words in the White House driveway reflected a new season of tension with a country that Bush has consistently called an important ally in the war on terror, and fueled a new battle between the administration and law-

Memo Warns Of New Plots To Hijack Jets

By SARA KEHAULANI GOO
and SUSAN SCHMIDT
Washington Post Staff Writers

Terrorists operating in teams of five may be plotting suicide missions to hijack commercial airliners on the East Coast, Europe or Australia this summer, possibly using "common items carried by travelers, such as cameras, modified as weapons," according to an urgent memo sent last weekend to all U.S. airlines and airport security managers.

The "information circular" issued July 26 was drawn from recent intelligence reports that detail the most specific terrorist plots involving passenger aircraft in the United States since four hijacked jetliners were used in the Sept. 11, 2001, at-

Disruptive Periods 2-7

When President Bush Pressured Israel
to Give Up Her Land

As with the last chapter on the September 11 terror attacks, I have documented that when President George W. Bush or one of his top officials pressured Israel to give up her covenant land, one or more of the following occurred:

- National terror alerts and warnings immediately followed and increased in frequency as the pressure continued to be applied on Israel.
- The Bush administration was required to defend its response to September 11, the war on terror, the economy, Iraq, etc.
- High ranking officials in the Bush administration resigned (White House Counselor Karen Hughes, Secretary of Treasury Paul O'Neil, White House economic adviser Larry Lindsey, White House Press Secretary Ari Fleischer and EPA Director Christine Todd Whitman.)

- The nation experienced record-setting tornadoes, hurricanes, rain and flooding, ice storms, and major forest fires.
- National anthrax scares, and heightened concerns over bio-terrorism and nuclear attacks.
- Major economic concerns: corporate bankruptcies and accounting scandals.
- Political, judicial and or legislative chaos.

After President Bush declared his commitment to a Palestinian state and/or was involved in the Middle East peace process there were immediate disruptive consequences.

The Second Disruptive Period:
October 1 - 31, 2001

Bush: Palestinian State 'Part of a Vision' if Israel is Respected

According to CNN, President Bush stated on October 2, 2001 that a Palestinian state was always "part of a vision" if Israel's right to exist is respected. He said the two parties needed to get to work "on the Mitchell process" which he said provides a clear path to solving the crisis in the Middle East.

He refused to say whether he had been prepared to announce his support for a Palestinian state prior to the September 11 terrorist attacks.

"We are getting hammered in the Arab world," said an administration official. "And it is not a mystery that one of the ways to diffuse this is to see some movement on the Israeli-Palestinian conflict."

Administration sources acknowledged that Arab support on the international coalition is crucial to winning the U.S.-led war against terrorism, and to send a signal the war is not against Islam, but against Osama bin Laden and his terrorist network.

The Bush administration also wanted Arab nations to cut the flow of money to bin Laden from wealthy Islamic supporters in their countries.

U.S. officials debated whether the administration should invite Palestinian leader Yasser Arafat to Washington to meet with Bush or Powell. Although Arafat had met Powell outside of Washington, he had yet to meet Bush.

Some in the administration believed inviting the Palestinian leader to Washington could give Arafat the "empowerment" he needed to deal with extremist factions of his Palestinian forces.

"Arafat needs a visit," one official said, noting that Arafat has publicly condemned terrorism and called for a cease-fire.

Anthrax and terrorism dominate new headlines:

Anthrax-laden mail was discovered throughout October in the U.S. Senate mail and mail in other federal buildings, plus Florida and New York. This discovery caused Congressional offices to be closed and sealed, the Supreme Court to be temporarily relocated, and the White House to quarantine its mail. Three people died. Following Bush's comments on a Palestinian state, October 2001 was dominated by anthrax and terrorism headlines as follows:

- Before Attacks, U.S. Was Ready to Say It Backed Palestinian State –October 1
- Bush: Palestinian State 'Part of a Vision' If Israel Respected–October 2
- Doctors determined Stevens, 63 [American Media Inc. photo editor], has anthrax. He is on a respirator, being treated with intravenous penicillin –October 3
- West Trenton, New Jersey post office letter carrier was hospitalized and a biopsy was performed–October 3
- Arab Leaders Warn No End To Terrorism Without Middle East Solution –October 3
- Government Stockpiles Supplies For Bioterrorism–October 5
- Officials: Anthrax Shown In Co-Worker and Work Place of Florida Man Who Died of Anthrax–October 8
- Ashcroft Issues New Mail Warning–October 12
- Three Exposed To Anthrax In New York Amid Fears of Bio-terrorism –October 14
- Anthrax Letter Sent To Daschle–October 15
- Anthrax, Smallpox, Plague: Reborn As Bio-weapons?–October 16
- Anthrax Found In New York Governor Pataki's Office–October 17
- U.S. House of Representatives To Adjourn Following More Anthrax Cases–October 17
- 31 Daschle Staffers Tested Positive For Anthrax–October 17
- Anthrax Scare Hits World's Mailrooms–October 19
- Anthrax Spores Found in House Building at U.S. Capitol Complex –October 20
- Postal Worker Very Ill With Inhalation Anthrax; 5 Others May Have It Also –October 22
- Anthrax Found At White House Annex–October 23
- Two Postal Workers Die of Anthrax–October 23
- State Dept Mailman Tests Positive For Anthrax–October 25
- Anthrax Found In Fifth Capitol Location–October 25
- Three Nations Known Capable of Making Anthrax Additive–October 25
- U.S. Anti-Terror Law Widens Police, Federal Powers–October 25

- Anthrax Scare Hits CIA–October 26
- Bin Laden Acquires Nuclear Materials–October 26
- Anthrax Spreads to CIA, Supreme Court, 3 House Offices on Capitol Hill, and an Army Institute–October 26
- FBI Renews High Alert Warning For Terrorism Against U.S. This Week –October 29

The Third Disruptive Period: November 2-27, 2001

Bush Calls for Palestinian State

On November 2, 2001, the Financial Times reported that the Bush administration was preparing to make a policy statement on the Middle East outlining U.S. commitment to the creation of a viable Palestinian state. Details of the U.S. blueprint were still being debated within the administration. Both Arab nations and Israel tried hard to influence the outcome.

In the context of Middle East negotiations, the word "viable" is generally understood to mean that the Palestinian state would have sufficient geographical, economic and political integrity to stand on its own. The statement, made by Colin Powell, U.S. Secretary of State, did not include prescriptions on the final status of Jerusalem and Palestinian refugees. The planned U.S. move made it easier for Arab allies to continue to support the war against terror.

In President Bush's first address to the U.N. General Assembly on November 10, 2001, he spoke briefly about his vision for Middle East peace. The following is an excerpt:

> The American government also stands by its commitment to a just peace in the Middle East.

> We are working toward the day when two states—Israel and Palestine— live peacefully together within secure and recognized borders as called for by the Security Council resolutions.

> We will do all in our power to bring both parties back into negotiations. But peace will only come when all have sworn off forever incitement, violence and terror.

Two days later, on November 12, 2001, within miles of the UN meetings American Airlines Flight #587 exploded over New York City. For the following 17 days, news headlines were dominated by President Bush's call for a Palestinian state, terror warnings, and the American Airlines tragedy.

The Fourth Disruptive Period:
April 20 to May 2, 2002

The Fallout from Bush's Palestinian State Declaration

The following events happened in a nine-day period as President Bush intensified his efforts in the Middle East talks.

On April 20, 2002, a 5.1 earthquake in New York was felt from Buffalo, New York all the way down to Boston, Massachusetts and Baltimore, Maryland. The epicenter was 50 miles from Saranac Lake, where President Bush would be delivering his Earth day address 48 hours later (April 22).

Within a few hours of the quake, in a national radio address, the President acknowledged the need for a Palestinian state and restated his vision for peace between Israelis and Palestinians.

The following Tuesday, April 23, Karen Hughes—a close confidant of the president—resigned as the White House director of communications.

On April 24, George H. W. Bush met with Crown Prince Abdullah of Saudi Arabia in Washington. The next day, President George W. Bush met Abdullah in Crawford, Texas while massive rains caused flooding.

On Friday, April 26th, President Bush's father met again with Abdullah in Houston. They took a train ride to College Station where Bush gave a speech at Texas A&M University.

Meanwhile, Wall Street closed down after experiencing the largest one-week capital loss since September 11.

On Sunday, April 28th, the United States brokered a deal with Israel for Arafat's release from captivity in Ramallah.

That day, tornadoes swept through southeastern Missouri, Illinois and western Kentucky, killing three people, and damaging homes and buildings.

A tornado that hit Maryland, rating F5 on the Fujita Tornado Damage Scale, was "a monster of a tornado." With winds in the 261-318 mph range, it was the strongest ever to hit Maryland, killing three additional people.

The Fifth Disruptive Period:
May 12 - 20, 2002

On May 12, 2002, Israel's Likud party voted against a Palestinian state. According to an article in the *Guardian* (UK), on May 13, 2002, President Bush held fast to his support for a Palestinian state.

"The President continues to believe that the best route to peace is through the creation of the state of Palestine and side-by-side security with Israel," White House spokesman Ari Fleischer said in response to Likud's decision.

As the President held fast on a Palestinian state, the following headlines and terror warnings were reported. The Bush administration defended its pre-September 11 actions and admission of the risk of bio-terrorism:

- 25 Islamic Extremists Have Entered the U.S.–May 13
- U.S. Prepares For Terror Attack In Food–May 13
- Bush Administration Was Warned of Potential Terror Event Prior To September 11 – May 15
- Dr. Condoleezza Rice Defends Bush Administration's Handling of pre-September 11 Terror Warning (White House Press Briefing)–May 16
- Democrats End United Support of Bush On War; Democrats Say Bush Must Give Full Disclosure–May 16
- Defense Secretary Says Another Terrorist Attack On U.S. Likely–May 17
- Bush Defends Pre-September 11 Actions–May 17
- U.S. Intercepting Messages Hinting At New Attack–May 18
- U.S. Bioterrorism Plan Inadequate–May 19
- Cheney Predicts More Attacks–May 19
- FBI's Director Mueller: Suicide Bombers Likely In U.S.–May 20
- Strife, Dissent Beset Hill's September 11 Panel: Bipartisan Group Disagrees On Mission–May 20

The Sixth Disruptive Period:
June 13 - 29, 2002

While President Bush and Secretary of State Colin Powell were completing the President's Middle East plan, terror warnings and two major suicide bombings in Israel were reported:

- Bush Polishing Palestinian State Proposal and Powell Suggests Interim Palestinian State–June 13
- Nation's Mayors Not Ready For Attacks–June 13
- Arab Leader Warns U.S. On Terror War–June 14
- Bush Gives CIA Power To Get Rid of Saddam–June 16
- Al Qaeda Plans Attacks On U.S. Targets–June 17
- Bush To Postpone Policy Speech Due To Terror Attack–June 18
- U.S. Expresses Reservations About Fence In Israel–June 18
- 19 Dead, 52 Wounded In Suicide Bus Bombing In Jerusalem–June 18
- FBI Searches Los Angeles Coast For Al Qaeda–June 18
- Suicide Bombing In Jerusalem–June 19
- Bush To Propose Provisional Palestinian Statehood As Soon As September –June 19
- President Bush Postpones His Middle East Message For the Second Time In Two Days Due To Jerusalem Bombings–June 19

- Lightning Disables Two of Four Fire and Medical Emergency Radio
    Antennas In Washington, DC–June 19
- Plane Prompts White House Evacuation–June 19

President Bush finally gave his Middle East speech the afternoon of June 24 from the White House Rose Garden. The following morning in Arizona, he declared the state a major natural disaster and the 500,000-acre fire one of the worst in western U.S. history. Later in the day WorldCom admitted to massive bookkeeping fraud. The headlines were as follows:

- Stocks Trade Near post-September 11 Lows–June 24
- Dollar Slides To Brink of Free Fall–June 24
- Bank of Japan Moves To Stop Dollar Plunge–June 24
- Worldwide Web of Debt Unravels–June 24
- United Seeks $1.8 Billion Federal Loan–June 24
- Bush Travels To Arizona Fire, Declares "Rodeo/Chediski" Arizona Fire As
    One of the West's All Time Worst and A Natural Disaster–June 25
- Massive Fraud Alleged At WorldCom–June 25
- World Leaders Stand With Arafat–June 25
- Stocks Plunge Amid Huge WorldCom Scandal News–June 25
- Bush Signs A Law Extending Benefits To Same-Sex Couples–June 25
- Worst Wildfire In Arizona's History–June 25
- 1st Time: Pledge of Allegiance Ruled 'Unconstitutional' In 9 States–June 25
- President and the Senate Call Pledge Decision Outrageous–June 25
- Judge Stays Decision On Pledge of Allegiance–June 27
- U.S. Senate Unanimously Condemns Pledge Ruling and Joins In Public
    Pledge–June 27
- Suspicion: Terror Web Attack On Our Nation's Power Grid–June 27
- 20,000 Gas Masks Have Arrived On Capitol Hill–June 27
- WorldCom Profits Scandal Shakes Stock Markets–June 27

The Seventh Disruptive Period:
October 1 to December 23, 2002

The Quartet met in New York in late September 2002 to formulate the Middle East Road Map. The Quartet consists of the UN, the EU, Russia and the U.S. The U.S. stock market had its worst September since the Great Depression and was at the lowest level since the September 11 terror attacks.

For three weeks in October, Washington, DC, was terrorized by a sniper who held the metro area hostage. Also, California suffered an earthquake, there was a major West Coast dock strike that forced President Bush to intervene, and Osama bin Laden issued a terror threat.

In November, 88 tornadoes slashed through seven states, which was one of the worst tornado outbreaks on record, especially since the tornado season is March through July, not November.

In early December, North Carolina and South Carolina were hit by the worst ice storm in their history, leaving two million homes and businesses without electrical power. President Bush was embarrassed by Senate Majority Leader Trent Lott's comments at Senator Strom Thurmond's 100th birthday party. Major terror warnings were again issued. There was talk of a national smallpox vaccine and debate over when to release the Quartet Road Map.

The Headlines from October 1 to December 23, 2002:

- U.S. Stock Markets Have Worst September Since Great Depression –October 1
- Bush and Congress Differ Over Jerusalem Bill Passed–October 2
- Shooting Spree In DC Suburbs; 5 Killed; Schools In Lockdown–October 3
- Strong Quake Hits In Gulf of California–October 3
- Intelligence Reports: Islamic Terrorists Target American Schools–October 4
- Doctors Warn of Bioterrorism Risks–October 4
- Bin Laden Tape Warns U.S.–October 7
- Arafat Signs Law On Jerusalem As Future Capitol–October 7
- Terror Threat For U.S. Ships In Yemen–October 8
- Whole Pacific Rim Is Suffering From Closure of All U.S. West Coast Ports –October 8
- DC Area On Edge As Sniper Eludes Cops–October 8
- Hurricane Lili Damage Set At $170 Million–October 8
- Court Orders West Coast Ports To Reopen On Bush's Request–October 9
- Tape of Al-Qaeda Deputy Warning of More Attacks On U.S. Appears To Be Genuine–October 9
- 'This Is Like A War Zone': Recurring Terror In D.C.–October 9
- Geologists Dissect Massive Alaskan Quake; The Biggest Earthquake In the World This Year–November 8
- 88 Tornadoes and Major Thunderstorms From the Gulf Coast To the Great Lakes, Affecting 13 States–November 9-10
- Five People Killed At Kibbutz Metzer In Israel–November 10
- U.S. Deputy Asst. Sec. of State David Satterfield Flies To Israel To Push the Quartet's December Deadline–November 10
- Satterfield Meets With Israeli Officials–November 11-12
- It's Like A War Zone Or Worse; Storms Leave Destruction and Death Across Eastern U.S.–November 11
- 4.2 Earthquake–30 miles (45 km) SSW from Charleston, South Carolina –November 11

CHAPTER 11

Disruptive Periods 8 & 9

The Eighth Disruptive Period:
April 30 to September 19, 2003

After the Quartet's Road Map was delivered there were many meetings between the U.S., Israel and the Palestinians. This was a period of great effort but nothing tangible was accomplished. This was also a very long and trying period of disruption for the Bush Administration as you will see below.

President Bush and the Quartet call on Israel
to give up her covenant land

After much delay, on April 30, 2003, the Quartet—the U.S., UN, EU and Russia—delivered the Road Map to the Israelis and Palestinians. It included a plan for Israel to divide her covenant land.

Secretary of State Colin Powell headed to the Middle East for meetings. In a meeting with Syrian President Bashar Assad on May 4, Powell stated his approval of Syria receiving the Golan Heights. Powell's associate William

Burns met with Israeli peace advocates on May 5, where he stated Christian fundamentalists were an obstruction to peace in the Middle East.

Two weeks later President George W. Bush and U.S. Ambassador Daniel Kurtzer called on Israeli Prime Minister Ariel Sharon to approve the Road Map. Here is what transpired:

- The U.S. decided to press Israel to approve the Road Map quickly. Ambassador Kurtzer delivered this message to Sharon on May 20, and Bush reiterated it in a telephone conversation with the prime minister the next day. Bush also talked with Palestinian Prime Minister Mahmoud Abbas that day.
- Bush said terrorism will not stop the Middle East peace process–May 22
- Discussions began on a Bush-Sharon-Abbas meeting in Egypt after the G-8 meetings–May 22
- President Bush planned a three-way summit with Sharon and Abbas in Jordan–May 27
- Colin Powell met Pope John Paul II at the Vatican to discuss Iraq and the Israeli-Palestinian conflict–June 2
- Bush met with Arab leaders in Egypt to discuss the Road Map–June 3
- Bush met with Jordan's King Abdullah II, Prime Minister Sharon, and Palestinian Prime Minister Abbas for the Aqaba Summit in Jordan–June 4
- Bush demanded a halt to Jewish settlements–June 4
- Bush said two states must share the Holy Land–June 4

Critical Five-Week Period Summary

The following will provide a perspective on what happened five weeks after the United States became actively involved with the Quartet's Road Map. The more the U.S. pressured Israel, the greater the intensity of events.

Week One, May 4-11, 2003: While Powell represented the U.S. in Syria and Israel, record setting tornadoes and major storms devastated the mid-western United States. Nineteen states suffered losses, and more than 40 deaths were blamed on the storms. No less than 412 tornados hit the area within 10 days.

Week Two, May 12-18: Powell continued his travels to Middle East countries and Russia to promote the Road Map, while Al-Qaeda terror bombings were aimed against Americans in Riyadh and Jews in Casablanca. The turning point for Ariel Sharon began when Powell blamed Sharon for the impasse (May 15) due to his refusal to freeze and dismantle settlements.

Then, following the Sharon and Abbas meeting, five suicide bombings in 48 hours broke the silence in Israel once again.

Week Three, May 19-25: The Bush administration called on Sharon to approve the Road Map. On the same day, the Homeland Security Office raised the terror alert status to Orange (high) and the Defense Department increased its terrorism threat to its top level. Fighter jets began patrolling the skies over Washington, DC. Also, Iran was being pressured over its alleged nuclear program and civil chaos increased in Iraq. Ari Fleischer resigned as White House Press Secretary.

Week Four, May 26-June 1: President Bush traveled to Poland, Russia, and France for the G-8 meetings. He then traveled to Egypt and Jordan to push the Road Map. His administration was put on the defense for embellishing the intelligence information that he used to justify the war in Iraq.

Week Five, June 2-7: Palestinian Prime Minister Abbas's cease-fire talks with Hamas failed. Hamas, Islamic Jihad and Al-Aqsa Intifada attacked and killed four Israelis at a Gaza Checkpoint. Israel attempted to assassinate the head of Hamas. Hamas blew up a bus in Jerusalem killing 16 Israelis and injuring 100. Israel struck back with missile attacks on militant leaders in Gaza. President Bush called for calm and condemned the killings, while his commitment to a solution was questioned.

Catastrophes in the U.S., Europe, Middle East and Indian subcontinent during May 2003:

- U.S.: Record 562 tornadoes, 535 windstorms, 1,385 hailstorms; 19 dead.
- Europe: Hottest summer in 500 years; 50% of crops lost; 22,000 dead.
- Mongolia-China: Locusts damaged 11 million hectares of crops.
- Saudi Arabia: Riyadh terror bombing killed 29 (10 Americans).

Bush Heads to Russia, Europe and the Middle East

After the Bush-Sharon-Abdullah-Abbas meeting in Aqaba, Jordan, on June 4, 2003, a major political crisis in Israel developed over the Road Map and the settlements. At the same time two of the most active proponents of the Road Map, U.S. and Britain, were experiencing a political crisis over intelligence reports claiming Iraq had weapons of mass destruction (WMD).

The Iraq crisis began to surface in the U.S. on May 30—the same day Bush left for his trip to Poland, Russia, France, Egypt, Jordan and Qatar.

After his meetings in Europe and Russia, President Bush met in Egypt with Arab leaders on the Road Map. He then went to Jordan to meet with Israeli Prime Minister Sharon and Palestinian Prime Minister Abbas.

While Bush focused on Israel's covenant land, in the U.S. there were allegations of faulty intelligence pertaining to Iraq's weapons of mass destruction.

Rice Raised Objections with Sharon on Security Fence

While meeting with Palestinian leaders on June 29, 2003, Dr. Condoleezza Rice, the national security adviser, listened intently to complaints about the Israeli fence walling off Palestinians in the West Bank. The next day, she raised objections to the fence with Prime Minister Sharon. American and Israeli officials said Sharon politely rebuffed Dr. Rice.

Administration officials said the exchange illustrated their new willingness to prod Israel and to get involved in the minutiae of the negotiations. "The very fact that Condi Rice raised the issue of the fence with Sharon is significant," said an administration official. "We will be back on this issue if things don't improve."

The exchange between Dr. Rice and Sharon showed a decision to direct pressure from both the White House and the State Department, which had long been warring over Middle East policy.

The week before Dr. Rice's visit, for example, Secretary Powell pressed Israel to withdraw from the Gaza Strip, even discussing individual checkpoints on maps of the area.

Bush Meets with Mahmoud Abbas at the White House

I was at the White House Rose Garden on July 25, 2003, for the U.S.-Palestinian peace talks between President Bush and Prime Minister Abbas. I watched as President Bush spoke and then observed him as he listened to Abbas. I really sensed he thought he could "will" peace into place with rhetoric, charm, creativity, military might and money.

It appeared Bush believed he could use his diplomatic skills to reverse thousands of years of hatred, and bring peace to the Middle East. Sadly, the United States continues to be the main perpetrator of the "land for peace" initiative and is using her assets to manipulate the participants.

Summary of President Bush's Rose Garden Address:

- Bush stated the government of Israel recognizes that its own interests will be served when the Palestinians govern themselves in their own state: a peaceful democratic state where the forces of terror have been replaced by the rule of law.
- He said Prime Minister Abbas is committed to a complete end to violence and terrorism, and recognizes that terror against Israelis, wherever they be, is a dangerous obstacle to the achievement of a Palestinian state.
- Bush stated he is committed to meet the goal that has been set. To accomplish that, the President believes that the daily lives of ordinary

Palestinians must be improved. Therefore, the President approved a grant of $20 million dollars to be directed to the Palestinian Authority.
- The President announced that the United States and the Palestinian Authority would establish a joint Palestine Economic Development Group. This group of American and Palestinian officials will meet regularly and be charged with finding practical ways to bring jobs, growth and investment to the Palestinian economy.
- Treasury Secretary John Snow and Commerce Secretary Don Evans will report directly to him on the steps that need to be taken to build a solid economic foundation for a free and sovereign Palestinian state.

The Main Points from Abbas' Rose Garden Address:

- Abbas promised to remain committed to the Road Map and to implement the security and reform obligations.
- Security for all Palestinians and Israelis is an essential element of progress, and they will achieve security based on the rule of law.
- Abbas said the Palestinians have had significant success in reducing violence, although Israel, with its military might, has failed.
- The Palestinians do not merely seek a state, but they desire a state that is built on the solid foundations of the modern constitution, democracy, transparency, the rule of law, and the market economy.
- Abbas will continue to negotiate with Israel on implementing its obligations. Some progress has been made, but effort needs to be made to free prisoners, lift the siege on President Arafat, see Israel withdraw from Palestinian areas, and increase freedom of movement for Palestinians.
- Abbas wants a sovereign, independent Palestinian state, with East Jerusalem as its capital.
- Palestinians want a just solution to the refugee question on the basis of UN Resolution 194.
- This vision cannot be realized if Israel continues to grab Palestinian land.
- If the settlement continues on Palestinian land, and construction of the so-called separation wall on confiscated Palestinian land continues, Palestinians might find that a free Palestinian state, living side-by-side in peace and security with Israel is impossible.
- Nothing less than a full settlement freeze will do because nothing less than a full settlement freeze will work. Abbas believes that for the sake of peace, and for the sake of future Palestinian and Israeli generations, all settlement activities must be stopped now, and the wall must come down.

A Summary of the Bush and Abbas talks:

• Prime Minister Abbas and President Bush covered a range of issues in their talks, discussing the impact of limited movement on the Palestinian people and the need to reduce the network of checkpoints and barriers.
• Abbas shared his concerns about Israeli settlements, confiscation of land, and the building of a security fence. He also expressed his strong desire to see the release of many more of the over 6,000 Palestinian prisoners.
• The government of Israel announced that it would take down more of the checkpoints that are making it difficult for Palestinians to travel to their jobs and schools.
• In addition, Israel will consider ways to reduce the impact of the security fence on the lives of the Palestinian people.
• Bush stated Prime Minister Sharon has demonstrated that he is also a partner committed to reaching a peace settlement. Sharon pledged to transfer the security responsibility for two West Bank cities to the Palestinian Authority and to make progress in removing settlement outposts.
• Bush stated that this is a time of great possibility in the Middle East. The people of the region are counting on all leaders involved to seize opportunities for peace and progress. Too many lives have been lost through resentment and violence. The Palestinian people, like people everywhere, deserve freedom, an honest government and peace.

Review of Bush Administration Plan and Involvement:

• President Bush allowed the Palestinians to state from the White House, that an independent Palestinian state would have East Jerusalem as its capital; that UN Resolution 194 would address the refugee situation; and that settlement activities on Palestinian land must be frozen. [Note: The White House event further legitimized the Palestinians claims; the East Jerusalem capital and the refugee issues are deal-breakers.]
• Bush gave Abbas the opportunity to call on Israel to stop building the West Bank security fence. He said it is not helpful to the peace process. [Note: The fence is to keep Palestinians from killing Israelis.] —
• President Bush in his June 24, 2002, Middle East message said there would be no more dealing with Arafat. [Note: Arafat was still calling the shots in 2003. He defined the role and provided the script for Abbas. In the Rose Garden, Abbas called for Arafat's release from his Ramallah compound.]
• According to the *Washington Times*, the Bush administration, in a gesture to Abbas, softened its stance on the militant group Hamas, saying it could survive if it became a purely political organization. Secretary Powell— who said in June 2003 that "It is no longer possible to separate one part of

Hamas from another part of Hamas" and called Hamas an "enemy of peace"—told reporters in Washington on July 24, 2003:

> If an organization that has a terrorist component to it, a terrorist wing to it, totally abandons that, gives it up, and there is no question in anyone's mind that is part of its past, then that is a different organization.

[Note: Bush stated numerous times in the last two months that the terror infrastructure in Israel has to be dismantled. Again, Powell and the State Department have entered the mix. In essence they are saying that the terror groups will be acceptable if the militants turn in their weapons and become political organizations instead.]

- The Council on Foreign Relations (CFR) remains in the political loop. Abbas addressed them on Thursday, July 14. [Note: The CFR farms people into State Department positions. Every U.S. Secretary of State since World War II has been a CFR member, Powell included.]
- After pressure from the White House and in preparation for Sharon's departure for Washington, Israel agreed to release 210 militants from Israeli prisons. [Note: Sharon's Cabinet voted 13 to 10 to release the militants. This was a complete change of course from earlier that week, and was due to White House pressure.]
- President Bush planned to send Treasury Secretary Snow and Commerce Secretary Evans to the region. [Note: Bush is using U.S. financial might and ingenuity to induce the Palestinians and the Israelis to parcel God's covenant land.]
- The CIA has peace monitors in Israel. [Note: The CIA has trained Palestinian sharpshooters to keep order within their own communities, who also turned their guns on Israelis.]

Bush and Sharon Met–July 29, 2003
–Not a Good Day at the White House

I was also in attendance for the Bush-Sharon White House Rose Garden event. Bush and Sharon gave brief speeches and then took a few questions from the U.S. and Israeli press.

I could tell from the beginning that the interaction between the two was very tentative, the worst in Sharon's eight trips to the White House.

Bush kept trying to get a positive response from Sharon but it wasn't forthcoming. Sharon acknowledged Bush a few times out of politeness, but he was reluctant. Sharon couldn't hide his dismay and he seemed very troubled.

What a contrast to the exuberance we witnessed in Sharon's last visit to the White House on October 16, 2002. Sharon said Israel has never had a better friend in the White House than Bush. Later that night Sharon and his staff sang Israeli songs at the Blair House. (He did not stay at the Blair House this time.)

The Israeli media was also very exuberant on October 16, 2002, but Tuesday, July 29, 2003 there was no life–you could sense their dismay. I spoke to two friends with the Israeli media, who tried to be positive but they couldn't hide inner feelings. Also, after Sharon's meetings, Israeli journalists tried to put a positive spin in their commentaries.

In my opinion, Sharon, who is a genius strategist, knew the White House maneuvered him into a very dangerous position. The sad irony is that this is the result of the White House and State Department's desire to help prop up Palestinian Prime Minister Abbas. Abbas had been under great political pressure from Arafat, and the heads of Hamas and other terror groups.

The White House made sure that both the Abbas and Sharon meetings and speeches started at the same time. Both Oval office meetings commenced at 11:20 a.m. The Rose Garden events both began at 11:50 a.m. Both Bush and Abbas, and Bush and Sharon, took a few questions from the U.S., Palestinian, and Israeli media before leaving for lunch with their combined staffs.

There was energy in the Bush-Abbas meeting but not in the Bush-Sharon meeting. Abbas was all smiles; Sharon seemed dejected. Bush went out of his way to be friendly to both leaders. Abbas responded; Sharon was reluctant.

I noticed Bush nudge next to Sharon for a smiling photo-op. Sharon smiled briefly, and then lost his place in his speech, and Bush helped him recover.

Sharon Pressured as Bush Feels the Repercussions–July 29, 2003

On the same day President Bush pressured Ariel Sharon to divide Israel's covenant land and to stop the construction of the security fence, Bush also faced some serious pressure.

Bush's people came under intense Senate questioning for the billions of dollars spent in Iraq and the almost daily loss of American life. President Bush met for two hours with an angry Saudi Foreign Minister who rushed to the United States over the September 11 report. He also faced scrutiny over the involvement of the Saudis in September 11. The President refused to release additional information to the American public or to the Saudi Foreign Minister about Saudi involvement. Meanwhile, U.S. security was heightened by an Al Qaeda terror threat and consumer confidence plummeted, catching many economists and the White House by surprise.

When the Bush Administration pressured Israel, they experienced pressure and disruption in America.

President Bush and his administration had invested a lot of time in Abbas, and Abbas's resignation devastated them. Bush had done everything he could to isolate Arafat and this event showed Arafat was still a disruptive force.

The Arafat Problem

On September 6, 2003, Mahmoud Abbas resigned as Prime Minister of the Palestinian Authority, stunning Bush administration officials. The event raised fresh questions about the administration's strategy of trying to isolate Yasser Arafat and work with so-called moderate Palestinians.

The official White House reaction to Mr. Abbas's resignation was cautious, hiding the administration's deep disappointment. A statement called on the Palestinian legislature to "act in a way that empowers the Prime Minister" no matter who is selected, and said that "all parties" needed to "consider carefully the consequences of their actions."

Realistically it would be extremely difficult for any successor of Mahmoud Abbas to do that.

The position of Palestinian prime minister was poisoned, and anyone who tried to stand up to Arafat was seen as a pawn of the United States and Israel.

Since President Bush took office, events in Israel have forced constant adjustments by the administration. First, administration officials were openly disdainful of the way President Clinton had become personally engaged in the Middle East peace effort. In the view of many, Bush's predecessor had actually made the situation worse by trying and failing to broker a deal in the waning weeks of his term.

Not until 2003, after the Iraq war, did the Bush administration become more involved, in large part because of pressure from Britain's Tony Blair, European allies, Crown Prince Abdullah of Saudi Arabia and other Arab allies. Bush also needed their money, troops and support in Iraq.

But there was never any doubt in the minds of the Europeans, Arabs and others that Arafat would prevent a crackdown by Palestinians on Palestinian militant groups—the prerequisite Israel demanded for taking actions of its own.

The Bush administration has been angered when its Road Map partners rebuff American pleas to stop meeting with Arafat when they visit Israel.

The U.S. and Israel both reaffirmed their refusal to work directly with Arafat. The EU said repeatedly that they will continue to work with Arafat.

On September 7, 2003, Chairman Arafat chose a senior official, Ahmed Qureia (Abu Ala), as his next Prime Minister. Qureia helped broker the 1993 Oslo accords between Israel and the PLO.

On the day of Queria's appointment, Secretary Powell and National Security Adviser Rice blamed Arafat for hindering Middle East peace and said he must relinquish control of security forces.

They opposed any expulsion of Arafat, which the Sharon government voted to do in the time of their choosing. They said expulsion could give the veteran Palestinian leader a wider stage from which to work.

We know the history of Arafat's involvement and time has proven he cannot negotiate with any tool other than terrorism.

Ironically, the White House stated they would not work with him, but in reality they were, because Arafat controlled the Palestinian prime ministers. It had also become a Bush vs. Arafat situation now that Abbas had resigned. On March 14, 2003 in the Rose Garden, Bush reaffirmed his commitment to an "Israel and Palestine" living side by side in peace and security, but Arafat was the major obstacle to that happening.

Secretary Powell said, "Israel would incite rage not only among Arabs, but also Muslims everywhere, by exiling or executing Palestinian Authority Chairman Yasser Arafat." (Note: A prime example of impact of terrorism.)

Powell, speaking from Baghdad on September 14, 2003, said that Israeli politicians are not helping the U.S.-sponsored peace process by making such statements as Vice Prime Minister Ehud Olmert's comment. Olmert said, "killing (Arafat) is definitely one of the 'options' under consideration by Prime Minister Ariel Sharon's government."

On September 16, the U.S. vetoed a UN Security Council bill that called on Israel to guarantee Arafat's security. U.S. Ambassador John Negroponte said the United States does not support the elimination or exile of Arafat and believes that his diplomatic isolation is the best course. He said the United States was forced to use its veto because the resolution failed to name groups such as Hamas and the Al-Aqsa Martyrs Brigade, which have claimed credit for numerous suicide bombings and other attacks against Israelis.

Also that day, the U.S. told Israel they would deduct money spent on settlements from their $9 billion loan guarantee. The U.S. stated they were considering whether to reduce money spent on the security fence from the loan guarantees. U.S. Treasury Secretary Snow reminded Israeli Finance Minister Benjamin Netanyahu that Israel is required to reduce its debt as another contingency of their loan guarantees. Due to Bush Administration pressure, Prime Minister Sharon delayed his cabinet meeting the following morning, when they would have discussed the course of the security fence.

Israel is Quick to Respond

Israel normally responds quickly to U.S. dictates and objections due to the financial and public support from the only nation continuing to favor them. With this in mind, the U.S. uses its money to maneuver Sharon only to the point of not angering Jewish and Christian voters. Most Jews want peace and have no problem using covenant land for it, but they also do not want to see Israel put in further danger. Of members of Congress, 61 percent attend replacement theology churches and seven percent attend Jewish synagogues. This 68 percent favor peace using Israel's land, as long as there are peace and security guarantees.

President Bush welcomes King Abdullah II to Camp David on September 18, 2003

First, I'm so pleased to welcome my friend, King Abdullah and Queen Rania to Camp David. I want to thank them so very much for rearranging their schedules to get up here ahead of Hurricane Isabel. Laura and I look forward to spending some quality time with two really fine people.

We're going to have some serious discussions today, then we'll have a nice lunch and then we'll batten down the hatches and spend a good evening with our friend.

Bush comments on Arafat in his Press Briefing with Abdullah from Camp David on September 18, 2003

Mr. Arafat has failed as a leader. And as I mentioned, Prime Minister Abbas was undermined at all turns by the old order, which meant Mr. Arafat. And the people of the Palestinian territory must understand if they want peace, they must have leadership who is absolutely 100 percent committed to fighting off terror. I believed Prime Minister Abbas when he told me at Sharm el-Sheikh, then at Aqaba, then in the Oval Office, he would do everything in his power to fight terror, that he would work to consolidate the security forces so that he could fight terror.

And his efforts were undermined, and that's why we're now stalled. I'm still committed to peace, because I believe the vast majority of people want peace; I'm committed to the Road Map.

But I'll remind those who focus on the Road Map that the first thing the Road Map said was that there must be security in order for peace to advance, that there must be a collective effort to fight off terror. Mr. Arafat has failed in that effort. And, hopefully, at some point in time, a leadership of the Palestinian Authority will emerge which will then commit itself 100 percent to fighting off terror. And then we'll be able to consolidate the power necessary to fight off terror.

And when that happens, the world will come together to provide the conditions for hope. The world will come together to help an economy grow so that the Palestinian people can have a hopeful future. The first thing that must happen is an absolute condemnation and defeat of those forces who will kill innocent people in order to stop a peace process from going forward.

Analysis: Bush vs. Arafat

To President Bush's credit, he never invited Arafat to the White House. He refused to meet with him or to negotiate with him. He attempted to isolate him in his dealings with Mahmoud Abbas, but Arafat continued to interfere until Abbas finally resigned in frustration.

President Bush has a lot riding politically in Israel and Iraq. He needs the world community's support for Iraq. Israel had been pressured previously due to that fact.

What Will Give?

As Michael Ledeen, Contributing Editor to the *National Review*, stated recently in a 700 Club interview with Pat Robertson: no peace agreement has ever been agreed to that did not first have a war. In other words, until the terror infrastructure in Israel is dealt with (which could bring in other Arab nations per Psalm 83 and Isaiah 17) there will not be a Daniel 9:27 peace agreement or any other.

Events & catastrophes in September 2003

- Arafat continued to hinder the Middle East peace process, particularly efforts by Prime Minister Mahmoud Abbas.
- Palestinian Prime Minister Abbas resigned.
- Hurricane Isabel hit east coast of U.S.; third most costliest in U.S. history.

The Ninth Disruptive Period:
December 17, 2003 - January 10, 2004

From November 24 to December 18, 2003, President Bush, Secretary Powell, the U.S. State Department, the EU, the UN, Russia, the Palestinians, the Egyptians, the Jordanians, members of the Arab League, the Vatican, members of the World Council of Churches, the National Council of Churches, Israeli peace activists, all pressured Israeli Prime Minister Sharon to return to the negotiating table and to make painful land concessions.

In the same time period Israel's "hard-line" Likud party reevaluated their position on the disputed land. Moreover, the Yesha council, which represents Israeli settlers, stated Sharon's government would fail if he tampers with the settlements.

Faulty Geneva Accord creates new pressure on Israel

The Geneva Accord was signed on December 1 in Geneva, Switzerland. It was an attempt by the French influenced EU to use the Accord to forge a compromise position between the Quartet's Road Map and the Geneva Accord, and to stir sentiment in Israel. Israeli and Palestinian opposition groups brokered the Geneva Accord after two years of secret negotiations. Information about the Accord was circulated to Israeli and Palestinian households in an effort to drum up support.

The Israeli government said they firmly opposed the Accord, and Jewish groups criticized Switzerland for "interfering" in internal Israeli affairs.

U.S. Secretary of State Powell wrote a letter to Geneva Accord sponsors Israeli Yossi Beilin and Palestinian Yasser Abed Rabbo expressing appreciation for their effort, and then met with them on December 5th.

Washington Post columnist Charles Krauthammer stated eloquently that the Geneva Accord was scandalous. Israel is a democracy; this agreement was negotiated in defiance of Israel's democratically elected government. If a private U.S. citizen negotiated a treaty on his own, he could go to jail under the Logan Act. If an Israeli does it, he gets a pat on the back from the U.S. Secretary of State.

The U.S. State Department sent an official from the U.S. Embassy in Bern to attend the signing of the Geneva Accord.

Former President Jimmy Carter unleashed a fierce attack against Israel and America in his speech at the Geneva Accord's ceremony in Switzerland. Carter blamed President Bush for anti-American sentiment and worldwide terror. "Bush's inordinate support for Israel allows the Palestinians to suffer," Carter said. "This is a source of anti-American sentiment in the world and encourages terror."

Carter said Israel's settlements in the West Bank and Gaza Strip and the security fence are the main obstacles to peace. He called repeatedly for the return of Palestinian refugees to the territories, beyond what is called for in the Geneva Accord.

"Settlements prevent the return of the refugees who left their homes after the 1948 and 1967 wars," Carter said. "No matter what leaders the Palestinians may choose, Israel must choose between peace and settlements."

UN Secretary General Kofi Annan also stated his approval of the Geneva Accord.

Ominously, the attempted siege of the Holy Land by Israel's enemies has entered a new phase. Peace proposals designed to undermine Israeli security are endorsed by past Israeli politicians, past sponsors of obsolete agreements, and most disconcerting, the EU and the U.S., whose continued support, and ultimate guarantee of Israel's security, looks more and more critical to any final peace agreement.

A quick review of the most perilous provisions of the recently signed Geneva Accord arouse deep concern:

- Reserve Maj.-Gen Yaakov Amidror is quoted as saying the Accord *conceded almost all the security arrangements for the West Bank and Gaza Strip sought by past Israeli governments* and would leave Israel without a *safety net* if the Palestinians violated the agreement.
- Israel would be forced to turn over sovereignty of the Jerusalem Temple Mount, closing the door to the rebuilding of the Third Holy Temple, and effectively sabotaging Jewish aspirations of resuming the Temple-based worship of God.
- Accord terms will be dictated by an Arab-biased group of nations (International Crisis Group) operating a European (Brussels based) conflict resolution organization.
- UN Resolution 194 (and others) would be the basis for resolution of the refugee problem. Its financial impact is potentially ruinous. Resolution 194 does not speak of the 'right' of return, but carries its own seed of discord to determine financial responsibility.

Secretary Powell spoke (December 2): "I have an obligation ... to listen to individuals who have interesting ideas."

President Bush spoke (December 4): "The Geneva Accord was productive, as long as terror is fought, there is security, and a free and democratic Palestinian state emerges."

U.S. Senators and Congressmen Present Plan

A group of 18 United States congressmen and five senators submitted a draft resolution in both houses of Congress, urging President Bush to adopt and promote two initiatives for an Israeli-Palestinian agreement formulated by members of the Israeli opposition and Palestinian interlocutors.

The two initiatives are The Peoples' Voice, launched by Ami Ayalon and Sari Nusseibeh, and the Geneva Understandings, drafted by Yossi Beilin and Yasser Abed Rabbo.

The resolution's sponsors included two Jewish senators, Frank Lautenberg and Dianne Feinstein, as well as veteran senator Patrick Leahy.

Clergy Urge More Active White House Effort for Middle East Peace
(Washington Post)

Thirty-two religious leaders representing many of the nation's largest Christian, Jewish and Muslim groups jointly urged the Bush administration to make more "active and determined" efforts to forge peace between Israel and the Palestinians. In a November 25, 2003, letter to the White House, the bishops, cardinals, rabbis and imams called for "renewed high-level U.S. engagement . . . to help both sides take the bold steps necessary to rebuild hope that peace is possible."

While praising President Bush's peace plan, known as the "Road Map," they were critical of the administration's effort to carry it out. So far, they said, the steps taken by Israel and the Palestinian Authority have been "far too timid" and the U.S.-led monitoring process has been "practically invisible."

The letter's signers included the presiding bishops of the Methodist, Lutheran, Presbyterian and Episcopal churches; the Roman Catholic cardinals of Washington and Baltimore; the Greek Orthodox primate in the United States; three prominent evangelical ministers; the heads of the Conservative, Reform and Reconstructionist rabbinical associations; and directors or founders of seven U.S. Muslim groups.

World Pressure

Putting this intense period into perspective, nations dramatically increased pressure on Israel to divide God's covenant land. Again, they called for the dismantling of Israeli settlements, condemned construction the new security fence (the U.S. deducted $289 million from Israel's loan guarantees), called for Jerusalem to be divided, called on Israel to leave most of the West Bank (Judea and Samaria), and called on Israel to deal with the Palestinian refugee situation. Meanwhile, Palestinian terror groups threatened to renew suicide bombings.

Sharon Responds with His Own Plan *(Jerusalem Post)*

In response to enormous pressure, especially from the United States, Prime Minister Sharon gave a major policy speech on December 18, 2003, pertaining to Israel's land and the peace talks. He made these major points:

Israel may begin to take unilateral steps to detach itself from the Palestinians while implementing the U.S.-backed Road Map peace initiative. Sharon said during his speech at the Herziliya Conference:

> According to circumstances, it is possible that parts of the 'Disengagement Plan' that are supposed to provide maximum security to the citizens of Israel will be undertaken while also attempting to implement the Road Map.

Sharon said that Israel would initiate "unilateral security steps" should the Palestinians not take the Road Map seriously. "The steps we will take are security-based and not diplomatically-based," he added.

Sharon said that in the meantime, Israel would begin to take security measures in order to protect its citizens.

> The 'Disengagement Plan' will include the redeployment of IDF forces along new security lines and a change in the deployment of settlements, which will reduce as much as possible the number of Israelis located in the heart of the Palestinian population. We will draw provisional security lines and the IDF will be deployed along them.

> The government, under my direction, adopted and is committed to the Road Map peace process. But I will not wait indefinitely for the Palestinians to fulfill their obligations.

The Prime Minister's speech comes after weeks of buildup. Sharon began speaking of undefined "unilateral steps" the previous month, indicating that he might consider moving West Bank Jewish settlements.

Calling on the Palestinians, Sharon said,

> I use this opportunity to turn to the Palestinians and say: We are not interested in controlling you but rather wish upon you a Palestinian state which has a normal relationship with Israel.

Sharon reiterated his recent statements whereby Israelis "would not stay in every place they are now."

> This reduction of friction will require the extremely difficult step of changing the deployment of some of the settlements. In the framework of a future agreement, Israel will not remain in all the places where it is today.

Sharon said he had made a commitment to the Bush administration to remove illegal settlement outposts, and "I plan to stand by that commitment."

Speaking of the Road Map peace plan, Sharon said,

This is a balanced plan with a progressive staged process to achieve peace and it is the best way to achieve real peace.

The Road Map is a clear and logical plan and therefore it must be implemented.

The perception, according to which the very signing of a peace agreement will produce security out of thin air, has already been tried in the past and failed miserably.

Sharon said that Israel has taken and will continue to take steps to improve the Palestinian's living conditions.

We will take away roadblocks and will ease passage for Palestinians. All these steps are meant to create a better life for the Palestinians who are not involved in terror.

Israel will only detach from the Palestinians under full coordination with the U.S. "We cannot hurt the strategic coordination with the U.S.," he said.

"If in a few months the Palestinians still don't begin to follow the Road Map then Israel will initiate a unilateral plan in order to give Israel maximum security," he said.

Sharon said that Israel wants to hold direct negotiations with the Palestinians "but we will not allow ourselves to be held hostage by the Palestinians. . . . As I said before, we will not wait for them forever."

Referring to the controversial construction of the security fence, the prime minister said, "The security fence will not be the permanent border for Israel."

Calling out to the Israeli people, Sharon said,

My life experience has taught me that peace like war, requires complete unity. I believe that this path of unity must be continued today. Whether we will be able to advance the Road Map, or will have to implement the "Disengagement Plan", experience has taught us that, together, through broad national consensus, we can do great things.

EU's Solana warns Sharon against unilateral action

EU foreign affairs chief Javier Solana warned on December 19, 2003, there was no "unilateral solution" to the Middle East conflict after Israel's leader threatened to take action of his own to bring about peace. Solana said,

There is no unilateral solution to this conflict. Any statements pointing in that direction will certainly not help to move the process forward.

I welcome Prime Minister Sharon's acknowledgement that a full and genuine implementation of the Road Map is the best way to achieve true peace between Israelis and Palestinians.

This important statement fully coincides with the EU's well-known position on this issue. But what is urgently required is that courageous and bold steps be taken in parallel by both sides for the effective implementation of the Road Map.

NRP: Sharon's speech harms Israel

National Religious Party (NRP) leader Effi Eitam said in response to Prime Minister Sharon's Herziliya Conference speech that the prime minister is inviting terror and harms the goals of the Jewish settlement movement.

"Unfortunately Sharon is continuing to make statements that invite continued terror, and harm the goal of Jewish settlement," Eitam said. "The NRP will judge Sharon according to his actions."

Eitam, the Housing and Construction Minister, said that the NRP would not be partners to a government that uproots Jewish communities and endangers the Zionist enterprise as a whole.

Sharon's threat to unilaterally disconnect from the Palestinians is an Israeli surrender to the war waged against it by Arafat for the past three years. Israel should learn from the Americans that the only key to achieve quiet and peace in the region is by militarily defeating terror, along with economic and diplomatic pressure.

NRP faction chairman Shaul Yahalom said, "The NRP will do every effort to assassinate the idea of unilateral separation."

Pinhas Wallerstein, a veteran leader of Israeli settlers, complained about the possible moving of settlements and warned that disengagement would create the "imposition of a siege on the Jewish settlements" inside the barrier.

Member of the Knesset (Israel's parliament) Shimon Peres said that he was very disappointed with Sharon's speech. "Instead of a decision, we were handed another delay, and a delay that is not necessarily in our favor."

Palestinian PM says Sharon 'threatens' Palestinians

Palestinian Prime Minister Qureia, reacting to a speech given by Prime Minister Sharon at a security conference in Herziliya, saying he was "disappointed" that Sharon's speech included "threats" to the Palestinians, in the form of unilateral steps.

Qureia said that if Sharon would negotiate with the Palestinians, peace could come "sooner than expected."

Asked by CNN what he would do if Israel started unilateral moves, Saeb Erekat, the Palestinian's chief negotiator said: "With this unilateral approach, they may make peace with Israelis and Israelis; they'll not make peace with Palestinians".

Erekat urged the Israeli prime minister to stick to the "Road Map" for peace, a blueprint backed by a Quartet. "We invite Mr. Sharon to come immediately with no conditions to the negotiating table on the basis of the Road Map and let the Americans, Europeans, Russians and the UN–the Quartet members–to be the judges of both of us."

Major increase in U.S. and world terror warnings, U.S. mad-cow outbreak, major earthquakes in California and Iran, chaos in Iraq, & suicide bombing in Israel

On December 17, 2003, Secretary Powell stated to the Palestinians, that a cease-fire deal would seal statehood.

On December 18, Israeli Prime Minister Sharon gave a major policy address on the future of Israel's land.

On December 19, President Bush's spokesman Scott McClellan reacted warmly to much of Sharon's latest plan for dealing with the Palestinians.

"We were very pleased with the overall speech," said McClellan in an apparent effort to offset reports that focused on his admonition that Sharon should not try to impose a settlement without negotiations.

"We believe that the Road Map is the way to get to the president's two-state vision" of a democratic Palestinian state existing alongside Israel by 2005, McClellan said.

These political statements were immediately followed by a significant increase in U.S. and world terror warnings, the U.S.'s first recorded mad-cow case, a major 6.5 earthquake in California, a 6.3 earthquake in Iran, an increase in insurgent chaos in Iraq, and a tragic suicide bombing in Tel Aviv, Israel.

On December 25, 2003, Israeli Prime Minister Sharon stated he would allow Likud members to vote on his plan for disengagement from the Palestinians, including the replacement of settlements and the approval of a Palestinian state. The move was intended to bypass the hawkish Likud central committee and the troublesome Likud Knesset faction and instead turn to the party's relatively moderate 300,000 grassroots members, who would be more likely to give the "Disengagement Plan" the party's stamp of approval. (A major suicide bombing occurred at a bus stop at the Geha Junction, east of Tel Aviv. The Popular Front for the Liberation of Palestine claimed responsibility for the attack.)

Again, as the nation of Israel was pressured to divide her land, the world experienced a major increase in terror warnings.

Summary

As I have shown in this chapter and previous chapters, when the Bush Administration is actively involved with negotiations pertaining to Israel's land, this has created periods of disruption for his presidency.

There have been numerous additional disruptive periods in 2004, 2005 and 2006 since this book was first published.

There was a disruptive period from May 23 – June 2, 2004, another from August 1 to September 24, 2004, another from August 17 to November 23, 2005, and we experienced yet another disruptive period beginning on January 11, 2006 and continuing through press time on May 15, 2006.

If the Bush Administration continues their participation in the land-for-peace process in Israel, you will see that this pattern continuing to repeat itself in the days ahead.

CHAPTER 12

Suicide Bombings Coinciding with U.S. or Israel "Land for Peace" Efforts

According to the Israeli government, an estimated 90% of planned terror events in Israel have been averted. Frequently, we hear about the large ones that have been miraculously prevented by the Lord's hand. Tragically, there are occasional suicide bombings or shootings where there is a large loss of life and multiple injuries.

Statements and Efforts by the Bush Administration Dealing with the Middle East that Coincide with Major Suicide Bombings

My research shows that when President George W. Bush intensified his involvement in the Middle East peace plan and backed a Palestinian state, for the period between late November 2001 and October 7, 2004, 26 out of 36 major suicide bombings occurred on the same day or within 24 hours of either major U.S. presidential pronouncements, or Israeli leadership statements or activities.

President Bush sees the suicide bombings as an attempt to disrupt the peace process. However, when the Bush administration is not meddling with Israel's land, the majority of suicide bombings are averted—only small bombings occur—or there are periods of calm.

What causes this phenomenon? Does the Lord lift His restraining hand of protection for a brief moment as His covenant land is being negotiated? Is the Lord protecting His people in Israel from even greater terror events? Is He keeping Israel from a peace agreement that would place her in indefensible borders with an enemy committed to her destruction?

The world community believes the Arab propaganda that the key to world peace is the land of Israel. How absurd! No nation in the world should require Israel to negotiate with terrorist regimes, and she should not be kept from defending herself and eliminating the terror infrastructure within her country.

Additionally, the God of Israel does not want to see His covenant land given to Israel's enemies.

Below is a list of major suicide bombings that corresponded with the Bush administration's intervention in Israel's affairs, from December 1, 2001–January 29, 2004.

- November 30–December 2, 2001: U.S. General Anthony Zinni was in Israel negotiating a cease-fire agreement between the Israelis and Palestinians.
  * December 1-2, 2001: Two major suicide bombings.

- March 8, 2002: President Bush stated he was sending General Zinni back to the Middle East.
  * March 9, 2002: A major suicide bombing.

- March 20-21 and 27-29, 2002: General Zinni was in Israel twice to negotiate a cease-fire agreement.
  * March 20-21, 27 & 29, 2002: Major suicide bombings.

- March 30, 2002: The UN and the U.S. called on Israel to withdraw from Palestinian cities.
  * March 30-31, 2002: Two major suicide bombings.

- April 10-12, 2002: U.S. Secretary of State Colin Powell went to Israel to jump-start peace talks.
  * April 10 & 12, 2002: Two major suicide bombings.

- May 7, 2002: President Bush met with Israeli Prime Minister Ariel Sharon at the White House.
  * Major suicide bombing occurred during their meeting in Oval Office.

- June 5, 2002: CIA Director George Tenet was in Israel negotiating a cease-fire deal.
  * June 5, 2002: A major suicide bombing.

- June 18-19, 2002: President Bush's Middle East address was postponed two days in a row due to suicide bombings.
  * June 18-19, 2002: Two major suicide bombings in Jerusalem.

- July 18, 2002: Secretary Powell stated the CIA was working on a plan to protect Israel from terror.
  * July 18-19, 2002: Two major suicide bombings.

- October 20, 2002: U.S. Assistant Secretary of State William Burns was in the Middle East to gain Road Map input.
  * October 21, 2002: A major suicide bombing.

- November 7, 2002: Revised "Road Map" called for immediate Israeli acceptance of Palestinian state.
  * November 7, 2002: A major suicide bombing.

- January 5, 2003: U.S. rejected Israel's objections to the Road Map.
  * January 5, 2003: A major suicide bombing.

- May 11, 2003: Secretary Powell went to Riyadh, Saudi Arabia to meet with Crown Prince Abdullah, the sponsor of the Saudi Middle East peace plan. They were to discuss the Israeli-Palestinian peace talks.
  * May 12, 2003: Four bombings occurred in Riyadh within hours of Powell's arrival. The bombings targeted Americans and were largest terror event directed towards Americans since September 11, 2001.

- June 9-10, 2003: Bush reiterated his commitment to the Middle East peace process following Israel's attempted assassination of Hamas leader.
  * June 11, 2003: A major suicide bombing in the center of Jerusalem.

- August 18, 2003: Under White House pressure, Israel was in the final stage of negotiations with the Palestinians before turning over security responsibility to four West Bank cities.
  * August 19, 2003: A major suicide bombing on a bus in Jerusalem.

- September 6-9, 2003: Palestinian Prime Minister Abbas resigned on September 6. The next day, PLO Chairman Arafat selected Ahmed Qureia as the new Palestinian Prime Minister. On September 9 (after pressure from the U.S.), Prime Minister Sharon's aides said that Qureia could be a partner if he carried out the Palestinians' obligations under a U.S.-backed peace plan, including disarming militants.
  * September 9, 2003 (afternoon): A major suicide bombing at the Tzrifin army base near Tel Aviv. Five hours later there was another major suicide bombing at the entrance to the Cafe Hillel restaurant (Emek Refaim Road), in the German Colony in southern Jerusalem.

- January 28, 2004: In Jerusalem, U.S. State Department envoys John Wolf and David Satterfield pressed Ahmed Qureia and Ariel Sharon to hold a

long-delayed summit to help revive the Quartet's Road Map.
* Within 24 hours, a major suicide bombing occurred in Jerusalem near
  Prime Minister Sharon's residence. The Al Aqsa Martyrs' Brigades
  claimed responsibility.

• February 19, 2004: Prime Minister Sharon briefed U.S. envoys on his
  proposal to uproot Israeli settlements in Gaza. He tried to sell Washington
  a unilateral plan that Palestinians fear will grab land they want for a state.
  "The prime minister is briefing them on his disengagement plan," a senior
  Israeli government official said about the talks with Elliot Abrams and
  Stephen Hadley, both national security advisers to Bush, and State
  Department official William Burns.
  * Within 72 hours of Sharon's meeting with U.S. officials, a major suicide
    bombing occurred on a Jerusalem bus. The Fatah Al Aqsa Martyrs'
    Brigades claimed responsibility for the attack.

• September 21, 2004: Bush spoke to the UN General Assembly on Tuesday
  morning: *he stated Israel should impose a settlement freeze, dismantle
  unauthorized outposts, end the daily humiliation of the Palestinian
  people, and avoid any actions that prejudice final negotiations.* Later that
  day, Sharon stated he was staying with the disengagement timetable and
  Israeli Foreign Minister Shalom assured the U.S. that Israel wouldn't
  enlarge settlements.
  * The same day, a major suicide bombing was carried out by a female
    terrorist at the French Hill junction in northern Jerusalem. The Fatah
    al-Aqsa Martyrs' Brigades claimed responsibility for the attack.

• October 31-November 1, 2004: On October 31, the United States rejected
  the list of unauthorized outposts in the West Bank. Israel listed 23 outposts
  established since Sharon's government assumed office in March 2001. The
  Americans believe the number of outposts built during that period is much
  higher. Israel and the U.S. awaited a report by Attorney Talia Sasson and
  the defense minister's advisor, Baruch Spiegel, on the ways outposts were
  to be set up and the legal means to get rid of them.
  * Within 24-hours, a major suicide bombing occurred at the Carmel
    market in Tel Aviv, carried out by a 16-year-old boy from the Askar
    refugee camp near Nablus.

Example of President Bush's response to Terrorist Attacks

President Bush condemned the June 11, 2003 terrorist attacks against Israel:

Today there was a terrible bombing in Jerusalem. I send my heartfelt condolences to those who suffered and lost life.

It is clear there are people in the Middle East who hate peace; people who want to kill in order to make sure that the desires of Israel to live in security and peace don't happen; who kill to make sure the desires of the Prime Minister of the Palestinian Authority and others of a peaceful state, living side-by-side with Israel, do not happen.

To the people in the world who want to see peace in the Middle East, I strongly urge all of you to fight off terror, to cut off money to organizations such as Hamas, to isolate those who hate so much that they're willing to kill to stop peace from going forward. I strongly condemn the killings, and I urge and call upon all of the free world, nations which love peace, to not only condemn the killings, but to use every ounce of their power to prevent them from happening in the future.

Peace Efforts or Statements by Israeli Leaders Coinciding with Major Suicide Bombings/Terror Events

- October 21, 2001: Prime Minister Sharon stated he might accept a Palestinian state if Israel's security is guaranteed.
  * Minister of Tourism Rechavam Ze'evi was fatally shot in the head in the Jerusalem Hyatt Hotel the morning of Sharon's public statement.

- May 18, 2002: Shimon Peres, Israel's Foreign Minister, called for an accelerated Palestinian state.
  * Within 24 hours: a major suicide bombing in Netanya.

- June 17, 2002: Sharon told U.S. he envisioned two states living in peace.
  * Within 24 hours, a major suicide bombing occurred at Patt junction between Gilo and Jerusalem; a second occurred in the French Hill intersection in northern Jerusalem within 48 hours.

- July 31, 2002: Israel transferred cash to the Palestinian Authority at U.S. insistence.
  * A major suicide bombing occurred on the Hebrew University's Mt. Scopus campus.

- September 18, 2002: Peres told UN that Israel was for a Palestinian state.
  * Within 24 hours: a major suicide bombing in Tel Aviv.

- October 21, 2002: Peres told EU that Israel favored a Palestinian state.
  * Within 24 hours, a major suicide bombing occurred on a bus from Kiryat Shmona to Tel-Aviv.

- November 14, 2002: Sharon said a Palestinian state was all but a given.
  * Within 24 hours, a major shooting occurred in Hebron.

- November 20, 2002: Jerusalem Mayor Olmert backed Ariel Sharon for the leader of the Likud Party.
  * Within 24 hours: a major suicide bombing in Jerusalem.

- November 28, 2002: Sharon won Likud election over Netanyahu, who was not in favor of a Palestinian state.
  * On the same day, there was a bombing in Mombassa, Kenya; two missiles missed an Israeli plane leaving Mombassa; and a shooting attack on a Likud branch in Beit She'an.

- January 5, 2003: Israel conducted secret statehood talks.
  * A major double suicide bombing occurred near the old Central Bus Station in Tel-Aviv.

- March 5, 2003: Sharon agreed to painful concessions for peace.
  * Within 24 hours, a major suicide bombing occurred of a bus in Haifa, en route to Haifa University.

- April 29, 2003: Sharon stated "we will do whatever we have to, to bring peace to Israel"; the Quartet Road Map was delivered on April 30, 2003.
  * A major suicide bombing occurred in Tel Aviv that day.

- May 17, 2003: Sharon met with new Palestinian Prime Minister Abbas.
  * May 18, 2003: a major suicide bombing occurred near French Hill in Jerusalem.
  * May 19, 2003: a major suicide bombing in Afula.

- August 18, 2003: Israel was in final negotiations with Palestinian negotiators prior to turning over security responsibility to four West Bank cities.
  * A major suicide bombing occurred in Jerusalem's Shmuel Hanavi neighborhood.

- December 25, 2003: Sharon said he would allow Likud members to vote on his plan for disengagement from the Palestinian areas. The plan included the replacement of settlements and the approval of a Palestinian state. The move was intended to bypass the hawkish Likud central committee and the troublesome Likud Knesset faction, and instead turn to the party's relatively moderate 300,000 grassroots members, who would be more likely to give the "Disengagement Plan" the party's stamp of approval.
  * A major suicide bombing occurred at a bus stop at the Geha Junction, east of Tel Aviv. The Popular Front for the Liberation of Palestine claimed responsibility.

- January 13, 2004: Prime Minister Sharon raised the possibility that Israel Defense Forces would one day leave the Gaza Strip (captured by Israel in the 1967 Six-Day War). "I hope the day will come when we will not have to sit in the Strip," Sharon said in a speech to Bedouin soldiers, broadcast on Army Radio. Sharon previously said Israel would have to yield some land for peace either in a deal with Palestinians, or as part of go-it-alone steps to end years of violence.

* The next day, four Israelis were killed and ten injured when a female suicide bomber associated with Hamas exploded at the Erez check point in the Gaza Strip.

• January 25-29, 2004: On January 25, Israel and Hezbollah finalized an agreement. Israel would free prisoners and return soldiers' remains if Hezbollah released Israeli businessman Elhanan Tennenbaum and the bodies of three IDF soldiers kidnapped in October 2000. On January 29, Israel freed 400 Palestinian prisoners; prisoners from Lebanon, Syria and other Arab states; and returned several dozen bodies to Lebanon. Israeli Foreign Ministry spokesman Jonathan Peled said, "We are releasing another 400 Palestinians with a very heavy heart, because we know that these 400 will return very quickly to the cycle of violence."

* January 29, 2004: A major suicide bombing occurred on a bus near the Prime Minister's residence in Jerusalem's Rehavia neighborhood. Al Aqsa Martyrs' Brigades claimed responsibility.

• March 14, 2004: Israeli and Palestinian officials met to prepare for the first summit between Israeli Prime Minister Sharon and Palestinian Prime Minister Ahmed Qureia. Israeli officials said the summit could determine whether Israel proceeds with peace talks, or adopts a unilateral plan to dis-engage from Palestinian areas. Sharon said Israel still supports the road map, but reserves the right to take its own unilateral steps if talks with the Palestinians do not succeed. Sharon said that the proposed unilateral plan is likely to include Israel withdrawing from most, if not all, of the Gaza Strip and parts of the West Bank.

* The same day two major suicide bombings occurred at Ashdod Port. Hamas and Fatah claimed responsibility.

• August 31, 2004: Israeli Prime Minister Sharon increased the size of his Gaza evacuations in response to pressure from the Bush administration.

* That day, suicide bombers on two Beersheba city buses killed sixteen people and wounded 100 others. Hamas in Hebron claimed responsibility for the attack.

• October 6, 2004: The United States asked Israel to clarify statements made by Dov Weisglass, a senior advisor to Prime Minister Sharon. Weisglass said that the disengagement plan means a "freezing of the peace process." U.S. State Department Spokesman Adam Ereli said the U.S. told Israel that Weisglass' comments do not match Israel's official government position as presented to the U.S. Secretary of State Powell told reporters

the U.S. does not doubt Sharon's commitment to the Road Map. On October 7, Prime Minister Sharon's office insisted that the diplomatic furor caused by Weisglass' comments is over.
* October 7, 2004: Twin terror bombings at two Sinai holiday resorts frequented by Israelis.

- November 1, 2004: The Knesset opened debate on the Evacuation and Compensation Bill, which would provide legal and financial underpinnings to Sharon's disengagement plan.
  * As the Knesset debate began, news reached the parliamentary chamber of a suicide bombing at the Carmel market in Tel Aviv. The bomber was a 16-year-old boy from the Askar refugee camp near Nablus. (Many of the Knesset speeches addressed the tragic bombing.)

The Cycle of Violence Continues

Presented below is the Israeli-Palestinian pattern that repeated itself from late November 2001 to January 29, 2004:

- The U.S. and the world community called for an end to violence in Israel and for new meetings between the Israelis and the Palestinians.
- The U.S. would sponsor a meeting between Israelis and Palestinians in Israel; a Bush-Sharon meeting would occur at the White House; Peres and Sharon would state Israel's approval of a Palestinian state; Mayor Olmert of Jerusalem and/or the Likud Party would back Sharon based on his pro-Palestinian state position; or Israel would agree to a large Palestinian prisoner release. As these events occurred, a major suicide bombing (or shooting event) would occur the same day or usually within 24 hours. A radical Islamic terror group would take "credit" for the act.
- President George W. Bush or his senior officials would condemn the killings in strong language, encourage the sides to get back to the table and ask Israel not to respond too harshly for the sake of peace.
- World leaders would strongly condemn suicide bombings and call for Israelis and Palestinians to go back to talks. Leaders would call on Israel to not respond too harshly and to leave the occupied land.
- Israel would respond forcefully to the tragedy by striking militant targets within Palestinian neighborhoods and tightening up its defenses. At times they called for the exile of Arafat, but the world community disapproved.
- If Israel responded too harshly, the U.S. State Department and the world community, led by the UN and EU, would chastise Israel for her use of force. The greater the proportion of military response by Israel the greater the world leader's outcry.
- The cycle would repeat itself again.

CHAPTER 13

U.S. Presidents & Middle East Leaders Involved in "Peace" Process and the Consequences

Since the early 1900's American Presidents have been very active in the support of Israel both before and after their statehood.

You can see below that the presidents who supported Israel were blessed and those who didn't experienced consequences. This is consistent with what the Bible says when dealing with the Jewish people. You will be either blessed or cursed. Genesis 12:3 declares: "And I will bless them that bless thee, and curse him that curseth thee: and in thee shall all families of the earth be blessed. Zechariah 2:8 proclaims: "For thus saith the LORD of hosts; After the glory hath He sent me unto the nations which spoiled you: for he that toucheth you toucheth the apple of His [God's] eye."

When the United States became actively involved in the Middle East peace process with the Israelis, Egyptians, Jordanians, Syrians and the Palestinians, the American president's began to experience the consequences. The greater the involvement and pressure on Israel to divide her land the greater the size and significance of the consequences.

U.S. President's Wilson, Harding, Coolidge, and Hoover[1]

In 1917, Lord Balfour sent a letter to Lord Rothschild, president of the British Zionist Federation, stating that the British Government would facilitate the establishment of a national home for the Jewish people in Palestine. U.S. President Woodrow Wilson expressed his support for the Balfour Declaration when he stated on March 3, 1919:

The allied nations with the fullest concurrence of our government and people are agreed that in Palestine shall be laid the foundations of a Jewish Commonwealth.

After Wilson left office, his successors expressed similar support for the Zionist enterprise. President Warren Harding said:

It is impossible for one who has studied at all the services of the Hebrew people to avoid the faith that they will one day be restored to their historic national home and there enter on a new and yet greater phase of their contribution to the advance of humanity.

President Calvin Coolidge expressed his "sympathy with the deep and intense longing which finds such fine expression in the Jewish National Homeland in Palestine."

Herbert Hoover observed:

Palestine which, desolate for centuries, is now renewing its youth and vitality through enthusiasm, hard work, and self-sacrifice of the Jewish pioneers who toil there in a spirit of peace and social justice.

Congress was no less sympathetic to the Zionist objective. One can look back to the joint Congressional resolutions of 1922 and 1944 that unanimously passed an endorsement of the Balfour Declaration. The Senate Foreign Affairs Committee stated in 1922:

The Jews of America are profoundly interested in establishing a National Home in the ancient land for their race. Indeed, this is the ideal of the Jewish people, everywhere, for, despite their dispersion, Palestine has been the object of their veneration since they were expelled by the Romans. For generations they have prayed for the return to Zion. During the past century this prayer has assumed practical form.

Legislatures in 33 states, representing 85 percent of the U.S. population, also adopted resolutions favoring the creation of a Jewish state in Palestine. Governors of 37 states, 54 United States senators, and 250 congressmen signed petitions to the President.

President Franklin D. Roosevelt - Mideastweb.org

During World War II, the United States was anxious to maintain good relations with Saudi Arabia. President Franklin D. Roosevelt had promised King Saud that the U.S. would make no policy decisions about Palestine without consulting the Arabs, though Roosevelt tried to enlist Saud's support for allowing Jewish immigration to Palestine. Following Roosevelt's verbal promise to Saud to consult the Arabs about Palestine policy, he reiterated the promise in writing on April 5, 1945. However, a week later, Roosevelt was dead. Replaced by Vice President Harry S. Truman, the end of the war created a different political reality as well as bringing the revelation of massive murder of Jews in the Holocaust.

President Harry S. Truman[2]

In early 1947, the British, who then administered a League of Nations mandate for Palestine, decided to bring the question of how to resolve the dispute between Arabs and Jews to the United Nations. The General Assembly decided to set up the UN Special Committee on Palestine (UNSCOP) to investigate the cause of the conflict in Palestine, and, if possible, devise a solution.

The majority of the UNSCOP concluded after its investigation that the question of ownership or right to Palestine was an insoluble antinomy. Rather than try to solve it, they chose the logical alternative of partition, in which both Jews and Arabs would be given sovereignty in their own separate states.

The Truman administration, despite internal disputes, endorsed the majority report and called on the General Assembly to approve partition. Ample evidence exists to indicate that U.S. influence played a critical role in securing the adoption of the partition resolution.

Less than six months later, Israel declared its independence and the United States was the first nation to grant de facto recognition to the new Jewish State—11 minutes after the proclamation. On May 26, 1952, Truman said,

> I had faith in Israel before it was established. I have faith in it now. I believe it has a glorious future before it—not just another sovereign nation, but as an embodiment of the great ideals of our civilization.

President Dwight D. Eisenhower[3]

When Israel made the decision to go to war in 1956, more than 100,000 soldiers were mobilized in less than 72 hours and the air force was fully operational within 43 hours. Paratroopers landed in the Sinai and Israeli forces quickly advanced unopposed toward the Suez Canal before halting in compliance with the demands of England and France. As expected, the Egyptians ignored the Anglo-French ultimatum to withdraw since they, the "victims," were being asked to retreat from the Sinai to the west bank of the Canal while the Israelis were permitted to stay just 10 miles east of the Canal.

On October 30, the United States sponsored a Security Council resolution calling for an immediate Israeli withdrawal, but England and France vetoed it. The following day, the two allies launched air operations, bombing Egyptian airfields near Suez.

President Dwight D. Eisenhower was upset by the fact that Israel, France and Great Britain had secretly planned the campaign to evict Egypt from the Suez Canal. Israel's failure to inform the United States of its intentions, combined with ignoring American entreaties not to go to war, sparked tensions between the countries. The United States subsequently joined the Soviet Union in a campaign to force Israel to withdraw. This included threats to discontinue all U.S. assistance, impose UN sanctions and expulsion from the UN.

On November 7, 1956, President Eisenhower addressed a note to Israeli Prime Minister David Ben-Gurion in which he advised Israel to abide by the UN Resolutions and withdraw its forces from Egyptian territory. Owing to communication delays, the message was received in Israel on November 8. On that day, Prime Minister Ben-Gurion informed the President that Israel would withdraw its forces when the appropriate arrangements were made with the United Nations regarding the entry of the international force into the Suez Canal zone.

Author Donald Neff wrote in his 1996 commentary—"Lyndon Johnson Was First to Align U.S. Policy With Israel's Policies"—that Dwight Eisenhower was distinctly cool toward Israel, seeing it as a major irritant in America's relations with the Arab world and U.S. access to oil. There were no powerful partisans of Israel in his administration and his secretary of state, John Foster Dulles, was a frequent critic of Israel.

President John F. Kennedy[4]

President John Fitzgerald Kennedy had a great intellectual and emotional commitment to the cause of nuclear nonproliferation, and he expressed his personal sense of urgency regarding proliferation both in public and private. In February 1960, France had become the fourth member of the nuclear club, and the question Kennedy faced was who would be next.

On May 19, 1963, President Kennedy stated in a "tough, extremely threatening" letter that Israel's capacity for developing nuclear arms could undermine world stability. The president demanded that Israel agree to periodic visits at the Dimona reactor by U.S. administration representatives. Israel was given no leeway. Acceptance of this demand would mean exposing the "Dimona Project" to possible liquidation, while non-acceptance would mean confrontation and possibly a severe crisis with the American administration.

A month later, on Saturday, June 15, 1963, Kennedy sent another letter to Ben-Gurion, in which he demanded vigorously and unequivocally that administration representatives be allowed to visit the sites in Dimona and that no time limits be placed on their stay there. The letter concluded with an unmistakable warning to Israel should it refuse to meet the president's demand. *The next day, Ben-Gurion resigned as prime minister.*

Ben-Gurion passed on the political hot potato to his successor, Levi Eshkol. From his first day as prime minister and almost to the time of his death, he energetically tackled this issue. His first step was handling the dispatch of John J. McCloy—U.S. special presidential envoy charged with the task of monitoring the arms race in the Middle East—who came to Israel for the express purpose of forcing the Eshkol government to agree to American inspection of Israel's "non-conventional activities." McCloy proposed establishing a link between the demand for monitoring Israel and a similar demand with respect to Egypt.

Egyptian President Nasser's reaction was negative. From Israel's standpoint, the proposal was a very positive one. In Zaki Shalom's book, "Between Dimona and Washington: The Development of Israel's Nuclear Option, 1960-1968," Shalom claims that the idea can be considered a notable achievement on the part of Eshkol's government. For the first time in many years, the American government accepted the principle for which Ben-Gurion had vainly fought: linkage between the American administration's demands regarding the monitoring of the "Dimona Project" and various Israeli demands of the administration—including the application of the same criteria to Egypt that the Americans sought to apply to Israel. Although the Kennedy administration chose to ignore Israel's other demands concerning Dimona, the acceptance of the principle symbolized a crack, albeit a tiny one, in Kennedy's tough positions vis-à-vis Israel.

This was Israel's first, and last, step in the dispute with the Kennedy administration. *On November 22, 1963, John F. Kennedy was assassinated in Dallas, Texas.*

President Lyndon B. Johnson[5]

Author Donald Neff wrote in 1996, in "Lyndon Johnson Was First to Align U.S. Policy With Israel's Policies":

> It was 33 years ago, on November 22, 1963, that President John F. Kennedy was assassinated in Dallas. While a traumatized nation grieved for its youngest president, he was succeeded by Vice President Lyndon B. Johnson, who was to become the most pro-Israel president up to that time. A sea change was about to take place in America's relations with Israel.

Johnson was quick to declare his support for the Jewish state. Shortly after being sworn in as president, Johnson reportedly remarked to an Israeli diplomat: "You have lost a very great friend, but you have found a better one." Commented Isaiah L. Kenen, one of the most effective lobbyists for Israel in Washington: "I would say that everything he did as president supported that statement."

The roots of President Johnson's feelings, like those of many other Americans, came from the Bible. As he explained in a speech before B'nai B'rith:

> Most if not all of you have very deep ties with the land and the people of Israel, as I do, for my Christian faith sprang from yours. ... The Bible stories are woven into my childhood memories as the gallant struggle of modern Jews to be free of persecution is also woven into our souls.

The United States and Israel share many common objectives ... chief of which is the building of a better world in which every nation can develop its resources and develop them in freedom and peace.

Israel's nuclear option returned to the American agenda in the talks Eshkol had with Johnson during a state visit to the U.S. in June 1964. Even before the first conversation, Johnson decided to maintain a low profile on the issue, notifying his advisers that he intended to adopt a restrained approach.

In Zaki Shalom's book, referenced above, he argues that the president's restrained position stemmed largely from domestic political considerations—for both Johnson and Eshkol. Johnson wanted to run for president in the November 1964 elections, and "Eshkol's support for him, so he very likely believed, would bring about a huge mobilization of Jewish voters to support him." Johnson feared that a head-on collision with Eshkol over such a sensitive, emotionally charged issue could undermine his political standing and strengthen Ben-Gurion's status in the major political battle between Ben-Gurion and Eshkol.

President Lyndon Johnson Was First to Align U.S. Policy With Israel's Policies

Not only was Johnson personally a strong supporter of the Jewish state but also he had a number of high officials, advisers and friends who shared his view. These included officials within the administration such as McGeorge Bundy, Clark Clifford, Arthur Goldberg, Harry McPherson, John Roche, the Rostow brothers, Walt and Eugene, and Ben Wattenberg.

These officials occupied such high offices as the ambassador to the United Nations, the head of the National Security Council and the number two post at the State Department. They were assiduous in putting forward Israel's interests in such memoranda as "What We Have Done for Israel," and "New Things We Might Do in Israel," and "How We Have Helped Israel."

The president was repeatedly urged by Israel's supporters to embrace Israeli policy, give the Jewish state increased aid, and distance America from the Arab world. So pervasive was the influence of Israel's supporters during Johnson's tenure that CIA Director Richard Helms believed there was no important U.S. secret affecting Israel that the Israeli government did not know about in this period.

Beyond the administration's supporters of Israel, one of Johnson's closest informal advisers was Supreme Court Justice Abe Fortas, another warm friend of Israel. Two of Johnson's closest outside advisers were Abraham Feinberg and Arthur B. Krim, both strong supporters of Israel. Feinberg was president of the American Bank & Trust Company of New York and the man whose "activities started a process of systematic fund-raising for politics [in the late 1940s] that has made Jews the most conspicuous fund-raisers and contributors to the Democratic Party," according to a study by Stephen D. Isaacs, Jews and American Politics. Johnson routinely consulted Feinberg on Middle East policy.

If one were forced to reduce the explanation for the unique relationship between the U.S. and Israel to one sentence, it was probably best expressed by Lyndon Johnson. When Soviet Premier Aleksei Kosygin asked Johnson why the United States supports Israel when there are 80 million Arabs and only three million Israelis, the President replied simply: "Because it is right."

The Six Day War[6]

Egyptian President Gamal Abdel Nasser announced on May 30, 1967:

The armies of Egypt, Jordan, Syria and Lebanon are poised on the borders of Israel ... to face the challenge, while standing behind us are the armies of Iraq, Algeria, Kuwait, Sudan and the whole Arab nation. This act will astound the world. Today they will know that the Arabs are arranged for battle, the critical hour has arrived. We have reached the stage of serious action and not declarations.

On June 5, 1967, Israel was indeed alone, but its military commanders had conceived a brilliant war strategy. The entire Israel Air Force, with the exception of just 12 fighters assigned to defend Israeli air space, took off at 7:14 a.m. with the intent of bombing Egyptian airfields while the Egyptian pilots were eating breakfast. In less than 2 hours, roughly 300 Egyptian aircraft were destroyed. A few hours later, Israeli fighters attacked the Jordanian and Syrian air forces, as well as one airfield in Iraq. By the end of the first day, nearly the entire Egyptian and Jordanian air forces, and half the Syrians', had been destroyed on the ground.

The fighting continued and by June 10, when U.S. Secretary of State Dean Rusk advised the Israelis "in the strongest possible terms" to accept a cease-fire, which Israel did, they had conquered enough territory to more than triple the size of the area they controlled, from 8,000 to 26,000 square miles. The Six Day War victory enabled Israel to unify Jerusalem. Israeli forces had also captured the Sinai, Golan Heights, Gaza Strip, and West Bank (Judea and Samaria).

On November 22, 1967, the UN Security Council adopted Resolution 242, which established a formula for Arab-Israeli peace whereby Israel would withdraw from territories occupied in the 1967 war in exchange for peace with its neighbors.

President Richard M. Nixon

President Richard Nixon didn't particularly care for Jews but he did provide support for Israel in the 1973 Yom Kippur war. His Secretary of State, William Rogers, was best known for his proposals for Israeli withdrawal from the West Bank to its 1967 borders. The Rogers Plan, as it became known, was rejected by Israel and Egypt when it was put to them in 1970, but formed the basis of future peace initiatives, including swapping land for peace and shared control of Jerusalem. Nixon's second Secretary of State, Henry Kissinger, was directly responsible for the drafting and approval of UN Resolution 338 which formally stopped the Yom Kippur War between Israel, Egypt and Syria. Nixon's peace efforts came to a halt after the Watergate crisis surfaced.

Yom Kippur War[7]

Throughout 1972, and for much of 1973, Egyptian President Anwar Sadat threatened war unless the United States forced Israel to accept his interpretation of UN Resolution 242 total Israeli withdrawal from territories taken in 1967.

On October 6, 1973—Yom Kippur, the holiest day in the Jewish calendar—Egypt and Syria opened a coordinated surprise attack against Israel. The equivalent of the total forces of NATO in Europe were mobilized on Israel's borders. On the Golan Heights, approximately 180 Israeli tanks faced an onslaught of 1,400 Syrian tanks. Along the Suez Canal, fewer than 500 Israeli defenders were attacked by 80,000 Egyptians.

At least nine Arab states, including four non-Middle Eastern nations, actively aided the Egyptian-Syrian war effort.

Thrown onto the defensive during the first two days of fighting, Israel mobilized its reserves and eventually repulsed the invaders and carried the war deep into Syria and Egypt. The Arab states were swiftly re-supplied by sea and air from the Soviet Union, which rejected U.S. efforts to work toward an immediate ceasefire. As a result, the United States belatedly began its own airlift to Israel. Two weeks later, Egypt was saved from a disastrous defeat by the UN Security Council, which had failed to act while the tide was in the Arabs' favor.

President Jimmy Carter Gets Land for Egypt, Brings Palestinians into the Process

After lengthy negotiations, President Jimmy Carter brought Anwar al-Sadat, President of Egypt, and Menachem Begin, Prime Minister of Israel, to Camp David. They met from September 5 to 17, 1978, and agreed to the Camp David Accords as the framework for peace in the Middle East. They invited other parties to the Arab-Israel conflict to adhere to it.

In the accords the U.S. and Israel recognized the Palestinians for the first time in a peace agreement. From this time forward they were connected to the land mentioned in UN Resolutions 242 and 338.

Isn't it ironic that Jimmy Carter, who brought the Palestinians into the peace process through the Camp David Accords was the head election official in Israel to oversee the January 25, 2006, Palestinian elections in which the terror group Hamas won in a landslide, gaining 74 of 132 seats in the Palestinian Parliament?

Since the election, Hamas refuses to acknowledge Israel's right to exist and lay down their arms, and has caused a political earthquake in Israel. The U.S. and EU are planning to stop funding the Palestinians. Iranian President Mahmoud Ahmadinejad, who has called for Israel to be wiped off the face of the map, has stepped in and offered Hamas $250 million. The Carter legacy continues in the Middle East.

The 6th Herzliya Conference[8]

Two days prior to the Palestinian election Jimmy Carter addressed "The 6th Herzliya Conference," in Herzliya, Israel. Here is an excerpt of Carter's speech:

A sovereign, contiguous, viable state for Palestinians recognized by the international community; a harmonious sharing of Jerusalem with arrangements that ensure unfettered access to holy sites for all; and the resolution of claims for displaced Palestinians that focuses on re-settlement in the new Palestinian state or equivalent compensation. The proposal calls for more than half of the Israeli settlers to remain permanently in the West Bank and strictly limits the return of Palestinian refugees.

Both Israel and the Palestinians will need a credible third party to help guide them through the process. Here, the role of the U.S. and in particular, the President of the U.S. cannot be underestimated. America remains the only power acceptable to both sides and the capability of leading the international community in planning for and delivering an effective implementation process once an agreement is reached.

There is little doubt that a lack of real effort to resolve the Palestinian issue is a primary source of anti-American sentiment throughout the Middle East and a major incentive for terrorist activity. The United States and almost all other nations recognize that Israeli settlements in the occupied territories are a violation of international law and the primary incitement to violence among Palestinians.

Quoting Colin Powell, "Israel must also be willing to end its occupation, consistent with the principals embodied in Security Council Resolutions 242 and 338, and accept a viable Palestinian State in which

Palestinians can determine their own future on their own land and live in dignity and security." A prerequisite for peacemaking is for antagonists to realize that good faith negotiations are preferable to sustained violence.

With increasing control of East Jerusalem, relatively secure behind the intrusive wall built in the West Bank, and with thousands of settlers protected by a strong occupying force, there is a temptation for many Israelis simply to withdraw from any further efforts to seek a just peace agreement proposals. The clear short-term benefits may very well subvert any further genuine efforts for a comprehensive and permanent peace.

This would leave the Palestinians with a prospective future impossible for them or any substantial portion of the international community to accept. Gaza, as presently defined and circumscribed, is a nonviable economic and political entity, and there is no possibility of an acceptable Palestinian state in what now remains of their territory in the West Bank East of the dividing wall. As acting Prime Minister Ehud Olmert pointed out years ago, efforts by Israel to perpetuate this situation will be increasingly difficult as the relative number of Palestinians increases inexorably both within Israel and in the occupied territories. The only rational response to these challenges is to revitalize the peace process, with strong influence exerted from America.

Ronald Reagan Administrations, 1981–1988

President Ronald Reagan's Middle East peace plan was released in September 1982, during his first term, with preliminary work by Secretary of State George Schultz.

The "Shultz Plan" drew upon the provisions of the Camp David accords and the September 1, 1982, Reagan peace plan, and was based on the well-known "land for peace" formula laid out in UN Resolution 242. The plan called for an international conference and implied that Israel would have to give up some of its "occupied" territories. Contained in the peace plan was an accelerated version of the time frame set out in the Camp David Accords, particularly the period required for autonomy before a permanent negotiated settlement could be reached. Shultz' efforts to meet the Arabs' need for an accelerated peace process and the Israeli need for an interim arrangement before handing territory back ran into predictable trouble.

President Reagan's Middle East peace efforts increased in the first year (1985) of his second term. The Israeli government was approached by the United States in August 1985, with a proposal to act as an intermediary by shipping 508 American made TOW anti-tank missiles to Iran in exchange for the release of the Reverend Benjamin Weir. Weir was an American hostage being held by Iranian sympathizers in Lebanon. The agreement stated that the U.S. would then ship replacement missiles to Israel. Robert McFarlane, the Assistant to the President for National Security Affairs, approached U.S. Secretary of Defense Caspar Weinberger and arranged the details. The transfer took place over the next two months. (source: Wikipedia.org)

In January of 1986, Reagan allegedly approved a plan for an American intermediary, rather than Israel, to sell arms to Iran in exchange for the release of the hostages, with profits funneled to the Nicaraguan Contras. In February, 1,000 TOW missiles were shipped to Iran. From May to November, there were additional shipments of miscellaneous weapons and parts. The proceeds from the arms sales were diverted via Lt. Colonel Oliver North, aide to U.S. National Security Advisor John Poindexter, to provide arms for the Contras (named from Spanish *contrarevolucionario*, "counter-revolutionary"). The Sandinistas' eventual loss of power in Nicaragua's national elections was seen by some as stemming from U.S. support for the Contras as well as the effects of a U.S. trade embargo initiated in May 1985. (source: Wikipedia.org)

The November 1986 Iran-Contra Affair complicated the Reagan Administration's Middle East peace efforts, and occupied much of their time and focus in 1987 leading into the election year of 1988. However, in early December 1987 the Palestinians living in the West Bank and Gaza initiated the intifadah, or uprising. This forced Secretary of State George Shultz to become reengaged in the peace process. Among others, Shimon Peres, Israeli foreign minister at the time, thought the only way to achieve a breakthrough in the peace process was to involve Jordan's King Hussein, under the context of an international conference. Shultz made three visits to the area in February, April and June 1988, trying to gain support for a revised Middle East peace plan.

On December 24, 1992, President George H. W. Bush pardoned all the principals charged in the Iran-Contra scandal. Walsh's eventual report, released in 1994, absolved Presidents Reagan and Bush for their role in the events.

George H. W. Bush Administration, 1989–1992

As a payback to the Arab nations and European allies who joined his ally base in the Desert Storm war with Iraq, President Herbert Walker Bush cosponsored the Madrid Conference with Russia on October 30-31, 1991.

Bush and his hard-line Secretary of State James Baker threatened to freeze $10 billion in loan guarantees if Israeli Prime Minister Yitzhak Shamir did not join the Madrid peace talks. Bush and Baker called on him to freeze settlement construction. On September 6, 1991, in a televised White House Oval Office appearance with the secretary of state, the President made his request:

It is in the best interest of the peace process and of peace itself that consideration of this absorption aid question be deferred for simply 120 days. And I think the American people will support me on this.

The funds were to be a "humanitarian measure" to provide housing for Jewish immigrants from Russia.

President Bush went from experiencing the highest approval rating in history (in the spring of 1991) to defeat by Bill Clinton in the November 1992 presidential election. The 1992 election was complicated by Ross Perot's candidacy, which helped consume Bush's focus. From October 1991, the only other significant Middle East peace meeting during his administration took place in Washington, DC, when peace talks reconvened on August 24, 1992.

Soviet President Mikhail Gorbachev, co-sponsor of the Madrid Conference with President George H. W. Bush, survived an attempted coup (August 18-22, 1991) less than eight weeks from the beginning of the Madrid Conference. The unsuccessful anti-Gorbachev coup by hard-liners shifted greater authority to the Russian Republic's President, and greatly accelerated change. Gorbachev dissolved the Communist party, granted the Baltic States independence, and proposed a much looser, chiefly economic federation among the remaining republics. With the formation of the Commonwealth of Independent States (CIS) on December 8, 1991, the federal government of the Soviet Union became superfluous, and *on December 25, less than eight weeks after the Madrid Conference, Gorbachev resigned as President.*

Bill Clinton Administrations, 1993–2000

President Bill Clinton was one of the key sponsors of the Oslo I Agreement, which was signed on the south lawn of the White House on September 13, 1993. Also, the Israeli-Jordanian peace deal was agreed to on October 26, 1994.

On January 21, 1998, the Lewinsky sex scandal was picked up by major news services and complicated Clinton's Middle East peace efforts. Clinton fought for his political life; he was already embroiled in Special Prosecutor Ken Starr's Whitewater inquiry and the Paula Jones sexual harassment case.

The Wye Plantation Agreement was agreed to on October 23, 1998.

Clinton became the second United States President to be impeached by the U.S. House of representatives on December 19, 1998.

On February 12, 1999, Clinton was cleared of all charges in his U.S. Senate impeachment trial, leaving him free to carry on as the United States President.

Clinton increased his peace efforts dramatically after his acquittal. He said it was an effort to atone for the Lewinsky sex scandal. He was also after a lasting legacy to help offset his very tainted two terms as president.

Clinton and James Carville, his campaign director, helped facilitate Ehud Barak's successful May 1999 election as prime minister of Israel. During 2000,

Barak offered more land than any other Israeli leader to the Palestinians and the Syrians. Barak negotiated with Syria in January 2000, and with Yasser Arafat at Camp David in July 2000. Both Syrian President Haffez Assad and PLO Chairman Arafat turned down enormously generous offers.

George W. Bush Administrations, 2001–Present

President George W. Bush wanted to be a facilitator and not an active participant in the Israeli–Palestinian peace process. But Egyptian President Hosni Mubarak and Jordan's King Abdullah II convinced him to become more involved in April 2001 when Israel was aggressively going after terror organizations in Israel. President Bush's administration was going extremely smoothly until he committed to becoming involved in the peace process. The more he became involved the worse became his political affairs and challenges.

President Bush approved of the Mitchell Plan, a "land for peace" plan prepared by former U.S. Senator George Mitchell and others on May 14, 2001.

Bush initiated the Tenet Cease-fire Agreement between the Israelis and the Palestinians; it was agreed to by the parties in June 2001, but never signed or implemented.

Bush was preparing the most comprehensive address on the Israeli-Palestinian issue ever to be presented by a U.S. President when the 9-11-2001 World Trade Center and Pentagon terror events occurred. He was going to call on the Israelis and the Palestinians to fulfill UN Resolutions 242 and 338, call for a Palestinian state, and for future negotiations on Jerusalem's borders.

Bush finally gave his vision for Middle East peace in the White House Rose Garden on June 24, 2002. It became a key part of the Quartet Road Map. [Quartet: U.S., UN, EU, Russia]

Bush was the key player in the Quartet Road Map, which was presented to the Israelis and the Palestinians on April 30, 2003.

Bush was the first U.S. president to ever call for a Palestinian state: Israel and Palestine living side by side in peace and security.

Leaders Who Attempted to Divide the Land

In researching the roles of U.S. administrations in the Middle East peace process, and in studying the defining events of each presidency, I found a distinct connection between the two. I discovered (and have pointed out in this book) that as the presidents and their administrations became involved with the Israeli-Palestinian peace process, major events developed that ultimately impacted and curtailed their future peace efforts and/or caused major disruptions in their political agenda.

The same scenario was true for Israeli prime ministers and Arab leaders.

Below is an example of the enormous personal and/or political price that U.S. presidents, Israeli prime ministers and Arab leaders have paid when involved in dividing God's covenant land:

U.S. Presidents

- Richard Nixon's peace efforts were stopped by the Watergate scandal of 1972-1974.
- Jimmy Carter, after his involvement in the Camp David Accord in 1978 and the Israeli–Palestinian Peace Treaty in 1979 between Israel and Egypt, experienced the following as president: record oil prices, record inflation, the Iran Hostage Crisis and a landslide loss to Ronald Reagan who received 489 electoral votes (Jimmy Carter received 49 electoral votes). Carter's presidency was considered a failure.
- Ronald Reagan's peace efforts were stopped by the Iran-Contra Scandal in 1986.
- George H.W. Bush's peace efforts were stopped when he was defeated in the 1992 Presidential election 12 months after he co-sponsored the Madrid Peace Conference in October–November 1991.
- Bill Clinton's peace efforts were stalled and impacted by the Paula Jones, Monica Lewinsky and the Chinese espionage scandals, as well as U.S. House impeachment and Yasser Arafat's missed opportunities. Arafat was the most frequent foreign visitor to the Clinton White House.
- George W. Bush agreed to become directly involved in the Israeli-Palestinian peace negotiations in April 2001. After the 9-11-2001 terror events, he became known as the War President. Bush is overseeing a trillion dollar war on terror, wars in Afghanistan and Iraq, and is witnessing many record-setting weather related disasters. He was also the first U.S. President to declare his commitment to a Palestinian state in 2001.

Israeli Prime Ministers

- Menachem Begin, the co-signor of the Camp David Accord in 1978 and the Israel-Egypt Peace Treaty in 1979, submitted his resignation as Israel's Prime Minister on September 15, 1983. He lived his final nine years of life in seclusion.
- Yitzhak Shamir became Israel's Prime Minister after Begin's resignation until the general elections in the fall of 1984. He was reelected in 1988. Shamir and Shimon Peres formed a new coalition government until 1990, when the Labor party left the government, leaving Shamir with a narrow coalition. In Shamir's second term his government failed in a no-confi-

dence vote in 1991 amid charges that Likud—by taking part in the Madrid Peace Conference—had effectively agreed to enter negotiations over Judea, Samaria and Gaza. Shamir was defeated by Yitzhak Rabin in June 1992.

- Yitzhak Rabin was assassinated on November 4, 1995, while he was active in the peace process.
- Shimon Peres became acting prime minister after Rabin's assassination. He lost in an election seven months later in May 1996 to Benjamin Netanyahu.
- Benjamin Netanyahu's government failed in a no confidence vote on January 4, 1999, ten weeks after he agreed to give up 13 per cent of Israel's Judea and Samaria at the Wye Plantation. Netanyahu lost to Ehud Barak in a landslide defeat in May 1999.
- Ehud Barak resigned as Israel's prime minister on December 9, 2000, five months after Yasser Arafat turned down his very generous offer at Camp David in July 2000. Barak lost to Ariel Sharon in a landslide defeat in February 2001.
- Ariel Sharon's government failed twice in his four years in office. He was reelected after the first no-confidence vote. On November 21, 2005, Sharon resigned from the Likud party, asked that the current parliament be dissolved, and announced that he would form a new centrist party called Kadima, the Hebrew word for "forward." On December 18, 2005, Sharon was struck by a minor stroke four months after completion of his disen-

gagement plan which had forced 9,000 Jews out of 21 settlements in Gaza and four settlements in Northern Samaria. On the evening of January 4, 2006, he suffered a major stroke and brain hemorrhaging, eleven weeks before the March 28, 2006, election. As of this writing, he is in a vegetative state in an Israeli hospital.

Middle East Leaders

- Egyptian President Gamal Abdel Nasser died of a heart attack on September 28, 1970, three years after being defeated in the Six Day War. He was 55.
- Egyptian President Anwar Sadat was assassinated on October 6, 1981. Sadat was a co-signer of the Camp David Accords in 1978 and the Israeli–Egyptian Peace Treaty in 1979. He was 63.
- King Hussein of Jordan died of non-Hodgkin's lymphoma, a form of cancer, on February 7, 1999. He co-signed the Israeli–Jordanian peace accord in 1995. He was 64.
- Syria President Hafez Assad died of a heart attack on June 10, 2000 while talking on the phone with the Lebanese Prime Minister Hariri about Ehud Barak's Golan Heights offer. He was 69.
- Lebanese Prime Minister Rafik Hariri was assassinated on February 14, 2005, as he was leaving the Lebanese Parliament. He was 61. Hariri was not active in the peace process but his country received land from Israel in 2000 as part of a deal with the Syrians. High ranking Syrian officials are alleged to have been responsible for Hariri's assassination.
- PLO Chairman Yasser Arafat died of AIDS on November 11, 2004, according to David Frum former White House speech writer for President George W. Bush, and John Loftus the author of the *Secret War Against the Jews*. Arafat was directly involved in the peace process until the time of his death. He turned down Ehud Barak's very generous land offers in July 2000 because he wanted control over the Holy Sites in the Old City section of Jerusalem. He was 75.

CHAPTER 14

Strange Parallels to Rabin and Sharon Political Endings

Hospital director: Letting Sharon go to Negev farm was negligent

On January 5, 2006 some prominent Israeli physicians raised questions about the quality of care Ariel Sharon received in the previous two weeks. The director of a large hospital told *Haaretz* that according to media reports of Sharon's medical treatment, he fears "there was indescribable negligence." One of the doctors stated,

> Yitzhak Rabin was not wearing a bulletproof vest that could have protected him from the murderers' bullets, and now, 10 years later, Sharon was not given the required medical treatment that could have saved him.

> Israel has not learned the lesson from Rabin's murder, and thus lost two prime ministers because of inadequate protection—one from weapons, the other from illness. I cannot understand how the prime minister could have been sent to stay in an isolated farm, more than an hour away from the hospital he was supposed to be treated in, two weeks after a stroke and one night before a heart procedure he was afraid of.

Sharon was slated to undergo a cardiac catheterization on Thursday, January 5, 2006, to fix a small hole between the chambers of his heart. Doctors said the hole contributed to his initial stroke. "A night before the catheterization he should have been hospitalized in Hadassah or at least made to stay in Jerusalem," the director said. "I also have questions about the dosage of blood-thinning medication he received. My feeling is that Sharon did not get the best medical treatment he deserved." A senior doctor told *Haaretz:* "Sharon's medical condition was iatrogenic—that is, induced by treatment of physicians, as it was likely that the blood-thinning medicine Sharon was receiving had caused the severe brain bleeding."

According to the doctor, "Clearly, Sharon needed complete rest at least until the catheterization, as anyone who had undergone a stroke would. But it is hard to say that Sharon's refusal to rest caused the hemorrhaging." Another senior doctor said he suspected "Sharon's treatment was partly faulty because he fell victim to the political-media spin intended to show the public he was back to work as usual." And added,

He paid a high price for this spin. ...

My concern is that non-professional considerations dictated the chain of medical events. The doctors took a dangerous but calculated risk when they gave him blood-thinning drugs at home instead of in the hospital under full supervision. Why wasn't the catheterization performed earlier; moreover, he should have been kept under constant supervision and certainly not allowed to return to work as usual.

Questions were asked about the decisions and the reason for the delays in getting Sharon help on January 4:

- How much time elapsed from the moment Sharon told his son, Gilad, he wasn't feeling well until his personal doctor arrived at Sycamore Ranch?
- Why wasn't there a doctor at his side since the first stroke, especially on the eve of the catheterization?
- Why did it take almost two hours from the time Sharon fell ill at his ranch until he arrived at the hospital emergency room?
- Why wasn't Sharon taken to the hospital by helicopter?
- Why was he taken to the distant hospital in Jerusalem, rather than to Be'er Sheva's Soroka Medical Center?
- To what extent did the treatment Sharon received after the first episode account for the hemorrhaging?

Sharon's aides said nobody thought he was in danger when he left his office for Sycamore Ranch on Wednesday afternoon. The paramedic of the Shin Bet security service's VIP protection unit, always at his side, accompanied him.

The initial plan was for a doctor to be with Sharon after the catheterization, when he returned to convalesce at the ranch. Since his release from Hadassah on Tuesday, December 20, Dr. Shlomo Segev (his personal physician) examined him frequently; he did not complain of pain or illness.

Sharon received two shots a day of the blood thinner Claxon to prevent clots and another stroke. His last shot was on Wednesday morning, January 4, so that its effect would wear off before the heart procedure.

When Sharon felt ill that Wednesday evening, his personal physician was called in from the center of the country. One report said Dr. Segev arrived at the ranch as Sharon was boarding an ambulance, and joined him on the trip. Another version said he met the convoy at the Masmia junction on the way to Jerusalem.

Sharon's aides said he did not want to be taken to a hospital, but wanted to wait until the next morning when he was scheduled for surgery. His son, Gilad, and the Shin Bet paramedic convinced him to go but, en route, Sharon told Segev he wanted to turn around.

Dr. Segev believed that Sharon had suffered another stroke, worse than the first one. He decided to proceed to the hospital in the ambulance rather than scramble a helicopter. He feared that the movement of the helicopter would harm Sharon more than a few more minutes in the car.

Apparently, Segev was the one who decided to take Sharon to Hadassah rather than the closest medical center. The trip to the hospital took 55 minutes, and Sharon's condition deteriorated. Fifteen minutes from arriving at the hospital Sharon experienced a massive stroke.

The Peres and Olmert Parallels

Daniel Pipes, Director of Middle East Forum, said that when Ehud Olmert became the acting prime minister of Israel that history was repeating itself. Shimon Peres led Rabin to the Oslo diplomacy and took over when Rabin was assassinated. Olmert led Sharon to the Gaza withdrawal and took over when Sharon was hospitalized. We shall see how far the parallel will continue.

Yitzhak Rabin - The Heart of Israel

Excerpts appear below from the *New York Times* book review of *Soldier of Peace. The Life of Yitzhak Rabin, 1922-1995*, by Dan Kurzman. (Review by Amy Wilentz, May 24, 1998)

When the big Cadillac arrived at Ichilov Hospital in Tel Aviv on the night of Nov. 4, 1995, no one in the emergency room knew the identity of the trauma victim who was being brought in. Only when the resident physician looked at the face of the white-haired man whose heartbeat he was vainly trying to find did he realize that his patient was Yitzhak Rabin. Rabin could have been pronounced dead on arrival, but none of the doctors could bear to let him go. They felt they had the history of Israel on their operating table. They were sure that the heart they held in their hands—the heart that refused to beat—was Israel's heart.

There was no doubt that after his death the world would be filled with Rabin biographies. Who could be more exemplary of the history of Israel than this freedom-fighting soldier and statesman, the first native-born Israeli Prime Minister, and one of the handful of giants whose lives paralleled the life of the nation? A man who began his political career issuing secret orders for Yasser Arafat's extermination, and who ended it shaking Arafat's hand before the eyes of the world.

It's impossible to write a book about Yitzhak Rabin without featuring his antagonist and doppelganger, the mercurial Shimon Peres. The problematic Rabin-Peres relationship began in earnest in 1973. Peres and Moshe Dayan were Ben-Gurion's boys and had always been the rivals of Yigal Allon, Rabin's mentor, and of Rabin himself. But when Rabin was elected Prime Minister for the first time, after the 1973 war, he had no choice politically but to name Peres as his Defense Minister. From that moment on, the two never stopped bickering, stabbing each other in the back, stealing each other's glory, hiding important facts and events from each other, trying to keep each other out of power.

A left-wing cabinet member once described to Samuel Segev, a former correspondent for the Israeli newspaper Maariv, how Peres and Rabin behaved toward each other in high-level meetings: "They looked to me like a couple married for 35 years, with no love but with mutual dependence. They lived together, apart." Peres was "capable of any stinking manipulation," Rabin once said. Kurzman writes that Rabin was satisfied with the plans for the Entebbe hostage-rescue raid —"even if Peres happened to agree."

Segev's descriptions of Peres as Foreign Minister during the second Rabin Government in the early 1990's, acting on major peace initiatives without the authorization or knowledge of his Prime Minister, are shocking. Not only were the Oslo talks begun without the Prime Minister's knowledge, but at a later date, according to Segev, when Rabin asked Peres to suspend the talks until after the American Secretary of State had completed a trip to the Middle East, Peres simply ignored the request. These unauthorized initiatives eventually produced the Oslo accords.

Rabin publicly ridiculed Peres' ideological bent and argued that the peace process was a strategic move forced on Israel with no alternatives. Rabin was constantly fighting with Peres. Peres moved the process at breakneck speed as Rabin's foreign minister and globetrotter. Rabin was very much the general, trying to marshal forces, keep his coalition together and survive the angry protests calling for his ouster.

Perhaps the finest example of Peres' and Rabin's symbiotic rivalry was the battle they had over who would grab Oslo's glory. Peres had been the motivating force behind the Oslo negotiations, eventually with Rabin's knowledge and blessing. Once the agreement was completed, Rabin and Peres decided that Peres and Abu Mazen, Arafat's deputy, would sign the declaration of principles at the White House ceremony. Rabin was too worried about Oslo's dubious ramifications to want to participate fully and publicly. But President Clinton had arranged to be host to Arafat, and he wanted Rabin as well, who was the top Israeli Government official. Under pressure, Segev says, Rabin finally capitulated.

Peres, who had scraped and fought and cajoled and wheedled throughout the niggling Oslo talks, who had spent the night writing and perfecting the speech he would give upon signing the declaration in Washington, had to hear on the radio that Rabin had effectively agreed to replace him as the leader of the Israeli delegation. "Why is he doing this to me all the time?, roared an angry Peres," Segev writes. Rabin, Peres continued, "has caused me enough damage. Why does he continue to walk on me? I brought the Oslo accords. He never believed in them. Now he wants to go to Washington? Fine. Let him go. Tell him that I am staying at home and I am resigning my position as Foreign Minister." Of course he went to Washington, watched the handshake from the sidelines and remained in his post. But this cri de coeur came from the man who, after Rabin's assassination, would tenderly call his old enemy "my elder brother."

Rabin's the Hero, Peres the Politician

Excerpts from *The Rabin Assassination, The Appointment of Gillon and the Pardon of Har Shefi: Israel in Darkness,* June 30, 2001.

Rabin was a key figure in Israel's war of independence and its first five decades as a nation. He helped build the Israel Defense Forces into one of the most powerful armies in the world and led his nation in battles for its survival. Peres is known as one of the most powerful politicians in Israel's history, hand-picked by Ben Gurion, who couldn't win an election even against himself. Rabin controlled Labor politics.

On November 4, 1995, Rabin was assassinated by Yigal Amir, a member of the religious Zionist camp. Amir believed Rabin was a traitor who deserved death, and that he was fulfilling the biblical command to take the law into one's own hands when Jewish lives were threatened.

Rabin's death allowed Peres, who could never have gained the premiership while Rabin was alive, to take control of the Labor Party and the government as acting Prime Minister. Peres lost in a close election to Benjamin (Bibi) Netanyahu of the Likud Party who becomes Israel's next Prime minister in May 1996.

As a result of the lost election, Shimon Peres also lost to Ehud Barak in Labor Party power struggle.

Later, during a One Israel (Labor) government headed up by Barak, Peres even loses a race for president of Israel (voted upon by members of the Israeli parliament, the Knesset, which his party controlled), against a politically meek opposition candidate from Likud, Moshe Katsav. Peres cemented his reputation as the most unelectable power politician in Israel's history.

Barak pushes Peres aside. Peres begins to focus on his Peres Center for Peace, which is able to generate millions of dollars in contributions.

Carmi Gillon was the head of the Shin-Bet, Israel's CIA/FBI during the period preceding the Rabin assassination and the period of the assassination itself. After the assassination Gillon is highly criticized for the poor security and protection given Rabin. Questions begin to be asked that intimate dark and sinister relationships.

It is uncovered that a Shin-Bet operative, Avishai Raviv, who operated as an agent provocateur, promoting Jewish undergrounds and revenge attacks, and who posed in the media as a right ring Jewish militant, had intimate knowledge of Yigal Amir's plans for assassinating Rabin well in advance of November 4. At the moment the information is to be broadcast publicly, the highest legal officers of the state, the attorney general and the state prosecutor, stamp the information top secret. The information is leaked over the Internet but it remains top secret in Israel. The question has yet to be answered: How much did Gillon know about his operative's involvement with Amir leading up to the assassination and how much of the events leading right up to the assassination were yet another attempt to discredit the political right and silence their opposition to Oslo?

Other questions have been raised. Questions so dark and sinister as to frighten even the most hardened Israeli. Why was Rabin so unprotected? When did Peres learn of the assassination? Was this whole thing an operation out of control or one very much in control? These questions continue to be asked.

A young, attractive religious woman barely out of her teens had been courted by Amir for some time. Amir told her of his plans to kill Rabin because he was killing Jews by betraying the Jewish state. Margalit Har-Shefi dismisses Amir, but at one point, does in fact ask a local rabbi if such a thing would be acceptable under Jewish law and would she be required to report such a thing in advance. The rabbi answered no to both questions. Har-Shefi goes on with her life. Amir kills the Prime Minister.

Soon thereafter, after a national witch hunt for anyone who said or heard anything derogatory about Rabin, Har-Shefi is charged with the crime of "knowing" or "having reasonable belief" that such a crime was to take place and not informing the police. In other words, Har-Shefi's very soul is investigated and found guilty of having a belief notwithstanding the fact that she insisted that she never believed that Amir would actually carry out such a heinous crime.

The political left hails the legal system's ability to penetrate a person's mind. The political right is still stunned by the accusations that it participated in the assassination via incitement and silence and little is said in Har-Shefi's defense.

Avishai Raviv, the Shin-Bet's agent, becomes a focus of attention. How is it that Har-Shefi is charged, tried and convicted before Avishai Raviv, who is suspected by everyone of at the very least knowing of Amir's plans, if not actually promoting it. Forces seemed to be at work to keep Raviv under wraps.

Finally charged after public pressure from the right and certain respected politicians like Micki Eitan, Raviv's trial is postponed several times. No evidence has yet to be taken. No one has a clue when the process might begin. Silence continues.

Har-Shefi wins a presidential pardon after serving 6 of 9 months in prison. The left is outraged over the pardon.

In the aftermath of the Rabin assassination, Gillon resigns as head of the Shin-Bet. He is severely criticized for the lax security arrangements to protect Rabin in light of the real and perceived threat from Arab terrorists and the Jewish underground elements.

Shimon Peres appoints Gillon to run his Peres Peace Center following his resignation—a position he holds until 1999. Gillon is reported to have received a hefty salary.

After Barak's failed attempt to give the Palestinians 90% of their demands at Camp David II, Likud's Ariel Sharon wins the premiership in a landslide victory. Barak is humiliated and announces that he is leaving One Israel (Labor) leadership and politics. Peres takes advantage of the vacuum and supports a unity government with Sharon. The deal is made and Peres becomes the number two man in charge of the foreign ministry once again.

Peres promotes his man Gillon to be Israel's ambassador to Denmark. Gillon is reported to have said that sometimes mild torture is necessary when dealing with terrorists to extract life saving information. The Danes erupt. The Danish justice minister is reported to have said that Gillon will be arrested if he reports to his post in Denmark.

Peres demands Gillon's posting and calls Gillon an honorable and peaceful man. Peres says he will not stand by to witness a *character assassination.*

[Source: http://www.iasps.org/nbn/nbn390.htm]

Ariel Sharon: Major General to Prime Minister

Ariel Sharon had a long history of service in Israel's military and government. He was active in all of the Israeli-Arab wars, and rose to the rank of major general by 1967. He distinguished himself as a strategist in the Six-Day War of 1967 and the Yom Kippur War of 1973. That same year he helped form the Likud party, and in 1974 was elected to his first term in Israel's parliament, the Knesset. Sharon served as Minister of Agriculture and then Minister of Defense under Menachem Begin, and led the Israeli invasion of Lebanon in 1982.

When hundreds of Palestinian refugees were murdered by Lebanese Christian militiamen, Sharon was severely criticized and forced to resign from the Knesset. He remained in the cabinet, however, and served as Minister of National Infrastructure under Benjamin Netanyahu.

In 1998, Sharon was named Minister of Foreign Affairs. Sharon capped his political comeback by becoming Prime Minister in February of 2001, unseating Ehud Barak in a landslide election victory.

Sharon Creates Disengagement Plan Under International Pressure

Prime Minister Ariel Sharon, under enormous pressure from the international community and the Israeli left, presented his vision for peace at the Herzylia conference in Israel on December 18, 2003. His vision became known as the Disengagement Plan. President George W. Bush backed the Plan in an April 15, 2004, meeting with Sharon at the White House.

The U.S. Senate voted on June 24, 2004, to embrace President Bush's support of Sharon's plan to withdraw from the Gaza Strip. The Senate's action came a day after the U.S. House approved a similar measure by a 407-9 roll call vote. The concurrent resolution states that Congress: (1) strongly endorses the principles articulated by President Bush in his April 14, 2004, letter to Prime Minister Sharon, which will strengthen the security and well-being of the State of Israel; and (2) supports continuing efforts with the international community to build the capacity and will of Palestinian institutions to fight terrorism, dismantle terrorist organizations, and prevent the areas from which Israel has withdrawn from posing a threat to the security of Israel.

The nonbinding Senate resolution, which passed 95-3, also said, "it is unrealistic" for any peace settlement between Israel and the Palestinians to require Israel to return to the borders that existed before the 1967 war. In addition, a Palestinian state would have to be part of a "just, fair and realistic framework" for peace with Palestinian refugees settling there, not in Israel. The resolution further stated that Palestinians must stop "armed activity and all acts of violence against Israelis anywhere."

Both chambers' resolutions endorsed Bush's April 14 letter to Sharon in which Bush backed Sharon's plan to remove Jewish settlements and some military bases and installations from Gaza and the West Bank.

(Source: http://www.jewishvirtuallibrary.org/jsource/US-Israel/hconres460.html)

Sharon's Practical, but not Biblical, Plan

Sharon's plan called for Israel's unilateral evacuation, forcing 9000 Jews from their homes in Gaza and four Northern Samaria settlements. He felt this would help minimize the enormous pressure he had experienced from the international community. Sharon also believed it was good to remove Israelis from harm's way in Gaza. After the evacuation, he planned to redeploy the 10,000 Israelis troops that had been protecting these communities. Sharon looked forward to controlling the Gaza borders and wanted to get tough with the Palestinian terror organizations.

I was told numerous times by government officials that Sharon planned to complete the disengagement and then park the peace process—believing that the Palestinian terror groups would continue their ways and Israel wouldn't have to go forward in the process.

After the evacuation, Sharon tightened the Gaza borders to the chagrin of the international community. He restricted the movement of Palestinians in and out of Gaza for security reasons and increased military hits on Palestinian terror groups. However, the international community pressured Israel to give more, despite the fact that the Palestinians continued to terrorize her.

Chronology: September 2005 – February 2006

Tuesday, September 13

"The United States will act to preserve the momentum in Israeli-Palestinian relations and is expected to press both sides to make progress," U.S. Secretary of State Condoleezza Rice told the *New York Times*. Due to Sharon's internal troubles and the Palestinian elections, the U.S. relayed a message to Europe and other nations to stop pressuring Israel to make further concessions.

However, the U.S. administration is apparently also concerned about stalling the process. During her meeting at the *New York Times*, Rice said the key on the Israeli side is to use the momentum, including the Sharm understandings, in order to go back to the U.S.-brokered Road Map peace plan. Rice noted both sides have obligations under the plan and said the U.S. will press both sides to deliver on their pledges.

Wednesday, September 14

Statements before Bush and Sharon meeting at the UN:

PRESIDENT BUSH: Mr. Prime Minister, thank you. I'm looking forward to our meeting. I've said several times publicly that I am inspired by your courageous decision to give peace a chance. And I know it was hard, but I admire your courage. And I look forward to talking to you about how we can get on the Road Map.

One thing is essential, and the world must hear, that now is the time for Palestinians to come together and establish a government that will be peaceful with Israel. And the Gaza is a good chance to start, and I know that the Israeli government wants to see that happen, as well.

The world needs to help the Palestinians. The Arab neighbors need to help the Palestinians develop an economy. Now is the time for people to step up. It's an opportunity that was created by a bold decision, and I want to work together to see the vision of peace come to be.

So, Mr. Prime Minister, thank you for being here.

PRIME MINISTER SHARON: Thank you. Mr. President, I'm glad to meet with you again. I'm glad that we are working together in order to achieve peace in the region.

Friday, September 16

Saudi Arabia's Crown Prince Sultan said that Israel should withdraw from more conquered Arab lands after Gaza, indicating in their words there can be no change in the collective Arab stand on Israel unless occupation ends.

Saturday, September 17

In New York City, President Pervez Musharraf of Pakistan told the American Jewish Congress that security for Israel will remain incomplete until the creation of a Palestinian state; Israel must "withdraw" from the West Bank; and final settlement must respect the character of Jerusalem. Exactly three weeks later, a record-setting earthquake measuring 7.6 hit northern Pakistan and the disputed Kashmir region, killing more than 74,000 people and leaving millions homeless.

On September 17, the U.S. State Department told Ariel Sharon not to interfere with Gaza elections even if Hamas was involved.

October 2005

Friday, October 14

Middle East Newsline reported that Israeli Prime Minister Ariel Sharon was weighing a unilateral pullout from 90 percent of the West Bank and had shared that with President Bush.

Sunday, October 16-17

On October 16, James D. Wolfensohn, the Quartet Special Envoy for Disengagement, sent a letter to UN Secretary General Kofi Annan and the foreign ministries of Britain, Russia and the United States, stating:

> The Government of Israel, with its important security concerns, is loath to relinquish control, almost acting as though there has been no withdrawal, delaying making difficult decisions and preferring to take difficult matters back into slow-moving subcommittees.

Accompanying the October 16 letter was a report written on October 17 regarding Wolfensohn's latest visit to Israel, from October 7-12. The introduction to the report stated:

> The Special Envoy was disappointed that none of the key movement issues has been resolved. Without a dramatic improvement in Palestinian movement and access, within appropriate security arrangements for Israel, the economic revival essential to a resolution of the conflict will not be possible.

Tuesday, October 18.

Bush met with Wolfensohn at the White House to discuss his report.

Wednesday, October 19

Secretary Rice made it clear to Israel that building settlements between Jerusalem and the Ma'aleh Adumim settlement contradicts American policy. In a speech before the Senate Foreign Relations Committee on October 19, Rice said that the United States is concerned about settlement construction and expansion around Jerusalem, adding that the U.S. administration reduced its financial support for Israel as a result of the continuous settlement activities.

Thursday, October 20

President Bush welcomed Palestinian President Abbas to the White House for a meeting. When they addressed the press in the Rose Garden after their meeting, Bush remarked:

> As I have stated in the past, achieving peace demands action from all parties. Israel must continue to work with Palestinian leaders to help improve the daily lives of Palestinians. At the same time, Israel should not undertake any activity that contravenes its Road Map obligations, or prejudices the final status negotiations with regard to Gaza, the West Bank, and Jerusalem. This means that Israel must remove unauthorized posts and stop settlement expansion. It also means that the barrier now

being built to protect Israelis from terrorist attacks must be a security barrier, rather than a political barrier. Israeli leaders must take into account the impact this security barrier has on Palestinians not engaged in terrorist activities.

November 2005

Monday and Tuesday, November 14-15

The final push began Monday night November 14. Secretary Rice launched a mediation session at 11 p.m. in her ninth-floor suite at the King David Hotel in Jerusalem, meeting alternately with Israel and Palestinian delegations and refusing to allow either side to go to bed until they reached the elusive deal.

The issue on the table was access to the Gaza Strip. Israel ended its 38-year presence in Gaza in mid-September, turning it over to the Palestinians, but had maintained tight control over the crossing points. During two months of sporadic violence, Palestinians and Israelis were unable to reach a border agreement, and the strip remained mostly sealed off.

According to a senior State Department official in the talks, Rice negotiated the long list of differences dividing the two sides "piece by piece."

By midmorning Tuesday, Rice announced an agreement between Israel and the Palestinian Authority to ease Gaza's isolation and provide reliable access for its goods and people to Israel and the outside world. She called the deal "a major step forward" that would allow the Palestinians to "live ordinary lives" and would establish a new "pattern of cooperation" between the two sides. "For the first time since 1967, Palestinians will gain control over entry and exit from their territory," she said, referring to the Middle East war when Israel took control of Gaza and the West Bank.

The deal defines the terms of operation for Gaza border crossings used to move cargo and people, resolving a deadlock that frustrated a team of international negotiators for weeks. It also establishes a system of bus convoys to shuttle Palestinians between Gaza and the West Bank, the two territorial components of what is envisioned as a future Palestinian state.

Monday, November 21, 2005

Israeli Prime Minister Sharon formally resigned from the Likud Party to form a new centrist party, "Kadima," or "Forward." His resignation triggered a far-reaching realignment of Israel's fractious political system. Sharon submitted a resignation letter to the Likud central committee chairman, Tzahi Hanegbi, making official his departure from the party he helped build into one of the country's most influential political movements and twice led to victory in national elections. Hours later, Israel's parliament voted overwhelmingly to dissolve itself in a move intended to lead to new elections by the end of March 2006, about eight months ahead of schedule.

December 2005

Friday, December 16, 2005

"Jerusalem must remain unified, open and accessible to all nations," said Shimon Peres speaking to Indian reporters.

Sunday, December 18, 2005

A source in Prime Minister Sharon's office said the 77-year-old leader had completed a full day of work in his Jerusalem office that included meeting with former Labor Party leader Shimon Peres and was en route to his ranch in the Negev Desert when he told aides he was not well. The source added that Sharon called one of his sons at 7:50 p.m. and told him he was ill. The convoy turned around and sped to Jerusalem's main hospital, arriving at 8:05 p.m., a spokesman at the medical center said.

Israeli media reported that Sharon was wheeled into the hospital on a stretcher, conscious but confused. "Our tests have shown that the prime minister had a mild CVA," said Dr. Yuval Weiss, deputy director of Hadassah Ein Keren Hospital, using medical jargon for "cerebral vascular accident," or stroke. The physician said Sharon initially had difficulty speaking but suffered no lasting sensory or motor impairment. "At the beginning, he had some problems with speech," Sharon's personal physician, Dr. Boleg Goldman said, "It started like that, but it was for a few moments and that's all."

The portly prime minister is not known to have had serious health problems in recent years. The health scare came from out of the blue, the BBC's Matthew Price stated. Sharon, who was overweight, had never released his medical records and stated he had no major health problems. Sharon's nickname was "the Bulldozer" for his stamina and long working hours. Goldman said Sharon's most recent physical examination was about three months ago, and the results were "excellent."

Sunday, December 25

Sharon returned to full duties after several days of rest and observation.

Tuesday, December 27

Doctors discovered a small hole in Sharon's heart wall as they conducted extensive tests on the former general. They believe the hole might have caused the stroke. Doctors said his stroke occurred when a blood clot lodged in the hole, restricting the flow of blood to his brain, though he never lost consciousness.

January 2006

<u>Monday, January 2, 2006</u>

The Israeli newspaper *Maariv* reported that Prime Minister Ariel Sharon planned on replacing the U.S. backed Road Map peace proposal with a new plan that would uproot Jewish communities in Judea and Samaria in exchange for American compensation.

Sharon reportedly would implement his new plan despite any deterioration in Israel's security situation due to an upsurge of terrorism from the Palestinian Authority. Details of Sharon's new plan were reported by sources close to former U.S. Secretary of State Henry Kissinger.

<u>Tuesday, January 3, 2006</u>

Dozens of settlers clashed with Israel Defense Forces soldiers and police who served them notices to leave Palestinian-owned buildings in a market in the heart of the West Bank city of Hebron.

Prime Minister Sharon's last interview

Prime Minister Sharon gave Japanese newspaper *Nikkei* an exclusive interview just one day before suffering a massive stroke. He said,

> I am a Jew, and that is the most important thing for me. Therefore when it comes to security, Israel will not make any compromises. If the Palestinians combat terror, I believe there is a chance to move forward in accordance with the Road Map initiative, which, with God's help, will bring peace.

<u>Wednesday, January 4</u>

Proof claim in Sharon bribery – Abraham Rabinovich, Jerusalem

A police document alleging bribery involving Prime Minister Sharon was revealed on Israeli television, rocking national politics three months before elections. The document refers to a three-year investigation into charges that Sharon illegally received large sums from abroad in connection with his first election campaign in 1999.

Prima facie evidence has been found that $3 million was transferred by two Austrian brothers "to the family of the Prime Minister, part for the return of illegal campaign contributions while part remained in the hands of the Sharon family," the document said.

It is the first time police have said they have prima facie evidence to substantiate the allegations and the first time there is a clear suggestion of personal bribery that goes beyond campaign contributions.

The Austrian brothers, Martin and James Schlaff, own casinos in several countries, and one in Jericho. That highly profitable business was shut down when the Palestinian intifada broke out five years ago. The establishment of the casino in territory under Israeli control required permission from the authorities, raising the possibility that any money channeled by the Schlaffs to Mr. Sharon was a quid pro quo.

<u>Wednesday, January 4</u>

A few hours before his major stroke, Prime Minister Ariel Sharon studied a new map showing potential borders that would allow for both a Palestinian state and for as many settlers as possible to remain in Judea and Samaria, Kadima politician Otniel Schneller told the *Jerusalem Post*.

He knows this, he said, because he was the map's maker.

Schneller, a religious settler from Ma'aleh Michmash turned centrist politician, told the *Jerusalem Post*, he was commissioned by Sharon to create a plan for Israel's future borders following the Gaza withdrawal last summer.

The two men met in Jerusalem for more than an hour late on the afternoon of January 4, said Schneller. "I showed him my plan. He said, 'It is very interesting. I would like to go with this principle and to work on this plan. Otni, I would like to meet you next week,'" Schneller recalled the PM saying.

"We finished our meeting at 4:30 p.m.," he said. The massive stroke Sharon suffered later that day cut short any future discussions about the map.

Source: Jerusalem Post – March 31:
    http://www.jpost.com/servlet/Satellite?cid=1143498772486&pagename=Post%2F
    JPArticle%2FShowFull

Prime Minister Ariel Sharon suffered a massive, life-threatening stroke Wednesday, January 4, 2006, and underwent lengthy overnight surgery to drain blood from his brain after falling ill at his ranch.

Summary of Strange Circumstances Surrounding Sharon's Health:

- Sharon's physical 90 days prior to his December 18 stroke showed he was in excellent health.
- Sharon met with Peres a few hours before his December 18 stroke.
- Israeli police released confidential information to the media on the upcoming indictment of his son Omri on January 4.
- Sharon studied a new map showing potential borders that would allow for both a Palestinian state and for as many settlers as possible to remain in Judea and Samaria, with Kadima politician Otniel Schneller; the meeting ended at 4:30 p.m. on January 4.

- Sharon had decided to stay at the ranch rather than go to the hospital the night before his Thursday afternoon, January 5, heart catheterization.
- Sharon was to start his fast at midnight, but began feeling ill at 9:30 p.m. on January 4.
- Sharon felt fine when he got in the ambulance—even felt good enough to ask to go back to his ranch.
- His doctor decided to go to Hadassah Hospital Ein Keren instead of Beer Sheva Hospital.
- Israeli media reports said that a helicopter had initially been summoned but that Dr. Shlomo Segev decided the situation was not urgent. Initial reports even said Sharon was able to sit up during the ride to the hospital.
- Sharon was reported to have had his major stroke 15 minutes before arriving at the Hadassah Hospital Ein Keren.

Ehud Olmert, Israel's Finance Minister and Vice Prime Minister was officially designated as acting Prime Minister after Sharon's massive stroke.

Thursday, January 5

Olmert had his first cabinet meeting at 9 a.m. He sought to calm financial markets by releasing a joint statement with the Bank of Israel Governor Stanley Fisher expressing confidence in the "strength of the Israeli economy." Olmert then scheduled a meeting with Deputy Prime Minister and Foreign Minister Silvan Shalom in order to receive a broad diplomatic briefing.

Polls indicated that Shimon Peres would be the top Kadima replacement, and would lead the Kadima Party to more Knesset seats than any other leadership candidate. Under Peres, Kadima would win 42 seats in the 120-seat Knesset in the election on March 28, 2006, according to a survey by *Ha'aretz* and Channel 10. The same survey showed Kadima would win 40 seats with Olmert, 38 with Justice Minister Tzipi Livni, or 36 with Defense Minister Shaul Mofaz.

Friday, January 6

Former Labor Party leader Peres met with Acting Prime Minister Olmert in Jerusalem to discuss the future of the government and the Kadima Party. During the meeting, Peres told Olmert he would support him as party leader.

"I'm no expert, I'm no doctor, just a simple citizen of this country, and I'm very worried about (Prime Minister Sharon's) health," Peres said.

"Olmert updated me regarding Sharon's condition. I'm not the person to relay medical announcements. I am, like everyone else, praying and very afraid," he said.

"Our meeting dealt with a central issue—how to continue the policies Sharon started in the national unity government, including the issue of war and a continual effort for the peace process," he said, adding that the two had "an extremely candid discussion" and agreed to continue talks at the beginning of next week.

"I believe there is also place for optimism, not just concern. Things which look difficult at the moment are not the end of the world," Peres explained.

"I hear there is general concern throughout the world and in Israel," he said. "Regard and honor for Sharon is constantly rising and everyone views him as a central figure, not just because of what he did but also because of the hope that he can continue to do it."

<u>Sunday, January 8</u>

Council of Foreign Relations' (CFR) Henry Seigman said four days after Sharon's massive heart attack that Sharon was never serious about lasting peace. Seigman has been involved with the peace process since 1991. His statements were insensitive and poorly timed. Seigman stated:

> In a remarkable transformation, the man now lying in a coma in an Israeli hospital has emerged these past five years as the single most dominant political personality in Israel's history, overshadowing even Ben-Gurion's mythic role as founding father of the state.

> Most Israelis came to believe that Ariel Sharon was the only person able to solve the Palestinian conflict. Alternatively, if the conflict were to continue, he was the man they trusted to manage it in a manner that assured Israel's stability and security.

> This view of Sharon is only partly correct. He was, indeed, uniquely able to make the compromises without which an agreement with the Palestinians is unattainable. It is difficult to imagine another Israeli leader who could retain popular support for the return of most of the West Bank, along the lines suggested in the Clinton proposal of January 2001, and compensate Palestinians for the retention by Israel of the major settlement blocs adjoining the pre-1967 border with comparable territory within Israel. The same is true of allowing the Arab-populated parts of Jerusalem to serve as the capital of a Palestinian state.

> If it were true that a negotiated agreement with the Palestinians incorporating these unavoidable 'concessions' were the strategic goal of the 'new' Sharon, his departure from the political scene would be grievous. But Sharon had no intention of making such concessions, nor is there any basis for the expectation that there will ever be a Palestinian leader willing or able to accept an agreement that does not include these provisions.

> Many in Israel saw Sharon's decision to disengage from Gaza as evidence of a new determination to end the conflict by dismantling the settlement enterprise, not only in Gaza but in much of the West Bank as well. I believe that to be a misreading.

The precedent Sharon sought to establish was not for additional disengagements from the West Bank (other than from isolated areas and major Palestinian population centers). Rather, he intended Gaza to serve as a precedent for a continuing unilateralism enabling Israel to retain de facto control of the West Bank, even if a nominal Palestinian state were to come into existence. Sharon believed a nominal state was the only way for Israel to deal with the demographic challenge posed by Palestinian population growth and—equally important—the only way to retain U.S. support for its unilateralism.

Sharon's ideas for an imposed solution to the Israeli-Palestinian conflict, based on a narrow conception of security that considers Palestinian national aspirations and Palestinian rights, a notion foreign to Sharon, as irrelevant, constitute a dubious foundation for peacemaking.

To be sure, an impediment to the resumption of the peace process is the chaos in Gaza and much of the West Bank, and President Mahmoud Abbas and his government bear responsibility for that. But so does Sharon, who violated virtually every promise he made to Abbas that would have eased the suffering of the Palestinians and given the President the credibility to face down rejectionists and advocates of violence.

In any event, the argument for unilateralism is dishonest, for nothing precludes Israel's implementation of policies that conform to international agreements. The argument for unilateralism has served as a pretext for the theft of Palestinian land and for arrangements in Jerusalem that violate existing agreements, including the 'Road Map'.

What hope there is for a revival of a peace process lies not with the success of Kadima, the new centrist party established by Sharon, but with an Israeli commitment to a Palestinian state on the West Bank and Gaza whose claims to security, viability and territorial integrity are entitled the same respect that Israel expects for its own claims.

Henry Seigman is director of the U.S./Middle East Project and former head of the American Jewish Congress.

Article: http://www.guardian.co.uk/israel/comment/0,,1681823,00.html

Sunday, January 8

Israeli police said they would reevaluate continuing their investigation into bribery allegations against Ariel Sharon due to his health condition. Police said that it was still too early to tell if the case would be closed but that the possibility would be considered. The investigation—dubbed the Cyril Kern loan affair [same as Schlaff case]—focuses on the nature of several money transfers made to the Sharon family by South African businessman Cyril Kern. Police suspect that Kern served as a front for Martin Schlaff—an Austrian-Jewish business-man—and that the money was meant to serve as a bribe to the prime minister.

Apparently, a possible police reevaluation wasn't comforting enough for Cyril Kern, who arrived from South Africa to be at Sharon's side soon after his massive stroke. The *Maariv* reported on January 10 that:

> Ariel Sharon's friend Cyril Kern arrived in the country to be by him. Kern arrived at Hadassah hospital two days ago and went to the sev-enth floor where the Prime Minister is interned. Sharon family sources explained that as soon as he heard Sharon was fighting for his life, he felt he had to be by his side. ... According to a State Comptroller's report, Sharon's son Gilad accepted an illegal 4.7 million shekel loan from Kern. ... Kern was not allowed to see the prime minister in his room but did meet with his sons for an update of the situation.

One of the messages Kern most likely delivered to the Sharon boys was, "You keep your mouths shut, or else."

<u>Tuesday, January 10</u>

Shimon Peres was expected to back Olmert in the elections in exchange for the number two spot.

Peres will apparently be placed second on Kadima's list ahead of the March elections, according to a deal that was struck in recent days between Peres, party chairman and Acting Prime Minister Olmert and Tzipi Livni.

New reports said Livni will be appointed foreign minister if Kadima forms the next government.

Rice Renews U.S. Support for a Palestinian State

In a phone conversation with Acting Prime Minister Olmert, Secretary of State Rice renewed the Bush administration's support for establishment of a Palestinian state. "That has been our policy and continues to be our policy," State Department spokesman Sean McCormack said afterward. With Sharon incapacitated and probably unable to resume his post, Rice's conversation with Olmert was intended to make sure there is no backtracking on the Palestinian statehood issue.

McCormack said Rice underscored to Olmert that "the United States sup-ports the two-state vision of two states living side-by-side in peace and securi-ty." Rice also spoke by telephone with Sharon's chief adviser, Dov Weisglass, and dispatched Assistant Secretary of State David Welch and Elliott Abrams of the National Security Council to the region to talk to Israeli and Palestinian offi-cials.

Meanwhile, unannounced, Rice sent one of her closest aides, Jim Wilkinson, to the Palestinian areas to help Palestinian leader Mahmoud Abbas and other officials to modernize their day-to-day operations. Wilkinson had already helped the Palestinians set up modern media facilities.

<u>Wednesday, January 11</u>

Secretary Rice welcomed Acting Prime Minister Olmert's statement that the government will convene Sunday in a bid to approve the decision to allow East Jerusalem residents to vote in upcoming Palestinian elections.

According to *The Jerusalem Post*, the United States government planned to invite Olmert to Washington before the March elections in Israel.

<u>Thursday, January 12</u>

According to Israel Radio, Olmert intended to visit Washington in February, where he was slated to discuss the upcoming Palestinian Authority elections, among other issues. *The Jerusalem Post* said the invitation indicated the U.S. government's support for Olmert and the Kadima ticket in Israel's upcoming elections.

Bush phoned Olmert, expressed admiration and concern for Sharon

Acting Prime Minister Olmert spoke with U.S. President George Bush, who telephoned and said: "I wanted to tell you that our hearts are with Ariel Sharon, his family, his friends and the entire Israeli people. We know that this is a difficult time for you and I will do whatever I can to help." Bush added that he appreciates the acting prime minister's responsibility and courage in taking the position upon himself. Olmert thanked President Bush for the call and his friendship with Prime Minister Sharon, and added that their relationship is very important for Israel.

At the end of their conversation, President Bush asked Olmert to convey to Omri and Gilad Sharon that he esteems their father very highly and that he has a partner in the U.S. who is concerned for his welfare. Bush said it is very important that Sharon recover and know that his friend in the U.S. is thinking about him and is concerned for him.

<u>Friday, January 13</u>

Peres tells Tel Aviv audience he and Olmert favor final status talks

According to Ynet News, Peres—who was guaranteed the number two spot on Kadima's list of Knesset candidates—was blamed for political extortion and subversion. Peres denied claims he demanded the second spot on Kadima's list, saying some party members understood the need to place him at the forefront.

Peres found it especially difficult to deal with the condemnations regarding his conduct in the aftermath of Sharon's hospitalization, as critics blasted him for "sewing suits as Acting Prime Minister Ehud Olmert's deputy, while others acted in a more dignified manner."

"I myself did not know whether or not I even wanted to join Kadima's Knesset list. But people told me 'It's important that you join,'" Peres said. "Then someone thought I should be in the number two spot, even though there were those who thought I should be number one. That's how it happened; and all this while my (former) party (Labor) is asking that I return."

'Olmert should head the government'

When asked whether he is considering running for prime minister in the future, Peres said with conviction, "I have other things on my mind now, and in any case I am not a candidate in the current political formation, so why delude myself? I do not want to be prime minister."

Peres said he trusts Olmert, but "not with my eyes closed";

I plan to support him, but express my opinions at the same time. I believe Olmert should head the government. It is the right choice, and as such I will support it. During my discussions with him I found that our political and economic viewpoints are similar enough for us to run together.

'A solution will be found for Jerusalem'

As to the ongoing Israeli-Palestinian negotiations, Peres says that many senior government officials contend that the permanent borders should be determined sooner rather than later. He said,

I believe this should take place during this term. I hope we will have someone to talk to as a result of the January 25 Palestinian elections.

We can talk to Hamas, but only if it lays down its arms. The organization is beginning to doubt whether it can triumph with guns and bombs. Hamas is the biggest obstacle to economic prosperity due to the fact that it is detrimental to peace.

So how will the region look in 2010? According to Peres, the permanent borders will be "more or less" set, with the necessary amendments to U.N. Resolutions 242 and 338. Peres further said,

A solution will be found for Jerusalem without dividing it, an Israeli-Jordanian-Palestinian economic troika focusing on Europe will be established, and we will look toward the *U.S.* for security-related and diplomatic guidance.

<u>Saturday, January 14, 2006</u>

The next day in a Tel Aviv speech, Shimon Peres said Kadima will attempt to reach a final-status peace agreement, and that Israel needs a strong political center to make tough decisions.

Peres further said that the next government would attempt to strike a final peace deal with the Palestinians in order to set Israel's permanent borders and put an end to terror.

I spoke now with Acting Prime Minister Ehud Olmert and we agreed on one major thing, to try and set final borders in the upcoming term, a situation that would put an end to the double conflict with the Palestinians on the one hand and with terrorism on the other hand. The Middle East is approaching a fork in the road—either becoming fanatical-Shiite-terrorist or modern and sane.

Arik (Prime Minister Ariel Sharon) surprised me in a positive way, he said "we're both no longer little kids and four years is plenty of time." With Ehud (Olmert) I found an even bigger drive to reach a peace deal.

Referring to the prime minister's decision to establish Kadima, Peres said,

Sharon's departure from the Likud is no less important than Israel's exit from Gaza. That's why I also took that step. As you know, before I made my decision I held thorough talks with Arik, who I wish a complete recovery.

Peres also spoke about Israel's political arena:

We must have a political spine that will allow for the implementation of decisions. If the political situation would have remained the way it is now, we would be going nowhere.

In recent years a situation emerged where radical rightist, radical leftist and anti-religious parties became powerful. We need a renewed political Center so we can make decisions ... today there's an opportunity to create a political Center not in accordance with marginal whims.

Regarding dividing Jerusalem as part of a future peace deal, Peres said,

The controversy over Jerusalem can be resolved even without dividing it. I'm not at all convinced Jerusalem should be divided. In my view, any situation can be resolved through creative ideas.

Source:
http://www.ynetnews.com/Ext/Comp/ArticleLayout/CdaArticlePrintPreview
/1,2506,L-3200088,00.html

Sunday, January 15

Shimon Peres left for the United States.

Wednesday, January 18

Peres: Israel ready to hold final status talks with PA after vote

Shimon Peres said that Israel would be ready to open negotiations with the Palestinians on a permanent peace accord after Israel holds elections March 28, 2006. The aim, he said after meeting for 45 minutes with Secretary of State Rice, would be to end the conflict between the two sides and establish permanent borders between them. Implying Israel was prepared to yield more territories, Peres told reporters, "We don't think of Gaza last, but Gaza first." *(The Associated Press)*

Olmert to Mofaz: Prepare to evacuate all illegal outposts

Charting a strident course toward illegal actions in the settlements, Acting Prime Minister Olmert directed Defense Minister Shaul Mofaz to present a plan for the evacuation of some 20 illegal outposts in the West Bank.

Olmert, speaking at a special security assessment on the situation in Judea and Samaria, also urged an immediate evacuation of the former wholesale market in Hebron and the Amona outpost near Ofra.

In the past two weeks, Olmert had come across much more determined than Prime Minster Sharon to take on the illegal actions of some settlers. Sharon, despite promises made to U.S. President Bush to remove the illegal outposts, seemed hesitant, for political reasons, to move against them. *(The Jerusalem Post)*

Thursday, January 19

Iranian President Mahmoud Ahmadinejad met in Damascus with the leaders of 10 radical Palestinian movements, including Islamic Jihad and Hamas. During the meeting, Ahmadinejad said he "strongly supports the Palestinian people's struggle," according to Popular Front for the Liberation of Palestine (PFLP) official Maher Taher. Taher said the militant chiefs pledged to Ahmadinejad that the "Palestinian resistance and struggle would continue" against Israel. Islamic Jihad chief Abdullah Ramadan Shala, Hamas leader Khaled Meshaal and PFLP-GC leader Ahmed Jibril were at the meeting, according to Taher. It is noteworthy that a suicide bomber struck in Tel Aviv about the time Ahmadinejad and Assad were meeting.

There is concern about Hezbollah's Katyusha rockets on the Israeli-Lebanese border and Islamic Jihad's threats of more suicide bombings. Iran and Syria fund Hezbollah and Islamic Jihad.

<u>Wednesday, January 25</u>

Hamas landslide victory in Palestinian elections

The story of all stories was the Islamic fundamentalist group Hamas' landslide victory in the Palestinian legislative elections on January 25, 2006. This victory is expected to reshape the political landscape of the Middle East. Since Hamas is openly determined to destroy Israel, and has said it will not acknowledge Israel's right to exist as a state, its landslide victory of 76 seats in the 132-seat Palestinian Parliament has produced a political earthquake that has sent shock waves throughout Israel, U.S., EU and the rest of the world.

Many thought Hamas would gain 35 seats or so. Former U.S. President Jimmy Carter, the head of the election monitors, told the annual Herzylia Conference this week he thought Hamas would receive 35 seats. The IDF expected about the same number, but no one expected 76 seats. This major political victory left Hamas with a clear majority and no need to form a coalition with Mahmoud Abbas and Saeb Erekat's Fatah (or any other group).

In perspective, while President Bush's call for democracy ("two democratic states—Israel and Palestine—living side by side in peace and security") helped produce this decisive victory for the democratic *process*, there's a big problem: a majority of the voters selected Palestinian terror entity Hamas as the group they want to lead the Palestinian Authority.

<u>Saturday, February 11, 2006</u>

Sharon was rushed into surgery after his condition deteriorated overnight. Saturday morning, doctors said the his life was in immediate danger. During the operation (four hours), doctors removed about one third of his large intestine.

Following the surgery the prime minister's advisors sounded more optimistic and said "the situation looks less severe at this time." Sharon's son Omri, as well as the prime minister's aides, rushed to the hospital Saturday morning after receiving word of the deterioration in Sharon's condition.

Rice nixes unilateral moves by Israel

Secretary Rice rejected the idea of Israel making additional unilateral pullouts one day after Acting Prime Minister Olmert indicated that Israel would move in that direction. Israeli politicians from the left, right and center who backed Prime Minister Sharon's unilateral pullout from the Gaza Strip and northern West Bank settlements last summer also objected to the idea of further unilateral pullouts from the West Bank.

Olmert said that Israel would "separate from the majority of the Palestinian population" that lives in the West Bank, something that would "obligate us to leave territories where Israel is today."

Following a meeting with Israeli Foreign Minister Tzipi Livni in Washington, Rice said the hope is that there will be a partner for peace on the Palestinian side. But under no circumstances should anyone attempt to make one-sided moves to prejudge the final outcome, she said.

No one should try and unilaterally predetermine the outcome of a final status agreement. That's to be done at final status.

The president did say that at the time of final status, it will be necessary to take into account new realities on the ground that have changed since 1967, but under no circumstances ... should anyone try and do that in a preemptive or predetermined way.

Livni, who was scheduled to meet with President Bush on February 16, urged the international community to make a united stand on the Palestinian Authority and Hamas and to send a "clear message that terror is not acceptable."

Rice said it was imperative that Hamas recognize Israel and its right to exist. "Israel is a member of the United Nations. It cannot be that you have a government that does not accept even its right to exist." *(CNSNews.com)*

Tuesday, February 14

Omri Sharon gets 9 months in jail

Tel Aviv Magistrate's Court Judge Edna Bankenstein, on February 14, sentenced Ariel Sharon's son, Omri, to nine months in jail, nine months probation, and a NIS (shekels) 300,000 fine. However, in light of his father's condition, the judge granted a postponement of his jail time for six months. The fine can be converted into jail time if Sharon does not wish to pay it.

Omri Sharon was convicted of concealing illegal donations of NIS 6 million to his father's election campaign for the leadership of the Likud Party in 1999. Bankenstein wrote in her decision, "These are very serious offences, and even if he committed them out of respect and admiration for his father, he should not have committed them." *(The Jerusalem Post*, February 14, 2006)

Summary

Yitkzak Rabin and Ariel Sharon were two of Israel's most decorated and courageous leaders. Israel would not be the nation it is today without the leadership of these national heroes.

In a continuation of the ongoing peace process, Presidents Bill Clinton and George W. Bush and the international community pressured Yitzhak Rabin and Ariel Sharon to participate in the "land for peace" process in Israel. Sadly, they both reluctantly cooperated and neither man would live to see the outcome of their efforts.

Shimon Peres, a political "cat with nine lives," moved into power after both of these men's tragic personal ends. Peres became Israel's acting Prime Minister when Rabin was assassinated.

Years later, Peres also met with Israel's acting Prime Minister Ehud Olmert less than 48-hours after Sharon's massive stroke. Peres said they had a candid talk. He agreed to support Olmert as the head of the Kadima Party; shortly thereafter, Peres was designated the number two person in the Kadima Party by Olmert. Peres is now (2006) the Vice Prime Minister of Israel and the Cabinet Minister for the Development of the Negev and Galilee.

Exactly two weeks after Ariel Sharon's stroke, while he was lying in a coma in a Jerusalem hospital, Peres met with Secretary of State Condoleezza Rice for 45-minutes at the State Department in Washington, DC. He told Rice that Israel would be ready to open negotiations with the Palestinians on a permanent peace accord after Israel's March 28, 2006 election. This was an aim to end the conflict between the two sides and establish permanent borders between them, implying that Israel was ready to yield more territories. Peres told reporters, "We don't think of Gaza last, but Gaza first."

A Fateful Evening

I was in Jerusalem the evening of Ariel Sharon's stroke and followed the Israeli news reports by the Internet. The Israeli press called it a political earthquake. A few days later, I went to Hadassah Ein Keren Hospital to join members of the world's media who had congregated to report on Sharon's condition. These were extremely tough days for Israel.

I pondered if Sharon's tragedy was yet another consequence for those who have attempted to divide the land of Israel. I asked the Lord in prayer to help me fully understand the very strange parallels of the Rabin and Sharon tragedies. I believe the Lord answered me with great clarity. He put on my heart that He was not responsible for the tragic turn in Rabin's and Sharon's lives, but that they were both victims of the "land for peace" process and the evil associated with it within Israel.

Rabin and Sharon (after completion of the Disengagement Plan) were both becoming more adamant and unyielding about going forward. Sadly, shortly thereafter, both men were out of the picture.

We very likely will never know the details of what happened to Yitzhak Rabin on the tragic night that his life was taken (there are people in Israel that are continuing to piece the events together), or what happened to Ariel Sharon the day he suffered his first stroke, the days before his planned heart catheterization, the hours before his final ride into Jerusalem and the massive stroke he suffered 15 minutes before arriving at the hospital. Some may say it was misfortune but there may be much more to both these stories.

CHAPTER 15

Israel's New Leader: Ehud Olmert

We are tired of fighting, we are tired of being courageous, we are tired of winning, we are tired of defeating our enemies, we want to be able to live in an entirely different environment of relations with our enemies.

– Ehud Olmert, June 2005
Address to the Israel Policy Forum in New York

Olmert's Kadima Party Wins Israeli Election—March 28, 2006

Popularity is not his strongest suit. "Olmert is arrogant, cold, cunning and unpleasant," said the historian and Haaretz columnist Tom Segev. "But he does have one advantage ... he is a professional politician."[1]

Ehud Olmert was born into a family of Russian origin in 1945 in the final years of British rule in Palestine. His father was an MP for the rightwing Herut party, in opposition to the then dominant Labor movement, which became part of Likud. He spent his national service as a correspondent for the army magazine, in stark contrast with the dazzling record of three of his predecessors, Generals Yitzhak Rabin, Ehud Barak and Sharon.

"I have the impression that Olmert has undergone a real change of view, unlike Sharon, for whom leaving Gaza was all about military tactics, a general retreating from one front," Mr. Segev argued. "Olmert has realized that his childhood dream of Greater Israel can't be realized. But it won't be easy to dismantle the settlements. I don't know if someone as grey and uncharismatic as Olmert can do it. Sharon he isn't."[1]

Family Ties Don't Bind Olmerts Politically

The leader of the centrist Kadima party is viewed among Israelis as a hawk. But his wife and their four children are firmly rooted in Israel's far left. "It would be the equivalent of George W. Bush running for election with a family full of communists," explains Efraim Inbar, a political science professor at Jerusalem's Bar Ilan University.[2]

Olmert's wife, Aliza, is a well-known artist and screenwriter. She supports Peace Now, a group that fiercely opposes Israel's security barrier and Kadima's plans to complete it. The group also promotes the division of Jerusalem for a Palestinian state and Israel's withdrawal to its 1967 borders.

The Olmerts' daughter Danna is a university lecturer of literature. She is a member of Machsom Watch, a group of Israeli women who monitor checkpoints for human rights abuses and often confront Israeli soldiers on behalf of Palestinians. Her older sister, Michal, holds a master's degree in psychology and runs creative thinking workshops. Married, she lives in Tel Aviv and is known to share her siblings' leftist political leanings, but is not as outspoken.

The Olmerts' son Shaul completed his military service and signed a petition of Yesh G'vul—a group of Israeli Defense Force soldiers who refuse to serve in the occupied territories—and now lives in New York.

The Olmert's younger son, Ariel, dodged military service altogether and is studying French literature at the Sorbonne in Paris. The Olmert's also have an adopted daughter, Shuli.

Olmert downplays any hint of conflict. "There is a complex and, I think, fascinating dialogue between my children and me," he said in a recent interview with the Hebrew daily Yediot Ahronot newspaper. "They have influenced me, and I am proud of it. I would like to think that I have also influenced them."

Ehud Olmert & Family: At Home in Israel's Corridors of Power[3]

When asked about what might be seen as her husband's great political fortune, Mrs. Olmert explains that it's actually an imposition, and by the way, no fun at all.

Now more of a moderate, her husband has also played the political provocateur, and Mrs. Olmert freely admits she has found his nationalism hard to abide. He grew up in what is often referred to as a nationalist settlement and enjoyed imagining broader borders for the Jewish state. Mrs. Olmert and her husband have had, she says, "a different basic understanding about this place," adding, "I couldn't cope with this rhetoric at all."

Israel's Unlikely Transformer[4] - David Makovsky

From a young confidant of Israel's conservative Likud leaders in the 1980s to the hawkish mayor of Jerusalem in the 1990s to the father of peace-activist children, Olmert has traveled significant ideological terrain. In many ways, Israeli society has traveled that road with him.

Much is riding on this journey. For the first 29 years of Israel's existence, the founding Labor Party dominated national politics. When Labor faltered following the traumatic 1973 war, Likud took over for most of the next 29 years. Last fall, former prime minister Ariel Sharon split Likud, upset that the party did not support him in the landmark Gaza pullout. The March 28, 2006 election marked the first time that a third party—Kadima, which Sharon founded a month before suffering a stroke last January—has won an Israeli election.

Settlements and occupation have not yielded peace with the Palestinians, and bilateral negotiations are remote now that Hamas—a movement sworn to Israel's destruction—is in power. Instead, Olmert campaigned on the promise of a new centrism, stressing the need to leave most of the West Bank and even parts of Jerusalem if there is no negotiating option that could yield final borders. He faces enormous challenges, ranging from the thousands of settlers furious about being evacuated from lands they consider Jewish biblical patrimony to the security nightmares posed by Hamas and like-minded groups. Olmert's political future—and perhaps the future of his nation—rides on that promise.

A famously non-religious man in an intensely religious city—for instance, he was well-known for attending weekly soccer matches on the Sabbath—Olmert often stood a few steps removed from the religious leaders citing biblical imperatives to reclaim ancestral lands.

As a fiery young Knesset member in the 1970s, Olmert had defied the venerable Menachem Begin over the 1978 Camp David accords between Israel and Egypt, which called for full withdrawal from the Sinai and offered a blueprint for Palestinian autonomy. And in 2000, he was furious over then-Prime Minister Ehud Barak's concessions in Jerusalem's Old City and on the Temple Mount as part of the "Camp David II" diplomatic effort. However, Olmert did not complain when Barak agreed to yield several Arab neighborhoods in East Jerusalem. He did not argue that the move violated the principle of what many Israelis consider "indivisible" Jerusalem—though such a reaction would have been in keeping with his earlier politics.

After nearly three years of the second intifada, 2003 brought some hope. The more moderate Mahmoud Abbas was the Palestinian prime minister, and many looked for him to lead his people away from the dead-end leadership of Arafat. However, within 130 days, Abbas resigned.

It was here that Olmert first suggested that if there were no prospects of peace talks, Israel would have to move unilaterally. Olmert felt time was not on Israel's side, a view at odds with Sharon, who felt time would either harmonize Israeli and Palestinian views or allow Israeli determination to prevail.

Olmert made his views explicit in a bombshell newspaper interview in December 2003. He stated that West Bank occupation could not continue indefinitely. He cited demographic trends that threatened the character of Israel as a Jewish and democratic state. He expressed concern that defeat of the two-state solution would give way to international calls for a "one-state" solution—a euphemism for the destruction of Israel.

The trigger for that interview was a memorial service a few days earlier. Sharon was due to give the annual speech at the gravesite of Israel's iconic founder David Ben-Gurion. Sharon canceled because of illness, and asked Olmert to stand in his stead. Speaking in the Negev's Sde Boker kibbutz, Olmert declared, "the greatness of Ben-Gurion was not just his capability to lift a vision of generations to the sky, but also to limit what was possible to the circumstances of time." Olmert went on to quote Ben-Gurion: "When it was a question of all the land without a Jewish state or a Jewish state without all the land, we chose a Jewish state without all the land."

David Makovski, Director of the Project on the Middle East Peace Process, saw Olmert in 2004 at his office in Jerusalem and asked what motivated the stirring gravesite speech. Olmert replied that when Sharon asked him to speak, he asked the prime minister to fax him his planned remarks. Those remarks were about the need to cede parts of biblical Israel. Olmert thus believed that he had Sharon's political imprimatur, but in the eyes of the Israeli public, it was Olmert who pressed Sharon.

With Sharon in a coma early in 2006, Olmert broke with Israeli conventional politics by declaring in the middle of an election campaign that if his party won he would seek to evacuate most of the West Bank settlements. This was Ben-Gurion's formula, updated for the times—a Jewish state without all the land.

The Voters of Israel Spoke

Israel's March 28, 2006 general election turnout was 63.2 percent of 4.5 million eligible voters, by far the lowest percentage in Israel's history. The election results show that Israeli voters favor unilateralism (Kadima Party) and a socialist agenda (Labor Party).

Amir Peretz's Labor Party performance shows that there is still a very significant socialist force in Israel.

Yair Lapid, a columnist from the Hebrew daily *Yedioth Ahronoth*, sums up the elections: "The people do not want to continue to hold on to the (occupied) territories, it supports the next disengagement, and it isn't willing to see its grandfather starve to death."

The Israeli public has said goodbye to the dream of a greater Israel, as shown by the poor performance of Benjamin Netanyahu's Likud Party and other hard-liners.

Bush Invites Olmert to Washington

The day after the Israeli general election, President George W. Bush called Acting Prime Minister Ehud Olmert, congratulated him on his election victory and inviting him to the White House promptly after he forms his government.

British Prime Minister Tony Blair also called Olmert to offer congratulations, saying Kadima's victory "changes the shape of Israeli politics."

"I look forward to meeting him soon to discuss his plans to take the peace process forward," Blair said in a statement released by his 10 Downing Street office. "I urge all parties to pursue a path of positive engagement as set out by the Quartet"—the EU, the U.S., the UN and Russia.

Javier Solana, the EU's foreign policy chief, said he phoned Olmert to congratulate him on his victory. "I encouraged Mr. Olmert to pursue all efforts to move toward a peaceful, negotiated resolution of the Middle East conflict," Solana said in a statement. "I assured him that the European Union stands ready, as always, to offer all its support in this process."

Olmert: Israel Entering a New Chapter

Acting Prime Minister Ehud Olmert said in his victory speech that the election marked a new chapter in Israeli history and that he plans to draw the country's final borders in the coming years. He said he is ready for new peace talks and is prepared to make painful compromises.

In the coming period, we will move to set the final borders of the state of Israel, a Jewish state with a Jewish majority. We will try to achieve this in an agreement with the Palestinians.

Addressing Palestinian leader Mahmoud Abbas, Olmert said:

We are prepared to compromise, give up parts of our beloved land of Israel, remove, painfully, Jews who live there, to allow you the conditions to achieve your hopes and to live in a state in peace and quiet. The time has come for the Palestinians to relate to the existence of the state of Israel, to accept only part of their dream, to stop terror, to accept democracy and accept compromise and peace with us. We are prepared for this. We want this.

Olmert's Plan on the Surface

On the surface, Olmert's unilateral plan makes practical sense in a perfect world:

- Israel will define the final borders (without being affected by the continual whim of Palestinians);

- Israel will choose the settlement blocs they want to keep (the Palestinians want all the land back to the 1967 borders);
- Israel will choose the parts of East Jerusalem that they want to keep and give the rest to the Palestinians for the capital of the proposed Palestine state (this will please the EU);
- Israel will evict settlers living in unauthorized settlements (to show Bush and the international community that Olmert is willing to comply); and
- Israel will finish their security fence (America is going to have a larger security fence, too) to protect them from the terrorists.

If these actions can be implemented (which isn't likely), the Palestinians will have a state (which will please Bush and the Quartet).

Furthermore, Israel will be isolating the Palestinians while showing the international community that they are serious about peace. The U.S. and the EU don't expect Israel to deal with Hamas, which will further isolate them and move them even closer to Iran and Syria.

What Olmert's Plan Doesn't Address

What about the missiles that could rain down on Israeli cities from Gaza, the West Bank or even from East Jerusalem?

What about the missiles that could be used from southern Lebanon, Syria and Iran?

How will Olmert deal with the acceleration of terror networks on Israel's borders and inside Israel?

I have sensed during my recent conversations with Israeli officials, who are almost giddy about the prospect of Israel determining their own boundaries, that for the moment they are not concerned with Hamas, the Muslim Brotherhood of Egypt, Islamic Jihad, Hezbullah, al Qaeda, Syria or Iran. I know they are well aware of the danger; but for now, they seem to want to bask in the thoughts and moments of peace. We can hardly blame them for wanting to dream of peace, but we know that this will be short-lived and costly.

The Disengagement Delusion[5]

Frank J. Gaffney, Jr., head of the Center for Security Policy, stated the first delusion is that the Israeli electorate is voting—as it has done time and time again over the past fourteen years—for someone who promises them security in the face of an increasingly virulent threat from the Palestinian community. Currently, the Palestinians are led by Hamas, a terrorist organization explicitly committed to the destruction of the Jewish State. A succession of previous prime ministers have run on such a platform, then proceeded to indulge in various diplomatic maneuvers that have put Israel at still greater risk.

The second delusion is that what amounts to cutting-and-running—in this case, it is running behind a security fence, yet remaining within easy range of artillery and rocket fire—will make matters better. In fact, Olmert's plan for turning over much of the high ground of the West Bank, its vital aquifers and strategic depth in the immediate wake of Hamas' electoral victory can only embolden those and other Islamofascist enemies of freedom. It will compound the danger they pose, not only to Israel but also to all of us.

This is not idle speculation. The results of Sharon's earlier disengagement from Gaza are already evident:

- The ascendancy of the most unabashedly hostile of Israel's foes;
- The creation of new Taliban-style safe-havens for terrorists (including al Qaeda); and
- A metastasizing threat as Russia, the European Union and the United Nations seek to legitimize Hamas, even as Kadima proposes to reward it with further territorial concessions.

Israel Avoids Victory[6]

Daniel Pipes, director of the Middle East Forum, stated, Arabs fight to eliminate Israel, Israel fights to win the acceptance of its neighbors. The first is offensive in intent, the second is defensive. The former is barbaric, and the latter civilized. For nearly 60 years, Arab rejectionists have sought to eliminate Israel via a range of strategies: undermining its legitimacy through propaganda, harming its economy through a trade boycott, demoralizing it through terrorism, and threatening its population via WMD.

With Likud getting only 11 seats it is clear how deeply unpopular Israelis presently find the idea of winning their war.

Pipes further said, they experiment with compromise, unilateralism, enriching their enemies, and other schemes. But as Douglas MacArthur observed, "In war, there is no substitute for victory." The Oslo diplomacy ended in dismal failure and so will all the other schemes that avoid the hard work of winning. Israelis eventually must gird themselves to resume the difficult, bitter, long, and expensive effort needed to convince the Palestinians and others that their dream of eliminating Israel is defunct.

Should Israelis fail to achieve this, then Israel itself will be defunct.

The U.S. Doesn't Object

Secretary Rice recently said that the Bush administration does not object to Israeli unilateral steps towards solving the Israeli-Palestinian conflict. However, she added that the preferred path to peace would include negotiations, not unilateral measures, since that is the essence of the Road Map.

Still, she noted that it is difficult to imagine contacts with Hamas, which does not recognize Israel or previous agreements between the Palestinians and Israelis. She added that the Palestinians have not yet provided a partner required for negotiations.

The U.S. and Israel are committed to isolation from the Hamas-led Palestinian Authority (PA), and will refrain from making contact with their representatives. Rice and Olmert say that the U.S. will continue its contacts with PA President Mahmoud Abbas, as he has proven to be a leader dedicated to ending the Israeli-Palestinian conflict.

Hamas Isn't Happy

Hamas warned that it would revert to "armed resistance" should Israel press ahead with further unilateral withdrawals from West Bank settlements under Acting Prime Minister Olmert's plan to impose borders with the Palestinians, British newspaper *The Guardian* reported.

Hamas' spokesmen in the Palestinian Legislative Council said the Palestinians have the right to renew violent attacks against Israeli targets in the West Bank, but fell short of threatening suicide attacks within Israel.

Bush and Olmert

In a Sunday, April 9, 2006, *TIME* magazine interview Ehud Olmert was asked how often he spoke to President Bush? Olmert said,

I've spoken to him maybe three times since I became Prime Minister. There is a very strong emotional bond between the two of us, every time we speak we both feel it deeply. I know how he feels and he [knows] how I feel. I think it grew out of his first trip to Israel, when I hosted him in Jerusalem. He knows that I like him. I very much depend on the understanding and cooperation of President Bush. The reason I think [disengagement] can be done is because of the trust and understanding we have for each other.

The U.S and Israel Accountable

Prime Minister Ehud Olmert told *The Wall Street Journal* on April 13 that he will seek broad international support for his plan to withdraw some 70,000 settlers from the West Bank. On his planned May 2006 visit to the U.S., Olmert will ask for financial backing for his plan, which will be completed within 18 months. Olmert said his "convergence plan" will cost up to $10 billion. In return, Israel will keep hold of large West Bank settlement blocks, where most of the evacuees will be relocated.

Ehud Olmert's government will continue to coordinate peace activities with the Bush administration.

To a certain degree, the White House was relieved when Sharon came up with his disengagement plan—even though it was outside the Road Map. President Bush officially endorsed the Sharon plan at the White House in April of 2004. Although it was Sharon's plan, it didn't stop the enormous parallel consequences of the White House's involvement during the Gaza and northern Samaria evacuations and, afterwards, in the peace process activity in August, September and October that occurred simultaneously with Hurricanes Katrina, Rita and Wilma.

The bottom line is: Israel is in a very dangerous position because of U.S. pressure to comply with U.N. Resolutions 242 and 338 and the Quartet Road Map. Although Israel has taken the initiative recently, the Bush administration has remained actively involved as the main facilitator and is not exempt from serious consequences.

Today, we are moving into an even more serious time, when God's covenant land could be divided and given to Muslims, a time when Jews will be forcefully evicted from their homes in Judea and Samaria [the West Bank], and the boundaries of Jerusalem could be determined. Ehud Olmert, Shimon Peres, President George W. Bush, Secretary of State Condoleezza Rice and the Quartet partners will all be responsible and fully accountable.

What will happen to Ehud Olmert?

We have documented in great detail what has happened to previous U.S. Presidents, Israeli Prime Ministers, and Arab leaders who have attempted to divide the land of Israel. Only the God of Israel knows the future of Ehud Olmert and recent history says it won't go well for him.

Summary

After his May 23, 2006 meeting with President Bush at the White House, Prime Minister Olmert said he was "very satisfied" with the understanding reached concerning his plan for possible unilateral withdrawal from parts of the West Bank.

According to the Jerusalem Post, in a briefing for Israeli reporters after the meeting, Olmert stressed that Bush's remarks about his new "realignment plan" were made in a "very clear and remarkable way." The president called Olmert's ideas "bold" and "important steps towards peace."

At a White House press conference with Olmert, Bush said,

Our preferred option, of course, is there to be a negotiated settlement. ...
On the other hand, as the prime minister said, that if he is unable to find
a partner in peace, if nothing can go forward, he is willing to think about
ways to advance the process forward.

The United States will seek international support before endorsing Olmert's
plan for unilateral withdrawal from parts of the West Bank. Bush was not yet
ready to adopt the unilateral Israeli move, though he did not oppose it.

The Bush administration does not have faith that Olmert has a government
coalition stable enough to sustain a parliamentary coalition during the firestorm
of political activity that will surround the implementation of the withdrawal.

Olmert currently has a governing coalition of 67 out of 120 Knesset seats.
Israeli governments composed of coalitions with less than 70 seats tend to be
problematic and short-lived.

The saga continues.

CHAPTER 16

Madrid to The Road Map & U.S. Statements

United States President George H. W. Bush and his Secretary of State James Baker along with President Mikhail Gorbachev of the Soviet Union, in the aftermath of the 1991 Gulf War, extended a letter of invitation to the Madrid Conference to Israel, Syria, Lebanon, Jordan, and the Palestinians.

The Madrid Conference was the beginning of the current peace process and lasted for three days from October 30 to November 1, 1991.

The subsequent meetings led to the Oslo Accords of 1993, the Israel-Jordan Treaty of Peace in 1994, the Wye Plantation Agreement in 1998, the Quartet Road Map in 2003 and various other agreements.

Former President George H. W. Bush stated on February 26, 2003, at the *Issam M. Fares Lecture,*

> The Madrid conference would never have happened if the international coalition that fought together in Desert Storm had acceded the U.N. mandate and gone on its own, if the United States had gone on its own, had gone into Baghdad after Saddam and his forces had surrendered and agreed to disarm.

> The coalition would have instantly shattered. And the political capital that we had gained as a result of our principle restraint to jumpstart the peace process would have been lost. We would have lost all support from our coalition, with the possible exception of England. And we would have lost all support from the smaller nations in the United Nations as well.

> And out of that momentum that we achieved at Madrid, we later saw that historic handshake on the south lawn of the White House between Rabin and Arafat, and the Oslo Accords that followed. And we saw King Hussein of Jordan, my late, dear friend, join the steady march on the path to peace.

How surreal that President Bush's statements about Iraq and his hopes for peace have actually seen the opposite result. The Middle East in 2006 is much more dangerous than it was in 1991. Furthermore, the peace process hasn't brought peace, but has placed Israel in much greater danger while Israel's neighbors and embolden and empower terrorist organizations who speak peace in English and "death to Israel" in Arabic.

The Madrid Conference
October 30 - November 1, 1991

Opening Speech by U.S. President George H. W. Bush

Prime Minister Gonzalez and President Gorbachev, Excellencies. Let me begin by thanking the Government of Spain for hosting this historic gathering. With short notice, the Spanish people and their leaders stepped forward to make available this magnificent setting. Let us hope that this Conference of Madrid will mark the beginning of a new chapter in the history of the Middle East.

I also want to express at the outset my pleasure at the presence of our fellow co–sponsor, President Gorbachev. At a time of momentous challenges at home, President Gorbachev and his senior associates have demonstrated their intent to engage the Soviet Union as a force for positive change in the Middle East. This sends a powerful signal to all those who long for peace.

We come to Madrid on a mission of hope – to begin work on a just, lasting, and comprehensive settlement to the conflict in the Middle East. We come here to seek peace for a part of the world that in the long memory of man has known far too much hatred, anguish, and war. I can think of no endeavor more worthy – or more necessary.

Our objective must be clear and straightforward. It is not simply to end the state of war in the Middle East and replace it with a state of non-belligerency. This is not enough; this would not last. Rather, we seek peace, real peace. And by real peace I mean treaties. Security. Diplomatic relations. Economic relations. Trade. Investment. Cultural exchange. Even tourism.

What we seek is a Middle East where vast resources are no longer devoted to armaments. A Middle East where young people no longer have to dedicate and, all too often, give their lives to combat. A Middle East no longer victimized by fear and terror. A Middle East where normal men and women lead normal lives.

Let no one mistake the magnitude of this challenge. The struggle we seek to end has a long and painful history. Every life lost – every outrage, every act of violence – is etched deep in the hearts and history of the people of this region. Theirs is a history that weighs heavily against hope. And yet, history need not be man's master. I expect that some will say that what I am suggesting is impossible. But think back. Who back in 1945 would have thought that France and Germany, bitter rivals for nearly a century, would become allies in the aftermath of World War II? And who two years ago would have predicted that the Berlin Wall would come down? And who in the early 1960s would have believed that the Cold War would come to a peaceful end, replaced by cooperation – exemplified by the fact that the United States and the Soviet Union are here today – not as rivals, but as partners, as Prime Minister Gonzalez pointed out.

No, peace in the Middle East need not be a dream. Peace is possible. The Egyptian–Israeli Peace Treaty is striking proof that former adversaries can make and sustain peace. And moreover, parties in the Middle East have respected agreements, not only in the Sinai, but on the Golan Heights as well.

The fact that we are all gathered here today for the first time attests to a new potential for peace. Each of us has taken an important step toward real peace by meeting here in Madrid. All the formulas on paper, all the pious declarations in the world won't bring peace if there is no practical mechanism for moving ahead.

Peace will only come as the result of direct negotiations, compromise, give-and-take. Peace cannot be imposed from the outside by the United States or anyone else. While we will continue to do every thing possible to help the parties overcome obstacles, peace must come from within. We come here to Madrid as realists. We do not expect peace to be negotiated in a day, or a week, or a month, or even a year. It will take time; indeed, it should take time – time for parties so long at war to learn to talk to one another, to listen to one another. Time to heal old wounds and build trust. In this quest, time need not be the enemy of progress.

What we envision is a process of direct negotiations proceeding along two tracks, one between Israel and the Arab states; the other between Israel and the Palestinians. Negotiations are to be conducted on the basis of UN Security Council Resolutions 242 and 338. The real work will not happen here in the plenary session, but in direct bilateral negotiations. This Conference cannot impose a settlement on the participants or veto agreements; and just as important, the Conference can only be reconvened with the consent of every participant. Progress is in the hands of the parties who must live with the consequences.

Soon after the bilateral talks commence, parties will convene as well to organize multilateral negotiations. These will focus on issues that cross national boundaries and are common to the region: arms control, water, refugee concerns, economic development. Progress in these fora is not intended as a substitute for what must be decided in the bilateral talks; to the contrary, progress in the multilateral issues can help create an atmosphere in which long-standing bilateral disputes can more easily be settled.

For Israel and the Palestinians, a framework already exists for diplomacy. Negotiations will be conducted in phases, beginning with talks on interim self-government arrangements. We aim to reach agreement within one year. And once agreed, interim self-government arrangements will last for five years; beginning the third year, negotiations will commence on permanent status.

No one can say with any precision what the end result will be; in our view, something must be developed, something acceptable to Israel, the Palestinians and Jordan, that gives the Palestinian people meaningful control over their own lives and fate and provides for the acceptance and security of Israel.

We can all appreciate that both Israelis and Palestinians are worried about compromise, worried about compromising even the smallest point for fear it becomes a precedent for what really matters. But no one should avoid compromise on interim arrangements for a simple reason: nothing agreed to now will prejudice permanent status negotiations. To the contrary, these subsequent negotiations will be determined on their own merits.

Peace cannot depend upon promises alone. Real peace–lasting peace –must be based upon security for all states and peoples, including Israel. For too long the Israeli people have lived in fear, surrounded by an unaccepting Arab world. Now is the ideal moment for the Arab world to demonstrate that attitudes have changed that the Arab world is willing to live in peace with Israel and make allowances for Israel's reasonable security needs.

We know that peace must also be based on fairness. In the absence of fairness, there will be no legitimacy – no stability. This applies above all to the Palestinian people, many of whom have known turmoil and frustration above all else. Israel now has an opportunity to demonstrate that it is willing to enter into a new relationship with its Palestinian neighbors; one predicated upon mutual respect and cooperation. Throughout the Middle East, we seek a stable and enduring settlement. We've not defined what this means; indeed, I make these points with no map showing where the final borders are to be drawn. Nevertheless, we believe territorial compromise is essential for peace. Boundaries should reflect the quality of both security and political arrangements. The United States is prepared to accept whatever the parties themselves find acceptable. What we seek, as I said on March 6, is a solution that meets the twin tests of fairness and security.

I know–I expect we all know–that these negotiations will not be easy. I know, too, that these negotiations will not be smooth. There will be disagreement and criticism, setbacks who knows–possibly interruptions. Negotiation and compromise are always painful. Success will escape us if we focus solely upon what is being given up. We must fix our vision on what real peace would bring. Peace, after all, means not just avoiding war and the costs of preparing for it. The Middle East is blessed with great resources: physical, financial, and, yes, above all, human. New opportunities are within reach–if we only have the vision to embrace them.

To succeed, we must recognize that peace is in the interest of all parties – war, absolute advantage of none. The alternative to peace in the Middle East is a future of violence and waste and tragedy. In any future war lurks the danger of weapons of mass destruction. As we learned in the Gulf War, modern arsenals make it possible to attack urban areas to put the lives of innocent men, women, and children at risk, to transform city streets, schools, and children's playgrounds into battlefields.

Today, we can decide to take a different path to the future to avoid conflict. I call upon all parties to avoid unilateral acts, be they words or deeds that would invite retaliation or, worse yet, prejudice or even threaten this process itself. I call upon all parties to consider taking measures that will bolster mutual confidence and trust steps that signal a sincere commitment to reconciliation. I want to say something about the role of the United States of America. We played an active role in making this conference possible; both the Secretary of State, Jim Baker, and I will play an active role in helping the process succeed. Toward this end, we've provided written assurances to Israel, to Syria, to Jordan, Lebanon, and the Palestinians. In the spirit of openness and honesty, we will brief all parties on the assurances that we have provided to the other. We're prepared to extend guarantees, provide technology and support, if that is what peace requires. And we will call upon our friends and allies in Europe and in Asia to join with us in providing resources so that peace and prosperity go hand in hand.

Outsiders can assist, but in the end, it is up to the peoples and governments of the Middle East to shape the future of the Middle East. It is their opportunity and it is their responsibility to do all that they can to take advantage of this gathering, this historic gathering, and what it symbolizes and what it promises.

No one should assume that the opportunity before us to make peace will remain if we fail to seize the moment. Ironically, this is an opportunity born of war–the destruction of past wars, the fear of future wars. The time has come to put an end to war–the time has come to choose peace.

Speaking for the American people, I want to reaffirm that the United States is prepared to facilitate the search for peace, to be a catalyst, as we've been in the past and as we've been very recently. We seek only one thing, and this we seek not for ourselves, but for the peoples of the area and particularly the children: that this and future generations of the Middle East may know the meaning and blessing of peace.

We have seen too many generations of children whose haunted eyes show only fear – too many funerals for their brothers and sisters, the mothers and fathers who died too soon – too much hatred, too little love. And if we cannot summon the courage to lay down the past for ourselves, let us resolve to do it for the children. May God bless and guide the work of this Conference, and may this Conference set us on the path of peace.

Thank you.

Source: http://www.mfa.gov.il/mfa/go.asp?MFAH0dg10

A Performance-Based Road Map
to a Permanent Two-State Solution
for the Israeli-Palestinian Conflict

White House Press Statement

Office of the Spokesman
Washington, DC
April 30, 2003

The following is a performance-based and goal-driven roadmap, with clear phases, timelines, target dates, and benchmarks aiming at progress through reciprocal steps by the two parties in the political, security, economic, humanitarian, and institution-building fields, under the auspices of the Quartet [the United States, European Union, United Nations, and Russia]. The destination is a final and comprehensive settlement of the Israel–Palestinian conflict by 2005, as presented in President Bush's speech of 24 June, and welcomed by the EU, Russia and the UN in the 16 July and 17 September Quartet Ministerial statements.

A two-state solution to the Israeli–Palestinian conflict will only be achieved through an end to violence and terrorism, when the Palestinian people have a leadership acting decisively against terror and willing and able to build a practicing democracy based on tolerance and liberty, and through Israel's readiness to do what is necessary for a democratic Palestinian state to be established, and a clear, unambiguous acceptance by both parties of the goal of a negotiated settlement as described below. The Quartet will assist and facilitate implementation of the plan, starting in Phase I, including direct discussions between the parties as required. The plan establishes a realistic timeline for implementation. However, as a performance-based plan, progress will require and depend upon the good faith efforts of the parties, and their compliance with each of the obligations outlined below.

Should the parties perform their obligations rapidly, progress within and through the phases may come sooner than indicated in the plan. Non-compliance with obligations will impede progress.

A settlement, negotiated between the parties, will result in the emergence of an independent, democratic, and viable Palestinian state living side by side in peace and security with Israel and its other neighbors. The settlement will resolve the Israel–Palestinian conflict, and end the occupation that began in 1967, based on the foundations of the Madrid Conference, the principle of land for peace, UNSCRs 242, 338 and 1397, agreements previously reached by the parties, and the initiative of Saudi Crown Prince Abdullah – endorsed by the Beirut Arab League Summit – calling for acceptance of Israel as a neighbor living in peace and security, in the context of a comprehensive settlement. This initiative is a vital element of international efforts to promote a comprehensive peace on all tracks, including the Syrian–Israeli and Lebanese–Israeli tracks.

The Quartet will meet regularly at senior levels to evaluate the parties' performance on implementation of the plan. In each phase, the parties are expected to perform their obligations in parallel, unless otherwise indicated.

Phase I: Ending Terror and Violence, Normalizing Palestinian Life, and Building Palestinian Institutions
– Present to May 2003

In Phase I, the Palestinians immediately undertake an unconditional cessation of violence according to the steps outlined below; such action should be accompanied by supportive measures undertaken by Israel. Palestinians and Israelis resume security cooperation based on the Tenet work plan to end violence, terrorism, and incitement through restructured and effective Palestinian security services. Palestinians undertake comprehensive political reform in preparation for statehood, including drafting a Palestinian constitution, and free, fair and open elections upon the basis of those measures. Israel takes all necessary steps to help normalize Palestinian life. Israel withdraws from Palestinian areas occupied from September 28, 2000 and the two sides restore the status quo that existed at that time, as security performance and cooperation progress. Israel also freezes all settlement activity, consistent with the Mitchell report.

At the outset of Phase I

Palestinian leadership issues unequivocal statement reiterating Israel's right to exist in peace and security and calling for an immediate and unconditional cease-fire to end armed activity and all acts of violence against Israelis anywhere. All official Palestinian institutions end incitement against Israel.

Israeli leadership issues unequivocal statement affirming its commitment to the two–state vision of an independent, viable, sovereign Palestinian state living in peace and security alongside Israel, as expressed by President Bush, and calling for an immediate end to violence against Palestinians everywhere. All official Israeli institutions end incitement against Palestinians.

Security

Palestinians declare an unequivocal end to violence and terrorism and undertake visible efforts on the ground to arrest, disrupt, and restrain individuals and groups conducting and planning violent attacks on Israelis anywhere.

Rebuilt and refocused Palestinian Authority security apparatus begins sustained, targeted, and effective operations aimed at confronting all those engaged in terror and dismantlement of terrorist capabilities and infrastructure. This includes commencing confiscation of illegal weapons and consolidation of security authority, free of association with terror and corruption.

GOI [Government of Israel] takes no actions undermining trust, including deportations, attacks on civilians; confiscation and/or demolition of Palestinian homes and property, as a punitive measure or to facilitate Israeli construction; destruction of Palestinian institutions and infrastructure; and other measures specified in the Tenet work plan.

Relying on existing mechanisms and on-the-ground resources, Quartet representatives begin informal monitoring and consult with the parties on establishment of a formal monitoring mechanism and its implementation.

Implementation, as previously agreed, of U.S. rebuilding, training and resumed security cooperation plan in collaboration with outside oversight board (U.S.–Egypt–Jordan). Quartet support for efforts to achieve a lasting, comprehensive cease-fire.

All Palestinian security organizations are consolidated into three services reporting to an empowered Interior Minister.

Restructured/retrained Palestinian security forces and IDF counterparts progressively resume security cooperation and other undertakings in implementation of the Tenet work plan, including regular senior-level meetings, with the participation of U.S. security officials.

Arab states cut off public and private funding and all other forms of support for groups supporting and engaging in violence/terror.

All donors providing budgetary support for the Palestinians channel these funds through the Palestinian Ministry of Finance's Single Treasury Account.

As comprehensive security performance moves forward, IDF [Israel Defense Forces] withdraws progressively from areas occupied since September 28, 2000 and the two sides restore the status quo that existed prior to September 28, 2000. Palestinian security forces redeploy to areas vacated by IDF.

Palestinian Institution-Building

Immediate action on credible process to produce draft constitution for Palestinian statehood. As rapidly as possible, constitutional committee circulates draft Palestinian constitution, based on strong parliamentary democracy and cabinet with empowered Prime Minister, for public comment/debate. Constitutional committee proposes draft document for submission after elections for approval by appropriate Palestinian institutions.

Appointment of interim Prime Minister or cabinet with empowered executive authority/decision-making body.

GOI fully facilitates travel of Palestinian officials for PLC [Palestinian Legislative Council] and Cabinet sessions, internationally supervised security retraining, electoral and other reform activity, and other supportive measures related to the reform efforts.

Continued appointment of Palestinian ministers empowered to undertake fundamental reform. Completion of further steps to achieve genuine separation of powers, including any necessary Palestinian legal reforms for this purpose.

Establishment of independent Palestinian election commission. PLC reviews and revises election law.

Palestinian performance on judicial, administrative, and economic benchmarks, as established by the International Task Force on Palestinian Reform.

As early as possible, and based upon the above measures and in the context of open debate and transparent candidate selection/electoral campaign based on a free, multi-party process, Palestinians hold free, open, and fair elections.

GOI facilitates Task Force election assistance, registration of voters, movement of candidates and voting officials. Support for NGOs involved in the election process.

GOI reopens Palestinian Chamber of Commerce and other closed Palestinian institutions in East Jerusalem based on a commitment that these institutions operate strictly in accordance with prior agreements between the parties.

Humanitarian Response

Israel takes measures to improve the humanitarian situation. Israel and Palestinians implement in full all recommendations of the Bertini report to improve humanitarian conditions, lifting curfews and easing restrictions on movement of persons and goods, and allowing full, safe, and unfettered access of international and humanitarian personnel.

AHLC [Ad Hoc Liaison Committee] reviews the humanitarian situation and prospects for economic development in the West Bank and Gaza and launches a major donor assistance effort, including to the reform effort.

GOI and PA continue revenue clearance process and transfer of funds, including arrears, in accordance with agreed, transparent monitoring mechanism.

Civil Society

Continued donor support, including increased funding through PVOs/NGOs, for people to people programs, private sector development and civil society initiatives.

Settlements

GOI immediately dismantles settlement outposts erected since March 2001.

Consistent with the Mitchell Report, GOI freezes all settlement activity (including natural growth of settlements).

Phase II: Transition – June - December 2003

In the second phase, efforts are focused on the option of creating an independent Palestinian state with provisional borders and attributes of sovereignty, based on the new constitution, as a way station to a permanent status settlement. As has been noted, this goal can be achieved when the Palestinian people have a leadership acting decisively against terror, willing and able to build a practicing democracy based on tolerance and liberty. With such a leadership, reformed civil institutions and security structures, the Palestinians will have the active support of the Quartet and the broader international community in establishing an independent, viable, state. Progress into Phase II will be based upon the consensus judgment of the Quartet of whether conditions are appropriate to proceed, taking into account performance of both parties. Furthering and sustaining efforts to normalize Palestinian lives and build Palestinian institutions, Phase II starts after Palestinian elections and ends with possible creation of an independent Palestinian state with provisional borders in 2003. Its primary goals are continued comprehensive security performance and effective security cooperation, continued normalization of Palestinian life and institution-building, further building on and sustaining of the goals outlined in Phase I, ratification of a democratic Palestinian constitution, formal establishment of office of prime minister, consolidation of political reform, and the creation of a Palestinian state with provisional borders.

International Conference: Convened by the Quartet, in consultation with the parties, immediately after the successful conclusion of Palestinian elections, to support Palestinian economic recovery and launch a process, leading to establishment of an independent Palestinian state with provisional borders.

Such a meeting would be inclusive, based on the goal of a comprehensive Middle East peace (including between Israel and Syria, and Israel and Lebanon), and based on the principles described in the preamble to this document.

Arab states restore pre-Intifada links to Israel (trade offices, etc.).

Revival of multilateral engagement on issues including regional water resources, environment, economic development, refugees, and arms control issues.

New constitution for democratic, independent Palestinian state is finalized and approved by appropriate Palestinian institutions. Further elections, if required, should follow approval of the new constitution.

Empowered reform cabinet with office of Prime Minister formally established, consistent with draft constitution.

Continued comprehensive security performance, including effective security cooperation on the bases laid out in Phase I.

Creation of an independent Palestinian state with provisional borders through a process of Israeli–Palestinian engagement, launched by the international conference. As part of this process, implementation of prior agreements, to enhance maximum territorial contiguity, including further action on settlements in conjunction with establishment of a Palestinian state with provisional borders.

Enhanced international role in monitoring transition, with the active, sustained, and operational support of Quartet.

Quartet members promote international recognition of Palestinian state, including possible UN membership.

Phase III: Permanent Status Agreement and End of the Israeli–Palestinian Conflict – 2004-2005

Progress into Phase III, based on consensus judgment of Quartet, and taking into account actions of both parties and Quartet monitoring. Phase III objectives are consolidation of reform and stabilization of Palestinian institutions, sustained, effective Palestinian security performance, and Israeli– Palestinian negotiations aimed at a permanent status agreement in 2005.

Second International Conference: Convened by Quartet, in consultation with the parties, at beginning of 2004 to endorse agreement reached on an independent Palestinian state with provisional borders and formally to launch a process with the active, sustained, and operational support of the Quartet, leading to a final, permanent status resolution in 2005, including on borders, Jerusalem, refugees, settlements; and, to support progress toward a comprehensive Middle East settlement between Israel and Lebanon and Israel and Syria, to be achieved as soon as possible.

Continued comprehensive, effective progress on the reform agenda laid out by the Task Force in preparation for final status agreement.

Continued sustained and effective security performance, and sustained, effective security cooperation on the bases laid out in Phase I.

International efforts to facilitate reform and stabilize Palestinian institutions and the Palestinian economy, in preparation for final status agreement.

Parties reach final and comprehensive permanent status agreement that ends the Israel–Palestinian conflict in 2005, through a settlement negotiated between the parties based on UNSCR 242, 338, and 1397, that ends the occupation that began in 1967, and includes an agreed, just, fair, and realistic solution to the refugee issue, and a negotiated resolution on the status of Jerusalem that takes into account the political and religious concerns of both sides, and protects the religious interests of Jews, Christians, and Muslims worldwide, and fulfills the vision of two states, Israel and sovereign, independent, democratic and viable Palestine, living side-by-side in peace and security.

Arab state acceptance of full normal relations with Israel and security for all the states of the region in the context of a comprehensive Arab–Israeli peace. [End]

Source: http://www.state.gov./r/pa/prs/ps/2003/20062.htm

President George W. Bush
Speech at Aqaba

Wednesday, June 04, 2003

George W. Bush, President of the United States:

King Abdullah, thank you for hosting this event.

Her Majesty, thank you for your hospitality.

It is fitting that we gather today in Jordan. King Abdullah is a leader on behalf of peace, and is carrying forward the tradition of his father, King Hussein.

I'm pleased to be here with Prime Minister Sharon. The friendship between our countries began at the time of Israel's creation. Today, America is strongly committed and I am strongly committed to Israel's security as a vibrant Jewish state.

I'm also pleased to be with Prime Minister Abbas. He represents the cause of freedom and statehood for the Palestinian people. I strongly support that cause as well.

Each of us is here because we understand that all people have the right to live in peace. We believe that with hard work and good faith and courage it is possible to bring peace to the Middle East. And today we mark important progress toward that goal.

Great and hopeful change is coming to the Middle East.

In Iraq, a dictator who funded terror and sowed conflict has been removed, and a more just and democratic society is emerging.

Prime Minister Abbas now leads the Palestinian cabinet. By his strong leadership, by building the institutions of Palestinian democracy and by rejecting terror, he is serving the deepest hopes of his people.

All here today now share a goal: The Holy Land must be shared between the state of Palestine and the state of Israel, living at peace with each other and with every nation of the Middle East.

All sides will benefit from this achievement and all sides have responsibilities to meet. As the Road Map accepted by the parties makes clear, both must make tangible immediate steps toward this two–state vision.

I welcome Prime Minister Sharon's pledge to improve the humanitarian situation in the Palestinian areas and to begin removing unauthorized outposts immediately. I appreciate his gestures of reconciliation on behalf of prisoners and their families, and his frank statements about the need for territorial contiguity.

As I said yesterday, the issue of settlements must be addressed for peace to be achieved. In addition, Prime Minister Sharon has stated that no unilateral actions by either side can or should prejudge the outcome of future negotiations. The Prime Minister also recognizes that it is in Israel's own interest for Palestinians to govern themselves in their own state.

These are meaningful signs of respect for the rights of the Palestinians and their hopes for a viable, democratic, peaceful Palestinian state.

Prime Minister Abbas recognizes that terrorist crimes are a dangerous obstacle to the independent state his people seek.

He agrees that the process for achieving that state is through peaceful negotiations. He has pledged to consolidate Palestinian institutions, including the security forces, and to make them more accountable and more democratic.

He has promised his full efforts and resources to end the armed intifadah. He has promised to work without compromise for a complete end of violence and terror.

In all these efforts, the Prime Minister is demonstrating his leadership and commitment to building a better future for the Palestinian people.

Both Prime Ministers here agree that progress toward peace also requires an end to violence and the elimination of all forms of hatred, and prejudice and official incitement, in schoolbooks, in broadcasts and in the words used by political leaders. Both leaders understand that a future of peace cannot be founded on hatred and falsehood and bitterness.

Yet these two leaders cannot bring about peace if they must act alone. True peace requires the support of other nations in the region.

Yesterday in Sharm el-Sheik we made a strong beginning. Arab leaders stated that they share our goal of two states, Israel and Palestine, living side by side in peace and in security. And they have promised to cut off assistance and the flow of money and weapons to terrorist groups and to help Prime Minister Abbas rid Palestinian areas of terrorism.

All sides have made important commitments, and the United States will strive to see these commitments fulfilled.

My government will provide training and support for a new, restructured Palestinian security service. And we'll place a mission on the ground, led by Ambassador John Wolf. This mission will be charged with helping the parties to move toward peace, monitoring their progress and stating clearly who is fulfilling their responsibilities.

And we expect both parties to keep their promises.

I've also asked Secretary of State Colin Powell and National Security Adviser Dr. Condoleezza Rice to make this cause a matter of the highest priority. Secretary Powell and Dr. Rice, as my personal representative, will work closely with the parties, helping them move toward true peace as quickly as possible.

The journey we're taking is difficult, but there is no other choice. No leader of conscience can accept more months and years of humiliation, killing and mourning. And these leaders of conscience have made their declarations today in the cause of peace. The United States is committed to that cause. If all sides fulfill their obligation, I know that peace can finally come.

Thank you very much and may God bless our work.

Where Does President George W. Bush Stand?
White House Press Conference – Ari Fleischer
June 9, 2003

In a White House press briefing on June 9, 2003, Press Secretary Ari Fleischer was asked the following questions:

QUESTION: Ari, there are millions of conservative supporters of the president who have signed letters protesting this Road Map for peace. Does the president see these letters, and does he give any consideration to this important constituent base of his?

MR. FLEISCHER: There's no question the president is aware of the risks to the Road Map. And the risks of the Road Map come principally from both edges of the debate. And, of course, within Israel there will be many people who oppose the dismantlement of these illegal outposts. But these are the actions that are required to be taken for Israel and Palestine to live side by side in peace and security.

And never stop asking yourself the question when it comes to the Middle East, how much longer can Israel and the Palestinian Authority live the way they are, with violence, with killing, with retaliation. Israel has the right to defend itself. But is there a better way? Is there a way that Israel and a Palestinian Authority can finally, at long last, live side by side as Israel and as a Palestinian state?

There have been Arab nations that have made peace treaties with Israel, and have honored them—Egypt has, Jordan has. Why does anybody have to assume that the Palestinian people don't want the same thing? There are terrorists who don't want it. And the terrorists are the enemy, not only of peace, but also of the creation of a Palestinian state. And that's why the president welcomes the words and is now looking for the results in the actions of the new Palestinian leader, as well as Prime Minister Sharon.

QUESTION: Do you know if President Bush plans a direct response to these letters or plans to meet with any of these conservative leaders?

MR. FLEISCHER: The president's response is widely known. The president is dedicated to implementing the Road Map.

QUESTION: Okay. Since the Palestinian Authority has done no more to fulfill its obligations to the Road Map than it did for the Oslo Accords, and since yesterday's [June 8, 2003] killings of five Israeli soldiers, my question is, can you cite any reason why, with the Road Map completely road blocked, the president should not end his exemption of Palestinian terrorists from his promise of war on all terrorists?

MR. FLEISCHER: The Road Map is just beginning. The Road Map is just being implemented.

QUESTION: What have they done? What have the Palestinians done to fulfill any of the requirements of last month for the Road Map?

MR. FLEISCHER: When you take a look at the statements that have been made by the prime minister of the Palestinian Authority, this President—

QUESTION: Statements? That's—

MR. FLEISCHER: This is exactly how the Road Map was designed to begin. The prime minister of the Palestinian Authority is determined to work with the United States and the Arab nations to rebuild their security forces so that he can, indeed, live up to the terms of the Road Map, which involve cracking down and dismantling terrorism. The president has confidence that over time, with the help of the United States and the help of the Arab nations and the help of Israel, that Prime Minister Abbas is the best hope for implementing the terms of the Road Map.

This is an issue that has always been fraught with extremists who seek to derail the Road Map. What is important now is that the Palestinian Authority is led by someone who is not an extremist, but somebody who is dedicated to implementing the Road Map. And the president will continue to work with both the Israelis and the Palestinians, despite the recent violence, to help them to implement the peacemaking sides of the Road Map.

[This was stated prior to Palestinian Prime Minister Mahmoud Abbas's resignation on September 6, 2003.]

Additional statement by U.S. President Bush - April 14, 2004

See: http://www.whitehouse.gov/news/releases/2004/04/20040414–3.html

Letter from President George W. Bush to Prime Minister Sharon

April 14, 2004

His Excellency
Ariel Sharon
Prime Minister of Israel

Dear Mr. Prime Minister:

Thank you for your letter setting out your disengagement plan.

The United States remains hopeful and determined to find a way forward toward a resolution of the Israeli– Palestinian dispute. I remain committed to my June 24, 2002 vision of two states living side by side in peace and security as the key to peace, and to the roadmap as the route to get there.

We welcome the disengagement plan you have prepared, under which Israel would withdraw certain military installations and all settlements from Gaza, and withdraw certain military installations and settlements in the West Bank. These steps described in the plan will mark real progress toward realizing my June 24, 2002 vision, and make a real contribution towards peace. We also understand that, in this context, Israel believes it is important to bring new opportunities to the Negev and the Galilee. We are hopeful that steps pursuant to this plan, consistent with my vision, will remind all states and parties of their own obligations under the roadmap.

The United States appreciates the risks such an undertaking represents. I therefore want to reassure you on several points.

First, the United States remains committed to my vision and to its implementation as described in the roadmap. The United States will do its utmost to prevent any attempt by anyone to impose any other plan. Under the roadmap, Palestinians must undertake an immediate cessation of armed activity and all acts of violence against Israelis anywhere, and all official Palestinian institutions must end incitement against Israel. The Palestinian leadership must act decisively against terror, including sustained, targeted, and effective operations to stop terrorism and dismantle terrorist capabilities and infrastructure. Palestinians must undertake a comprehensive and fundamental political reform that includes a strong parliamentary democracy and an empowered prime minister.

Second, there will be no security for Israelis or Palestinians until they and all states, in the region and beyond, join together to fight terrorism and dismantle terrorist organizations. The United States reiterates its steadfast commitment to Israel's security, including secure, defensible borders, and to preserve and strengthen Israel's capability to deter and defend itself, by itself, against any threat or possible combination of threats.

Third, Israel will retain its right to defend itself against terrorism, including to take actions against terrorist organizations. The United States will lead efforts, working together with Jordan, Egypt, and others in the international community, to build the capacity and will of Palestinian institutions to fight terrorism, dismantle terrorist organizations, and prevent the areas from which Israel has withdrawn from posing a threat that would have to be addressed by any other means. The United States understands that after Israel withdraws from Gaza and/or parts of the West Bank, and pending agreements on other arrangements, existing arrangements regarding control of airspace, territorial waters, and land passages of the West Bank and Gaza will continue. The United States is strongly committed to Israel's security and well-being as a Jewish state. It seems clear that an agreed, just, fair, and realistic framework for a solution to the Palestinian refugee issue as part of any final status agreement will need to be found through the establishment of a Palestinian state, and the settling of Palestinian refugees there, rather than in Israel.

As part of a final peace settlement, Israel must have secure and recognized borders, which should emerge from negotiations between the parties in accordance with UNSC Resolutions 242 and 338. In light of new realities on the ground, including already existing major Israeli population centers, it is unrealistic to expect that the outcome of final status negotiations will be a full and complete return to the armistice lines of 1949, and all previous efforts to negotiate a two–state solution have reached the same conclusion. It is realistic to expect that any final status agreement will only be achieved on the basis of mutually agreed changes that reflect these realities.

I know that, as you state in your letter, you are aware that certain responsibilities face the State of Israel. Among these, your government has stated that the barrier being erected by Israel should be a security rather than political barrier, should be temporary rather than permanent, and therefore not prejudice any final status issues including final borders, and its route should take into account, consistent with security needs, its impact on Palestinians not engaged in terrorist activities.

As you know, the United States supports the establishment of a Palestinian state that is viable, contiguous, sovereign, and independent, so that the Palestinian people can build their own future in accordance with my vision set forth in June 2002 and with the path set forth in the roadmap. The United States will join with others in the international community to foster the development of democratic political institutions and new leadership committed to those institutions, the reconstruction of civic institutions, the growth of a free and prosperous economy, and the building of capable security institutions dedicated to maintaining law and order and dismantling terrorist organizations.

A peace settlement negotiated between Israelis and Palestinians would be a great boon not only to those peoples but to the peoples of the entire region. Accordingly, the United States believes that all states in the region have special responsibilities: to support the building of the institutions of a Palestinian state; to fight terrorism, and cut off all forms of assistance to individuals and groups engaged in terrorism; and to begin now to move toward more normal relations with the State of Israel. These actions would be true contributions to building peace in the region.

Mr. Prime Minister, you have described a bold and historic initiative that can make an important contribution to peace. I commend your efforts and courageous decision which I support. As a close friend and ally, the United States intends to work closely with you to help make it a success.

Sincerely,
George W. Bush

U.S. Senate & House Embrace
President Bush's Support of Sharon's Plan

The Senate voted on June 24, 2004, to embrace President Bush's support of Israeli Prime Minister Sharon's plan to with-draw from the Gaza Strip. The Senate's action came a day after the House approved a similar measure by a 407–9 roll call vote.

The concurrent resolution states that Congress: (1) strongly endorses the principles articulated by President Bush in his letter dated April 14, 2004, to Israeli Prime Minister Ariel Sharon which will strengthen the security and well-being of the State of Israel; and (2) supports continuing efforts with the international community to build the capacity and will of Palestinian institutions to fight terrorism, dismantle terrorist organizations, and prevent the areas from which Israel has withdrawn from posing a threat to the security of Israel.

By 95–3, Senators approved nonbinding language that also said "it is unrealistic" for any peace settlement between Israel and Palestinians to require Israel to return to the borders that existed before the 1967 War. In addition, the resolution said a Palestinian state would have to be part of a "just, fair and realistic framework" for peace with Palestinian refugees settling there, not in Israel. The Senate resolution also said Palestinians must stop "armed activity and all acts of violence against Israelis anywhere."

Both chambers' resolutions endorsed Bush's April 14 letter to Sharon in which Bush backed Sharon's plan to remove Jewish settlements and some military installations from Gaza, and some military bases and settlements from the West Bank.

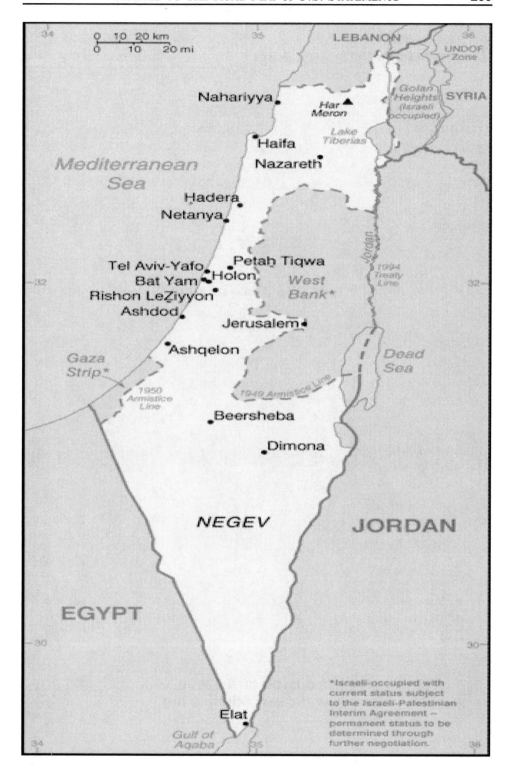

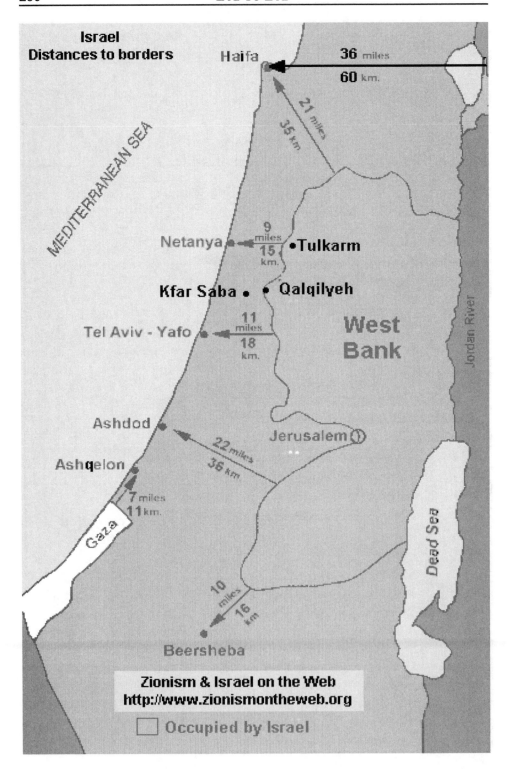

Israel
Distances to borders

Haifa

36 miles
60 km.

MEDITERRANEAN SEA

21 miles
35 km

Netanya   9 miles •Tulkarm
           15 km.

Kfar Saba •   • Qalqilyeh

Tel Aviv - Yafo   11 miles   West
                   18 km.   Bank

Jordan River

Ashdod   22 miles
          36 km   Jerusalem

Ashqelon

7 miles
11 km.

Gaza

Dead Sea

10 miles
16 km

Beersheba

Zionism & Israel on the Web
http://www.zionismontheweb.org

☐ Occupied by Israel

Conclusion

President Bush is Sincere

President George W. Bush has been sincere in his attempts to bring peace to Israel and the Middle East, but the land of Israel is not to be divided.

Despite his and previous president's good intentions, the United States' administrations, beginning with the Nixon Administration, have unknowingly sponsored and participated in a plan by Israel's enemies to eliminate the nation of Israel by forcing her into indefensible borders.

Consequences

President Bush's problems and challenges are directly attributable to his involvement with the Israeli–Palestinian peace process. The more he has been involved the greater the catastrophes, corresponding events, political disruptions and challenges.

Here is a partial list of what has happened since the September 11, 2001 terror events, the largest terrorism events in world history:

- A trillion dollar hit on the U.S. economy due to the 9-11-2001 terror events and the war on terror;
- A $300 billion and growing war in Iraq and Afghanistan;
- Numerous costly national terror alerts;
- America (and Israel's) enemies are attempting to obtain weapons of mass destruction for one purpose—the elimination of the United States and Israel;
- Continued concern that there will be a weapon of mass destruction attack on the U.S.;
- Relationships with the U.S. government and embassies worldwide have been strained over the war on terror;
- Relationships with world leaders have been strained over Iraq and the war on terror;
- Bush's political and legislative agenda have been severely affected despite controlling two house of Congress, and his political party is losing confidence in him and beginning to distance themselves politically for fear he could hurt them in their re-election efforts;

- Osama bin Laden, al Qaeda, Iraq and the war on terror are mentioned more than education, faith-based initiatives or any other topic;
- An underestimation of the size and complexity of the Middle East terror war;
- Major complications in post war Iraq between the Sunnis, the Shiites and the Kurds;
- Suicide bombings which have greatly disrupted lives in Iraq and could lead to a civil war;
- Secretary of State Rice admitted there have been many errors in Iraq;
- Washington, DC, is becoming a fortress, many U.S. cities are tightening their security, and security cameras are being placed in communities throughout the country;
- Radiation sensors are being placed in public transportation buildings and public places;
- Individual rights and privileges are being usurped by the Patriot Act;
- Unprecedented eavesdropping of private citizens by the government;
- A National ID program is in the offing;
- Airport security requires the removal of shoes, coats and sweaters;
- Massive financial losses and bankruptcy filings by the nation's airlines, along with service cutbacks;
- Border problems with Mexico are becoming more complicated due to terror fears;
- Borders are being tightened in an effort to stop a single terrorist from getting into the U.S.;
- Regulations for container shipments into America are becoming costly and burdensome;
- A growing concern over who is in charge of U.S. ports;
- Record deficits—the U.S. federal deficit has gone from $5.9 trillion in late 2000 to $8.397 trillion on April 9, 2006, and Congress increased the debt ceiling to $9.2 trillion;
- Seventeen billion-dollar disasters during Bush's first five years in office —only a few of which did not happen at the same time Israel was being pressured to divide their land;
- Bush has traveled to New Orleans ten times to review Hurricane Katrina's devastation and rebuilding program.

God is Warning us in the Scriptures

To know where the world is headed in the coming days and weeks, keep your ears and eyes on the words and actions of the world leaders as they pertain to Israel. Most, if not all of them, are not aware of what is awaiting them. They have a Divine appointment with the God of Israel, the God of the Bible.

What is happening and going to happen is written in the Word of God. Here are a few of the final-day Scriptures:

- A world leader will come on the scene with a plan for peace (Daniel 9:26,27).
- Leaders and nations will experience enormous consequences (Joel 3:2; Matthew 24; Ezekiel 38-39; Psalm 83).
- Jerusalem will become a burden (Zechariah 12:3).
- God will deal with the nations that come against Jerusalem (Zechariah 12:9; Zechariah 14).
- Russia, Iran, Turkey, Sudan, Libya and former Soviet Union countries from the Caucasian Mountain region will come together for a future war against Israel (Ezekiel 38-39).
- Earthquakes will continue to increase in size and intensity and be felt in diverse places—Indonesia, Japan, Pakistan, Chile, Iran and other nations (Matthew 24:7).
- Famine will worsen—Africa, India, China and other nations (Matthew 24:7).
- Pestilence will spread worldwide—AIDS, avian flu and small pox (Matthew 24:7).
- The sea and waves will roar—Indian Ocean tsunami; hurricanes and cyclones will devastate other nations (Luke 21:25).
- Men's hearts will fail them for fear, and for looking after those things which are coming upon the earth (Luke 25:26).
- Many will be deceived by false prophecies, false prophets, false signs and wonders (Matthew 24:4, 11, 24, 1 Timothy 4:1).
- Wars and rumors of wars will increase (Matthew 24:6).
- Nations shall rise up against nations and kingdoms against kingdoms (Matthew 24:7).
- Persecution of Christians will increase (Matthew 24:9).
- Signs in the sun, moon, and stars will increase (Luke 21:25).
- Nations will be distressed and dismayed, and be perplexed because they don't understand what they see—this may include wars on terror and weapons of mass destruction (Luke 21:25).
- Radical Islam will continue to penetrate and disrupt Europe, the U.S. and other nations (Luke 21:26).

- Damascus will be destroyed (Isaiah 17:1).
- Iraq will become a wasteland (Isaiah 13:9).

The Messiah is Returning

The ultimate "peace solution" lays with the return of the Messiah, the Lord Jesus Christ to Jerusalem, who will reign for 1,000-years in Israel.

Repent of your sins. Ask the Lord for His forgiveness. Surrender your life to Jesus Christ as your Lord and Savior and get ready for the return of the King of Kings.

For God so loved the world, that He gave His only begotten Son, that whosoever believeth in Him should not perish, but have everlasting life (John 3:16).

Behold the tabernacle of God is with men, and He will dwell with them, and they shall be His people, and God Himself shall be with them and be their God. And God shall wipe away all tears from their eyes, and there shall be no more death, neither sorrow, nor crying, neither shall there be any more pain: for the former things are passed away (Revelation 21:3-4).

Come Quickly Lord Jesus!

ADDENDUM 1

Open Letter to Israel

To the Nation of Israel from William Koenig

June 28, 2002

We want you to know that your best friend in the world is the passionate Christian who would live and die for you. Please call on us and we will be there for you whenever you need us. Just look next to you, and you will see that we are there also!

God is allowing current world events to bring our times to completion and to bring many more to Him. Yes, all that is happening does have a purpose in His plan; our prayers for the Peace of Jerusalem are about to be answered.

Please know that the Lord is speaking to you these days. It is time for you to get your life right with the Lord, Israel.

If you keep sinning, you will keep paying the price, because sin does have consequences!

If you keep denying Him, you will also continue paying the price, because many are called but very few are chosen!

If you keep subscribing to the "land for peace" mantra of "peace and security," you must know that there will be no lasting peace. Your only peace is in the Messiah!

Man has not been given the ability to comprehend or understand the purpose of death and the tragedies that you are facing, but know that your God, the God of the Bible, loves you. Nothing in the world happens over which He does not have control.

The God of Israel is not millions of miles away. To the contrary, He exists in those who have called on Him; He will come into your life if you ask Him.

If you have doubts about His existence, ask Him to show Himself. He will answer your petition just like He has many others who have doubted Him but who have reached out and were given proof of His existence.

Out of His love for you and desire to be everything in your life, He wants you to reach out your hand, and then He will take yours. Learn to walk in His presence; there is nothing like it. Trust me, your life will never be the same!

It is time to press into the power that can only come through Jesus Christ.

I am not here to evangelize you, but I do want to tell you about the One who can deliver you, and to tell you about those Christians who would put their lives on the line to be there for you.

It is the existence of Jesus Christ in us that has given us this love for you and for your nation. Those who have the heart of Jesus Christ will also have a heart for Israel and for the Jewish people.

Please read these words spoken by Jesus Christ 2,000 years ago alongside the Sea of Galilee. Take time to ponder and pray over them because they will bless you and give you the hope for today, for the future, and for eternity.

Matthew 5: 1-12
The Sermon on the Mount – The Beatitudes

Now when He saw the crowds, He went up on a mountainside and sat down. His disciples came to Him, and He began to teach them saying:

"Blessed are the poor in spirit, for theirs is the kingdom of heaven. Blessed are those who mourn, for they will be comforted. Blessed are the meek, for they will inherit the earth. Blessed are those who hunger and thirst for righteousness, for they will be filled. Blessed are the merciful, for they will be shown mercy. Blessed are the pure in heart, for they will see God. Blessed are the peacemakers, for they will be called sons of God. Blessed are those who are persecuted because of righteousness, for theirs is the kingdom of heaven. Blessed are you when people insult you, persecute you, and falsely say all kinds of evil against you because of Me. Rejoice and be glad, because great is your reward in heaven, for in the same way they persecuted the prophets who were before you."

Our God loves us all, but He is especially fond of you, the nation of Israel and His Chosen People; you are the "apple of His eye" (Zechariah 2:8).

In the New Testament Letter to Romans, Paul (formerly Saul, a Jew and a Pharisee who was devoted to serving the God of Israel by strict adherence to the Law) wrote that followers of Jesus Christ have been grafted into the olive tree of Jewish inheritance and blessing (Romans 11:17). We are your brothers and sisters, and we are there for you too!

For now, we will continue to stand by you, to comfort you and to be there for you ... in the bad times and in the good times ... in the Spirit of His love for you! We are your best friends!

We love you, Israel. We love the Jewish people! We love Jesus Christ! All to His Glory!

ADDENDUM 2

United Nations Resolutions

UN Security Council Resolution 242
November 22, 1967

Following the June 1967, Six-Day War, the situation in the Middle East was discussed by the UN General Assembly, which referred the issue to the Security Council. After lengthy discussion, a final draft for a Security Council resolution was presented by the British Ambassador, Lord Caradon, on November 22, 1967. It was adopted on the same day.

This resolution established provisions and principles which, it was hoped, would lead to a solution of the conflict. Resolution 242 was to become the cornerstone of Middle East diplomatic efforts in the coming decades.

The Security Council,

Expressing its continuing concern with the grave situation in the Middle East,

Emphasizing the inadmissibility of the acquisition of territory by war and the need to work for a just and lasting peace in which every State in the area can live in security,

Emphasizing further that all Member States in their acceptance of the Charter of the United Nations have undertaken a commitment to act in accordance with Article 2 of the Charter,

1. Affirms that the fulfillment of Charter principles requires the establishment of a just and lasting peace in the Middle East which should include the application of both the following principles:
   • Withdrawal of Israeli armed forces from territories occupied in the recent conflict;
   • Termination of all claims or states of belligerency and respect for and acknowledgement of the sovereignty, territorial integrity and political independence of every State in the area and their right to live in peace within secure and recognized boundaries free from threats or acts of force;

2. Affirms further the necessity:

- For guaranteeing freedom of navigation through international waterways in the area;
- For achieving a just settlement of the refugee problem;
- For guaranteeing the territorial inviolability and political independence of every State in the area, through measures including the establishment of demilitarized zones;

3. Requests the Secretary General to designate a Special Representative to proceed to the Middle East to establish and maintain contacts with the States concerned in order to promote agreement and assist efforts to achieve a peaceful and accepted settlement in accordance with the provisions and principles in this resolution;

4. Requests the Secretary-General to report to the Security Council on the progress of the efforts of the Special Representative as soon as possible.

Source: http://www.mfa.gov.il/mfa/go.asp?MFAH00p40

UN Security Council Resolution 338
October 22, 1973

In the later stages of the Yom Kippur War—after Israel repulsed the Syrian attack on the Golan Heights and established a bridgehead on the Egyptian side of the Suez Canal—international efforts to stop the fighting were intensified. U.S. Secretary of State Henry Kissinger flew to Moscow on October 20, 1973. The Soviet Government agreed to support the U.S. on a proposed cease-fire resolution in the UN Security Council. The Council met on 21 October at the urgent request of both the U.S. and the USSR, and by 14 votes to none, adopted the following resolution:

The Security Council,

1. Calls upon all parties to present fighting to cease all firing and terminate all military activity immediately, no later than 12 hours after the moment of the adoption of this decision, in the positions after the moment of the adoption of this decision, in the positions they now occupy;

2. Calls upon all parties concerned to start immediately after the cease-fire the implementation of Security Council Resolution 242 (1967) in all of its parts;

3. Decides that, immediately and concurrently with the cease-fire, negotiations start between the parties concerned under appropriate auspices aimed at establishing a just and durable peace in the Middle East.

ADDENDUM 3

Signatories of letter from church leaders quoted in Chapter 2

The 18 U.S. Church Leaders who signed a letter to U.S. Secretary of State Colin Powell, June 7, 2001:

The Most Rev. Frank T. Griswold, Presiding Bishop and Primate,
The Episcopal Church

Bishop Vicken Aykazian, Diocesan Legate and Ecumenical Officer,
The Armenian Orthodox Church

The Very Rev. Brother Stephen Michael Glodek, S.M.,
President, Catholic Conference of Major Superiors of Mens' Institutes

Rev. John L. McCullough, Executive Director,
Church World Service

Bishop Donald J. McCoid, Southwestern Pennsylvania Synod, Chairman,
Conference of Bishops of the Evangelical Lutheran Church in America

Rev. Fr. Alexander Karloutsos for Bishop Dimitrios of Xanthos,
Ecumenical Officer, Greek Orthodox Archdiocese of America

Bishop William B. Oden, Immediate Past President,
The Council of Bishops, The United Methodist Church

(Endorsing Heads of Churches follow)

The following heads of churches and faith-based organizations join the delegation in this expression of concern and appeal to Secretary of State Colin Powell:

Bishop McKinley Young, Presiding Bishop, 10th Episcopal District,
African Methodist Episcopal Church

The Rev. Dr. Robert H. Roberts, Interim General Secretary,
American Baptist Churches USA

Mary Ellen McNish, General Secretary,
American Friends Service Committee

Metropolitan PHILIP, Primate, Antiochian Orthodox Christian,
Archdiocese of North America

The Rev. Dr. Richard L. Hamm, General Minister and President,
Christian Church (Disciples of Christ) in the U.S. and Canada

Rev. Judy Mills Reimer, Executive Director,
Church of the Brethren General Board

The Rev. H. George Anderson, Presiding Bishop,
The Evangelical Lutheran Church in America

Michael E. Livingston, Executive Director,
International Council of Community Churches

Rev. Dr. Seung Koo Choi,
General Secretary of Korean Presbyterian Church in America

Dr. Ron J. R. Mathies, Executive Director,
Mennonite Central Committee

Rev. R. Burke Johnson, President,
Moravian Church - Northern Province

Rev. Dr. Bob Edgar, General Secretary,
National Council of the Churches of Christ in the USA

The Rev. Clifton Kirkpatrick, Stated Clerk,
Presbyterian Church (USA)

Wesley Granberg-Michaelson, General Secretary,
Reformed Church in America

Archbishop Cyril Aphrem Karim, Archdiocese of the
Syrian Orthodox Church of Antioch for the Eastern USA

John Buehrens, President, Unitarian Universalist Association

The Rev. John H. Thomas, General Minister and President,
United Church of Christ

Bishop Melvin G. Talbert, Ecumenical Officer,
Council of Bishops, The United Methodist Church

Koenig's International News

"Monitor of World Events"   William R. Koenig

October 22, 2001

Mr. George W. Bush
President of the United States
The White House
1600 Pennsylvania Avenue
Washington D.C. 20500

Re: God's Covenant Land (Israel)

Dear President Bush,

In the Bible, God speaks to Abraham, father of the Jews and the nation of Israel, and directs him to the land of Canaan (Israel):

I will make you into a great nation, and I will bless you,
I will make your name great, and you will be a blessing.
I will bless those who bless you,
and whoever curses you I will curse;
and all peoples on earth will be blessed through you.
(Genesis 12:1-3, NIV)

With all due respect, America is now experiencing the consequences (curses) of Middle East policies which have been opposed to God's Word and the preservation of His covenant land. Ever since the Madrid Conference over ten years ago, this country's participation in Israel's destiny has been flawed when put in the context of Holy Scripture.

The events of September 11 were a national wake-up call. However, this nation continues to support the Mitchell Plan, affirming a "land for peace" approach, and if Secretary of State Colin Powell proclaims your Middle East "vision" for a Palestinian state, with a foothold in Jerusalem, to the United Nations General Assembly, America can expect to experience the lifting of the Lord's protective hand in an even greater measure.

It is a fact that Israel's very existence is in grave danger, because of our nation's sponsorship of "land for peace" plans which have led her to the brink of war.

What is happening in the world, and especially in the Middle East, these days is truly remarkable. But then again, Bible believers (like yourself) shouldn't be surprised, because the Old Testament prophet, Zachariah, pre-warned us about these times over 2,500 years ago:

"On that day, when all the nations of the earth are gathered against her, I will make Jerusalem an immovable rock for all the nations. All who try to move it will injure themselves" (Zechariah 12:3 NIV).

"On that day, I will set out to destroy all the nations that attack Jerusalem" (Zechariah 12:9 NIV).

The attached documents lists five examples of warning events which have taken place since you have been in office. These events all happened at or near times when you were involved in dialogue or decisions pressuring Israel to trade her Covenant land for peace, contrary to the Word of God. These warnings are examples of the Lord trying to get your attention.

May I suggest, Mr. President, that the way in which you are currently responding while the United States homeland is at risk is not unlike the manner in which the Lord responds when His promised land (Israel) and His chosen people (the Jews) are at risk.

The land of Israel is unique and special, like no other land in the world. It is God's land, and this fact is well documented throughout the Old Testament. "O descendants of Israel his servant, O sons of Jacob, his chosen ones. He is the Lord our God; his judgments are in all the earth. He remembers his covenant forever, the word he commanded, for a thousand generations, the covenant he made with Abraham, the oath he swore to Isaac. He confirmed it to Jacob as a decree, to Israel as an everlasting covenant: "To you I will give the land of Canaan as the portion you will inherit" (I Chronicles 16:13-18 NIV).

I realize that these words I have written will not likely change your decision, but I am hoping and especially praying that they will. Please understand, Mr. President, that I am fulfilling part of my calling, which is to warn you and those who advise you about the seriousness of your pressure on Israel to give up her Covenant land. The Bible is very clear that our loving and fair God will always warn His people before judgment comes.

You are a very good man with an enormous responsibility and a fine administration. It is obvious that you love the Lord and desire to do God's will. Many people, including myself, are praying for you.

In Christ,

William R. Koenig

Cc:
Mr. Dick Cheney
Mr. Andrew Card
Dr. Condoleezza Rice
Mrs. Karen Hughes
Mr. Carl Rove
Mr. Ari Fleischer

THE WHITE HOUSE
WASHINGTON

November 9, 2001

Mr. William R. Koenig
White House Correspondence
Koenig's International News
Post Office Box 671127
Dallas, Texas 75367-1127

Dear Mr. Koenig:

Thank you for your letter and the materials you sent.

I welcome information from Americans across the country,
and I value your input.

Sincerely,

George W. Bush

Koenig's International News

"Monitor of World Events"   William R. Koenig

March 25, 2002

Mr. George W. Bush
President of the United States
The White House
1600 Pennsylvania Avenue
Washington D.C. 20500

Re: God's Covenant Land (Israel)

Dear President Bush,

On October 22, I wrote you a letter about the importance of Israel's covenant land in the context of the Middle East Peace Process and our country's involvement in the "land for peace" proposals.

That letter cited same day events that have taken place when you or your administration made public comments or were actively involved in meetings that would have an adverse impact on God's covenant land of Israel.

Our new book, "Israel: The Blessing or the Curse," which deals specifically with this subject, was also sent to you by Ruth Mizell a friend of your parents and was sent to the First Lady by a friend of yours from Midland.

In addition, I was able to personally give a copy to Vice President Dick Cheney and to Karen Hughes and 450 copies of the book were distributed to legislators on Capitol Hill.

By now, you certainly must be aware of Sen. James M. Inhofe (R-OK) and his address on the Senate floor this week. Sen. Inhofe stood courageously in the face of world opinion and presented seven powerful reasons why Israel is entitled to possess her covenant land.

His seventh reason was and is, by all accounts, the most important. Quoting Scripture, he said that Israel has a right to the land, and that we ought to support her in this, because God said so. "This is not a political battle at all." he said. "It is a contest over whether or not the Word of God is true."

Surely you would agree, Mr. President, that Israel's very existence today is in grave danger, not only because of the Palestinian Authority and other Muslim states who seek her demise, but because of our nation's sponsorship of "land for peace" plans which have led her to the brink of war.

The Bible is very clear that our loving and fair God will always warn His people before judgment comes. He has warned our nation many times since the Madrid peace talks in which your father was an active party and participant. Those warnings are clearly documented in "Israel: The Blessing or the Curse."

However, the Lord is preparing to lift His protection on our nation and against those other nations who are pressuring the nation of Israel to give up her land (God's covenant land) according to United Nations Resolutions 242 and 338. Those resolutions are an affront to our Lord.

Allying with the enemies of Israel in a war against terrorism, in return for siding against Israel, is not only illogical and erroneous, but it will be a miserable failure. Most importantly, it will draw the Lord's anger and wrath. What is happening in the world, and especially in the Middle East these days, is truly remarkable. But then again, Bible believers (like yourself) should not be surprised, because the Old Testament prophet, Zechariah, pre-warned us about these times over 2,500 years ago:

"On that day, when all the nations of the earth are gathered against her, I will make Jerusalem an immovable rock for all the nations. All who try to move it will injure themselves" (Zechariah 12:3 NIV).

"On that day, I will set out to destroy all the nations that attack Jerusalem" (Zechariah 12:9 NIV).

Mr. President, you have been very clear about choosing sides in the battle of good versus evil. In that perspective, the world continues to side with the Palestinians and the Arab nations against Israel, the country that is called the Promised Land in the Bible and home to the Jews who are called God's Chosen People in the Word of God.

Millions of Bible-believing Christians and observant Jews around the world are currently lifting prayers to God on behalf of Israel, the integrity of her covenant land, and for the United States that you, your Administration, and members of Congress will choose to support Israel, with faith and courage, in the face of increasing pressure.

In my previous letter, I expressed my feeling that the words I have written may not affect or change your decisions regarding Israel, but I am hoping and especially praying that they will.

Please understand, Mr. President, that I am fulfilling part of my calling, which is to warn you, and those who advise you, about the seriousness of any pressure on Israel to give up her Covenant land.

Many people, including myself, are praying for you, and they will continue praying for you daily.

In His Service,

William R. Koenig

"And I will make of thee [Israel] a great nation, and I will bless thee, and make thy name great; and thou shalt be a blessing: And I will bless them that bless thee, and curse him that curseth thee: and in thee shall all families of the earth be blessed" (Genesis 12:2,3).

THE WHITE HOUSE

WASHINGTON

May 1, 2002

Mr. William R. Koenig
White House News Correspondent
Koenig's International News
Post Office Box 671127
Dallas, Texas 75367

Dear Bill:

Thank you for the copy of *Israel: The Blessing or the Curse*,
forwarded by Ruth Mizell.

As we strive for lasting peace in the Middle East, I am continually
impressed by the deep historical context of this conflict. I appreciate
your gift of a book that addresses the different aspects of this situation.

I am grateful for your kind words of support and your prayers. Laura
joins me in sending our best wishes.

Sincerely,

George W. Bush

Koenig's International News

"Monitor of World Events"   William R. Koenig

June 5, 2002

Mr. George W. Bush
President of the United States
The White House
1600 Pennsylvania Avenue
Washington D.C. 20500

Re: God's Covenant Land (Israel)

Dear President Bush,

Thank you for your kind note acknowledging receipt of our book, "Israel: the Blessing or the Curse," which goes into great detail about what happens when the United States pushes on Israel to give up her covenant land. In our newly revised book we have added some additional words on your wonderful staff on (pages 149-151).

You are the man the Lord has chosen for this hour, it is incredible to see how our Lord has positioned you at the most crucial time in biblical history. The United States is so blessed to have you as our President and your administration representing us.

As you continue to call on Israel to accept UN Resolutions 242 and 338 and a Palestinian State I would like to warn you as a fellow Christian that the United States will reap major repercussions and magnitude as never before. The Lord has sent many warning signs as we outlined in our book since October 30, 1991 and due to the intensity and seriousness of the moment in Israel the future repercussions will be enormous.

In the October 21, 2001 Washington Post article, "Putting a Price on 'What Ifs' it mentioned the three largest insurance events in U.S. history. I might add all three of these events had a same day Israel component.

On September 11, 2001, the World Trade Center and Pentagon terror attacks produced the most expensive event in U.S. history ($30 to $50 billion estimate). Saudi Arabia Prince Bandar bin Sultan went from being "the happiest man in the world" on Monday night, 9-10, to experiencing the worst crisis of his career on 9-11. Dreams of a new Mid East peace initiative evaporated. The realization that most of the hijackers were Saudis "fell on me ... like the whole house collapsed over my head," Bandar said later. He couldn't imagine a way to "do more damage or worse damage to Islam or to Saudi Arabia."

On April 23, 1991, the $19.6 billion Hurricane Andrew the most expensive event in U.S. history, hit Florida at the very moment the Madrid talks convened in Washington.

On January 16, 1994, President Clinton and Syrian President Haffez Assad called on Israel to leave the Golan Heights. Within 24 hours the third largest event in U.S. insurance history the "Northridge Earthquake caused a loss of $16. 2 billion.

Please reconsider being the one sponsoring the "land for peace" efforts in Israel. They are contrary to God's word. If you don't stop the effort the United States is going to experience enormous repercussions.

As I have stated before, please understand Mr. President, that I am fulfilling part of my calling, which is to warn you, and those who advise you, about the seriousness of any pressure on Israel to give up her Covenant land.

Many people, including myself, are praying for you, and they will continue praying for you daily.

In His Service,

William R. Koenig

Cc:
Mr. Dick Cheney
Mr. Andrew Card
Dr. Condoleezza Rice
Mrs. Karen Hughes
Mr. Carl Rove
Mr. Ari Fleischer

"And I will make of thee [Israel] a great nation, and I will bless thee, and make thy name great; and thou shalt be a blessing: And I will bless them that bless thee, and curse him that curseth thee: and in thee shall all families of the earth be blessed" (Genesis 12:2,3).

September 30, 2003

Mr. George W. Bush
President of the United States
The White House
1600 Pennsylvania Avenue
Washington D.C. 20500

Re: Petition with 26,000 signatures

Dear President Bush,

We have submitted 26,000 signatures on the enclosed petition from people concerned about your role in the parceling of God's covenant land in Israel. Please remember your efforts will have eternal consequences.

Surely you would agree, Mr. President, that Israel's very existence today is in grave danger, not only because of the Palestinian Authority and other Muslim states who seek her demise, but because of our nation's sponsorship of "land for peace" plans which have led her to the brink of war.

What is happening in the world, and especially in the Middle East these days, is truly remarkable. But then again, Bible believers (like yourself) should not be surprised, because the Old Testament prophet, Zechariah, pre-warned us about these times over 2,500 years ago:

"On that day, when all the nations of the earth are gathered against her, I will make Jerusalem an immovable rock for all the nations. All who try to move it will injure themselves" (Zechariah 12:3 NIV).

"On that day, I will set out to destroy all the nations that attack Jerusalem" (Zechariah 12:9 NIV).

Israel, the country that is called the Promised Land in the Bible and home to the Jews who are called God's Chosen People in the Word of God is not to be parceled. The nations who parcel God's land will be judged harshly by our Lord (Joel 3:2).

Many people, including us, are praying for you.

In His Service,

William R. Koenig   George Whitten
Koenig's International News   Worthy News

Koenig's International News

September 1, 2005

President George W. Bush
The White House
1600 Pennsylvania Ave. NW
Washington, DC 20500

Re: <u>Gaza Evacuation and Hurricane Katrina</u>

Dear President Bush:

I have written before about the consequences of dividing the land of Israel. We are once again experiencing these painful consequences through Hurricane Katrina, the four major Florida hurricanes of 2005 and the challenging situation in Iraq.

Below is the news from the past two weeks — right at the time Jews were being forced from God's covenant land and thereafter.

I am delivering this letter with a copy of my book, *Eye to Eye: Facing the Consequences of Dividing Israel*. I pray that the information in the book will cause you to see the reason for these consequences.

Once again, as a fellow believer in Jesus Christ, I pray that you will reconsider your position on the land of Israel — for the sake of our country and for you.

We will continue to pray for you during these extremely difficult times.

In His service,

William R. Koenig

William R. Koenig

cc: Dick Cheney
        Condoleeza Rice
        Andrew Card
        Karl Rove
        Scott McClellan
        Karen Hughes

President George W. Bush   -2-
Washington, DC 20500   September 1, 2005

To say the least, much has happened since the disengagement eviction began in Israel on
August 17 (with preliminary work actually taking place during the 9th of Av — sundown
on Saturday, August 13, to sundown on Sunday, August 14. The government of Israel
didn't want the disengagement eviction to begin until August 17 due to the curse of the
9th of Av for the Jewish people.)

On Monday, August 22, the last Jewish settlement in Gaza was evacuated — wrapping
up Israel's historic pullout from the coastal strip after settlers held a farewell march
behind Torah scrolls and a massive menorah, then boarded armored buses and left.

Israeli Prime Minister Ariel Sharon and Palestinian leader Mahmoud Abbas spoke by
telephone and expressed their commitment to peace -- the first conversation between the
two since the pullout started, a senior Palestinian negotiator said.

The leaders spoke for about five minutes, with Mr. Abbas telling Mr. Sharon, "We are
your partners for peace," according to negotiator Saeb Erekat.

The next day, August 23, the day after the completion of the Gaza evacuation, the
government of the Bahamas issued a tropical storm warning for central and northwestern
Bahamas. (Putting this storm into perspective, many of the tropical storms and hurricanes
begin off the western coast of Africa and typically take ten days to two weeks before
affecting the Bahamas, the Caribbean and/or the U.S. coastline. Not Katrina.)

By 11 a.m. on Wednesday, August 24, the newly formed tropical depression was
upgraded to Tropical Storm Katrina; and by 5 p.m. on Thursday, August 25, Katrina
became a hurricane.

In a period of only 72 hours, tropical depression 12 developed into a hurricane and hit
southeast Florida (the only area untouched by the past six hurricanes).

Hurricane Katrina is now expected to be the costliest weather related disaster in U.S.
history. It was devastating in intensity and in size. If it hadn't been for a

last-minute break in the eye wall, it would have very likely destroyed the city of New
Orleans and cost hundreds of billions of dollars.

Government agencies and private relief organizations flew into action yesterday in what
some are describing as the largest mobilization ever for a natural disaster.

President George W. Bush   -3-
Washington, DC 20500   September 1, 2005

Following is the main news from the past two weeks:

- Israel begins preparation for Gaza evacuation — August 13-16
- US warns of new attacks on London and U.S. Cities — August 14
- The United States issue tender for up to 80 million doses of a smallpox vaccine, worth more than $1 billion, to guard against terrorist attack — August 17
- Israel begins the evacuation of Gaza and northern Samaria settlements — August 17
- IDF storms Gaza synagogue — August 17
- "Everyone empathizes with what the Israelis are facing. [But] it cannot be Gaza only," says U.S. Secretary of State Condoleezza Rice — August 17
- Russia reminds United States that attacking Iran militarily will cause major problems for the world — August 17
- The first-ever joint Chinese and Russian military exercise begins, meant to send political signal to the United States — August 18
- The United States plans to send assessment teams to Israel to decide on U.S. economic aid for the Galilee and Negev regions — August 18
- Bad Iraq war news worries some in GOP on '06 vote — August 18
- Katyusha rocket attacks on U.S. ships in Eilat and Aqaba — August 19
- Israel completes Gaza evacuation — August 22
- Ariel Sharon and Palestinian leader Mahmoud Abbas speak by telephone and express commitment to peace — August 22
- Gaza home demolitions continue — August 22
- A tropical depression forms near the Bahamas — August 23
- Tropical Storm Katrina forms — August 24
- Katrina becomes a hurricane — August 25
- Hurricane Katrina hits southeast Florida — August 26
- Hurricane Katrina increases in intensity in the Gulf of Mexico — August 27
- Russia and China complete their first eight-day military maneuvers — August 26
- Suicide bomber targets Israeli bus station: Two guards critically wounded in first suicide attack since Gaza withdrawal — August 28
- U.S. war on terror: more costly than 'the war to end all wars' — August 29
- Sharon: More West Bank settlements would go for peace — August 29
- Katrina kills 55 in Miss.; governor calls storm a 'grievous blow' — August 29
- Katrina floods downtown Mobile, beaches, bayous — August 29
- Hurricane Katrina could slow U.S. economic expansion — August 29
- New Orleans facing environmental disaster — August 29
- Gov. Bush warns residents of gas shortages — August 29

President George W. Bush   -4-
Washington, DC 20050   September 1, 2005

- Tens of thousands to be homeless for months due to Katrina — August 29
- American Red Cross launching its largest relief operation ever — August 29
- Largest mobilization ever for a natural disaster — August 30
- Bush returning to White House to monitor hurricane effort — August 30
- Oil hits new record near $71 after Katrina — August 30
- Katrina may cost insurers up to $25 billion — August 30
- President Bush says U.S dealing with one of the worst natural disasters in our nation's history – August 31

"I will make you a great nation. ... I will bless those who bless you, and I will curse him who curses you; and in you all the families of the earth shall be blessed" (Genesis 12:2-3, NKJV).

"I will also gather all nations, and bring them down to the valley of Jehoshaphat; and I will enter into judgment with them there on account of my people, my heritage Israel, whom they have scattered among the nations; they have also divided up my land" (Joel 3:2, NKJV).

THE WHITE HOUSE

WASHINGTON

September 12, 2005

Dear Mr. Koenig,

Thanks for sending a copy of *Eye to Eye: Facing the Consequences of Dividing Israel*. I know it will be a great read. I appreciate your thoughtfulness.

Thanks again.

Sincerely,

Karl Rove
Deputy Chief of Staff and Senior Advisor

Mr. William R. Koenig
Koenig's International News
Post Office Box 25812
Alexandria, Virginia 22313

KR:sml

ENDNOTES

Chapter 1

1 – MYTH "The Jews have no claim to the land they call Israel." Jewish Virtual Library. http://www.jewishvirtuallibrary.org/jsource/myths/mf1.html#a

2 – Israel and the Arab-Israeli Conflict: A Brief Guide for the Perplexed, by David A. Harris, Executive Director – http://www.ujc.org/content_display.html?ArticleID=68620

3 – Legal Right Of Israel For All The Land West Of Jordan http://invitation.to/dance/israel-balfouragreement.htm

4 – HISTORY- Foreign Domination http://www.mfa.gov.il/MFA/Facts+About+Israel/History/HISTORY-+Foreign+Domination.htm?DisplayMode=print

5 – The US & Israel – Peter Grier http://www.csmonitor.com/2001/1026/p1s1-uspo.htm

6 – Edward Jacobson: http://en.wikipedia.org/wiki/Edward_Jacobson

7 – The 1948 War – Mitchel Bard http://www.jewishvirtuallibrary.org/jsource/History/1948_War.html

8 – The 1956 Sinai Campaign http://www.unitedjerusalem.com/HISTORICAL_PERSPECTIVES/Israel_Wars_Maps_History/israel_wars_maps_history.asp#anchor2_1956map

9 – The 1967 Six-Day War - by Mitchell Bard, Jewish Virtual Library – http://www.jewishvirtuallibrary.org/jsource/History/67_War.html

10 – The Yom Kippur War – By Mitchell Bard http://www.jewishvirtuallibrary.org/jsource/History/73_War.html

11 – The U.S. & Israel – Peter Grier: www.csmonitor.com/2001/1026/p1s1-uspo.htm

Chapter 2

1 – The Error Of Replacement Theology http://www.therefinersfire.org/replacement_theology.htm

2 – Documentation: Text Of 18 U.S. Church Leaders' June 7, 2001, Letter To U.S. Secretary Of State Colin Powell – http://www.ncccusa.org/news/01news69d.html

3 – Documentation: Text Of Dr. Edgar's Letter To President Bush, August 30, 2001 – http://www.ncccusa.org/news/01news69a.html

4 – Presbyterians Position on Christian Zionists www.layman.org/layman/news/2004-news/overture-opposes-christian-zionism.htm

5 – Assembly endorses Israel divestment http://www.pcusa.org/ga216/news/ga04121.htm

6 – Israel Troubled by World Council of Churches Divestment Campaign By Julie Stahl - CNSNews.com Jerusalem Bureau Chief – February 23, 2005 http://www.cnsnews.com/ViewForeignBureaus.asp?Page=/ForeignBureaus/archive/200502/FOR20050223d.html

7 – Overture opposes Christian Zionism http://www.layman.org/layman/news/2004-news/overture-opposes-christian-zionism.htm

Chapter 3

Catastrophe #1

Middle East Peace Chronology – 1989-1991
   http://usinfo.state.gov/regional/nea/summit/chron2.htm
The Oakland-Berkeley Hills Fire: An Overview
   http://www.sfmuseum.org/oakfire/overview.html
Drought in the United States
   http://www.glaciermedicaled.com/Earthquake_html/Drought/draught6.html

Catastrophe #2

Bush opens historic Mid East peace conference – October 30, 1991
   news.bbc.co.uk/onthisday/hi/dates/stories/october/30/newsid_2465000/ 2465725.stm
The Madrid Conference Speeches – October/November 1991
   http://www.mfa.gov.il/mfa/go.asp?MFAH0dg10
The Perfect Storm – October 1991:
   www.ncdc.noaa.gov/oa/satellite/ satelliteseye/cyclones/pfctstorm91/pfctstorm.html
Bush Kennebunkport Home Damaged by Perfect Storm
   http://wampum.wabanaki.net/archives/000349.html

Catastrophe #3

Chronology of Events, June 1992 - December 1994
   http://www.mfa.gov.il/mfa/go.asp?MFAH0je60
Middle East Peace Chronology – 1992-1993
   http://usinfo.state.gov/regional/nea/summit/chron3.htm
Hurricane history – Andrew: http://www.usatoday.com/weather/wandrew5.htm
Hurricane Andrew – Ten Years Later
   http://www.noaa.gov/hurricaneandrew.html

Catastrophe #4

Ross Perot: Political Timeline: http://www.cnn.com/ALLPOLITICS/1996/
   conventions/long.beach/perot/political.timeline.shtml
H. Ross Perot: http://www.famoustexans.com/rossperot.htm
Only the stupid could think it'll be the economy: Comparing the Bushes –
   May 7, 2003: http://www.jewishworldreview.com/0503/blankley050703.asp

Chapter 4

Catastrophe #5

1993: World Trade Center bomb Terrorizes New York – February 26, 1993
   news.bbc.co.uk/onthisday/hi/dates/stories/february/26/newsid2516000/ 2516469.stm
U.S. Secretary of States Visits to Israel – 1953-2002
   http://www.state.gov/r/pa/ho/trvl/12924.htm

Catastrophe #6

Visits to the U.S. by Foreign Heads of State and Government – 1993
   http://www.state.gov/r/pa/ho/15737.htm
Chronology Of Events, June 1992 - December 1994
   http://www.mfa.gov.il/mfa/go.asp?MFAH0je60
Storm of the Century – The Blizzard of 1993, March 12-15, 1993
   http://snrs.unl.edu/amet498/sherman/blizzard93.html

Catastrophe #7

The Oslo Peace Process
 http://news.bbc.co.uk/1/shared/spl/hi/middle_east/03/v3_ip_timeline/html/1993.stm
Israel-Palestinian Negotiations: http://www.us-israel.org/jsource/Peace/ispal.html
Middle East Peace Chronology – 1992-1993
 http://usinfo.state.gov/regional/nea/summit/chron3.htm
Effects of the Great Midwest Flood of 1993 on Wetlands
 http://water.usgs.gov/nwsum/WSP2425/flood.html
Looking Back: The Great Midwest Floods of 1993
 http://www.redcross.org/news/ds/floods/030806midwest93.html

Catastrophe #8

Opening statements by President al-Assad and President Bill Clinton at a
 news conference, Geneva, 16 January 1994: http://domino.un.org/UNISPAL.NSF/
 0/0ba7b126ad99f8c78525605b00722335? OpenDocument
Case Studies in Sanctions and Terrorism – U.S. v. Syria
 http://www.iie.com/research/topics/sanctions/syria.htm
Earthquake: http://www.eqe.com/publications/northridge/northridge.html

Catastrophe #9

Treaty Of Peace: Between the State of Israel and the Hashemite Kingdom of Jordan –
 October 26, 1994: http://www.mfa.gov.il/mfa/go.asp?MFAH00pa0
Middle East Peace Chronology – 1994-1997
 http://usinfo.state.gov/regional/nea/summit/chron4.htm
U.S. Flooding Disasters: http://snrs.unl.edu/amet351/oppenheim/disasters.html
One Hundred Years of Southeast Texas Weather (1900-2000)
 http://www.srh.noaa.gov/hgx/climate/holidays/hundred.htm#2

Catastrophe #10

Israeli–Palestinian Interim Agreement on the West Bank and the Gaza Strip
 – Washington, D.C., September 28, 1995 –
 http://www.israel.org/mfa/go.asp?MFAH00qa0
Opal – September 27-October 5, 1995: http://www.nhc.noaa.gov/1995opal.html

Chapter 5

Catastrophe #11

Arafat arrives in Washington: Tensions rising between Israel and the
 Palestinians – March 2, 1997: http://www.cnn.com/WORLD/9703/02/arafat/
March 1997 Tornadoes and Flooding
 http://www.ncdc.noaa.gov/oa/reports/marchflooding/marchflooding.html
Tornado outbreak, flood index
 http://www.usatoday.com/weather/wmar0197.htm
March 1997 Tornadoes and Flooding
 http://www.ncdc.noaa.gov/oa/reports/marchflooding/marchflooding.html
FEMA Highlights and Statistics for 1997
 http://www.fema.gov/library/fact97.shtm

Catastrophe #12

President Clinton and King Hussein Discuss Ways to Revive Middle East
 Peace Process – April 1, 1997
 http://www.usembassyisrael.org.il/publish/peace/documents/clnt0401.htm

1997 Red River flood index: http://www.usatoday.com/weather/wsflood1.htm
1997 northern Plains flooding at a glance
  http://www.usatoday.com/weather/wgredfld.htm
The Flood of the Century: A look into the 1997 Red River Flood
  http://www.geo.mtu.edu/department/classes/ge404/mlbroder/during.html
Burns: U.S. Talks With Netanyahu "Serious" – April 7, 2004
  http://www.usembassy-israel.org.il/publish/peace/documents/brns0407.htm
Transcript: Clinton/Netanyahu Oval Office Q&A with Reporters – April 7, 1997
  http://www.usembassyisrael.org.il/publish/peace/documents/cln0407b.htm
Blizzard adds to weather woes in upper Midwest – April 7, 1997
  http://www.cnn.com/WEATHER/9704/07/flood.update/

Catastrophe #13

Israel condemns UN vote on Har Homa – April 27, 1997
  http://www.jpost.com/com/Archive/27.Apr.1997/News/Article-1.html
UN condemns new Israeli settlements in Jerusalem
  http://southmovement.alphalink.com.au/southnews/July18.htm
Emergency Special Session of General Assembly Condemns Israel's Failure to Cease
  Building of New Settlement in East Jerusalem: By 131-3-14 Vote, Assembly Also
  Demands that Israel Reverse Immediately All Illegal Actions against Palestinian
  Jerusalemites – July 15, 1997: http://domino.un.org/UNISPAL.NSF
  /0/4dfef4edb0bdae8585256c8b0072c05f?OpenDocument
Russia's Financial Crisis – June 8, 1998
  http://csf.colorado.edu/students/Hosomi.Eiji/russian-crisis.html
"Contagion Indicators" for an Ailing Global Economy
  http://www.rand.org/publications/randreview/issues/rr.winter98.9/market.html
Contagion
  http://www.guardian.co.uk/globalisation/story/0,7369,768336,00.html

Catastrophe #14

Transcript: Ross Remarks To Press In Jerusalem – January 7, 1998
  www.usembassyisrael.org.il/publish/peace/archives/1998/january/me0107a.html
Northeast ice storm index: http://www.usatoday.com/weather/wice98.htm

Catastrophe #15

Transcript: Clinton, Netanyahu Oval Office Q&A With Reporters – January 20, 1998
  www.usembassyisrael.org.il/publish/peace/archives/1998/january/me0120b.html
Clinton Works To Move Middle East Peace Process Forward – January 20, 1998
  www.usembassyisrael.org.il/publish/peace/archives/1998/january/me0120c.html
Clinton Denies Affair With Intern, Cover-up Attempt – January 21, 1998
  http://www.cnn.com/ALLPOLITICS/1998/01/21/clinton.starr.am/
Transcript: Clinton/Arafat Oval Office Q&A With Reporters – January 22, 1998
  www.usembassyisrael.org.il/publish/peace/archives/1998/january/me0122c.html
Clinton Meets With Palestinian Authority Chairman Arafat – January 22, 1998
  www.usembassyIsrael.org.il/publish/peace/archives/1998/january/me0122d.html
Firestorm Consumes White House – January 22, 1998
  http://www.cnn.com/ALLPOLITICS/1998/01/22/clinton.main/
New Details Emerge About Sex Allegations Against Clinton – Dec. 23, 1998
  http://www.cnn.com/ALLPOLITICS/1998/01/23/clinton.main/
A Chronology: Key Moments In The Clinton-Lewinsky Saga
  http://www.cnn.com/ALLPOLITICS/1998/resources/lewinsky/timeline/

Catastrophe #16

Transcript: Clinton, Netanyahu Oval Office Q&A With Reporters – January 20, 1998
www.usembassyisrael.org.il/publish/peace/archives/1998/january/me0120b.html
Clinton Meets With Palestinian Authority Chairman Arafat – January 22, 1998
www.usembassyisrael.org.il/publish/peace/archives/1998/january/me0122d.html
Transcript: Albright To Try Again To Jump-Start Mideast Peace – January 28, 1998
www.usembassyisrael.org.il/publish/peace/archives/1998/january/me0128a1.html
Us Must Find A Way To Continue Peace Process, Official States – February 6, 1998
www.usembassyisrael.org.il/publish/peace/archives/1998/february/me0206a.html
Albright Reaffirms U.S. Commitment To Middle East Peace – February 10, 1998
www.usembassyisrael.org.il/publish/peace/archives/1998/february/me0210a.html
1998 off to a very warm, wet start in USA
http://www.usatoday.com/weather/climate/warm98.htm
California Flooding and Florida Tornadoes – February 1998
www.ncdc.noaa.gov/oa/reports/febstorm/february98storms.html#CMORE

Event #17

Chronology of Events, 1998-1999: http://www.israel-mfa.gov.il/mfa/go.asp?MFAH0h1n0
Transcript: Gore, Netanyahu 5/1 Joint Press Conference – May 1, 1998
http://www.usembassyisrael.org.il/publish/peace/archives/1998/may/me0501b.html
Vice President Gore, Saudi Crown Prince Joint Statement, May 2
www.UsembassyIsrael.Org.Il/Publish/Peace/Archives/1998/May/Me0504a.Html
Chinese Missile Allegations: Key Stories:
http://www.washingtonpost.com/wpsrv/politics/special/missile/keystories.htm

Catastrophe #18

Transcript: Clinton Remarks After Meeting With Netanyahu, Arafat. September 28, 1998
http://usembassyaustralia.state.gov/hyper/WF980929/epf202.htm
Hurricane Georges comes ashore near Biloxi – September 28, 1998
http://www.cnn.com/WEATHER/9809/28/georges.02/
Revised Middle East peace deal gets Arafat's OK – September 29, 1998
http://www.cnn.com/WORLD/meast/9809/29/mideast.03/
Hurricane Georges: http://www.nhc.noaa.gov/1998georges.html

Catastrophe #19

Middle East Peace Talks Wye River October 16-23, 1998
http://www.usembassyisrael.org.il/publish/peace/october98/news.html
Texas reeling from tornadoes, floods – October 18, 1998
http://www.cnn.com/US/9810/18/texas.storms.03/
Rivers crest as Texas flood toll climbs – October 23, 1998
http://www.cnn.com/WEATHER/9810/23/texas.floods.02/
The Wye River Memorandum – October 23, 1998
http://www.mfa.gov.il/mfa/go.asp?MFAH07o10

Event #20

Conference raises $3 billion for Palestinians: Arafat meets Clinton at White House –
November 30, 1998 – http://www.cnn.com/WORLD/meast/9811/30/mideast.01/
Transcript: Clinton Remarks to Mideast Donors Conference – Nov. 30, 1998
http://usembassy-australia.state.gov/hyper/WF981130/epf102.htm
Stock markets tumble worldwide as meltdown fears grow – December 2, 1998
http://archives.tcm.ie/irishexaminer/1998/12/02/fbhead.htm

Event #21

Judiciary approves three articles of impeachment – December 11, 1998
http://www.cnn.com/ALLPOLITICS/stories/1998/12/11/impeachment.01/
President Clinton's Trip to the Middle East – December 12-15, 1998
http://www.usembassyisrael.org.il/publish/president/photos.html
Clinton says he will not resign – December 13, 1998
http://www.cnn.com/ALLPOLITICS/stories/1998/12/13/impeachment.02/
Palestinians affirm Israel's right to exist – December 14, 1998
http://www.cnn.com/WORLD/meast/9812/14/clinton.gaza.03/
Arafat, Netanyahu, Clinton gather to seek Mideast peace – Dec. 15, 1998
http://www.cnn.com/WORLD/meast/9812/15/mideast.03/
Judiciary Committee wraps up its case against Clinton – Dec. 15, 1998
http://edition.cnn.com/ALLPOLITICS/stories/1998/12/12/impeachment.02/
Republicans skeptical of Iraq attack on eve of impeachment vote – December 16, 2003
http://edition.cnn.com/ALLPOLITICS/stories/1998/12/16/congresstional.react.02/
House impeaches Clinton: President will face Senate trial on perjury, obstruction of
  justice charges – December 19, 1998
http://edition.cnn.com/ALLPOLITICS/stories/1998/12/19/impeachment.01/
Israel to Hold Early Elections, Netanyahu Government Fails – Dec. 21, 1998
http://www.cnsnews.com/in-depth/archive/199812/IND19981221g.html
Netanyahu decries 'fantasies' of political rivals – December 22, 1998
http://www.cnn.com/WORLD/meast/9812/22/israel.01/

Event #22

Arafat meets with U.S. leaders to discuss statehood – March 23, 1999
http://www.cnn.com/WORLD/meast/9903/23/arafat.01/
Clinton urges Arafat to delay declaration of Palestinian state – March 24, 1999
http://www.cnn.com/ALLPOLITICS/stories/1999/03/24/clinton.arafat/
NATO attack on Yugoslavia begins – March 24, 1999
http://www.cnn.com/WORLD/europe/9903/24/kosovo.strikes/

Catastrophe #23

Oklahoma/Kansas Tornado Outbreak – May 3, 1999
http://www.nssl.noaa.gov/headlines/outbreak.shtml
U.S. President Clinton will send a message to Palestinian President Arafat, pushing
  him to postpone the declaration of the Palestinian state on May 4 – April 19, 1999
http://www.arabicnews.com/ansub/Daily/Day/990419/1999041909.html
Hillary Clinton: Palestinian State Important For Mideast Peace – May 6, 1999
http://www.usembassyisrael.org.il/publish/peace/archives/1998/may/me0506b.html
Mrs. Clinton backs Palestinian state – May 7, 1999
http://www.cnn.com/US/9805/07/palestinians.hillary/

Catastrophe #24

Transcript: Albright Remarks On Meeting With Palestinian Officials – August 30, 1999
www.usembassyisrael.org.il/publish/peace/archives/1999/august/me0830a.html
Hurricane Dennis Impact Studies; Peculiar Storm Path
http://coastal.er.usgs.gov/hurricanes/dennis/
Hurricane Dennis weakens, heads away from North Carolina coast
  – August 31, 1999: http://www.cnn.com/WEATHER/9908/31/storms.02/

Catastrophe #25
Israel, PA launch final-status talks tonight – September 13, 1999
  http://www.jpost.com/com/Archive/13.Sep.1999/News/Article-0.html
Final Status Talks: 'Middle East Peace In New Millennium?' – September 16, 1999
  http://www.fas.org/news/israel/wwwh9s16.htm
Floyd's floods hit N.C., N.J. hardest – September 17, 1999
  http://edition.cnn.com/WEATHER/9909/17/floyd.floods.01/
Hurricane Floyd – September 7-17, 1999
  http://www.nhc.noaa.gov/1999floyd.html

Events #26
Barak Plans to Dismantle Some Settlements, Expand Others – October 12-13, 1999
  http://www.us-israel.org/jsource/Peace/barakot.html
Hurricane Irene – October 13-19, 1999
  http://www.nhc.noaa.gov/1999irene_text.html
Hurricane Irene makes landfall in SW Florida – October 15, 1999
  http://edition.cnn.com/WEATHER/9910/15/irene.05/
Greenspan fuels market meltdown: Dow nose-dives 267 points – October 15, 1999
  http://starbulletin.com/1999/10/15/business/market.html
Barak lauds deal with settlers – October 15, 1999
  http://www.jpost.com/com/Archive/15.Oct.1999/News/Article-0.html
The M7.1 Hector Mine Earthquake – October 16, 1999
  http://pasadena.wr.usgs.gov/hector/index.html

Event #27
Wall Street Takes a Beating, Nation Burns, the Land in Drought Washington's Role In
  The Syrian–Israeli Peace Talks: Do's And Don'ts – February 4, 2000
  http://www.heritage.org/Research/MiddleEast/BG1345.cfm
Barak, Arafat holding third day of talks – March 9, 2000
  http://www.cnn.com/2000/WORLD/meast/03/09/mideast.talks.02/
Remarks By The President and Prime Minister Ehud Barak Of Israel – April 11, 2000
  http://www.usembass-israel.org.il/publish/peace/archives/2000/april/me0412b.html
Clinton Meets Barak at White House – April 12, 2000
  http://www.newsmax.com/articles/?a=2000/4/12/61439
$1,000bn wiped off U.S. stocks – Saturday, 15 April 2000
  http://news.bbc.co.uk/1/low/business/711505.stm
Finance: April 2000 Stock Market Fluctuation; $2.1 Trillion NASDAQ Fluctuation –
  574.57 points: http://mt.sopris.net/mpc/finance/$2.1.trillion.html
Remarks by The President in Photo Opportunity with Chairman Yasser Arafat of the
  Palestinian Authority – April 20, 2000
  www.usembassyisrael.org.il/publish/peace/archives/2000/april/me0421b.html
Transcript: Senior Official Briefs On Clinton–Arafat Meeting – April 20
  www.usembassyisrael.org.il/publish/peace/archives/2000/april/me0421c.html
U.S. Has Its Warmest Spring and Year-to-Date on Record, NOAA Reports – 2000
  http://www.noaanews.noaa.gov/stories/s443.htm

Event #28
The Middle East Peace Summit at Camp David – July 2000
  http://www.mfa.gov.il/mfa/go.asp?MFAH0hls0
Camp David timeline – July 2-25, 2000
  http://news.bbc.co.uk/2/hi/world/middle_east/848968.stm

As Barak goes abroad, his coalition collapses – July 10, 2000
  http://www.jewishworldreview.com/0700/collapse1.asp
Climate of 2000: U.S. Drought, Heat Waves, and Wildfires – June-August
  http://lwf.ncdc.noaa.gov/oa/climate/research/2000/sum/us_drought.html
2000 Fire Season Most Expensive In History
  http://www.Taxpayer.Net/TCS/Pressreleases/12-14-00fromtheashes.Htm
Hot Spots: Forecast: Bad Year For Wildfires In Northwest
  abcnews.go.com/sections/scitech/DailyNews/wilfire010527forecast.html
The Year of the Wildfires
  http://www.riverdeep.net/current/2000/09/091800twildfires.jhtml
U.S. Drought Monitor – October 10, 2000
  http://www.drought.unl.edu/dm/archive/2000/drmon1010.htm

Event #29

Latest attempt to form Israeli emergency government fails – Oct. 29, 2000
  http://www.cnn.com/2000/WORLD/meast/10/29/mideast.violence.03/
Amid Florida presidential tumult, GOP can still count on House and Senate
  – November 8, 2000:
  www.cnn.com/2000/ALLPOLITICS/stories/11/07/campaign.wrap/index.html
Blow-by-blow account of Gore's concession, and retraction – Nov. 8, 2000
  http://www.cnn.com/2000/ALLPOLITICS/stories/11/08/gore.election/index.html
U.S. names Mitchell to head Mideast fact-finding commission – Nov. 8, 2000
  http://www.cnn.com/2000/WORLD/meast/11/07/mideast.02/index.html
After meeting with Clinton, Arafat's next stop is UN – November 10, 2000
  http://www.cnn.com/2000/WORLD/meast/11/09/mideast.06/index.html
Jerusalem explosion starts new day of Mideast violence; Arafat to push UN
  for security force – November 11, 2000
  http://www.cnn.com/2000/WORLD/meast/11/10/mideast.02/
Bush and Gore marshal legal forces for the Battle of Florida – Nov. 13, 2000
  www.swdtimes.com/swdtimes/html/Daily1/MONDAY/nov13/002.html
Legal big guns for Bush and Gore head for showdown at Florida high court
  – November 20, 2000
  http://www.cnn.com/2000/ALLPOLITICS/stories/11/19/president.election/
'I'm ready for elections,' says Barak – November 29, 2000
  http://www.jpost.com/Editions/2000/11/29/News/News.16464.html
Bush goes to U.S. Supreme Court to counter effects of Florida ruling – Dec. 8, 2000
  http://www.cnn.com/2000/ALLPOLITICS/stories/12/08/election.wrap/
Barak resigns in move to sidestep push for new elections – December 9, 2000
  http://www.cnn.com/2000/WORLD/meast/12/09/barak.resigns.02/
Sharply divided U.S. Supreme Court stops Florida recount – Dec. 10, 2000
  http://www.cnn.com/2000/ALLPOLITICS/stories/12/09/president.election/
Gore concedes presidential election – December 13, 2000
  www.cnn.com/2000/ALLPOLITICS/stories/12/13/gore.ends.campaign/index.html
Sharon defeats Barak in a landslide – February 6, 2001
  www.zipple.com/newsandpolitics/israenews/20010206_landslide-victory.shtml

Chapter 6

Event #30

Remarks by Pres. Bush & Egyptian Pres. Mubarak in Photo Opportunity–April 1, 2001
  http://www.whitehouse.gov/news/releases/2001/04/20010402-4.html

U.S. aircraft collides with Chinese fighter, forced to land – April 1, 2001
http://www.cnn.com/2001/US/04/01/us.china.plane.03/
Statement by President on American Plane & Crew in China – April 2, 2001
http://www.whitehouse.gov/news/releases/2001/04/20010402-2.html
Remarks of the President and His Majesty King Abdullah of the Hashemite
Kingdom of Jordan in Photo Opportunity – April 10, 2001
http://www.whitehouse.gov/news/releases/2001/04/20010410-1.html
Remarks by Pres. on Release of American Servicemen in China–April 11, 2001
http://www.whitehouse.gov/news/releases/2001/04/20010411-3.html

Event #31
Text: Powell Endorses Mitchell Report on Mideast Violence – May 21, 2001
www.usembassyisrael.org.il/publish/peace/archives/2001/may/0521a.html
Bush Discusses Mitchell Report with Leaders of Egypt & Jordan –
May 22, 2001: http://www.usembassy.it/file2001_05/alia/a1052201.htm
Bush Calls Sharon, Arafat About Mitchell Report – May 23, 2001
http://www.usembassy.it/file2001_05/alia/a1052305.htm
President Bush meets with the Dalai Lama – May 23, 2001
http://www.whitehouse.gov/news/releases/2001/05/20010523-3.html
Jeffords leaves GOP, throwing Senate control to Democrats – May 25, 2001
http://www.cnn.com/2001/ALLPOLITICS/05/24/jeffords.senate/

Catastrophe #32
CIA's Tenet Meets Sharon, Arafat – June 8, 2001
http://www.newsmax.com/archives/articles/2001/6/7/190806.shtml
Bush Hails Israeli–Palestinian Cease-fire Agreement – June 13, 2001
www.usembassyisrael.org.il/publish/peace/archives/2001/june/0614a.html
NOAA's National Weather Service Releases Service Assessment Report for Tropical
Storm Allison Texas / Louisiana Flood Event – October 31, 2001
http://www.noaanews.noaa.gov/stories/s797.htm
Allison's Impact: A Look Back at a Killer Storm that cost $4 Billion in Damage
http://www.disasterrelief.org/Disasters/010622AllisonReview/
Tropical Storm Allison Floods
http://www.srh.noaa.gov/hgx/projects/allison01.htm

Catastrophe #33
September 11: Chronology of terror
http://www.cnn.com/2001/US/09/11/chronology.attack/
Statement by the President in His Address to the Nation – Sept. 11, 2001
www.whitehouse.gov/news/releases/2001/09/20010911-16.html
Marriage of Convenience: The U.S.–Saudi Alliance – February 10-12, 2002
Three-part article by Bob Kaiser & David Ottaway published in Washington Post
http://www2.aya.yale.edu/classes/yc1964/activities/kaiser.htm
Review of the Studies of the Economic Impact of September 11, 2001 Attacks on the
World Trade Center: http://www.gao.gov/new.items/d02700r.pdf
How much did the September 11 terrorist attack cost America?
http://www.iags.org/costof911.html

Catastrophe #34
Bush: Palestinian state 'part of a vision' if Israel respected October 2, 2001
http://www.cnn.com/2001/US/10/02/gen.mideast.us/index.html

Before Attacks, U.S. Was Ready to Say It Backed Palestinian State – October 3, 2001
  http://www.globalpolicy.org/security/issues/israel-palestine/2001/1003uspal.htm
Chronology of anthrax events: http://www.sun-sentinel.com/news/local/southflorida/
  sfl-1013anthraxchronology.story?coll=sfla-home-headlines
Anthrax Threat – October 31, 2003
  http://www.pbs.org/newshour/bb/health/july-dec01/anthrax10-30.html

Catastrophe #35

President Bush Speaks to United Nations – November 10, 2001
  http://www.whitehouse.gov/news/releases/2001/11/20011110-3.html
Powell: Bush's use of `Palestine' deliberate – November 12, 2001
  http://www.haaretzdaily.com/hasen/pages/ShArt.jhtml?itemNo=93580&;
  subContrassID=1&;sbSubContrassID=0&;listSrc=Y
American Flight 587 crashes into residential Queens: 260 dead – Nov. 12, 2001
  http://www.uwire.com/content/topnews111301002.html

Catastrophe #36

President Bush Meets with Crown Prince of Saudi Arabia – April 25, 2002
  http://www.whitehouse.gov/news/releases/2002/04/20020425-4.html
Statement by the President on the Middle East and Arafat's Release – April 28, 2002
  http://www.whitehouse.gov/news/releases/2002/04/20020428.html
F5 Class Tornado Strikes Southern Maryland on April 28, 2002
  http://www.somd.com/news/2002/04/tornado/
Killer tornado becomes one for the books in Maryland – April 29, 2002
  http://www.cnn.com/2002/WEATHER/04/29/storm.deaths/
Tornadoes rip through towns from Missouri to Maryland, killing six – April 29, 2002
  http://www.ardmoreite.com/stories/042902/new_tornado.shtml

Catastrophe #37

President Bush Meets with Egyptian President Mubarak – June 8, 2002
  http://www.whitehouse.gov/news/releases/2002/06/20020608-4.html
Hayman Fire Unstoppable: 137,000-acre blaze out of control after started
  http://www.fs.fed.us/rm/main/pa/newsclips/02_11/1114_hayman01.html

Catastrophe #38

Hell comes to the White Mountains – June 18-26, 2002
  http://www.azcentral.com/news/specials/wildfires/
President Bush Calls for New Palestinian Leadership – June 24, 2002
  http://www.whitehouse.gov/news/releases/2002/06/20020624-3.html
President Visits Displaced Families in Arizona – June 25, 2002
  http://www.whitehouse.gov/news/releases/2002/06/20020625-4.html
WorldCom admits massive fraud: $3.8 billion scheme, inflated profit; financial exec fired
  – June 25, 2002: http://www.siliconvalley.com/mld/siliconvalley/3545267.htm
Adelphia is filing for Chapter 11 – June 26, 2002
  http://www.forbes.com/2002/06/26/0620adelphiapackage.html
President Reiterates Path for Peace in Middle East – June 26, 2002
  http://www.whitehouse.gov/news/releases/2002/06/20020626.html

Catastrophe #39

Bush Hesitates on Moving U.S. Embassy to Jerusalem – October 1, 2002
  http://www.foxnews.com/printer_friendly_story/0,3566,64565,00.html
Bush, Congress clash over Jerusalem status – October 2, 2002
  http://www.jewishsf.com/bk021004/us11.shtml

Chronology: Sniper attacks Began – October 2, 2002
   http://www.cbc.ca/news/features/sniper_victims.html
Lili damage estimated at $600 million – October 5, 2002
   http://www.cnn.com/2002/WEATHER/10/05/lili/
Hurricane Lili NOAA Report: http://www.nhc.noaa.gov/2002lili.shtml

Catastrophe #40

President Hosts Iftaar [Ramadan] Dinner – November 7, 2002
   http://www.whitehouse.gov/news/releases/2002/11/20021107-11.html
Twister: A Case Study of the November 10-11, 2002 Tornado Outbreak
   http://www.personal.psu.edu/users/j/l/jln177/Twister/
Tornado Outbreak: Overview and brief look at SPC forecast decision process –
   November 10, 2002: http://www.spc.noaa.gov/staff/evans/talk1/talk1_frame.htm
Boucher Says Mideast Peace Roadmap Not "Frozen" – November 13, 2002
   http://www.usembassy.it/file2002_11/alia/a2111302.htm

Catastrophe #41

President Commemorates / Remarks on Eid al-Fitr
The Islamic Center of Washington, D.C. – December 5, 2002
   http://www.whitehouse.gov/news/releaes/2002/12/20021205-5.html
Winter comes early to Carolinas: Forecasters say 1 million could be without power –
   December 5, 2002: http://www.cnn.com/2002/WEATHER/12/04/wintry.storm/
Duke Power Responding to Worst Storm in History – December 5, 2002
   http://www.prnewswire.com/cgibin/stories.pl?ACCT=105&STORY=/
   www/story/12-05-2002/0001852841

Catastrophe #42

Address at the National Conference of World Affairs Councils of America,
   Secretary Colin L. Powell – Washington, DC – January 31, 2003
   http://usembassy.state.gov/seoul/wwwh43fy.html
President Bush Meets with Prime Minister Blair – January 31, 2003
   http://www.whitehouse.gov/news/releases/2003/01/20030131-23.html
President Addresses Nation on Space Shuttle Columbia Tragedy – February 1, 2003
   http://www.whitehouse.gov/news/ releases/2003/02/20030201-2.html
Again on TV, riveting scenes and gathering of grief – February 2, 2003
   http://www.boston.com/news/packages/shuttle/globe_stories/ Again_on_TV_rivet-
   ing_scenes_and_gathering_of_grief+.shtml

Catastrophe #43

'Road map' to pact in Mideast is delivered – May 1, 2003
   http://www.iht.com/articles/94928.html
Second Oklahoma City twister caps nation's worst tornado week – May 10, 2003
   http://www.usatoday.com/weather/news/2003-05-10-stormyweek_x.htm
Record Number Of Tornadoes, NOAA Reports – May 11, 2003
   http://www.noaanews.noaa.gov/stories/s1144.htm
May tornado count sets record – May 11, 2003
   http://www.usatoday.com/weather/news/2003-05-11-tornadoes-may_x.htm

Catastrophes #44

EU says Mideast 'road map' does not belong to U.S.
   http://middleeastinfo.org/article.php?sid=2519
New study finds Europe's severe heat wave during the summer of 2003 was a 1-in-
   46,000 event: http://eces.org/articles/000741.php

Europe's hottest summer for 500 years – September 24, 2003
  http://eces.org/articles/000741.php
Behind this summer's wild, tragic weather
  http://www.csmonitor.com/2003/0815/p01s02-usgn.html
London breaks record for heat, wildfires plague Europe – August 8, 2003
  http://www.smh.com.au/articles/2003/08/07/1060145794919.html
Have Apocalyptic Weather Changes Begun? – Hal Lindsey – Aug. 18, 2003
  http://www.hallindseyoracle.com/articles.asp?ArticleID=3243
Climate of 2003 – Annual Review U.S. Drought:
  www.ncdc.noaa.gov/oa/climate/research/2003/ann/drought-summary.html#natldrot

Catastrophe #45
Powell In Mideast, Pushing 'Roadmap' – May 11, 2003
  http://www.cbsnews.com/stories/2003/05/11/world/main553333.shtm
Secretary Powell's Visit to the Middle East Photo Gallery: Meets Egypt's Mubarak and
  Jordan's King Abdullah II – May 12, 2003
  http://usinfo.state.gov/regional/nea/summit/sectrip2photos.html
Bush Denounces Terrorist Attacks in Saudi Arabia – May 13, 2003
  http://www.usembassy.it/file2003_05/alia/A3051301.htm
U.S. worried about more al Qaeda attacks: U.S., Saudis suspect terror group in Riyadh
  bombings – May 13, 2003
  http://www.cnn.com/2003/WORLD/meast/05/13/saudi.blast/
Bombings Show 'War on Terrorism Goes On,' Rice Says – May 14, 2003
  http://www.defenselink.mil/news/May2003/n05142003_200305144.html

Catastrophe #46
Palestinian Officials Meet With Congress – July 17, 2003
  http://www.guardian.co.uk/uslatest/story/0,1282,-2916166,00.html
Hurricane Claudette moves inland after lashing Texas coast – July 17, 2003
  http://www.augustachronicle.com/stories/071603/nat_claudette.shtml

Events #47
Blair addresses U.S. Congress: UK Prime Minister Tony Blair is addressing the United
  States Congress at the start of a visit to Washington, dominated by Iraq and the
  Middle East peace process – July 17, 2003
  http://news.bbc.co.uk/2/hi/uknews/politics/3073193.stm
Remarks by Palestinian Authority Prime Minister Mahmoud Abbas to the Council on
  Foreign Relations – July 24, 2003: http://www.cfr.org/publication.php?id=6156
President Bush Welcomes Prime Minister Abbas to White House – July 25, 2003
  http://www.whitehouse.gov/news/releases/2003/07/20030725-6.html
Navy Secretary Nominee's Death Ruled Suicide – July 25, 2003
  http://www.foxnews.com/printer_friendly_story/0,3566,92896,00.html
Abbas Seeks U.S. Assistance in Prodding Israel – May 25, 2003
  http://www.foxnews.com/printer_friendly_story/0,3566,92909,00.html

Catastrophe #48
Abbas resigns as Palestinian prime minister – September 6, 2003
  http://www.washtimes.com/world/20030907-124732-9980r.htm
Bush briefed on hurricane; White House battens down – September 17, 2003
  http://www.hamptonroads.com/stories/br0917bush.html
Isabel Essentially Shuts Down Capital Region – September 18, 2003
  http://www.news8.net/news/stories/0903/103048.html

Bush, Jordanian King Continue Work on Mideast Peace – Sept. 18, 2003
  http://www.foxnews.com/printer_friendly_story/0,3566,97681,00.html
President Bush, King Abdullah of Jordan Meet at Camp David – September 18, 2003
  http://www.whitehouse.gov/news/releases/2003/09/20030918-4.html
Statement on Federal Assistance for Maryland – September 20, 2003
  http://www.whitehouse.gov/news/releases/2003/09/20030919-5.html

Catastrophe #49

President's Ramadan Message – October 24, 2003
  http://www.whitehouse.gov/news/releases/2003/10/20031024-10.html
The White House Ramadan 2003 Section
  http://www.whitehouse.gov/infocus/ramadan/index.html
'The Perfect Non-Storm': Why Southern California Is Burning – October 27, 2003
  http://abcnews.go.com/sections/wnt/SciTech/fires031027why.html
Remarks by President at Iftaar with Ambassadors & Muslim Leaders – Oct. 28, 2003
  http://www.whitehouse.gov/news/releases/2003/10/20031028-9.html
Bush: Fence will impede emergence of Palestinian state – October 28, 2003
  http://www.haaretzdaily.com/hasen/spages/354749.html
One of the largest known solar flares erupted – October 29, 2003
  http://www.cnn.com/2003/TECH/space/10/28/solar.flare/
Fire Roars Through San Bernardino Mountains – October 30, 2003
  http://www.foxnews.com/story/0,2933,101512,00.html
Second huge solar storm hits Earth – October 31, 2003
  http://www.theage.com.au/articles/2003/10/31/1067233358702.html
Sun on Fire, Unleashes 3 More Major Flares – November 3, 2001
  http://www.space.com/scienceastronomy/solar_flares_031103.html
President Bush Thanks Firefighters & Volunteers in California – November 4, 2003
  http://www.whitehouse.gov/news/releases/2003/11/20031104-4.html

Catastrophes #50, 51, 52 and 53

Charley death toll at 13
Downgraded to tropical storm, Charley moves up East Coast
  http://www.cnn.com/2004/WEATHER/08/14/storms/
Heavy cost of Hurricane Frances
  http://news.bbc.co.uk/2/hi/americas/3684804.stm
Insurers to Pay $6 Billion on Claims for Hurricane Ivan
  http://www.insurancejournal.com/news/national/2004/10/15/46927.htm
Jeanne Eyewall hits Florida
Eye of Category 3 storm just miles from town of Stuart
  http://www.cnn.com/2004/WEATHER/09/25/hurricane.jeanne/
Responding to Hurricanes Charley and Frances:
  http://www.whitehouse.gov/news/releases/2004/09/20040914-14.html
President signs $14.5 billion disaster bill — October 14, 2004
  www.usatoday.com/weather/hurricane/2004-10-14-aid-billx.htm?POE=WEAISVA
Oil Production Likely Slow for Months — October 19, 2004
  www.nwanews.com/story.php?paper=adg&section=Business&storyid=96091
Florida's Hurricane Train (October 2004)
  http://www.afn.org/~savanna/hurricanes.htm
Insurers Expected To Tap Florida Catastrophe Fund For $3 Billion
  — October 19, 2004: http://www.local10.com/news/3831621/detail.html

Chapter 7

Catastrophes #54, 55, 56 and 57

PM's Statement On London Explosions
   http://www.britishembassy.ie/press/Speeches_Archive/PMs
   Statement_on_London_Explosions.htm
7 July 2005 London bombings
   http://en.wikipedia.org/wiki/7_July_2005_London_bombings
Hurricane Dennis
   http://en.wikipedia.org/wiki/Hurricane_Dennis
Israel: Gaza pullout moving quickly - August 16, 2005 – CNN
   http://www.cnn.com/2005/WORLD/meast/08/17/gaza.pullout/
Gaza Evictions Go More Smoothly – CBS
   http://www.cbsnews.com/stories/2005/08/19/world/main787247.shtml
An End and a Beginning – CBS
   www.cbsnews.com/stories/2005/08/19/opinion/diplomatic/main788387.shtml
78% of Gaza evacuees are out of work – Jerusalem Post
   http://www.unitedjerusalem.org/index2.asp?id=670872
"World Reacts to Katrina's Devastation."
   http://www.foxnews.com/story/0,2933,168002,00.html
Advisen Estimates Record Insurer Losses of $57.6 Billion Related To 2005 Hurricanes
   https://www.advisen.com/HTTPBroker?action=jsp_request&id=articleDetailsNot
   Logged&resource_id=44327057

Chapter 9

Bob Kaiser is Associate Editor of the Washington Post. He and David Ottaway co-
   authored a three-part article published in the Post on February 10, 11 & 12, 2002
   http://www2.aya.yale.edu/classes/yc1964/activities/kaiser.htm
September 11: Chronology of terror
   http://www.cnn.com/2001/US/09/11/chronology.attack/
Remarks by the President After Two Planes Crash Into World Trade Center
   http://www.whitehouse.gov/news/releases/2001/09/20010911.html
Statement by the President in His Address to the Nation
   http://www.whitehouse.gov/news/releases/2001/09/20010911-16.html
The Milken Institute: http://www.milkeninstitute.org/

Chapter 10

Remarks by President in Address to Nation – Homeland Security Department Funding
   http://www.whitehouse.gov/news/releases/2002/06/20020606-8.html
President Bush Signs Homeland Security Appropriations Bill – Oct. 1, 2002
   http://www.whitehouse.gov/news/releases/2003/10/print/20031001-4.html
FY 2004 Budget Fact Sheet – Homeland Security
   http://www.white-house.gov/news/releases/2003/10/20031001-7.html
Thompson Releases Report on Fiscal Impact of 9/11 on New York City
   – September 4, 2002
   http://comptroller.nyc.gov/press/2002releases/print/02-09-054.shtm

Chapter 13

1 – Roots of the U.S.-Israel Relationship - Mitchell G. Bard
http://www.jewishvirtuallibrary.org/jsource/US-Israel/roots_of_US-Israel.html

2 – President Harry S. Truman and U.S. Support for Israeli Statehood
http://www.mideastweb.org/us_supportforstate.htm

3 – Suez War of 1956
http://www.jewishvirtuallibrary.org/jsource/History/Suez_War.htm

4 – History of a hot potato: Here is innovative research into the major changes in U.S. administration's thinking on Israel's "nuclear option" in the 1960s – Yehiam Weitz
http://www.tau.ac.il/jcss/haaretz14012005.html

5 – Lyndon Johnson Was First to Align U.S. Policy With Israel's Policies - by Donald Neff - November/December 1996, page 96
http://www.washington-report.org/backissues/1196/9611096.htm

6 – The 1967 Six Day War – Mitchell Bard
http://www.jewishvirtuallibrary.org/jsource/History/67_War.html

7 – The Yom Kippur War – Mitchell Bard
http://www.jewishvirtuallibrary.org/jsource/History/73_War.html

8 – Jimmy Carter's Speech from The 6th Herzliya Conference – January 23, 2006
herzliyaconference.org/Eng/_Articles/Article.asp?ArticleID=1435&CategoryID=215

Chapter 15

1 – "Daunting task for a cold but pragmatic politician," Ian Black in Jerusalem – Thursday, March 30, 2006
http://www.guardian.co.uk/israel/Story/0,,1742685,00.html

2 – Sonia Verma, "Family Ties Don't Bind Olmert's Politically," Newsday, March 26, 2006: http://www.newsday.com/news/nationworld/world/ny-wofa-mi264676980mar26,0,7289699,print.story?coll=ny-worldnews-print

3 – Ned Martel, "Ehud Olmert and Family: At Home in Israel's Corridors of Power," New York Times, March 28, 2006: http://www.nytimes.com/2006/03/28/arts/ televi-sion/28mart.html?_r=1&oref=slogin&pagewanted=print

4 – David Makovsky, "Israel's Unlikely Transformer"
washingtonpost.com/wpdyn/content/article/2006/04/01/AR2006040100010.html.

5 – Frank J. Gaffney, Jr., "The Disengagement Delusion," Jewish World Review – March 28, 2006: http://jewishworldreview.com/cols/gaffney032806.php3

6 – Daniel Pipes, "Will the Jewish state be allowed to become defunct?" – Jewish World Review, March 28, 2006
http://www.jewishworldreview.com/0306/pipes2006_03_28.php3?printer_friendly

Bill Koenig's Biography

Bill began his business career in 1978 with Coldwell Banker (now CB Richard Ellis) a major-international real estate company. He began work in Phoenix, Arizona transferring to Dallas, Texas in 1979. He was associated with two other commercial real estate companies in Dallas before starting his own brokerage and investment company in 1984.

In a career change, in the summer of 1996, Bill began publishing Koenig's Watch" a weekly summary of important Middle East news from Dallas. He moved onto the Internet in 1997, expanding the coverage to international news and changing the name to "Koenig's International News" (http://watch.org).

The news service, with constantly updated stories from a large variety of news sources, today has readers and e-mail subscribers in all 50 states and 79 countries around the globe.

In early 1999, he produced the audiotape, "Countdown 2000," discussing ten major events to watch moving into the new millennium.

In late 2001, Bill co-authored with John McTernan, Israel: The Blessing or the Curse, a book on the history of Israel's land, a history of the peace process, the consequences to those who have participated in the "land for peace" process and political insight.

Bill was a member of First Baptist Dallas and the Dallas Theological Seminary's Presidents Council, before moving to Washington D.C. He has been very active in both local and national Christian activities. He has attended four National Religious Broadcaster (NRB) conventions, two in Washington, D.C. and two in Nashville.

He graduated from Arizona State University with a B.S. in Communications.

Bill and his wife Claudia reside in the Washington D.C. area where he is a White House correspondent.